John Singer Sargent

JOHN SINGER SARGENT

A self-portrait at the age of thirty-six

John Singer Sargent

A Biography

CHARLES MERRILL MOUNT

New York · W · W · NORTON & COMPANY · INC ·

KRAUS REPRINT CO.
New York
1969

Reprinted with the permission of the author

KRAUS REPRINT CO.
A U.S. Division of Kraus-Thomson Organization Limited

Printed in U.S.A.

To *Winthrop Sargent, Jr.*

Contents

Acknowledgment is made to the following for the photographs appearing in this book: The Brooklyn Museum, Chicago Art Institute, Corcoran Gallery of Art, Detroit Institute of Arts, Fogg Museum of Art, Imperial War Museum, Metropolitan Museum of Art, Musée Rodin, Museum of Modern Art (Paris), National Academy of Design, National Gallery of Art, National Portrait Gallery, St. Louis Museum, Tate Gallery, Babcock Galleries, Knoedler Art Galleries, Bulloz, Henry Dixon & Son, Peter A. Juley & Son, Paul Laib, J. A. Lavaud.

Illustrations

Preface to the Third Edition

THIS new publication of what may be the most unauthorized biography ever written appears fittingly on a note of triumph. Its pages still throb with passion from the crusade it launched, though all its purposes have been accomplished and everything for which it stood has been vindicated. Sargent has returned to his lofty pedestal. The unique enchantment of his vision is widely appreciated and he reigns the supreme example of a vigorous and penetrating artist. All this is singularly gratifying. And best of all, unlike Isaiah or Jeremiah I have lived to see the fulfillment of a prophetic vision, even though like Joan of Arc I too for a time despaired.

Few books are undertaken specifically to resurrect a fallen master. Today it appears improbable that my purpose was called folly and an eccentricity of taste. Yet well do I recollect the scathing comment of that former time. To withstand assault the book was strongly constructed on a heavy foundation of documents unearthed in many parts of the world. In place of the purely reverent attitude expected of biographers I attempted from the start to penetrate and explain Sargent's individual genius. To depict his living organism as it functioned unconventional biographic techniques were developed. The examination of motivations was a further distinct innovation for that time. Because the artist was sometimes stripped to clinical nakedness a horrified relative attempted to stifle this book at publication. By passing falsehoods to an influential critic she nearly succeeded. Even after thirteen years I fancy the artist's own ghost sniffs at me in reproof. It is sad to reflect that despite my devotion were Sargent and I to meet we could not be friends. Or perhaps I wrong him. The man whose brush wrought so many devastating portraits might well understand biographic exigencies.

xa

Publication took place in November 1955, a few weeks before the dawn of Sargent's centenary year. Response was immediate and gratifying and at Christmas The New York Times listed *John Singer Sargent* in its BEST BOOKS OF THE YEAR. Shortly the John Simon Guggenheim Foundation viewed its merit so favorably that despite my excessive youth they financed researches which in time produced my further biography MONET. As an aberration the biography of *Gilbert Stuart* was produced along the way. During that centenary year 1956 therefore I had ample reason to be elated, but was profoundly discouraged. Nothing could hide from me that though this book was received enthusiastically as a literary work everywhere its message was evaded.

Newspapers, radio, magazines, and scholarly journals, permitted themselves to be employed for my persistent exhortations. Even so the great crusade languished. I retained a distinct impression that aside from providing a reasonable entertainment as a preacher I was my own only convert. Nor did anyone credit my genuine anguish that a call to arms was praised for its literary quality. From the better vantage of a long retrospect it is now astonishing how widely the seed was planted during that time. After a few winters it sprung up in miraculous bloom. By 1961 the London sale of the Alvin T. Fuller collection gave the movement a sudden dramatic impetus. Everywhere there was a new demand for Sargent's works. I myself was put into service by Washington's Corcoran Gallery to scour Europe for a loan exhibition that ultimately toured the United States. That first electrifying revelation of Sargent in his full glory accomplished what I had hoped this book would do alone. Nine years of hard campaigning had been required, but at last the job was done.

Were I writing freshly today, when the literary climate and attitudes toward Sargent have drastically altered, undoubtedly my candour would be greater. Occasional sexual phantasies among his drawings and paintings demand a more pungent Freudian examination. New evidence also could be used, such as revelations concerning Louise Burckhardt and Sargent's repeated offers of marriage to Flora Priestley. Though fact and understanding could now be taken further the total effect might be no more than to confirm what I wrote thirteen years ago.

All questions of Sargent's artistic stature would, on the contrary, be revised upward. For *Monet* I defined Impressionism as *An art employing chemically constituted pigments to create a synthetic coloration and more powerful accents without the use of black or brown.* By chance this revealed the true significance of Sargent's outdoor work. He had been an *Impressionist,* but far more, and certainly no follower. Sargent is the master who brought Impressionism to final fruition by imposing the necessary ultimate discipline on a disordered fabric created by Monet. By perfecting the most significant artistic discovery since the Renaissance Sargent was greater by far than my 1955 estimate of him suggests.

The catalogue raisonné appended to this new edition has been thoroughly revised. Entries have been rationalized, duplications eliminated, dates thoroughly re-examined, and ownership records brought up to date. Better than anything this last demonstrates how great has been the movement in Sargent's works since first publication of this book. History supplies no parallel of an artistic reputation so completely reappraised. Sargent has returned to his lofty pedestal. This third publication of the book undertaken to bring that about fills me with extreme pride.

Charles Merrill Mount
Dublin, Ireland
November 12, 1968.

Preface

SOME eleven years ago, when I was studying portraiture to make it my profession, as it has become, I cast about for a teacher, and found a model instead. Though I also gratefully received instruction from living artists, it must be acknowledged that I owe whatever I may know of my profession to a man who died too early for our lives to have crossed. This book was undertaken in gratitude to that artist.

It is the product of some four or five years' continuous effort to uncover the facts of a man's existence. During that time I had the good fortune to find many new materials not available to those writing on him previously: diaries, private papers, wills, passports, newspaper files, plus many hundreds of his own letters, which had to be located in the possession of the persons to whom they were written or of their heirs. As his own papers were destroyed in the cleaning out of his studio subsequent to his death, in each case it has been necessary to reconstruct events from what could be found among the papers of others. The sequence thus constructed was further filled out by interviews with people who were his friends, sitters, relations, and their families, as well as the records of his transactions in public institutions. Working so long with these materials it was inevitable that I should discover unknown paintings as well, most of them still in the possession of the original owners or their families, and they also filled out little-known incidents of his career. Over these years I visited many of the places in which he lived and worked, especially Fladbury and Broadway, and his studios in Boston, London, and Paris, in that way further familiarizing myself with the atmosphere and the places he knew. My one wish in all this has been to reconstruct the most accurate and correct account of the man possible.

A biography is a compilation of facts and ideas relative to the life of an individual. Its value depends on the objectivity and trustworthiness of the facts brought forth. In writing of anyone so controversial as John S. Sargent this is of particular importance, for the success that attended him in full career was so staggering that it bewildered two generations and gave rise to wholly erronious speculations which have since been set down as fact. We are so far removed from the Sargent era that both the man and the times can be seen with more detachment than was possible during intervening years, and as I have made a special effort to establish the *facts* of the matter, it is *not* surprising that a new image grows from these pages. Blinded by the brilliance of his career, the world for too long lost sight of both the humble beginnings and the quiet man who lived sequestered within the legend. For in a personal sense Sargent's splendid career was a cloak over three notable tragedies: the scandal that forever wrecked his youthful career in France; the realization in middle life that his integrity precluded and was irreconcilable with the practice of portraiture; and his failure to marry a woman who would have made him happy.

He lived in neither the best nor the worst of times. It was an era that in some ways was extravagant and in others brilliant, when, despite the apparent signs of optimism, there were those who labored unseen in the depths of despair and others who, had they the strength, could have lifted themselves out. Genius still had some relationship to sanity, and the capacity to take infinite pains; competence was not yet despised. It was an age in which strong men still achieved their ambitions — and this is the story of one man who did.

Times change and styles change, and fashion, that plaything of the winds, is an unreliable weathervane. For the winds are varied and subject to invisible eddies and currents, though in the end fashion, the weathervane, has only come full circle.

A book such as this places its author under grateful obligation to the multitudes of people who have helped him in his work, and without whom it would not have been possible to compile the necessary information. How much disinterested kindness there is in the world soon becomes apparent. Unfortunately, the simple

limitations of space make it impossible to account for most of the
help I have received, which in each case I have tried to acknowledge to the individual. Saying thanks never seems sufficient,
though I hope it is understood with what warmth and honest gratitude it was meant. Still, overwhelming nature of the aid I received
in some few cases must be acknowledged here. An institution like
the Frick Art Reference Library, with its treasures of photographs,
exists almost as an inducement to research, and the understanding
cooperation of its staff, including the two smiling young men who
bring carloads of material to the reading room, is an assistance
superior to any other in the world. The Museums that possess so
large a part of Sargent's work deserve equal thanks for their
courtesy in placing records at my disposal, especially Albert Ten
Eyck Gardner, archivist at the Metropolitan Museum in New
York. Many were the curatorial staffs I bothered to open store-
rooms and make available paintings and studies not on exhibition,
in which connection Miss Muriel Oxenburg of the Metropolitan
Museum, Mary Chamot of the Tate Gallery, and James D.
Breckenridge of the Corcoran Gallery were especially gracious.
Helen Willard of the Fogg Museum in Cambridge deserves special
thanks for allowing me to dig at my own pace through the extensive collection of drawings under her care. The Massachusetts
Historical Society, Knoedler's, and the Royal Academy are other
institutions under whose wings I found shelter and aid. Mr. Hutch-
inson, the energetic librarian of the Royal Academy, was especially
kind, placing at my disposal everything I could wish, explaining
systems I could not otherwise have understood and conducting
me through the rooms of the Academy despite the fact they were
shut up at the time. To its president, Sir Gerald Kelly, who invited
me to a dinner he made me pay for myself, and made it a most
delightful evening which I shall never forget, I owe gratitude beyond measure. Morris Carter, Director at Fenway Court, allowed
me the use of all the letters of Sargent, his sister Emily, Dennis
Miller Bunker, Charles Martin Loeffler, and Henry James, which
were received by Mrs. Gardner, and spent his precious time with
me in a hunt for photographs that never materialized among the
locked boxes of Mrs. Gardner's rooms. To Paul Manship, Dean
Cornwell, Timothy Cole, Mrs. Hertha Wegener of the Brooklyn

Museum, Sir Sidney Cockerell, Jean Helleu, Madame Phillipe
Cruse, Madame Suzanne Meyer-Zundel, Jean Louis Vaudroyer,
Robert Bourget Pailleron, Bernard S. Carter, his sister Mildred,
Countess of Gosford, Vernon C. Porter of the National Academy,
and Mr. Mayes of the Imperial War Museum, to each in separate
measure for the time, patience, and energy they spent in my behalf I owe thanks. To Lady Mary Baillie, who now graces the
house at 31, Tite Street, and her neighbor, Mr. Craig, on the other
side of the wall once knocked out by their famous common prede-
cessor, I owe my knowledge of the interior of his living quarters.

To Sir Walter Lamb go thanks for the thoughtful preparation
that went into his expression to me of Sargent's influence at the
Royal Academy during the years of his secretaryship. Sir Alec
Martin allowed me the use of the inventory he had prepared of
Sargent's property at the time of his death, and Alfred Yockney
gave me not only free access to his memories of Sargent's association with the first war, but letters and newspaper clippings I had
not found elsewhere. Mrs. Richard Hale allowed me the use
of the wonderful letters in her possession, with the added service
of deciphering them as well; Mrs. W. C. Endicott showed me
the spot where she had posed so many years before, and stood so
that I could see the light as it fell on her in that bygone time. Mrs.
Fiske Warren provided wonderfully interesting sidelights on her
portrait, then ransacked her house for photographs. Miss Sally
Fairchild provided perhaps the greatest single store of memories,
taking me back by her lucid prose to periods that could never have
been reconstructed without her aid. Robert Mathias, Esq., and
his son John helped me to unravel the tangled relations with the
Wertheimer family. To his daughter, Baroness Soyer de Bosmelet,
I owe particular gratitude for the fine sportsmanship with which
she climbed flights of dingy stairs to act as interpreter during my
interviews in Paris; and in like measure thanks go to Mademoiselle
Christiane Poirson, the charming granddaughter of Sargent's landlord, who conducted me about Paris, made inquiries, introduced
me to people who were able to help this work, and finally climbed
six flights in Montmartre to be present at the discovery of a picture
that had been unknown since it was painted in 1879. Dr. John
Alfred Parsons Millet provided not only the key that unlocked the

strange personality of the artist, but special knowledge concerning Broadway, and the artists associated with it; Mme. Denise Bagues did the same concerning her grandfather, Carolus-Duran; and Philippe Fauré-Frémiet added to my knowledge of his father's friendship with Sargent, as well as telling me about the first of the early portraits I suspected might exist in Paris. Miss Elizabeth Williamson was my chief source and guide through the maze surrounding her grandmother, Mrs. Charles Hunter, and I took advantage of her knowledge of Hill Hall and its intimates to check many of my correlations. Mrs. Nathaniel Bowditch Potter allowed me the use of the many charming letters in her possession, augmented by her memories and explanations; and, finally, I cannot forget how thoroughly I am indebted to the Marchioness of Cholmondeley, whose fabulous charm and wit turned research into a pleasure, and whose kindness and help have followed me.

Lately, I come to those whom I cannot thank without an admission of some of the affectionate regard in which I hold them. Mr. Welles Bosworth, who provided a wealth of anecdote concerning the portraits of Rockefeller and was of inestimable aid while I did research in Paris; Mr. Ralph Curtis, whose knowledge of the Venetian years and whose help and hospitality were limitless; Mrs. Edgar Speyer, who aided me in every way, both by providing material and by reading early drafts, which showed bravery above and beyond the call of duty; and lastly, Winthrop Sargent, Jr., of Haverford, Pennsylvania, who placed at my disposal all his materials on the Sargent family, collected through many generations, whose unequaled knowledge of Gloucester and New England history frequently came to my rescue, and whose kind guidance, criticism, and many opinions were of tremendous aid in this work. Last of all, I cannot forget, and will always be grateful for, the kindness and help of the artist's sister, Mrs. Francis Ormond, with whom I spent evenings plunged into a world known only to the two of us.

C. M. M.

JOHN SINGER SARGENT
As a very young man

John Singer Sargent

Art is a bit of creation seen through
the medium of a powerful temperament.

— Emile Zola

Capriccio Italien

RAIN FELL during the night, leaving London damp and gloomy the morning of April 15, 1925. Along Chelsea Embankment the pavements still showed two colors where wet and dry came together, footsteps trailing the one into the other, as a few silent students gathered in Tite Street, their doleful attitudes a mute testimony of respect. Already, this chill gray morning, news had spread that John Sargent died in the night, and now they stood opposite his green door, quiet figures, shifting in the wet and watching dim windows on the other side. At noon they saw the frock-coated form of Sir Philip Sassoon, Trustee of the National Gallery, arrive with a floral wreath, then a few minutes later step back across the pavement to his car and hurry away.

Only a few persons entered the house: the coroner, Sargent's two white-haired sisters, and the inevitable reporters, trailing along to ask questions no one wished to answer. It was not through their dispatches, which spread the news that night to the world, but rather through the batch of memoirs soon appearing in friendly tribute that some of the nebulosity so long surrounding Sargent began to drift away. Some facts had always been known: that he had been born in Florence of American parents, that he strongly maintained he was an American. But only now, when his huge, upright figure would no longer be seen trotting with short quick steps down Tite Street, head erect and cigar in mouth, was

3

the ill-defined haze surrounding him pierced. It did not wholly evaporate, as those who knew him best were aware, and something of the mystery of the man died with him.

Big, bulky, and flushed, Sargent scanned the world about him with full, rather bulging, inquisitive eyes, taking in everything and keeping it secret. London saw his probing, roving glance and noted something in his attitude that implied a sense of loneliness, but knew it was what he wanted. His armor was thick, consisting in part of a suspicious reserve that few penetrated and none really saw removed. A glance might be caught now and again of what seemed to be a gentle, much-mortified spirit inside, but there could be no certainty. All he allowed to be seen was his art, and that served as a screen between himself and the world, behind which the man remained in seclusion.

He could be blunt when he chose, fixing his eye and shooting out a few words that disposed of troublesome people with dispatch. Long years had taught him that it was really the most humane approach, for otherwise there was a dashing of hopes built on his hesitation; people were insistent and he impatient. Yet he never liked to hurt if it could be avoided, and when he chose, or when he found a sympathetic presence, he betrayed a responsiveness to humanity that was drawn from his own keenly sensitive nature. He had a quiet boyishness that became familiar to his friends and was the hallmark of his pleasure, the sign that he was enjoying himself. They learned to look for it, knowing its appearance was a compliment. But at other times his raking vision and surly expression could arouse a feeling almost of physical danger in anyone on whom they were focused, which was as easily dissolved when those wide eyes became gentle and hooded. Or they might narrow and twinkle with gaiety, as this bearded colossus of a man forgot restraint and dignity, pulled up his trouser legs and, with rolling hip and vampish jiggle, gave an imitation of the modern woman's walk.

His humor was keen, rather caustic perhaps when it mirrored his acute observations of the life around him. He had whimsy too; his letters were filled with it, and it flowed from his tongue with joking quotations and parodied mottoes. When he showed such high humor, in the roar of laughter, there was for a few mo-

ments a feeling that part of his true self was visible; then he withdrew within himself again, leaving in those who had seen the
flash of revelation a wish to know him better in that other light.
Such moments were all too rare, and were seen only by those who
knew him apart from the ordinary routine of his professional life.
To that wider world which saw him without the advantage of
intimacy, he remained completely incomprehensible. Perhaps during his later years the shadow of personal tragedy was too heavy,
and it is open to question what he might have been like had he
been less embittered, more sure of himself, and less withdrawn.
Much of his searching suspicion had root in honest doubts concerning the intentions of those who addressed him. But even then
the boyishness that occasionally burst forth made him an attractive person.

Impressions of him in his early years, when that boyishness was
more prominent, lack a certain substance. It was as though he
passed through the lives of others, leaving his mark in their memories and, while drawing so much out of them, giving in return
but a momentary charm and a pervading sense of mystery. His
intimates were under the spell of his personality; they expressed
a deep affection for him and they felt, and rightly so, that in his
stolid way he returned their affection. There were those who
knew they were beloved with great and obvious warmth. Even
so, in any realm other than his art, the qualities of John Sargent
were baffling.

It is largely this sense of mystery that survives from his earliest
years. From the time he was twenty-one and first catapulted into
prominence, he lived under the glare of public scrutiny. With
few exceptions, the events of his life were played out before the
readers of contemporary journals and newspapers, yet from the
beginning a habitual reserve guarded the inner fastnesses. He did
not talk of himself, rarely even of his work, for which he offered
neither explanation nor defense. With a bland reserve reminiscent
of his Bostonian father, he filled in no details.

To those who knew that elder Sargent, though he could not
have been very tall, his head seemed higher than other people's, his
thin back longer and stiffer. On the Continent, where he wearily
spent half his life in the empty, shifting, wasting years of the

expatriate, he was that strange thing, more British than any Briton, a Bostonian gentleman. To John Sargent as a boy his father always seemed to speak with an austere twang, and the impression early sank in upon him that his words implied disapproval. It must have been more the tone than the words, for his father showed great interest in him and his childish games. Even so, the high dome of his forehead, the widespread troubled eyes that mirrored Puritan conscience, gave his face a look of suffering that made the boy uneasy. The very atmosphere surrounding him seemed to have in it some of the chill of northern winters, irreconcilable with the warm, sunny land where they lived. For all the classic surroundings in which the young Sargent was raised, he remained keenly aware that somewhere across the sea was a different kind of land where the people were like his father, speaking and acting as he did. It was a difficult realization for a boy, giving him a slight sensation of being different, of not belonging to the world in which he found himself, the only world he knew. The persistent feeling of another land, spectral and imperceptibly present beyond the sea, which had a call on him, prevented complete acceptance of what was incontrovertible reality — Europe, the languages he heard about him, the sights, sounds, and smells that were the only sights, sounds, and smells he knew.

This feeling of isolation, the odd strangeness to all that was so familiar, carried over into his later life so that he experienced no strangeness in whatever land he was and he never really felt that any particular place was his own. In London he made himself an integral part of that great city, yet no one was so bold as to think him a Londoner, any more than in America he bore the stamp of the American or the Bostonian. The truth was, he felt no association with any of these places. None of them had any particular call on his heart. None excited him when he thought of them or visited their shores.

Perhaps Italy alone roused some feeling. For that land of his youth was the background of all his earliest memories and was perhaps the only land where he ever felt at peace. In his early years, before he realized the complexity of his heritage, Italy had become, in that nameless, placeless, wordless, moving tableau of early memory, accepted. And if so, then he accepted it as he was never again to accept any land or city; for though the greatest part of his life was spent in London, still he was an American, and perhaps equally, a Florentine. His taste bespoke the classic and his development during formative years amidst the treasures of antiquity and the Renaissance. His earliest recollection was of a bit of porphyry in the gutter of the Via Tornabuoni that he passed on daily walks with his nurse. Later, when little Johnny Sargent grew into a skittery boy, bounding about Rome in a pepper-and-salt Eton jacket, his juvenile games included bombarding the pigs outside the Porta del Populo with acorns and pebbles from the Pincian Terrace. His childish play for a time was concentrated on hunts for pieces of antique marble, which he dug from the pavement with an umbrella, loitering in the still desolate regions between the arum-fringed walls of the Esquiline and the Viminal until his father's stern accents rang out "Come on, children," and he knew the day had come to a close.

The energy and enthusiasm he threw into this play did not cease with maturity; he was as vigorous in his London life, entering into all his activities with the same gusto that he had displayed in bombarding the Roman pigs so long before. With maturity, though, and away from the land of his youth, the strangeness increased, for there was no longer even the sentimental attachment to things seen and felt that he had experienced in Italy. England was strange when he first arrived there at twenty-eight; he could make it a home, become part of it, but never feel more than a tenuous association. America he never saw until he was twenty; certainly none of the European legacy of his youth could apply there. This land was completely new. If there was any faint sense that it was a country to which he belonged, there must also have been the conscious knowledge that he had nothing in common with any inhabitant.

One of the delights of his young life was to receive his own personal letters from his grandmother in Philadelphia. He read these himself, then read them to his sister Emily, and together they were astonished that a letter should have come so far. Then there began the prodigious task of answering: writing first on a slate, having it corrected, the grammar and spelling checked; and how many sheets blotted, how many fingers stained with ink, how much strenuous effort, before the letter would be presentable, and finally fitted into an envelope for its journey across the sea. A month was not a long time for the family to work on such a letter for America.

To his American cousins, who had never seen him, he was often pointed out as an example of childish virtue. He grew up a good and well-behaved boy, unusually desirous of complying with parental wishes. And from the letters written back to America his cousins acquired the strange belief that he arose at dawn to practice for hours on the piano, an instrument he probably made himself and certainly tuned; his favorite pastimes were playing scales and brushing his teeth; and he had two sisters who were equally rare and perfect creatures, though one was sickly. How wonderful it seemed to have thus been born in a foreign land surrounded by all that was beautiful and good. The exotic strain coloring their impressions of him, when it did not move them to envy, indicated a life that was exemplary, and the only positive contact with him, the childish letters written to grandparents he was never to see, seemed in their impeccable spelling and clear script to support such an inference.

Two years before his death, Sargent took sufficient interest in a family genealogy being prepared by his cousins Winthrop and Charles Sprague Sargent to provide the required information pertaining to his own immediate forebears. It is remarkable that he did even this, for the strictness of his personal values was being violated by the fact that this genealogy would be published, though only for private circulation, and as the most famous member of that family he was aware that his was the first heredity to be investigated by the curious. Still, not only did he co-operate, but he allowed the insertion of a rather cryptic reference to his mother, which evidently expressed his own idea of her: *She is believed to have been the dominant force in the family and to have obtained everything she really wanted.* This was all he would allow said of her, but the fact that he considered the inclusion of this note proper implied that he thought it was relevant. It is the only direct reference we have from him to any member of his family.

Mrs. Sargent was indeed the dominant force of the family,

guiding husband and children with a firm will. Hers was the restless temperament that drove them all to a vagabond existence
through Europe. Never ceasing to move, overcoming all obstacles
by sheer force of will, she filled her family with the warmth
of a nature overflowing with affection. She lavished her love on
them all, delighting to feel them close, where she could express her
strong and tender attachment and where her own need of affection
was served by their presence. The very move to Europe, made a
few years after her marriage, was entirely the idea of this tenacious
woman, who continued to justify an incessant love of movement
with the claim, vigorously supported, that it was more economical
than to be established in one place. There were times when they
found themselves in some less fashionable parts of the Continent
and it seemed that economy actually was dictating a sterner regi-
men. Then such exigencies seemed to pass, and they would move
again to Pau or Biarritz, returning in the winters to Florence or
Nice.

Perhaps Mrs. Sargent's social aspirations must also bear some
responsibility for the perambulations to which she subjected her
family. As a girl, brought up in Philadelphia, she resented the
provincial atmosphere, the stifling attitudes still in vogue, and
sought the wider world of Europe, the glamour of which seemed
larger than life to her. She had once traveled in Italy, and the
memory of it never ceased to fascinate her. She quickly accustomed herself to foreign ways, becoming versed in the constant
cycle of "days," and the receptions which Americans who were
made acceptable by the possession of moderate wealth could attend.
Perhaps, too, she had hopes of advancing beyond that stage to an
even more glittering world.

As the oldest of three children, and the first to reach the maturity
from which he could examine her motives, John grew painfully
aware that he was part of a family that was perhaps open to scorn.
There was something shameful and lacking in dignity about the
way his mother ceaselessly courted people who cared little or not
at all for her; and though he was incapable of expressing his feelings,
he was deeply hurt. It was not a realization that any child could
accept with equanimity, this being wronged through no fault of
his own, guilty by association with events in which he had no part

and from which his own sympathies were withdrawn. His mother's dominating affection was nonetheless an overpowering factor to be wrestled with before he might see objectively. As he grew older he realized that he had adopted many of her ideas and viewpoints, that these had not arisen from any reasoning of his own. Perhaps it was at this point that he first saw that emotions could cloud the objectivity of his vision. He saw this happening to himself as he accepted what his mother pointed out to him as fine music or good painting. Her taste, he began to realize, was not perfect; there were serious faults in her judgment. Her eye was more that of a tourist than a connoisseur; her culture was that of the wanderer, and often she was attracted by what was ostentatious rather than fine.

When he was eighteen, he was amazed at how different from his parents his father's sister was when she came to visit. She had none of the attributes he associated with Americans through seeing them abroad. She was plain, rather simple, with gentle eye and blunt speech. And from her knitted cap to her Bible she was of a type he did not associate with himself. During later years in London, when his mother and sisters were only a few blocks from him in Chelsea, only a few most intimate people knew that he had any family or that they were in England. It was naturally assumed that his relations all lived in America and that perhaps he too had cultivated there the personal austerity clinging so heavily to him. Often he brought a few of those closest to him to dinner at his mother's apartment or, after her death, to his sister Emily's, for they were people with a delightful sociability. Henry James, who shared something of the same European youth and New England background, was one of these intimates. To him Sargent told the story of his Continental boyhood, the sojourns in half the lands of Europe, the smiling faces of strangers who smiled without conviction but seemingly out of habit and weariness. To James, this vision of a child who saw through the pretenses of his parents, loathing the vagabondish, too openly aspiring lives they led, was wonderful material. With sufficient change to render the characters unrecognizable, and with the improvements and exaggerations of a facile imagination, he turned his friend's childhood into a short novel, *The Pupil*.

The name Sargent had long figured in the colonial shipping trade of Gloucester, Massachusetts, where since the early sevententh century the family had been important merchants and shipowners. The first Sargent, William, had come to Massachusetts early in the sixteen-thirties, and was married there during April of 1633. It was his grandson, Epes Sargent, born in 1690, who established the far-flung mercantile interests that were to make the family's fortune. When toward the end of his life Epes Sargent posed to Copley for perhaps the most famous portrait done by that painter, it was as a man of solid wealth and respectability, who in his massive features and stubby hands bore striking resemblance to John Singer Sargent. The number of portraits Copley was commissioned to do for members of his family attests to their wealth at that period, if not to their patronage of the arts. The family owned land in and around Gloucester, and as a further sign of their position, they contracted marriage with the Winthrops. These tough, nervous, tenacious, and restless New Englanders, materially ambitious and prone to introspection, carried on a trade with distant parts of the world in schooners and brigs measuring sixty to ninety feet in length and rarely of more than a hundred tons. With such ships, in the eighteenth century, the port of Gloucester, and the interests of the Sargents, took a virtual monopoly of the trade in fish and molasses with Surinam, Dutch Guiana. For more than a hundred years Gloucester ships were better known there than those from any other North American port. The Revolutionary War caused no hiatus in their activity, introducing them to the even more profitable enterprise of privateering. Winthrop Sargent was designated General Washington's agent on Cape Ann, and members of his immediate family sent out at least twenty-three privateers. At times their success was spectacular, as when the *General Stark* set sail in April 1779, with a crew of one hundred thirty-five men and boys, and eighteen guns. On her outward passage she took four enemy ships, then spent the winter refitting at Bilbao, where in the spring she captured a Guernsey privateer at the invitation of the port and was rewarded with a bounty of a thousand dollars, plus the sixten hundred realized from the sale of the prize. Crossing the ocean once more, she captured four more prizes, which arrived at

Gloucester, one by one, before the *Stark* itself returned in September of 1780.

When the China trade opened, the three most important families of Gloucester — Sargent, Parsons, and Pearce — formed an association to engage in this East India trade, as it was called. Initially they sent out the 104-ton ship *Winthrop and Mary*, the loss of which, off Sumatra on her homeward journey in 1800, ended the association. Undaunted, the Sargents pressed on by themselves, sending ship after ship on the year-long passage across the Atlantic and around the Cape of Good Hope, to call at Canton, the only Chinese port where foreigners were tolerated. Particularly adapted to this China trade because of their privateering experience, they continued to prosper, with ownership and part interest in as many as eighty-two vessels. Except for some few commodities like sandalwood, sea otter pelts, and opium, silver was the only acceptable medium of exchange at Canton, which made it necessary to call first at other ports, where the outbound cargo from Gloucester might be exchanged for silver with which to purchase the silks, lacquerware, dishes, and tea that brought unusually high percentages of profit. The lack of silver in Massachusetts forced the discovery of expedients, the first of which was to round the tip of South America, spend six months or a year among the Indian villages of the northwest coast, until a cargo of Massachusetts hardware could be exchanged for sea otter pelts. They in turn might be traded for sandalwood in Hawaii, where Daniel Sargent had an exclusive treaty with King Kamehameha, or taken directly to Canton. The original worth of the cargo out of Gloucester was thus twice pyramided before it was exchanged for the profit-making Cantonese goods. Trading with the Indians was a dangerous business, however, for their peacefulness was subject to sudden fluctuations. The vessels were well armed, and when a flotilla of dugouts surrounded them, only a few natives were allowed on deck at one time, while men armed with blunderbusses were stationed in the tops lest the waiting customers lose patience.

FitzWilliam Sargent (1768–1822) established the India Company for trading with Baltic ports and Russia, where pelts were available, and Calcutta, where other cargoes of value might be found, before arriving at Canton. Winthrop Sargent found it worth while to carry crockery from England to Canton, where it was decorated while his ships lay over through the winter, then carried back to Gloucester.

The years following the War of 1812 saw the expansion of this pattern of European and China trade, then a slow decline of American overseas commerce in general. The individual enterprise that had built the mercantile fortunes of the end of the previous century counted for less against the larger combinations in world trade, and profits dwindled while the risk of voyages remained constant.

Young Winthrop Sargent, the grandfather of John, who took over control about this time, joined in the move to larger ships, with their greater consequent overhead, and suffered a series of disastrous losses. When the 200-ton brig *Juliana* went down in August 1828 while bound for Port-au-Prince, it marked the beginning of the end. The brig *Mary*, a small ship but a new one, was lost off the Carolinas, and hopes were pinned to the imminent arrival of an indigo cargo from India. The business was now in desperate condition. Whether a gale that ripped through Gloucester harbor that November, sending nineteen schooners high and dry in Fresh Water Cove, was a contributing factor or not cannot be proved; but the ship from India never came in. The result was bankruptcy, with a total loss of the family's property. Thus five generations of Yankee enterprise came to an end. FitzWilliam Sargent, the father of John, was then nine years of age, growing up in straitened circumstances but with the traditions of past glory.

FitzWilliam was born at Gloucester in 1820, and despite the adversity that greeted his early life, after the removal of the family to Philadelphia, where they engaged in a commission business, he was sent to the University of Pennsylvania, graduating in 1837. He went on to study medicine, as a younger brother did after him, receiving his degree in 1843 and practicing medicine and surgery in Philadelphia for eleven years. During that time he wrote a book, *On Bandaging, And Other Operations of Minor Surgery*, which he illustrated himself. He seems to have made himself some reputation in the city, and in 1850 married Mary Newbold Singer, the only child of a prosperous merchant in hides and leathers.

Mary Singer was a passable musician, and painted in watercolor with a higher degree of skill than that of many other young ladies who also dabbled. Her father was a devoted parent, willing whenever possible to grant the wishes of his headstrong daughter, and after his death the income left her was equal to the seven hundred dollars a year that Dr. Sargent earned from his practice at best. The means were thus at her disposal to take her husband to live in Europe, and finally, in 1854, Dr. Sargent surrendered to his wife's insistent importuning, resigning his position at the Wills Hospital. If he had any serious reservations, it was only the first of many occasions on which Mary Newbold Sargent would prove capable of carrying the day. Finding it impossible to deny his wife anything, Dr. Sargent was now committed to allowing his family to live, and himself to be largely dependent, upon the half-yearly remittances she received from Philadelphia. No doubt that added to the weight of her wishes; as time passed, whatever her eager, bubbling nature craved, there was none to deny her.

If they had any one home in Europe during the early years of their life abroad, it was the city of Florence, to which they returned most often. There on January 12, 1856, while they lived at the Casa Arretini, facing the river, a son was born to them and named after his grandfather, John Singer. He was the second child, and as the first had already died, his health was much feared for. However, it was early established that he was extraordinarily healthy, and he grew to be a strong, dark, blue-eyed, animated young fellow. His father thought him not especially fond of reading and, for one of such strict conscience, displayed a remarkable leniency about it, writing to relatives in America that the boy was displaying good sense, for "his muscles and bones are of more consequence to him, at his age, than his brains; I dare say the latter will take care of themselves."

Young John grew up speaking Italian and English equally well, and a German nurse early added a knowledge of her own tongue. His education was taken in hand by his father, along with that of his little sister Emily, who was born at Rome in 1857. They were supplied with books on natural history, illustrated with pictures of birds and animals; the editions were carefully chosen, with a text simple enough for them to make out themselves. In his childish way John became a close observer of nature, recognizing various birds familiar from his books. At the same time, true to the Puritan background of the Sargents, he was also given Bible stories to read. The question of whether or not to teach his children a catechism worried Dr. Sargent, who realized he no longer remembered his own word for word, though he knew well enough the meaning of the answers. But his love of God was of extraordinary simplicity and faith, and eventually he decided to teach a rather comprehensive idea of right and wrong, along with the meaning of sin and salvation, hoping it would bore the children less than the tedium of memorizing an exacting catechism. He wished to teach his children as much as possible without the disagreeable notion entering their heads that they were studying.

For a number of years during the sixties Nice, where numerous American families were living, became the Sargents' winter headquarters, and the Maison Virello, in the Rue Grimaldi, acquired some little sense of permanence in their scheme of things. So long as they had money enough this was a wonderful place to spend the winters, though the increasing cost of the apartment and food brought grave doubts about how long they would be able to remain there. Johnny was only six when prices thus became a matter of concern. Nor were their problems helped that winter by the cheating cook, who insisted that Dr. Sargent, who alone ate apple dumplings in the family, consumed twenty-four pounds of brown sugar in one month, though dumplings were served him only once a week. "Of course we got rid of her as quickly as possible," wrote the doctor. "This is a specimen of the Nice cooks; they have no bowels whatever." That straitened winter was also marked by the presence of chicken pox in the city. For six weeks, one after another, John and Emily, then the newest little sister, Mary Winthrop, were down with it, all of them surviving, though many in the city did not.

Near the Maison Virello was a garden of pepper trees that bloomed through the winter with arid magenta and lilac-colored flowers. Next door to six-year-old Johnny Sargent was Ben del Castillo, of the same age. Often the two went with their sailboats to a pond in the larger common garden adjoining the apartments of the Maison Corinaldi, where a collection of American children were ready to play hide and seek, or take part in historic improvisations, like the decapitation of Mary Queen of Scots with the fire shovel. Another day the contrite Earl of Essex offered his neck to an imperious Queen Elizabeth; the Queen perhaps a trifle too imperious, for she was a British girl and liable to overdo the pomp of the thing. Violet Paget was her name, and through that and later winters in this garden she played a prominent part in the Sargents' lives, the two families establishing a regular coming and going between houses.

Emily was rarely able to join in their play, for, young as she was, three years of her life had already been spent lying flat on a hard bed suffering from a strange disease. Unable to walk, barely able to move, she was carried with the family as it went from place to place, sometimes with the forlorn hope that a warmer climate or clearer air would heal her pain-racked body. Her bed was fitted with a small platform, supported on C springs, that her father contrived, and with the joltings and shakings of the railway carriages thus diminished, they continued on their journeyings. Despite her pain, this frail little girl held on year after year with remarkable tenacity. London seemed to promise aid in the form of famous surgeons, for which they crossed the Channel. While Johnny played in Regent's Park, opposite their house, through the summer of 1862, Emily's condition was "favorably spoken of by her examiners." Lest the strain on her back be too great, it was thought unwise to let her sit up at once, and only gradually was she allowed to assume an upright position. Then they noticed that her spine, due to the disuse of the muscles, seemed imperfectly developed, her high-shouldered posture betraying the deformity left by her disease.

John and Emily grew up together. With only a year separating them, they had begun to read together, taught first by their Swiss nurse, who was proficient only in her native French; their father reasoning that the language in which they learned to read made no difference, for the letters were the same. These early years were punctuated not only by the come and go of nurses, and the moves from place to place, but sadly, too, by the arrival and death of little brothers and sisters whose aptitude for the expatriate life was less strong than theirs. When little Mary Winthrop joined them, at Nice in 1860, John found her some new sort of curiosity, and the sad history of decline and early death can be traced in the letters of this observant brother. "Poor little Minnie is getting thinner every day," he wrote when he was nine. "She does not care for anything any more. Emily and I brought her some beautiful Easter Eggs but she would not look at them. She never talks nor smiles now." With unerring instinct he noted the symptoms of his sister's human decay, mentioning not the progress of her disease but the fact that she cared for nothing and neither talked nor smiled.

His father's attitude was less worldly, colored by his deeply religious nature. When he realized the child could not live, for all his grief, he wrote to America:

> Geneva, June 23, 1864
>
> Humanity is selfish. We know that our children, if they die young, will go to heaven surely, and that they will be happy together. Yet we shudder at the idea of their being removed from this world, where they are sure to meet with trials and suffering and unhappiness, simply because the idea of parting with them and the actual partings are so painful to us, and because if we have had experience, the void left in our family circles, by their death, is so great and so slow to fill and so full of sorrow.

After the Civil War a squadron of the United States Navy was stationed in the Mediterranean, and the officers were often seen at Florence, where in fact the wife of the commander, Admiral Goodrich, taught a Sunday school. With all the eagerness of the expatriate, Dr. Sargent watched this squadron arrive and depart, for perhaps in his idleness and his unhappiness over the maritime and medical careers that had eluded him, there was the wish that just for a short time he could be out there, where Sargents belonged. He was a patriot in a very true sense, watching the fortunes of his country with a wistfulness one could not but notice, viewing the agony of the Civil War from afar, not without qualms of conscience, which in her gay way his wife must have been called upon to put at rest. Undoubtedly he felt some call of duty, all of it centered in the hope, indeed the plan, that one day his son would be the man he was not, to take his place, marked out by heredity, sympathy, and every tie of country.

He was so chagrined that he attempted in what small way he

could to help his stricken country and wrote a book in the hope
of influencing the pro-Southern sympathies he had found in England. *England, the United States, and the Southern Confederacy*
was the title, and he ransacked the libraries and consulates in and
around Nice for figures of investments and production with which
to state his case. Though his expatriate heart was wrung by the
bloody agony of the homeland, an indication of his entire attitude
toward life can be found in his comments on the progress of the
war: "Grant's victory seems to have been a grand one. Let us
give God the Glory!"

When little Johnny was taken to visit the ships calling at Mediterranean ports, his father was pleased by the interest shown by
the boy in all the paraphernalia of sails, steam, guns, and shot.
But he could not fail to notice that his son seemed more interested
in sitting down to draw all he had seen; his hand was eager to
record what his eye noted, almost as if the drawing was as important as the inspection, being with men and ships, and feeling
the sea beneath one's feet. A letter little Johnny wrote to Ben
del Castillo, when he was nine, regrets leaving Bordeaux so early
in the morning on the way to Pau that he was unable to draw the
ships in the harbor; "but they would have been too difficult for
me, I think," he adds ruefully. It was simple childish foolishness,
his father thought, and nothing to become angered about: how
could the boy fail to see that out beyond the sight of land was
the real life; not this dabbling with paints and music, and sentiment
over past ages, and things unbecoming to a man?

Whatever his father's view, Mrs. Sargent was certain her son
displayed talents in several directions. She taught him to play
the piano and he took to the instrument wonderfully well. When
she was not able to help him further she turned his instruction
over to a professional, who introduced the study of theory, training him to solfeggize passages that at first seemed too difficult. It
seemed he could have a musical career if he were determined to
excel. And often when Mrs. Sargent went forth armed with
camp stool and paint box to sketch some sun-flushed monument —
for she kept a running account of her travels in her sketchbooks
— John went along and took his turn at that too. In time he
had his own outfit. Here too he was soon past the point where

she could instruct him. One thing she did insist upon, though. So that he would understand one could not simply play with these things that were arts and of great importance to the finer people of the world, no matter how many drawings he might start each day he had to select one and finish it, working with precision and getting into the refinements of the subject. One did not learn by hasty improvisation, and it was not well to allow children to feel that something grown difficult could simply be abandoned. His sketches seemed to show some cleverness, even a little understanding of the nature of the materials; but of course it was only a pleasant toy for the child, for everyone knew, how could they fail to know, that Dr. Sargent's little boy was headed for a career in the United States Navy. The sea was part of the Sargent heritage. If for lack of ships Dr. Sargent had not been able to go to sea, America now had a navy, and there was the career he himself would have wanted. Wherever he was, Dr. Sargent saw a fascination in the deep waters, frequenting admirals and ships, cherishing an enmity toward Britain over the *Alabama* business and the soft attitude toward "rebels." So Johnny was taken to entertainments on board ships, and his sailboat was almost the badge of his future.

Through these years the factor of rising costs was becoming increasingly troublesome. By the time John was twelve it was evident that the Sargents would have to try new places to live, where expenses might be kept more moderate. Their first essay was the Brittany coast. If the country had not the lush verdure of Italy, it was nonetheless pleasant and picturesque. The women still wore their caps of white muslin, which were decidedly becoming, and every elevated spot was capped by its windmill, with a thatched cottage by the side for the miller and his family; the latter of course included his cow, pig, and chickens. Looking around in June, they were pleased to discover a house at St.-Enogat, just opposite the ancient gray walls of St.-Malo harbor. The rent was only three hundred francs a month. It was a nice-looking place, the large garden filled with fig and fruit trees; and since the rental included furnishings right down to linens and silver, it seemed an economical step to have taken. Unfortunately, as the summer progressed the rent began to show fluctuations, boosting to four hundred francs in July, to remain at that figure through

September. Their reward came in October, however, when it miraculously tumbled to one hundred twenty francs, and since food also was cheap and plentiful in the neighborhood, they considered staying on, perhaps as late as December, "simply because it is cheap." A considerable saving would be made through those autumn months, which inspired Mrs. Sargent to talk of taking John and Emily to see their grandparents in America the following year.

Here was an exciting prospect! They chattered about passage, deciding it would be wisest to leave in May, so their visit need not be hurried, and they might still return before the equinoctial storms of the fall. Dr. Sargent elected to remain abroad with the baby as an economy measure, explaining, "Such trips cost a great deal of money, and unfortunately we must live after the trip shall be over, but they are all very anxious to go 'home' as they say. . . ." Like so many others, this trip did not materialize, and by October, when the summer tenants vacated their apartment in Nice, the Sargents shifted back. The cost of living in the south was still headed upward. Now they discovered that fruit was too costly for them to touch, excepting grapes and figs in season, while peaches, pears, and apples were selling by the pound instead of the bushel as an added means of increasing the cost. Another worry was that it was time for Johnny to start school. His father inquired around the city, finally selecting an academy because it was run by an English clergyman, in whose judgment he could feel secure. Latin, Euclid, and algebra suddenly surrounded the boy, who made manly efforts to meet the challenge. At eight-thirty in the morning he was off to lessons that lasted until half past one. Lunch was finished by two, then games of football took over, for this was the balanced English curriculum. At four he arrived home to begin preparation of the following day's lessons. Despite all the enthusiasm with which he threw himself into this new life, it did not last long. His mother was conscious of how little could be done with her limited income at Nice, and when her second son, FitzWilliam Winthrop, became ill, she was certain that neither the climate nor the expense was suitable to them. She rented out their apartment and they moved south.

A month later they were in Florence, from where Dr. Sargent

explained something of their circumstances to his brother Henry, who had asked if he could find people abroad to purchase land in Virginia. ". . . the fact is my acquaintance among Capitalists is actually nil; we lead a very quiet sort of life, balancing between winter quarters and a summering place; we have very few acquaintances, and those which we have are in the same category with ourselves, — people who have, as a rule, no superfluity of means . . . As to ourselves, Mary's income is only such as enables us to live on with a constant effort to spend as little as possible consistently with the requirements of rather delicate health in all of us, which makes it necessary to resort to places of residence which are more expensive than we should think of going to if we were well enough to avoid them."

That winter of 1868 they finally settled in Rome, the mighty and eternal city, much shrunken from her former greatness, whose ancient population exceeding two million was now scarcely one hundred twenty thousand. On his way to daily rides Dr. Sargent passed through areas of waste and desolation, entirely uninhabited, even before reaching the city walls. Outside, due to the prevalence of malaria a large part of the year, the campagna was equally uninhabited, seemingly given over to wild foxes, rodents, and even wilder looking herdsmen clad in rough goatskins, who watched over vast flocks of sheep and cattle. Since their last residence there, the streets looked even dirtier, the Pope a little older and more feeble. Otherwise Rome was the same as it had always been, its most telling disadvantage remaining in the fleas with which each house was permanently infested.

It was while vehemently scratching after these eternal inhabitants of the eternal city that little Johnny Sargent, his hair plastered down to his round skull, his face grown full, with brows set close over wide eyes and a full pouting mouth, made his way through the miles of Vatican Galleries, even stopping to make hurried forbidden sketches of statues selected as easy to do. The Pagets were in Rome that winter also, John, Emily and Violet forming a compact group delighted in rambling through the city, where they saw red-robed cardinals, and perhaps even the Pope himself, a white sash around his portly middle, distributing benedictions among the bay hedges and mossy fountains of the Villa Borghese.

There were early winter mornings when with secret biscuits and chocolate they were packed in among black-veiled ladies in St. Peter's, to witness some pontifical mass. But there were afternoons in tinsel-hung churches where tapers shone through the haze of stale incense and the little organs seemed out of tune with the throaty falsetto of the prayerful. From their windows the children sometimes watched Cinderella coaches pass with scarlet-robed figures seated in all the earnestness of state. Perhaps, too, on some particularly restless day, when it was too cold for them to venture out, they might all play in the Sargents' empty bedroom, where they did the Sistine Chapel, John warbling in striking mimicry of the sounds heard in that larger Sistine Chapel not far away. Then as the afternoon grew dark, a porter arrived from some cookshop, balancing on his head the tin box containing dinner, expressly ordered by the Pagets to regale the Sargents; not without the charlotte russe, pièce de résistance and special delight of the children.

The winter was cold. Nightly temperatures plunged to twenty degrees, freezing over the basins of numerous fountains, while long icicles ornamented the horned tritons and the dolphins. Off in the distance the Sabine and Volscian mountain ranges were capped with snow, while the gay contrast appeared near at hand of almond trees in bloom. Ice was a rarity to the children, and their obvious delight was increased by lessons in sliding, Gloucester style, administered by their father on a patch two yards long, discovered on the Pincian Hill. Other afternoons John would use Violet's paintbox, which she employed in place of the words she could not spell and the sights she could not express. She had watercolors and porcelain tablets, and albums of tinted papers, and perhaps it was these that attracted him to this girl who persistently took the wrong side of the *Alabama* affair. For, though he had never seen the land to which he owed allegiance, he was nonetheless letter-perfect in the opinions his father expressed on the rebellion back home. The *Alabama* crisis split the English-speaking population of Southern Europe right down the middle, English and Americans each clinging to their own opinions. Over the lure of paints, however, the two consumed refreshments, conversing the while on elevated topics, he in the quiet grave way now beginning to typify him, she with forceful gesture of hand and face.

At Rome, too, Mrs. Sargent had her "day," when the hired cook made special efforts, and artists and writers and distinguished Americans gathered in the drawing room of her rented quarters, between the busts of Washington and the goddess Isis that were part of the standard furnishings of a Roman lodging. John, Emily, and Violet waited below stairs while legendary figures conversed above, and young FitzWilliam Winthrop crawled about the floor, babbling to himself part in French, part in English, and the rest in Italian. Then there came the joy of being brought the disarranged, though still sumptuous, remains of the dinner party, when Johnny's renowned appetite, already the marvel of parents and friends, found good use.

Occasionally Mrs. Sargent, in her irrepressible way, would show some of her son's sketches to those now-forgotten "immortals" who cluttered her drawing room one day a week. One of her guests that winter of 1868 was the German-American painter Carl Welsch, who, like so many artists, had established his studio in Rome, then, and for a few years to remain, the artistic center of the world. As Mrs. Sargent's guests generally did, Welsch thought the sketches showed promise. A boy of twelve has scarcely time to find abiding interests, and it was amazing that this youngster, who spent hours over a drawing of some rock on a hillside, should then go back the following day of his own volition to see if a second attempt might improve what he had done. Welsch invited the boy to his studio, where he might study from paintings and watercolors, and through the winter John applied his mornings to copying.

The plan of a naval career seemed further off now than ever, his mother quietly suggesting that he might be better suited by nature to some career where his aptitudes would have expression. It was a difficult time for Dr. Sargent. It seemed God had given him a son with unusual artistic abilities; still, was it right to encourage in his young soul foreign mores and frills? His wife seemed to gain pleasure from these artists. But was it right to sacrifice a son to this doubtful caste, and a career by no means certain? However, Dr. Sargent saw God's work everywhere, and it could not long have escaped him that God, who dispensed all blessings, had given his son a talent. If he was going to sacrifice his own prejudices, it would be best to do so completely, giving the boy every facility and encouragement. For if a thing was to be done it had to be done well, and the boy would not be an amateur, but a professional and a master.

Thus that winter of 1868 in Rome it was decided. From thenceforth John was specifically to be a painter. His efforts, which had been of a stern sort, would now be more sternly applied. Perhaps the most important result of those years, which had so great an effect on his future development, was not any technical advance he made, nor the undoubted steady improvement of his skill, significant as that was, but the development of his eye. For it cannot be forgotten that to his mother painting was an important adjunct of sightseeing; it was recording in a specific and specialized way, and when he went out to paint by her side, it was the clarity of his vision that she concentrated on. To him, too, drawing and painting in watercolor was the specific recording of what he selected from the visual world. Of course, he also drew now and again from illustrations in the American magazines his father read, but the fact remains that he rarely attempted anything that was not before him. He was conscious of the world about him, interested as the traveler, perhaps even as the budding historian, might have been, in this residue of great civilizations. He read accounts of the history of the places he visited, and when he drew often as not it was with knowledge of some obscure event associated with the place. Yet what he drew was in each instance an objective recording of what he saw, not of what he might know.

In an age devoted to the poetic sentimentalization of ancient and medieval worlds, it was remarkable that he remained so individually preoccupied with the visual aspects of what passed before him. His earliest letters, many of them written to Ben del Castillo, are crammed with accurate descriptions, dates, and measurements, and stress the restlessness of his visual faculty. During these formative years, when impressions were stored up for the future, Sargent had before him the wreckage and remains of the great classic civilizations. The shapes and forms, the proportions and textures of ancient art were impressed upon him. The gardens and the hilltops he noted, which he was careful to draw in proper proportion, were the product of Renaissance taste. Even the stray oleander that clambered across some wall had been placed there in an earlier time to achieve a desired effect. The fountains, the statue-strewn gardens, the cathedral towers he drew, all indelibly impressed themselves on his forming taste. He had also the advantage of seeing collections of paintings scattered over Europe, and becoming familiar with masterpieces of the first order which could be sought out and studied and drawn where they were. The attention he paid these pictures is attested by the detailed descriptions of them that went into his letters, in some of which he even directed visitors to the particular gallery in which they hung.

Spring arrived in Rome with a spell of warm weather, and the family, fearful for its various sickly members, went off to get some refreshing air at Naples. It seemed a healthy change after the winter in Rome, where the soil, thought Dr. Sargent, "was composed of the dust of the ages, dead men's bones, and all infirmities, temporal and clerical." The effects of sea air, however good, were appreciated for only a week before they moved north to Bavaria, to drink the mineral waters of Kissingen. Shortly after they arrived, little FitzWilliam Winthrop became ill, and following a fortnight's illness he died.

The waters seemed less important then, and they went on, in August, to Clarens, in Switzerland, where John and his father fished for trout in the lakes and mountain streams. With scarcely any arable land in sight, the entire view consisted of small lakes and glaciers, with snowcaps dominating the distances; minds naturally turned to mountain climbing. John joined a group of men who wanted to climb the highest peak in the region, something over ten thousand feet, and this sturdy thirteen-year-old had a wonderful view from the top, then came down and returned home "brisk as a bee." Meanwhile it amused Dr. Sargent to see that the Swiss, simple-minded and openhearted by reputation, were actually a people sharp at moneymaking. Their grapes, growing plentifully on the hillsides, were not of a quality to compete with the French in winemaking, so they started a new fad, the Grape Cure. People were flocking from all sides to Clarens, and ate from six to ten pounds of grapes a day. All through the little town they marched, basket in hand, eating and eating, constantly eating grapes. From six in the morning until bedtime the process was industriously carried on. A little Russian woman staying at the same house with them ate ten pounds a day, until inevitably the evil effects set in, and there were endless discussions over whether it was due to eating too few grapes or too many.

By October of 1870 they returned once again to Florence to settle down for the winter. "I am tired of this nomadic sort of life: — the Spring comes, and we strike our tents and migrate for the summer: the Autumn returns, and we must again pack up our duds and be off to some milder region in which Emily and Mary can thrive. I wish there were some prospect of our going home and settling down among our own people and taking permanent root," wrote the doctor. But it was not to be, nor did he ever reach home; and his weary life, to his last hour, was spent in this same endless, shifting pattern.

John was entered in a boys' school run by a political refugee from France, and from the Latin primer he jumped directly into Livy. Nightly his father refreshed his own youth by working with him; "but he studies well, and he is well and strong, eating heartily and sleeping soundly and playing joyfully whenever it is playtime, so that we hope he will get on well." John was also attending a dancing class, and soon was taking courses in drawing at the Accademia delle Belle Arti. This was his first really systematic training in art and served to prove the value of what had gone before, for in his first year he won the annual prize.

In May John's teacher had given a good account to Dr. Sargent, and he was invited by Carl Welsch to tour with him through the Tyrol in the summer, on the understanding that they would sketch when the light was good, fish when it failed. Their actual route, with the dates when they were at each point, can be traced by the notations carefully made on each of the drawings in John's notebook. It seems that the fishing was as good as the weather was bad, and there was an amusing incident when Johnny caught eight trout in one day, only to lose the two largest to a cat.

John's family traveled close by, for sudden deaths so easily overcame their children that they dreaded being kept apart. And all the while the question of better schooling was thrashed out in his father's mind. That autumn, therefore, accompanied by a new little girl, born the previous February at Florence and named Violet, they moved up to Dresden. There they found the people as civil to strangers "as fish hooks are to fish." Somehow they preferred the oily-mannered Italians, who lied to their visitors and gouged them unmercifully, but did so agreeably and pleasantly. However, it was for education that they had come north. The German system was considered very thorough, and John was at once placed in the care of teachers who were to tutor him privately in Latin and Greek, while a bright boy from each class was to get him on with mathematics, geography, history, and especially German, in which through lack of use he was now deficient. The school year began at Easter, when he was to be ready for classes. Though the same care was not taken with Emily, she too was involved with a curriculum laid out by her father until it was seen that her health was suffering in the cold German winter. By February it was realized that the Dresden climate might be disastrous for her, so Johnny was not entered in school after all, but taken back to Florence.

The baths at Carlsbad were on the itinerary for the next summer, after which they set out by train for a lake in the Tyrol, near Innsbruck. John complained of headaches and chilliness on the train, and was looking very sick by the time they rolled into Munich. Remittent fever was his father's first diagnosis. Finally his illness was discovered to be a mild typhoid, and for three weeks he was nursed and fed on broth, until he was ready to travel again.

John was sixteen, and as tall as his father, though a trifle heavier, when they returned to Florence. His former art teacher had been able to return to France following the fall of Louis Napoleon, leaving a void in the matter of schooling facilities. Cold weather brought measles for them all, and also another, new glimpse of Italian life. Discharging a servant, Dr. Sargent found himself threatened with a court summons unless he paid an extra two weeks' salary, with board and lodging. This was an idle threat to the son of privateers, and he said to fire away. But he soon found himself before a judge's tribunal, or court of reconciliation. The most amusing part of the hearing was to find all the Americans in Florence present, brought in on the same charge, apparently a favorite among the Italians they hired. To live in Italy was not all classic dream, as they knew exceedingly well, and the fact was further proved the following summer when they stayed in Venice, awaiting Dr. Sargent, who had gone off alone to see his parents in America. Shortly after his departure the heat became unbearable, the canals began to stink, disease spread through the city, and there was a sudden loss of appetite in the family. When a woman in their house died of cholera, they packed for Switzerland, where all arrived deathly sick. When their lone traveler returned, his work was cut out for him.

By the early seventies it was acknowledged that the artistic primacy of Italy once again had faded, and the best training was to be got only in Paris or in the several German cities then popular with American students. Various of the people the Sargents met made strong and often eloquent appeals in behalf of some particular city and school. But the question of where was still a matter for keen consideration; for was not Paris the center of that grotesquely immoral Bohemian life? Still, from all they could gather, it seemed certain that Paris offered the best training to be had, and so, with a conscience more than faintly uneasy, it was decided that Paris would be the place for John. In the meantime he continued to work in the Academy at Florence, where he used charcoal and stump, and was taught severely rigid standards. It was an unhappy institution, of which as time passed he became more and more critical. Finally, late in the winter, it was closed down for some months, while the faculty discussed with the Minister of Public Instruction ways to improve a situation that had grown impossible. When, three months later, the school reopened (the Sargents had taken the opportunity to visit Venice), John saw no change.

Shortly after the reopening, his youthful exuberance took the form of jumping down flights of stairs. He missed his footing one day, spraining his right ankle. For several weeks he was unable to stand, and a model was hired for him at home, who played on native instruments and when he grew tired of holding his position amused them all by dancing the tarantella. When John was able to get about again, despite colds and reports of more cholera, the family were off once more to Venice. There they met Whistler, who expressed himself enthusiastically over John's watercolors and drawings. Then, in the second week of May, 1874, they moved on to their final destination and John's first permanent home in Europe, *Paris*.

Paris: Atelier Carolus-Duran

STOOPING to accommodate his new height, John Sargent arrived in Paris awkward and gangling. He stood with shoulders hunched and head thrust forward, a boyishness in every gesture revealing the uneasiness with which he viewed his scrawny self. At first sight his small, round face disguised something of his leanness, but that too proved bony, abruptly fusing into a short, birdlike nose that was his most prominent feature, protruding like a blunt beak, entirely unsuited to the rest of his face. Beneath it were the fuzzy beginnings of a mustache still too immature for grooming, a transparent brier patch framing the upper limits of a full mouth. The whole head was a trifle small in proportion to the long body it sat upon, a union further troubled by his outsized Adam's apple, so often dancing about that it rendered humorous the vast seriousness of his expression. Nature, otherwise liberal in her endowments, gave him few external graces, and at eighteen he had not yet licked himself into shape.

It was the second week of May, and the Sargents experienced difficulty locating themselves with the economy they had known in the south, for due to the continued cold weather people were not yet leaving the city and there were few vacancies. Emily and Violet, whose colds were still troublesome, came down with whooping cough. John and his father were coughing too, though less heavily, theirs probably being no more than garden variety colds. While they were getting settled, John selected a portfolio

30

of drawings, added a few watercolors, and with them under his arm he started off with his father for Montparnasse, and the studio of Carolus-Duran.

The gray, stiff-backed gentleman and his scrawny son made their way up to the Boulevard Montparnasse, past the huge open intersection before the Gare Montparnasse, with its tangled mass of pedestrians, buses, and hacks, then down the wide sidewalk a few steps to the left, where they came upon a cobblestoned alley. This little alleyway led back from the boulevard, where it was closed by a gate. Their ankles twisted as they made their way past the industrial buildings that lined it on the left and the back walls of residences on the right. At the end, on the right, they found a wooden gate marked with the number 81. It opened into a small, musty-looking court around which two tiers of studios were ranged. Sculptors clearly occupied the lower row, their product evident through the partly opened doors, and strewn into the court, while the tier above was reserved for painters. In the middle of these studios, at the far end of this miniature court, was the home of Madame the Proprietress, looking anomalous in this musty, statue-strewn atmosphere; and above it, on the third floor, was the largest studio of all. The entrance was by a stairway that issued from the alley in which they stood, at the foot of which a sign read: *L'Atelier des Elèves de Monsieur Carolus-Duran.*

That was it, then, and they made their way up. Dr. Sargent knocked at the door, gently, quietly, firmly, as was his way, and it was opened from within by a pale-faced little student who motioned for them to remain quiet, explaining the "patron" was within. He looked over the tall young man with the portfolio and appraised him as an applicant to the studio. Dr. Sargent spoke politely in French and then, hearing the accent of the student, switched to English, all in subdued tones. From where they stood near the door they could see a short thick man, wearing a strange wide collar and a coat with velvet lapels. He was pretentiously examining the work of the students, putting his hand out now and again for a brush. Those at the door could not make out what he said, but they could see the entire class following him from easel to easel, eager to catch every word, to see every correction made by his hand. Soon he had finished and turned to the Sargents.

They were introduced, and Carolus-Duran took the portfolio offered him, spreading the contents on the floor for all to see. His eyebrows rose and his lips pursed as he examined the drawings; complete silence reigned. There were some low murmurs of approval as he fanned the papers out, and it was obvious that Carolus too was pleased, even startled, by what he found. At length he announced that he found "much to be unlearned" and, pausing for emphasis, continued, "but promise above the ordinary." Yes, he approved the boy's entry into his class.

John started work the following Monday morning, rising early to get a good place before the model. To be officially admitted he paid his entry fee of twenty-five francs to Carroll Beckwith, the class monitor; the same pale student who had opened the door for them. One formality still remained, to "treat the crowd," generally no more than a toast at noontime in one of the numerous cheap restaurants whose awnings and sprawling chairs lined the Boulevard Montparnasse in both directions. He began work at the atelier that first spring at seven each morning, continuing until eleven-thirty, when he made his way home for lunch. Afternoons he generally spent at the various galleries with which Paris abounded, and with which he had to become familiar. Beckwith, rather shy at first, proved friendly. Possessed of a similar capacity for concentration and drawn together by a sympathetic awareness of each other's reserve, they were soon close. Beckwith explained his intention of taking the examination for the Ecole des Beaux-Arts. He was devoted to Carolus, who he readily explained was the best teacher in Paris, "and therefore the world," but he felt that his teacher did not concentrate sufficiently on drawing. At the Ecole he would continue to perfect his draftsmanship while he painted with Duran. It seemed a good idea to John, for if both were admitted, they could take a late afternoon class and fill out the day's work. But this would have to wait, for, as summer approached, Mrs. Sargent packed her family for the seashore, where it was hoped the salt air would favor all the coughers in the family.

At the end of August they returned to Paris and found more permanent quarters at number 52, Rue Abbatucci (now Rue La Boëtie), which curved upward from the fashionable Champs-

Elysées toward the Avenue de Friedland. This was still a new section of the city, and a long way from the atelier on Montparnasse on the other side of the river. The inconvenience of long hours of travel was added to the daily routine of work.

Once back in Paris, John immediately went off to join a sketch class at the Ecole des Beaux-Arts, for every bit of practice and study would help in the awful examination at the end of September. The class was filled with others suffering the same pre-examination anxiety. Among them was Beckwith, who, seeing the distance his younger friend traveled each day, invited John to work after class at the little studio he had taken near the school, in the Rue des Saints-Pères. Together the two walked daily between school and studio; Sargent, tall and lanky, stepped briskly with a preoccupied manner not calculated to invite conversation, while a pace or two behind, and constantly on the verge of running, the short, nervous Beckwith tagged along. They shared the five-franc cost of a model each afternoon, which enabled them to continue the figure drawing they knew would count so heavily on the examination. As early as that October 13, Beckwith confided to his diary: "My talented young friend Sargent has been working in my studio with me lately and his work makes me shake myself."

The entrance examinations at the Ecole des Beaux-Arts began on September 26 and went on until October 18. They were unlike anything invented since, consisting of separate sessions in perspective, anatomy, design, and life drawing, plus a language requirement designed specifically to exclude the foreign students, who otherwise would crowd in. Sargent's sentiments while in the midst of this torturous experience were expressed in a letter to Ben del Castillo:

52, Rue Abbatucci
Oct. 4ᵗʰ, 1874

My dear Ben,

Caro il mio ben. I am in the midst of my exam . . . which seems unreasonably long difficult and terrible . . . Two weeks are still to come . . . But the supreme moment is one of twelve hours wherein we must make a finished drawing of the human form divine.

Heaven only knows whether I shall get through; also Heaven alone could bring such a miracle to pass; therefore let us implore its aid and do our best. After this Concours my regular winter work will commense at the atelier [Duran's].

Has this summer been pleasant to you? I have never passed a more delightful one. We have been as you know in the habit of spending our summer in the land of rocks and cheeses as Violet [Paget] calls it, and the seashore has been such a pleasant change that I have no doubt we will return to Normandy or Brittany next year.

. . .

> Believe me ever
> Yr. very affect. old friend,
> John S. Sargent

When at length the examinations were over and his admission was posted, it was proof that he was as good as the best France could produce. Beckwith, for his part, swallowed disappointment and determined to try again. Three days later the two went along to the reopened studio of Carolus-Duran. At the foot of the wooden stair every morning Sargent glanced over the sign, while Beckwith gave it a more scrutinizing look, for as monitor of the class it was his duty to see that none of the pranksters from the Beaux-Arts added anything unfortunate. That first Tuesday in November, Carolus arrived fresh from his summer's painting at his country home and proceeded to give the class its first criticism. Every respect was naturally paid him, in the exaggerated French way, as the master, the "patron," of the studio. Just before he was due to arrive, Beckwith nervously scrambled down the stair to be sure the sign was still respectable. Then, with a proper flourish, seated pupils rose in their places, those standing ceased to work, and Carolus appeared. Little was said, and as he spoke no English, Carolus habitually called on Beckwith to interpret for those insufficiently acquainted with French. At no other time was English permitted in the studio, a strict ten-franc fine restraining even the French students grown proud of the few words they had picked up.

In those early days, when the studio of Carolus-Duran was a new institution, it had the well-deserved reputation of being the most advanced in Paris. Sargent's determination to join it had required a certain amount of courage, and no doubt was based on Carolus' reputation of being the most brilliant younger portraitist in the French Capital. It is quite probable that this first year with Duran was something of a trial, for once Sargent passed the examination for the Ecole, he undoubtedly realized that, should he be displeased with the modernism of Carolus, he could readily find a place in the more conservative school.

Like his friend Edouard Manet, who did his portrait, Carolus was an advocate of new methods, derived from a study of Velásquez. In his youth he had met the fate common to innovators. After ten years of want, during which time he wandered about France, unable to do portraits at even twenty-five francs, suddenly, in 1869, his *La Dame au Gant* created a sensation at the Salon. In successive years, as he continued to exhibit striking portraits of prominent sitters, he consolidated his position, receiving official honors and a commission from the state to paint a mural for the Luxembourg Palace.

Carolus had done no teaching until 1872, when a young American called on him with the request that he be taken on as a student. Never immune to flattery, and in his first fabulous success somewhat lacking in modesty and reserve, Carolus was known to accept compliments designed to make a bronze statue blush. Now, however, he acted with discretion, telling his caller that a French student had come to him with the same request. If the two wished to rent a studio accessible to his own, he would give them criticism on Tuesday and Friday mornings. In this same way all the studios of Paris had been formed, the master giving of his time entirely for the prestige to be gained from training notable pupils, and often, too, with remembrance of similar instruction received when young. Starting with eight or ten students, the studio on Montparnasse grew to twenty-four by the time Sargent entered it two years later. Each student paid a small fee toward the maintenance of the premises, heat, and hiring of models. Later Carolus also taught a separate women's class, which, like this one, was particularly popular with Americans.

What Carolus taught is best summed up by the single word "painting." His primary concern was to show his pupils the proper application of pigment. He outlined a procedure for them to follow as they laid in a canvas, and when frequently they all

adjourned to his studio, in the Passage Stanislas, he demonstrated
a methodical, but highly variable, approach. He was most insistent
upon correct values, simplified to a few, and taught that the eye
could be relied on adequately to grasp the structure of the subject.
Derived from Velásquez, his was the impressionistic doctrine that
it was not necessary for the painter to have any understanding of
the organic nature of the objects to be painted. He advised his
pupils to paint what they saw, as it appeared, allowing only for
simplification that stressed the larger forms; but sternly he cautioned them to educate their eyes, and see correctly. Most mis-
takes could be traced, he taught, to slipshod vision and faulty
painting. The advantage of his methods to a student were that they
built a sound approach, permitting the student to tackle anything
so long as he looked at it carefully. Because it was a method of
approach and not an imposed technique of the sort other masters
gave their pupils, individual tastes could be incorporated, and Carolus in no sense thwarted individuality, a distinction he alone had
among the teachers of Paris. Compared with the rigid teaching
of the time, his instruction was of extraordinary flexibility. Its
principal shortcoming lay in the fact that a pupil not already an
able draftsman was unable to benefit from his instruction. An
unerring sense of line was required to place paint on canvas and
model it into human form entirely by means of variations in color,
and Carolus himself was too impatient to correct drawing. Once,
while touching over a pupil's work, it seemed obvious that his
delicate nuances were beyond the pupil's understanding. Beckwith, who was interpreting, broke in to say, "Yes, dear master, but
that is not how you did it when you *began*." Realizing his error,
Carolus put down the student's palette and brushes, saying, "No,
no, I drew like Holbein."

Carolus' teaching, while a model of soundness and flexibility,
required model pupils, who were well trained in drawing and had
the intelligence to grasp its significance. Carolus produced few
pupils of note. But from the very start he seems to have sensed that
Sargent was apt, possessing all the requirements of intelligence and
previous training, with over and above these a diligence itself
worthy of praise. A genuine affection, which increased with time,
grew up between this impatient master and the pupil who could

follow him. Nor was Carolus altogether so abrupt as might be expected from the nature of the interviews in the studio. It was to his credit that he was willing to interrupt the busy practice of portraiture to help these aspirants, and his additional kindnesses bear witness to an innate generosity. He proved remarkably sympathetic to them all individually, and when a student began an ambitious project for submission to the Salon, he visited the student's quarters to lend his advice. Any absence that might denote illness brought him calling with a marked sense of responsibility, especially for those who had come all the way from America. His very reference to them all, "my children," denotes his attitude. And a small entry in Beckwith's diary, noting the repayment of a four-franc "old debt to Carolus," makes it appear he also lent small sums of money.

But youth can be vexing to even the most patient of teachers, which most assuredly Carolus never was. He was known also as a sculptor, which inspired periodic efforts in that medium, sometimes leaving about the floor such unlikely matter as a bucket of clay-soaked water. On one occasion one of the more spirited among those rather grave young painters found a sponge left in such a pail, which seemed momentarily to give him the inspiration he failed to gain from his work. Taking the sponge, with a considerable ceremony he placed himself on a stool just inside the door, from which seat of majesty he proclaimed his intention to "let Becky have it" when he came in from the anteroom. The door duly opened, and his aim proved good; but the recipient was not Beckwith. Carolus-Duran, resplendent in the blue velvet coat and yellow silk shirt he wore on the days when he felt most conceited, had arrived for his weekly criticism. He slowly backed out, closing the door behind him and leaving the class stunned, hardly knowing whether to run, beg forgiveness, or perhaps go through the windows en masse. Either way it appeared to make little difference, for clearly it was the end of the atelier Carolus-Duran; and what if Carolus, who was the best swordsman in Paris, insisted on dueling with his assailant? In the meantime, with the assistance of Beckwith, who was still in the anteroom, Carolus managed to repair the damage. When he reappeared, looking very grave, feeling a little foolish, he had no chance to speak before receiving profuse apologies. He was assured that a terrible mistake had been made, and declared himself satisfied, gaining respect by his quiet dismissal of a silly episode.

Despite such peccadilloes, the studio of Carolus-Duran was probably the quietest in Paris. The model was ready to mount the platform at eight-thirty every morning; students began to file in at eight, except on Mondays when places were taken for the week. Mondays were a race, for, according to custom, positions were chosen in the order of arrival. More than one enterprising student, returning late from an enterprising Sunday night, thought it wiser to remain awake the few hours until class, or sleep on the cobblestones outside, rather than spend a week crowded against the wall. Sargent, despite his long trip, usually managed to be first in the studio, and his first choice of position was not begrudged him, for it was soon noted that he had an unerring eye for the best angle. Once the model was placed, he looked about from this side and that, his eyes now wide, now narrow, his head thrown back, until at length he planted himself with his easel; and the others, in the order of their arrival, were content to crowd near, confident that he had chosen wisely.

Considering that he had made no use of oil before entering the studio, it is remarkable how well Sargent took to this tricky medium. There were no official gradings in the studio; each member covertly measured himself against the others, assuming with complete lack of self-consciousness that he was alone in doing so. Beckwith had concluded that only three of the others compared favorably with him, when the advent of Sargent upset his calculations. Soon others, too, were finding it rewarding to watch and imitate Sargent struggling to master his difficulties, for Carolus was present only twice a week, and in his absence it was good to watch someone even a single step in advance of the class.

In January the studio gave its annual dinner to Carolus. As would be expected of a Latin Quarter affair, it was a gay and noisy party. Three weeks later, still obviously thrilled, Sargent wrote to Ben del Castillo:

> ... we cleared the studio of easels and canvases, illumined it with
> venetian or coloured paper lanterns, hired a piano and had what is

called "the devil of a spree." Dancing, toasts, and songs lasted until 4, in short they say it was a very good example of a Quartier Latin Ball . . . I enjoyed our spree enormously, I hope not too much; probably because it was such a new thing to me.

Carolus, himself only thirty-six, could enter into the prevailing gaiety more easily than other masters; he performed well on the guitar and, though of only remote Spanish ancestry, liked to play the Spaniard. To think of him singing Spanish songs, surrounded by his "children," makes more sympathetic his somewhat foppish and overweening character. And when the jubilation was over, he took three of his pupils, Hinckley, Parker, and Sargent, for a short winter vacation to Nice. Beckwith was not asked along, and felt badly, for though he remained among the most faithful of Carolus' pupils he was never again among the stars.

High above the Boulevard Montparnasse at one end was the tomb of the first Napoleon in the Hôtel des Invalides. In the other direction the avenue was lost by fusion into the complex of the Boulevard St.-Michel. Near the atelier it was gaily decorated by a fringework of colored awnings and tables belonging to the many cheap restaurants that lined it. The Montparnasse railway station was visible from the entrance to the alley, across the way at an angle, rising above the clatter of the wide multiple crossings that fed it at the head of the Rue de Rennes. There were numerous studios on both sides of the boulevard, and one better hotel and restaurant, Lavenue's, which nestled into the corner of the Rue de Rennes immediately across from the turmoil of the station. On the boulevard the church of Notre-Dame-des-Champs was slowly being built, and the trees, newly planted to replace those cut for firewood three years before during the siege of 1871, gave a stamp of newness not entirely deserved. For new as some of Montparnasse appeared, surrounding it were still the narrow dusty little streets with overhanging walls and cracking stucco through which the boulevard had been cut. Montparnasse was new, but it could not change the environment in which it was set.

This was decidedly a student quarter, and the second-tier studios surrounding the court at number 81 were filled with Duran's pupils. A single window rising ten feet from the floor occupied an entire wall of these small, lofty rooms. Opposite, and at the same height, was a projecting platform, which by the use of a ladder became a bachelor bedroom. Periodically efforts were made at a conjugal home life in these lofty perches, but Madame the Proprietress, who represented all there was of law and order within her confines, frowned on them. She was a deep-voiced, portly woman, sworn by various of her tenants to have sported a better mustache than any of them managed with considerable care to cultivate. The unfortunate concierges led unhappy lives with the motley assortment of forty artists sharing their premises. Obliged to answer the bell on the outer gate whenever it rang, no matter the hour or the season, there were few occasions when M. Pavent, appearing out of the dark in his nightshirt, did not give vent to a colorful idiomatic usage.

Among the inhabitants of the second tier at number 81, as they all referred to that combined circus and workshop, was R. A. M. Stevenson. As a Cambridge graduate, and a few years older than the others, "Bob" Stevenson commanded the respect due a "university man." Anything but a conscientious student, his was the distinction of being the evil genius first to discover, by rapping it with a stick, that the hollow lion in the courtyard bellowed! Once found, the process became a common delight, used first by Bob when he wanted to attract the attention of Will Low on the second tier and then growing into a common greeting for all occasions. Stevenson was a graceful talker, not at all dogmatic as many another with his "superiority" might have become, but one whose quiet words instilled doubts into others, and in that he was something of a healthy influence, for the tendency of the atelier was to idolize the master. He specialized in hilarious poems on the general subject of Carolus, which gained great currency at the time, but unfortunately are lost to us because they were not of a nature to be put on paper.

When Edinburgh weather became oppressive, or he felt particularly "seedy," Bob's cousin, Robert Louis Stevenson, often came to stay in the second tier. A more bohemian pair there never was, nor one more attractive to their friends. Frequently in the evenings, when American students from all the ateliers of

Paris met together at Picot's restaurant, these two British dandies turned up with Will Low; and a sight they were! Louis Stevenson in his velvet jacket; Bob Stevenson peg-trousered, tam-o'-shantered, well sashed; and Will Low, who as a gesture to respectability religiously went about Paris with a high silk hat crowning his ensemble of ill-fitting and ragged clothes. Low confided to the others that in Paris a man was always properly dressed so long as he wore a high hat. Disdaining the company of others speaking English, these three were generally found with the few French who would put up with their eccentricities, notably the sculptor Adrien Gaudiez.

Exchange of patriotic sentiment was common at Picot's, for the Americans seemed to have a knack for running afoul of the authorities. *L'Oncle Sam*, a play ridiculing America, was making a successful run in Paris, its popularity apparently attributable to the fact that Americans often appeared ridiculous in French eyes. One rather handsome youth named Pardessus, who hailed from Brooklyn, and was studying sculpture in Paris, went to see it, getting himself drunk at a nearby café between the acts. As the audience filed out, he felt called upon to deliver a patriotic tirade that brought police to the scene. To their chagrin they found that he was not only a public speaker of parts, but also an able boxer, who proved difficult to quiet. He was hardly stilled, and his name vanished from the cafés of Paris, when Neville Cain, of Louisville, Kentucky, arrived from Munich to join the Duran studio. He had been sitting one evening in a Munich restaurant when he suddenly put a large coin in one eye, thus insulting an army officer who thereupon insisted they duel. City officials, who would have been embarrassed to find a dead American on their hands, held Cain in custody until they could put him on a train for Paris. Clearly Americans were peculiar.

Sargent, who took his meals at home, seemed to prefer inviting friends into that circle rather than loitering in the noisy gathering at Picot's. Largely this was because he had less leisure than the others. He remained in the studio after the model left to paint from any friend he could persuade to pose or to analyze his day's progress, plotting the work that remained. At five he went down the Rue Bonaparte to a class at the Ecole des Beaux-Arts, where he worked until seven, then home across Paris to the Rue Ab-batucci for dinner with his family. In the evening he was off again to the studio of Léon Bonnat, where a class lasted until ten. Plainly he was too absorbed by work to join in the lighter side of Latin Quarter life, though he saw it on all sides of him, intruding into working hours in the studio and present in the court. He was applying himself to his task. If that required long hours and physical strain, he was willing.

His disregard of the pleasures normally associated with a stay in Paris came of no moral convictions, though it is true that to some he seemed to have a touch of the strict morality and puritan-ism of his father. If so, it was more than balanced by the natural hedonism of youth, the hearty laughter and the love of food associated with him. He was a good student of the expressive idiom employed by the studio concierge, able to use it at times with profound results. His temper, never far beneath a tranquil exterior, was known to be explosive, and tales had followed him to Paris of an episode in Florence, when he visited a rather wild form of justice on bullying colleagues. Considering his size, few cared to trouble him, and if he was not one who would enjoy him-self at Picot's, that was his affair. Probably he had no need to seek a companionship which in all likelihood he would have found un-congenial. Not affecting the eccentricities of his fellow students, friendship with the French was easier for him, and he was well supplied with friends for what time was left free.

The odd, fanciful quality that already appeared in his conversa-tion and crept into letters, introducing a note of humor and ease, made his company attractive. Those with whom he became more intimate remarked on his charm, the indescribable way he said a little something, saying it hesitantly, as though it were painfully coming forth; yet managed to be interesting and to create a bond of sympathy with his listener. That sympathy, nothing more than the capacity to communicate a sense of quiet good-fellowship, was the essence of his friendship. He was always a slow talker, one from whom conversation did not flow, though the impression lingered that he would have said more had the words not danced so elusively in his brain. Paul Helleu, whom he met at about this time, was amazed at the way he spoke French without accent, in a manner indistinguishable from that of a cultured Frenchman. Helleu was in many ways an odd associate for this rather sentimental and seemingly austere lad of puritanical tendency, for he was filled with adventures among the fair sex about which he talked delightfully. These satisfactions, pleasant though they were, were not what a sensitive boy like Sargent could readily respond to. At twenty his heart was already feeling its own romantic impulse and was not to be lightly traded for the few moments Helleu made sound so delightful.

The summer of 1875 was spent on the seacoast again, this time in Brittany, where the Sargents arrived at the end of June. When the fall came, the family elected not to return with John to all the expenses of Paris, but to remain at the little village of St.-Enogat, putting the economies thus effected toward a trip to America the following year. Back in Paris, John moved into the Hôtel des Etats-Unis on the Boulevard Montparnasse, from where he was able to walk the few blocks of broad sloping sidewalk to the studio at number 81.

In April of 1876, Sargent and Helleu went around to the gallery of M. Durand-Ruel in the Rue Le Pelletier. A group of revolutionary painters were exhibiting there whom the critics dubbed "impressionists." More even than Carolus, these impressionists were taken up with color and light, yet they, too, sought visual effects of the sort to which Carolus' teachings and theory had sharpened Sargent's natural perception. These pictures now extended the very principles he was familiar with into the realm of color. It was exciting to see the effects obtained by such logical extension of means, and he was most attracted to Claude Monet, who seemed the particular master of that phase of impressionist work.

As the two boys moved from picture to picture, analyzing the canvases, so different from anything they had previously seen, Monet entered the gallery. Sargent spotted his broad bearded figure and, filled with youthful admiration, he went precipitantly to introduce himself. Then quickly he invited the amazed artist to dinner, arranging to meet him that night at the Café de la Paix. During what remained of the afternoon he rounded up as many members of the Duran atelier as could be located, and when they all arrived, Monet, seeing the size of the troupe, suggested they eat at the Café Helder, where they could have a room to themselves and talk more easily. On arriving at the restaurant he was embarrassed to find the place filled with his own paintings, which had at various times been left in payment, or as pawns, for previous dinners.

Sargent later declared that at first sight of Monet's pictures he was "bowled over." He had never before seen such a throbbing sense of life as impressionism gave to paintings, and this fascination became more pronounced as he grew older. In the early years of their friendship he was content to learn from Monet as much of the impressionist practice as he could, though it was Carolus-Duran, and his approach, that was still, and would ever be, the underlying structure of his work. At first he learned from Monet something of the fine sense of placement to be found in the older man's work — the haphazard arrangements of landscape, the appearance of having noted quickly, from an unusual angle, which now and again appeared in his compositions. In time Monet became a more decisive influence, but now their friendship would have to be interrupted.

On May 15 the Sargents were off on the trip to America, though not precisely as planned. The economies of that winter on the seacoast were not sufficient to buy passage for them all, and Dr. Sargent stayed behind with little Violet in Switzerland, living meagerly at a pension, while John, Emily, and their mother saw America on their own.

This was John and Emily's first crossing of the ocean to the country which loomed so large in their father's mind, and to which they, too, owed allegiance. It was a strange experience for a youth of twenty to be going to a homeland he had never seen, and of which his entire knowledge consisted of hearsay. He naturally greeted the adventure with the same enthusiasm he would all his life bring to new adventures, but there must also have been a great uneasiness that the dream, the distant land across the sea, might not be as expected. In Philadelphia they discovered that a temperature of seventy-six degrees in the shade could be worse, with its accompanying humidity, than any heat they had known. They visited with Aunt Emily and Uncle Gorham, and saw the Centennial

Exhibition, where it was difficult to tear John away from a Japanese exhibit.

From Philadelphia they traveled a well-worn tourist circuit through Saratoga and Newport, where they stayed with Admiral Case's family, then on to Niagara, Chicago, Quebec, Montreal, Lake George, New York, Washington, and Philadelphia again. Covering all this in four months meant almost constant movement. Wherever John was, he continued to sketch in his notebooks, as he had during his earlier European travels. Much paper was covered with his impressions of America, and yet, strangely, the effect of this visit upon him cannot be learned. There is nothing even suggestive of his reactions. What he saw was a new and vigorous land, unlike any he had known; it was a different atmosphere from that in which he had been raised. Its standards and his were hard to reconcile. His forebears were so intimately connected with American history that it is difficult to believe he would not have some pride of association with the country he now saw before him, where five generations of his ancestors had lived, and the civilization they had helped shape and defend. But the evidence for any such supposition is lacking.

In the fall John once again settled in Paris, while the rest of the Sargent family congregated at Geneva, where Dr. Sargent expressed anxiety over the cost of the trip just completed. He questioned his younger brother about the likelihood of writing articles, of any sort, for the American newspapers, with the hope of increasing their income. It was a vain hope though, for American publications paid almost nothing. Still, they managed somehow to scrape along on their inadequate funds, and John, entirely dependent on what was sent him in Paris, had an allowance seemingly sufficient for his needs. Everything was comparatively cheap in Paris, except dwelling, which became expensive through the extraordinary French penchant for charging the necessities as extras: towels, ice, soap, a bath, everything was extra. As a result, the necessities of life were commonly neglected, and French cleanliness, unlike the daily tub to which John had always been accustomed, consisted solely in washing the face and hands, and wearing clean linen, where it could be seen. However, he was able to live on a scale which in comparison to his fellow students at least seemed expansive.

He had grown even taller during the summer, and his friends were astonished at the six-foot lad who returned from America. Often he breakfasted with Helleu at Lavenue's, eating the typical French petit dejeuner of a bowl of coffee filled half with milk, and accompanied by a foot of bread cut from a six-foot loaf. They shared the table with Rodin, Paul Bourget, and Gustav Natorp, Rodin's wealthy pupil. A common devotion to art was the only thread holding this group together. Rodin's coarse and clumsy manners noticeably clashed with the boulevardier aspect of Bourget, who was easily the most talkative. Bourget, soon to have tremendous popularity as a drawing-room favorite, ranged over a variety of topics, his talk shimmering with wit and occasionally raising a humorous reply from Sargent, when his mouth was not too full or he was not busily motioning to the waiter for more bread.

Early in 1877, with Carolus' approval, Sargent decided to chance sending a picture to the Salon. The *Portrait of Miss Watts* that went was accepted. For the first time he knew the elation of being represented among acknowledged masters. But first pictures were generally hung unbelievably high on the walls of the Salon, and when he saw it his enthusiasm may have been dampened. Furthermore, his was not an extraordinary picture, evidencing a certain affectation of pose and self-consciousness in execution. Even so, it is a creditable performance for a young man of twenty-one, and a remarkable fact that the jury of the Salon, probably the strictest extant, should be pleased by his efforts.

Curiously, both that year and the next he gave his birthplace in the Salon catalogue as Philadelphia, which revives speculation over what his feelings may have been when he first saw America on his recent visit. It would be easy to see in it an indication of some patriotic motive — did he wish to be thought American in a more forthright fashion than his European birth would allow? It is difficult to say, and any speculative excursion risks finding patriotic motives in an act which may have been merely youthful affectation.

During that same winter, Carolus was at work on a ceiling

decoration for the Luxembourg Palace and, finding himself unable to keep up with his portrait sittings while engaged on it, asked both Sargent and Beckwith to assist him. He did them great honor by asking, for, although it was employed during the Renaissance, the practice of using students to work on a master's paintings had long since disappeared. Even by the seventeenth century, in those few instances where the practice persisted, it was not students but other members of the guild who were employed by such painters as Rubens and Van Dyck. Carolus in fact was not only showing great confidence in them, he was also paying a huge and unparalleled compliment.

When the opportunity came to introduce heads into the composition, the two boys painted in portraits of each other, and then Sargent added a portrait of Carolus. The master expressed particular satisfaction with Sargent's part of the work, as well as with some little sketches Sargent made of him while they were all three at work. He consented to sit to his pupil for a portrait, the very greatest compliment he could bestow, and proof, were any needed, of the esteem in which he held this, his most accomplished fledgling. Sargent, however, found that to paint Carolus was a trying experience, rather like having a second conscience hovering over to inhibit every impulse. Because of his excessive vanity and flamboyant manners, Carolus was not an easy model to please, and it is not surprising that the finished portrait, though an effective piece of work, has a polite restraint about it. Every suggestion of the coarseness of Carolus' features is carefully polished away, as is every indication of a wrinkle, even the vertical folds between the eyes, so characteristic of the painter. Remarkably, the likeness remains, plus a dandified nonchalance well suited to the subject, while the dexterous quality of the execution covers the pains it cost. Beckwith, who had not the enterprise to think Carolus would sit to a pupil, was probably not envious of the exertions Sargent's task entailed.

After Sargent's first Salon, he went off to the Brittany coast with another American student, Eugene Lachaise, for the summer. They settled down at Cancale, attempting to make use of the principles learned from Monet, painting directly on the beach to make studies of the fisherfolk who passed over the wet sands gathering mussels at low tide. It was a new sort of work, and very difficult, much of it having to be discarded at first, for without experience in working out of doors they did not compensate for the brilliant light, and sketches that seemed sparkling were murky when brought indoors. Early on the morning of August 22 they were back in Paris, waking Beckwith in his little room to fill him with their plans. That night all three would leave for St.-Germain, where Lachaise's parents lived and where a gay week was in prospect. Though embarrassed by the same lack of funds that had kept him in Paris through the summer, while all his friends went off in groups and pairs, Beckwith finally decided that the studio money, which was in his charge, made a convenient source for a quick loan.

It proved to be a delightful week. Added to the pleasure of painting out of doors was the boating, fishing, and especially for Sargent, the swimming. Always of good appetite, he satisfied his robust tastes with the large quantities of fine food served. When the week ended he went off to join his parents in Switzerland. Beckwith followed on the eighth of September, for a walking trip through Switzerland, doubtless influenced by Louis Stevenson in this choice of a cheap, healthy vacation. Several times Louis had demonstrated his predilection for an outdoor cure, and his *Walking Tours*, written from experience gained while seeking better health, put a rosy glow over his exertions. Ten days later Beckwith burst in on the Sargents at Bex. When he started back for Paris, Mrs. Sargent, Emily, and John accompanied him by train as far as Lausanne. Writing of the Sargents in his diary, Beckwith noted, "I do not see why they come into this valley of the Rhone to stay unless it be for economy," and it is true they were not staying at any hotel of luxury, for he also noted that his two days with them had cost him twenty-one francs ($4.20) with meals.

As winter came on, the members of the Carolus-Duran atelier drifted back to Paris from summer haunts at Grez, Fontainebleau, and Brittany. Beckwith rather optimistically took a large studio on the fifth floor of a building only four or five blocks from the Duran atelier, which was to cost him a thousand francs for the year. How he ever hoped to meet such a rental is difficult to imagine, and soon the immensity of it struck him too, for he was asking his friends to come and work there with him, to help pay the rent. At different times, and often together, Frank Fowler, George Becker, Theodore Robinson, and Fanny and Isobelle Osbourne, shared it with him. Sargent developed the habit of joining him too. It was a particularly severe winter, and Beckwith, who was in perpetual difficulties with the rent, found it impossible to replenish his small supply of coal for the stove. The very first month a loan of one hundred twenty-five francs from Sargent paid the rent. In time Beckwith repaid this, and when he did his friend brought him coal. Sargent seems also to have purchased a little picture from him, agreeing to pay the price in installments, the first of which Beckwith notes on February 15: seventeen and a half francs. Considering that he himself existed on means that were extremely limited, it is remarkable that after December Sargent already appears to have shared the support of the studio equally with Beckwith.

The unaccustomed presence of women in this studio caused hearts to flutter. During the summer Isobelle Osbourne had caught the eye of Frank O'Meara, a strange moody Irishman, full of the alternate sunshine and rain of his homeland and a boon companion to the Stevensons. For a time it seems there bloomed a romance, and while it did O'Meara induced Sargent to paint a little head of him, that might be given "Belle." Before long the little portrait was all that remained of the romance. By the time Sargent had finished that chore and turned to work on the sketches brought back from Cancale, a second romance was budding. Louis Stevenson, now a member of the Edinburgh bar, was in Paris that winter, and could be found regularly at Beckwith's. The actual state of affairs was first known to the little group in the studio, who, as winter progressed, saw signs of affection between Louis and Fanny Osbourne grow into something more lasting.

With all this romancing, Sargent continued to work the Cancale sketches into a large picture for the Salon. Purely a studio product, based entirely on sketches, conservative in the careful delineation of the figures, the finished picture nonetheless had impressionist influence. The feeling of the outdoors and the importance given occular effect are both unmistakably products of his admiration for Monet. It was part of the vanguard of impressionism at the Salon, for, though the actual members of that group were still largely banned, Sargent's picture, based on their principles, was awarded Honorable Mention. Aside from being a signal achievement by a young man of twenty-two, it was a step in breaking down the barriers of the official world to an art form that one day would be pre-eminent.

Now that he was winner of an Honorable Mention at the Salon, that proving ground of professionals, it was obvious that he no longer needed to maintain active status in the atelier. Though he remained close to Carolus, he preferred working in Beckwith's studio, 73 bis, Rue Notre-Dame-des-Champs. After his picture was sold, and for the first time in his life he had a sum of money in his pocket, he suggested that they ought to keep the studio together, sharing expenses. It was an agreeable notion to Beckwith, who was glad of his friend's continued presence and pleased to have half the weight so conveniently lifted from his shoulders. Sargent's attendance at number 81 became sporadic, though his output remained continuous at the studio a few streets away, where he was able to do canvases that were more in the nature of pictures than studies from models. A few of these little pictures sold too, after that first flurry of interest following his award, and his happiness knew no bounds.

Friday afternoon at the atelier had always been something of a revel. The entire crew flowed into the Boulevard Montparnasse before settling at one or another of the cheap restaurants, where with much commotion they proceeded to relax in gaiety from their week's exertions. Sargent now made it a habit to join them, and was counted an important acquisition. He had never been without youthful spirit, and at this moment in his life, when he had so much to be pleased with, he allowed himself more normal expression with those about him.

At about this time Sargent, along with Will Low and Beckwith, became acquainted with the sculptor Augustus St.-Gaudens, who was in Paris working on his famous statue of *Admiral Farragut*. Low and Beckwith were facing the prospect of returning to America and were taking a great interest in New York affairs. The conservative nature of the National Academy of Design in New York was a topic of general interest, for many of the young Americans in Paris had sent their best work across the ocean, pictures that had often been accepted at the Salon, only to experience the ignominy of rejection by the Academy. It was galling beyond words to them, who thought, in their advanced vision, that their work thoroughly dated the Hudson River School, which was still being hung with honors. Something had to be done, and a series of meetings were inaugurated at St.-Gaudens' studio, where they voted endless resolutions and created the *Society of American Artists*, intended not to buck the line of the Academy, but to give newer ideas a place where they might be seen. St.-Gaudens, one of the first officers of the new association, thought Sargent an important addition to the ranks, and their friendship dated from these meetings, when the sculptor was struck with "the tall rather slim, handsome fellow." St.-Gaudens had just done a medallion of Jules Bastien-Lepage, the darling of daring Paris, and a painter for whom Sargent had no particular respect. In return for a copy of it, Sargent gave St.-Gaudens a watercolor.

It was probably at this time that he met another friend of the sculptor's, who was often about the studio having a plaque made of himself. He was Frank Millet, an American who, only ten years older than Sargent, already had behind him a rather legendary career, beginning with service in the Civil War as an assistant contract surgeon when he was not yet fifteen. Lively companion though he was, Millet's time was much taken up by a black-eyed Bostonian miss named Lily Merrill, whom he married soon after.

In the four years since Sargent had come up from Italy he had not returned, though through the rest of his life, wherever he was, his footsteps seemed always drawn there. It was the principal home of his childhood, the land of his youthful associations, and it seemed to exercise a great hold. Probably he preferred it to any other environment he knew. In the summer of 1878, Beckwith packed for his return to America and left Sargent in sole possession of the studio. Bubbling with his achievement at the Salon, with money of his own, and a personal establishment in Paris to support, he set off for Naples. He engaged a studio there and, despite the heat, began to work from models. It did not go well. He lay awake at night quarreling with mosquitoes, fleas, and all imaginable beasts, then felt used up in the heat of the following day. He tried to follow the Italian custom of an hour's siesta during the noonday heat, either in an armchair smoking a cigarette or on his bed. Suddenly at five o'clock he would awaken from a deep sleep of several hours. The local custom of adding drugs to the wine made him uneasy too, and he forced himself to drink the bad Neapolitan beer, to avoid the strange drunkenness prevalent in the restaurants. One week of this proved enough, and he decided he would go over to Capri, where conditions for work might be better.

Capri was not then the resort it has since become; it was still very much cut off from communication with the mainland, and getting to the island proved a formidable task. A steamer ran from Naples, but it had no particular day for leaving. He was assured that, if he went down to the quay of Santa Lucia every morning with his baggage and if the saints were smiling, he would get off in less than a week. This required checking in and out of lodgings at Naples twice a day, and after doing it several times it hardly seemed worth while. Eventually he located a market boat and sailed to Capri packed in tightly with the vegetables, fruits, and garlic. The only hotel of sorts was the Marina, and he moved in there. The only other occupant was a German, who was not much company, since he spoke of nothing but his sweetheart's moral irreproachability. The servants were careful to inspect every guest's traps, and the word that an American artist had come quickly spread over the island. Soon a message arrived from a painter named Frank Hyde, who had established himself in an old monastery that was everything required for a studio and picturesque surroundings. Sargent went to call and he found Hyde most hospitable, extending an invitation to come work with him. The two settled down to a succession of native models, from whom Sargent hoped to do a number of small pictures of the sort he had already found salable.

Several French painters were working on different parts of the island also, some of whom Sargent possibly knew from Paris, and at his suggestion they all agreed Capri needed a little touch of life to awaken its slumbering spirit. Collecting an orchestra of tambourines and guitars, they spent a wild night in the careening whirl of tarantellas on the flat roof of the hotel, their madly gesturing figures set against a vast outer silence. When at last the violet mass of the sky turned orange before the impending day, Sargent ordered supper served.

The Education of John Sargent

NEW STUDENTS at the Carolus-Duran atelier during 1878 and 1879 were conscious when Sargent occasionally joined them for a day that they were in the presence of one who had arrived. His appearance caused a greater stillness, and out of deference to his intense concentration, the others seemed to work harder. He was not talkative and, though it was said by some of the older students that he was hospitable to anyone calling at his studio, he extended no invitations. Those wise in the ways of the atelier told new members that if they were in need of a dinner they could not do better than call on Sargent before dinner-time; if he was not dining out, which he did more frequently now, he was certain to invite his caller along to a restaurant. Once a month, when on a Thursday morning the entire class adjourned to Carolus' studio, a few short blocks away in the Passage Stanislas, Sargent was generally there, sometimes taking it upon himself to conduct a new member among the framed paintings lining the dark, heavily draped walls. Once a painting of his own was discovered among the master's, and rumor had it that Carolus now and again signed one as a compliment to his favorite pupil.

Obviously the two were close. Sargent had achieved a technical proficiency that made him no longer a student. There was no longer any reason for him to trouble himself with the stilted poses and studio-looking sketches that were all that might be produced in an atelier. His time might be employed more profitably in his own studio. But though he had finished with study in the academic sense, he realized that there still was much he might learn from Carolus in other ways. Despite his posturing, Carolus was an individual capable with both brush and brain, able to guide another through the maze to success. As a busy portraitist he had already threaded the course Sargent would have to follow, and it was useful to have advice from one who knew the currents in that sea where so many careers were wrecked. His habits, the means by which he conducted his affairs, were worthy of study, for there was more to success than exhibiting at the Salon.

To assess properly the activities of Carolus-Duran and the atmosphere into which Sargent was thrust on leaving the atelier, they must be seen in their longer historic context. What Sargent aspired to was success in the well-rounded meaning of that term. He wanted to be a fine practitioner of his craft, he wanted to know the approbation that came of producing works of unqualified artistic value, and he wanted the financial security coming to any professional who did his job well. Until history suffered a rewriting in our time, it was well known that the old masters, the same masters we still revere so highly, were all amazingly affluent, and their works widely sought. Looking about him during the nineteenth century, any student of the arts could see practicing masters who lived in splendor, and had recognition of their contemporaries for their achievement. They saw a continuity from past times to their own which implied that if a man was a real artist, one of greatness, he would achieve success on a large scale, with all the attributes of honor, wealth, and position. Popes and princes vied with one another for the services of Michelangelo, and that master was not above contracting with him who offered the most appealing terms. Rembrandt early in life built himself a large house in Amsterdam, where he lived to within ten years of his death, the poverty of his last years resulting as much from the combined effects of economic change and personal scandal as from the alteration of his vision. Van Dyck, who was perhaps something of a lackey at heart, lived at royal expense in London, traveling abroad in a coach and six. El Greco maintained a mansion in

Toledo. Goya lived at court, using every manner of influence to get his appointment to the King. During his prime, Sir Joshua Reynolds averaged one hundred fifty portraits a year, and was sufficiently adept at business to make large profits in addition to earnings from his craft. Rubens also dealt in Italian masters, classic statues, jewels, tapestries, and even contemporary paintings; at least once he was caught passing the latter off as his own.

It was not yet the era of impecunious painters when Carolus-Duran held sway, and the young Sargent sat at his feet. Only since then, with our interest in psychology, has come the new confusion of values which demands that an artist cry in the wilderness and cower with fears from within and without. The wretchedness of a man's life has come to count as an indication of artistic integrity, as though (further confusion) integrity alone could produce art. No one has ever challenged the integrity of Titian, who painted largely to order and whose workshop was so crowded that he took three years to finish and deliver a picture. Nor, among portraitists, has the integrity of Gainsborough ever been compromised, though he kept a room of his fashionably located house open to the public as a gallery hung with his paintings, using as bait the royal portraits that he frequently painted. And Titian, again, had Pietro Aretino, that most feared blackmailer of the Renaissance, circulate sonnets in praise of his work — the work itself in no wise suffering from the sonnets. Frans Hals was certainly among the most uncompromising realists ever to wield a brush. Yet if we venture to count the number of finely outfitted gentlemen and their ladies that he painted we must conclude that the difficulties of his later years arose (as contemporaries thought) from badly managed affairs and incessant drinking. Was there ever the equal of Holbein for painstaking delineation? Holbein, who did a portrait of Henry VIII's son as a Christmas present for that monarch. The examples are without number, the inference is always the same; the old masters were, each of them, adept at selling their works, producing to order their most prized masterpieces. Each in his own way bowed to the necessity or the custom of his time, employing methods that to us may be summed up as "good business." None of these men felt that he was belittling his art by seeking to sell it, employing the best means he knew to do so.

Sargent, at the beginning of his career, was naturally aware that the Salon was the most important means for an artist to bring himself before the French public and before the visitors who yearly flocked to it from all over Europe and America. The objections to the Salon were put succinctly by Ingres, who called it "a picture shop, a bazaar in which the tremendous number of objects is overwhelming," and that distinguished master, idol of students, because he also was not in need of patronage, refused to show there. The importance of the Salon was largely attributable to the unsettled political and economic conditions existing in France from the beginning of the century. Each new regime brought an inevitable rise and fall of favorites, while the nobility, from whom art patronage was normally drawn, found itself weakened and unable to lend continued support. Artists dependent upon any particularized patronage might see it swept away with the next barricade. To spread the base of patronage and make up for the loss of the nobility, it was necessary to recruit new groups into the market, and the arts were fast turning toward a rising bourgeoisie. It was at the Salon that an artist could present his works, achieve a reputation that had a wide acceptance, be awarded the honors that counted so much to those who could not judge a painting for itself, be welcomed by the press, and project himself by all these means into the arms of the new public.

To Carolus-Duran the Salon was well and good. His original success had been achieved there and he continued to think it a fine arena in which to display his abilities, though he did not rely on it as a sole means of making sales or receiving portrait commissions. The Salon added prestige to a man's name and was the general advertising that preceded him wherever he went. But for himself, he knew it was *Carolus* who sold his own wares. In his scheme of things the Salon was important because he never had to sell an unknown product. He knew also that it was well to have dealers handle work, though so long as the Salon remained the dominant attraction in Paris they were held to the margins of the patronage community, never achieving the importance they have since acquired. Still, he was careful to cultivate them, doing a portrait of the distinguished dealer, M. Haro, without charge. Dealers would sell a picture now and then, possibly a landscape or a nude that had come back from the Salon, and to have one's name before the public anywhere did no harm. Sometimes they were able to send him an applicant for a portrait, though even then the final task of making the sale and setting the price fell to him. Everything proved to him that an artist was his own best dealer, his success depending, first, on the quality of his work — that was of greatest importance — but, second, upon himself. He knew that his own success rested upon how well he was known in the drawing rooms of Paris and the châteaux of France and had made himself a sought-after guest from the Vendôme to Ferrières.

In point of fact Carolus was an excellent example of the French artiste and homme d'esprit. His dashing horsemanship was well known in the Bois de Boulogne, where in the early hours he had also founded his reputation as a swordsman and duelist. He was able to speak engagingly on many subjects: art, poetry, music, and language. He had a way of putting things well, making one overlook the fact that the substance of his remarks often vanished upon further consideration. His mots were worth remembering, and often repeated, gaining a certain currency in the proper quarters of Paris. He was familiar with the still-revolutionary operas of Wagner, from which he sang snatches in illustration of his thought, no matter how esoteric. Typically French, he spoke with much warmth about his own heart, its flames and embers. His mention of the accumulating years, which he feared made him less attractive to amours (he was forty-two), could send a genteel titter through any gathering where he held the stage.

To all this Sargent was a witness, not all of it striking him as tasteful, much of it decidedly offensive to a sensitive youth of his restraint; but, conscientious student that he was, he certainly gave it earnest thought. A great affection existed between himself and Carolus, based on the mutual satisfaction of a teacher and pupil well suited to each other, the one pleased to see the progress of his protégé, the other flattered by the interest maintained in him by his famous and busy master. Whether or not all he saw was pleasant, whatever his personal reactions to some of Carolus' more foolish moments, he was receiving his practical education, studying still with the same intensity that had characterized him when he applied himself to a lesson.

In 1879 Sargent sent his portrait of Carolus to the Salon. Why at this juncture he sent a portrait executed fully two years before is obscure. Had it been done specifically for exhibition it would more likely have gone the previous year, if not before that. Most likely Carolus and Sargent both thought that this portrait, painted with a certain flair, might get the young man launched. It was sufficiently conventional, so giving no offense to the jury, while at the same time commanding interest for pose and subject. If this was the purpose it had been calculated to a nicety. The picture proved popular, and though there was no hint of academic approval, it was reproduced on the cover of *L'Illustration* as a means of honoring both master and pupil. The public liked this watered-down portrait, discovering in it a new talent of importance. His little success brought Sargent some notoriety, and a half dozen portrait commissions, for by chance he had chosen his year well, and France had now definitely emerged from the depression hanging over it since 1873. There were invitations for the young man, too, and he began to get abroad and make himself known.

Now twenty-three, his beard had grown more full and was worn close cropped about the chin and sides of his face. His large blue eyes, habitually opened wide as though through a desire to see more than others, contrasted well with a complexion grown florid. He was still slim, though his large frame was no longer so spare as it had been, the awkwardness of youth having left and taken with it the slight stoop that had formerly marked him. Though certainly not a handsome man, he might have passed for distinguished.

To hostesses he was useful, for they often needed an extra man, someone single, agreeable, and well mannered. He was an excellent pianist, thus even more advantageous to have about, for this was the age when every woman sang, and required an accompanist. He soon found his way into the literary and artistic salon of Mme. Roger-Jourdain, one of the Parisian hostesses who exercised an incessant watchfulness for new elements to join their salons, judiciously combining them with the permanent members who were the chief performers. This was a rather natural place for him to gravitate, for Roger-Jourdain himself, though of independent wealth, happily maintained the fiction that he too was a professional artist and would have been the first to become aware of Sargent's little success. As a compliment to Mme. Jourdain, a slim little woman, notoriously unfaithful, he did a charming little sketch portrait of her dark-eyed daughter, and on some outing a watercolor of herself lying stretched on the grass with her parasol.

Probably at Jourdain's, or some similar home, he met Edouard Pailleron, the prosperous playwright, who was astonished at Sargent's comprehension of literature. The portrait he was soon doing of Pailleron was the first commission he received following that all-important Salon. It was an order he could feel proud of, for it was being done for a man who understood his art and held promise of being a patron. Not all of his work at this time was done on such elevated terms. He was also making two little children's portraits about which he felt less exuberant. A landscapist friend, Louis Le Camus, had induced an Alsatian relative named Kieffer to have his two children, of five and seven, painted, telling him that, while the young Sargent was of tremendous talent and promise, he presently needed work and his prices were low. He placed it on the basis of a mutually advantageous transaction; the artist happy with the work, while they would be acquiring pictures that would rapidly increase in value. A third child's portrait came his way, too, this also done for little money. Apparently as a compromise between what he was willing to do for the price and the demands of the people, he began a full-length portrait of the child with his dog, making it half life size. And so, when his parents came to Paris that June, on their annual visit to see how he was getting on, they "were very much gratified with the progress he had evidently made during the year." During the two months they remained in the city he was constantly engaged on his commissions, working with equal application on them all, even making last-minute alterations in the clothing worn by little Jeanne Kieffer, when she came for what was to be a last sitting devoted to reshaping her hair ribbons. She had been promised that afterward she might go down the Rue Vavin to play in the Luxembourg Gardens, only a block from the studio, and thus arrived dressed in a frilly pink pinafore. It was more appropriate to a child's portrait, he thought, and brushed it over the black costume she had previously worn, improvised arms, then carried some of the lighter tones up into the background, where he scrubbed them over the previous somber tone.

Sargent was filled with plans, too, for Pailleron had found him such a delightful companion that he invited him, as soon as he was free to leave Paris, to come along to the family estate near Chambéry, in Savoie, to do an even bigger order — a full-length portrait of Mme. Pailleron. What elation! Before he left Paris in August he was planning a winter tour through Spain, then across into Africa, elaborating on this to his father. To Pailleron, during the six weeks' visit, it was a matter of wonder how the mind of this young artist teemed with the French poets. It is the first mention we have of the extraordinary memory that apparently retained everything he read, in later years giving him an almost omniscient quality in the fields he concentrated on. It seemed he had only to read a poem to know it, and be able to rattle off portions of it in conversation.

A gaiety was present that summer which for the first time makes him seem very young. He spent long hours running with the Pailleron children, his laughter proclaiming that, while there was difference in age, it meant little in spirit. They delighted to see him bound long-legged over fences, and his carefree, infectious good humor seemed to permeate the house long after the children had gone to bed. When on a day's outing the family went mountain climbing, he carried the lunch basket, dancing a jig with it. Then he turned to strumming a banjo, singing the Negro songs he must have learned in America, the words and accents falling on French ears with twice the wit. Youth, so tardy in asserting itself, now burst into the open.

Even with the high spirits he displayed, it was not a time for play alone, for often he sat under a large white umbrella, as he had seen Monet do, to work on some little piece of landscape that later he destroyed. He also attempted to get the Paillerons' daughter, Marie Louise "the little savage," to pose. That was hopeless, for aside from the child's normal distaste for holding still, Marie Louise was an animal lover who found him much too cruel to be approved of. How often she saw him stand motionless watching butterflies in flight and then, with the ferocity of an assassin, pounce on them the moment they lit! He did manage to do a sketch portrait of her lying out in the open with straw hat and fichu, but this was under protest; and through all he continued the extended sittings for the portrait of her mother, for which, with remarkable courage, he asked Mme. Pailleron to pose in the garden. The very idea of undertaking a portrait in the open was revolutionary, something not present in the work of Carolus-Duran, and an early instance of the independence of Sargent's taste and judgment.

This outdoor picture betrayed a style that had evolved considerably from the manner employed in the portrait of M. Pailleron some months before. A more varied character was slowly creeping into his formal work, while the sketches of the period showed sudden and often striking variations in their style and technical aspects. He was undergoing a period of growth in every sense, the obvious changes in his personality constituting outward symbols of his inner metamorphosis from intense student to confident individual. Becoming more conscious of this growing confidence, he was determined to distinguish his paintings more fully from those of his master and was searching for a personal style.

Since the time when he did the little sketch head of O'Meara, he had gained considerable experience executing very swiftly some exceedingly vivacious sketches of his friends, which are without doubt finer than the more formal manner he was then employing in his commissioned portraits. Many qualities of his later more typical work are apparent in these studies, rather than in portraits such as those he did of Carolus-Duran and Edouard Pailleron. A sketch he made of his friend, the painter Frémine, is a feast of improvisation, and because in it we see his own vision and no troubling over the smoothness of the technical means, it is a head that makes immediate impact on the observer for the sense of life it conveys. Willing to explore possibilities, indulging himself to discover the nature of his abilities in each direction, he was crossing ground that would have banned him from the Salon. Other sketches of his friends Helleu, Duez, Lefort, and Juillerat are all more vigorous, better characterized than his Salon entries dared to be.

Another facet of these works becomes apparent as they are examined. While he was seeking greater freedom in his handling of the brush and trying to root his natural predilections in a style less suggestive of Carolus, he indulged in surface play, minor affectations of brushwork, and roughness for its own sake, which Carolus, with the good sense of a mature artist, avoided. The *Juillerat* is characterized by a straight chipping stroke, ending in a ragged edge wherever he thought it noticeable. Unfortunately the head itself, which is a marvel of clean draftsmanship, was not built by means of such strokes, but developed in the sound manner learned from Carolus, and these bold touches, effects of dash and courageous brushwork, are added on the surface for motives largely disingenuous. When painting Frémine he employed another sort of ragged touch, inherent in the structural portions of the work (he had learned that lesson himself, no doubt by examining the previous canvas), but now there is an ostentatious squaring of the ear lobes, a staccato treatment of the hair, that are still youthful affectation. Probably these quirks are products of an exuberant nature as much as they are affectation of manner, and it is not entirely just to use the one term without stress on the other, for his was never a disingenuous nature, nor one that allowed excesses of vanity. He was falling into the pitfalls that await anyone possessed of his tremendous abilities without a compensating maturity. And the large fact to be understood from these minor failings is that, though he was already vastly skilled and learned in his craft, with an over-all cleverness to carry him through difficulties another would find insurmountable, he was still too immature to grasp that true style, which was what he sought, was something larger and deeper than surface treatment.

A definite cleavage developed between his important works, those he considered his ambassadors sent forth into the world, and the sketches, where he was free to indulge his caprice. Wherever it appears, the more restrained style, still close to Duran, is an indication of the frame of mind in which he undertook a canvas. In June of 1880 he did a small bust portrait of the father of a young lady with whom he was then friendly, the dry manner of the execution implying that, though it was an informal work, not commissioned, he hoped commissions might be obtained from the family. The young lady, Valerie Burckhardt, and later her younger sister, Charlotte Louise, were much in his company, and two years later he sent a full-length of Louise to the Salon. He afterward inscribed this to her mother, so that we see a compliment offered to that quarter also. Whatever business motivations lay behind his generosity toward this family, there is also the added consideration that these young ladies were pleasant company, answering some of his needs. His puritanical streak had led him far from the exciting realm in which Helleu lived, with its momentary ardors, into another where he saw visions of a more elevated passion, shared more equally and enduringly. For a while it seemed that one and then the other of these sisters fitted the image he had formed, and his kindness sprang from personal motivations that were perhaps equally important.

During the winter of 1879 he carried out his plan to travel through Spain and Morocco. Discovering Velásquez at Madrid, though for years he had been applying the lessons of that master, as taught by Carolus, he appears to have been overwhelmed when he saw canvas after canvas, low keyed and restrained, lining the walls of the Prado. For the first time since as a boy he had done innumerable pencil drawings he undertook earnest copying. Coming at this point, it was a factor in his growing maturity; for he was now ready for the lesson of this master. He was possessed of the technical resources, coupled with the intellectual growth, necessary to understand what he saw, and the nature of his own essays into originality betrayed a need of the disciplining process that Velásquez would provide for him. His intellectual capacities were evident in the way he went about his task, plumbing the depths of these works unerringly, analyzing them in terms of structure, form, and color, to find the essential qualities that distinguish them. His copies were no slavish imitations, no stroke by stroke following of the master hand, nor did he alter his own technique of pure oil paint to simulate the tempera and oil glaze of the Spaniard. None of his copies would be mistaken for an original by the master, for they are essentially free translations, analyses, pure and simple, capping the lessons of the Paris atelier with the final depth of understanding necessary to form the mature artist. When his interest centered on a large picture, like the *Las Hi-*

landers, he was content to do a reduced version, knowing it was conception and the infinite refinement of values that he must look at, rather than the scale. And when he turned to portraits, like the *Don Balthazar Carlos,* he copied the heads separately, then did a reduced version of the entire picture to study its structure. He spent no more than a month in Madrid, working earnestly all the while, but the lesson was thoroughly learned, and in the work that came from his brush after this point there are none of the earlier adolescent faults, none of the puerility of surface work.

He dispatched his completed canvases to Paris, and with the two French artists Daux and Bac he rode through the mountains to Gibraltar. It was an adventurous undertaking for someone who had never sat a horse well and who might at any moment find himself projected into rocketlike flight. Carolus was such a gay figure trotting through the Bois de Boulogne that we may conceivably find the inspiration of this adventure in his dashing air as he paraded before the beau monde of Paris. Sargent no doubt hoped that after the personal mortification of this trip he would return to Paris a good enough horseman to join the morning canters that were a fashionable diversion. Carolus was his model, and he would try to follow the well-trod path. But horses and Sargent were always certain to come to disagreement, and soon there was that sudden parting of the ways that typified his relations with even the gentlest beast.

By January 1880 the party arrived in Morocco, after months of bad weather, hail, and rain, that spoiled the trip for painting, and allowed them only the most dismal view of Spain. Sargent thought he had done so much jogtrotting on atrocious horses and mules that he would be unable to sit down even to write the letters expected of him, and the heat of Morocco came as a sudden change from the fluid climate of the Spanish mountains.

The three painters rented a Moorish house in Tangier, which they discovered they were unable to tell from the other uniformly white houses of the town, wandering the tortuous little streets in the hope that they might suddenly recognize some keyhole doorway, or tile pattern, that would bring them to their own dinner. On little wooden panels, which fitted snugly into his sketch-box, he began to study the alleyways as evening fell across them, the shadows risen halfway up the white stucco; or some brilliantly lit wall cut by a horseshoe window, and set off by rough-stoned streets. They were fluent and exceedingly charming sketches, in feeling totally unlike his other work; and when he returned to Paris the little panels were lost amongst the turmoil of his sketches. They were never varnished, retaining to the present day the freshness of touch and immediacy of vision that originally characterized them, with much of the vague poetry of foreign places that caused them to be done.

Along his way through Spain he had jotted down the folk music for Violet Paget, now grown into a strange mannish young woman, writing under the name Vernon Lee. She had asked him to collect authentic Spanish folk material for her. Once he began to do so he enthusiastically wrote down what he heard in the mountain cafés, noting words and music across his drawings of the performers, though back at Paris he reported to Vernon that the finest things were mostly "dismal restless chants" of African origin, which he found it impossible to note or even render into syllabic sequence.

Each year Vernon Lee arrived in Paris to see the Salon, and the honor of escorting her, and being exposed to her pugnaciously held views, fell to Sargent. She was a disturbing person to be with, unfeminine, and much too certain of her opinions, expressing them with full-armed gestures that he found distasteful. But old obligations had to be honored; they had been friends once, their families remained so, and Emily seemed quite attached to Vernon, as she now wished to be called.

When the Salon opened he once again did his duty of escorting her, and in the course of their conversation, which under her guidance frequently took a theoretic turn that he found uncomfortable, he described himself as an impressionist, entirely given up to the faithful reproduction of "les valeurs." It is a different attitude toward impressionism than we now have, but more akin to the aims of those practicing the art at that time, and it was as far as he would go with her toward theory. He had no use for the abstruse speculations on art she indulged in, nor did he ever, for it smacked of dilettantism and was vaguely sacrilegious. Vernon was beginning to apply psychology to art, and was taken up with writing some short pieces in that vein later published in book form. He did not like the look of it, deliberately admonishing her, rather hotly it seems, to let that sort of thing alone and confine herself to literature. It was the first voicing of a view that he adhered to strongly in later years when it was no longer a personal issue but involved a large part of the British public, and it is interesting to see from what deep springs his notions grew and how consistent he was over the years. The clear implication was that she might know something of literature, an art form she practiced, but painting was best understood by those with training. He saw no psychological problem in art, nor could he admit that such an aspect was fair game for the layman. In his view the whole complexity of art was a matter for its priests. Vernon was obstinate in her views, even rather aggressive once attacked, and as he could rarely be contradicted, their conversation turned to other things: books, music, and people.

His own pictures of M. and Mme. Pailleron, which they saw at the Salon on their visit, brought him a new order, and he began painting a fashionable young Chilean woman, Mme. Ramón Subercaseaux, traveling for each sitting out to her house in the Avenue du Bois-de-Boulogne. He had already begun work in his own studio on a double portrait of the two children of the Paillerons, when in the course of one of Marie Louise's sittings there came a knocking at the door and he found two Americans on the landing, come to inquire about a portrait. In the studio he had few things to show them, but he was sufficiently confident to ask 1,500 francs for a portrait of head and shoulders, to which the prospective sitter, Henry St. John Smith, whose motives are interestingly explained in his diary, agreed:

Today I walked with Gussie Jay to Sargent's studio, 73 (bis) Notre Dame des Champs, and arranged to have my portrait painted. Sargent is said to be the best pupil of Carolus-Duran and Duran is one of the most celebrated (many say the best) portrait painter in Paris. The few things I saw in his studio I did not like much; I go, in choosing him, chiefly on the advice of Frank Chadwick who has been painting here seven years and ought to know about artists. Arthur Roach of Boston also recommended him highly to Gussie

Jay. Roach said he would rather have a portrait by Sargent than by Millais, but of course, that is bosh. Sargent seems like a man twenty-seven or eight years old.

When the two had left, Sargent was eminently pleased, dancing a jig about the studio before getting back to work. This rather pleasant side of his personality was obvious to Smith also when, in a few days, he began coming for his sessions. Several times he wrote "a pleasant sitting" in his diary, and on various occasions Ralph Curtis, a cousin of Sargent's, was present as he sat, or Beckwith, who was back from America for a short stay, came by to talk. There were discussions of Velásquez, whom the young artist just back from Madrid spoke of with enthusiasm; and then, at the next to last sitting, he presented Smith with a frame for the portrait. Soon after he departed for Holland with Curtis, Chadwick, and Helleu, to study Frans Hals.

At Haarlem he followed the same procedure as in Spain, making reduced versions of the *Regenten* groups, in which the striking quality is the balance of light and dark, and painting full-sized copies of small groups of two and three heads from the *Doelen* groups, which were more lively in content. Perhaps the most decisive lessons he had to learn from Hals were those of animated expression and the proper handling of the sweeping brush. As master of perhaps the most vigorous brush ever, Hals never allowed it to obtrude, or predominate over the form, and the beauty of Hals's brushing, as Sargent now realized, was not the boldness of it, but the perfection with which each stroke is made precisely the right size and shape to do its task. Hals's brush, he discovered, was not so much free as it was economical, achieving effects with minimal effort and stating briefly what others labored after.

He was hardly back in Paris before he went with the Subercaseaux on a trip to Venice, where he joined his family for the summer. The old Palazzo Rezzonico had been divided up into studios and turned into a veritable barracks of artists. Native Italians, students down from Paris, and some of Frank Duveneck's boys in from Germany, all shared an industrious existence in the noisy halls of the fifteenth-century palace. Sargent took a room on an upper floor, finding there a happy, short, squat Italian named Boldini who, though nine years older than himself, was something of a kindred spirit. He was great fun to be with, for he overflowed with Rabelaisian humor, and one day while Sargent stood chaffing the Italian, a mahlstick stuck through his elbows and across his back, Boldini had the bright idea that he wanted to do a little portrait of him in the position he had struck. Their merriment bubbled over during the few sittings, and except for the broomsticks, rockets, dots, dashes, and frequent exploding missiles Boldini allowed to clutter the background, what he produced was a small-scale full-length portrait imbued with much of Sargent's air of overgrown boyishness. In the fall, when his family returned to Nice, Sargent retained his studio in the Rezzonico, painting some small figure pieces in the halls, trying his hand again at watercolor out of doors, and making notes on wood panels of details of architecture, variations of color in the weather-worn walls of the city, and the same effects of failing light that he had studied in Morocco.

Visitors to the Paris studio, when he returned, found him at work on two large canvases. The group portrait of the two Pailleron children was still in progress, and it was joined now by a full-length of the exotic Dr. Pozzi, a friend of Carolus-Duran's. Periodically Carolus himself delighted the Rue Notre-Dame-des-Champs by coming out of the Passage Stanislas, just across from number 73, in full flamboyant dress, to see his pupil's progress, mounting the five flights of dark stairs with a jaunty air and later leaving eminently satisfied. The studio crowded, his evenings filled with the calls of society, Carolus assuring him of the quality of his work, Sargent had reason to be content. He envisioned himself as *the* rising young artist of Paris and showed his new confidence in the more racy character of his talk. To some extent it was a deliberate attempt to counter the serious cast of his mind, and as camouflage it proved excellent, for he blended well with the Parisian scene of which it seemed he was shortly to become a fixture.

Dr. Pozzi, a dashing Latin type, was interesting to paint. This fashionable Parisian physician, sleek, and still quite young, posed in a scarlet dressing gown, sporting beneath it a ruffled shirt, the frills framing his proud head and elegantly held fingers. Alternating with his sittings were those of Marie Louise Pailleron, who came to sit with her older brother. When she arrived war was declared in the Rue Notre-Dame-des-Champs! Exceedingly careful about the clothing worn in his pictures, at each point he had chosen what she liked least. He insisted on arranging her hair, which exasperated her, but worst of all, through the spring and winter he demanded eighty-three sittings. When at length it was finished, his words came as a reprieve to the two condemned children. They watched with interest as he once more danced his little jig of contentment before the new work, but were unprepared to see him suddenly throwing the studio furnishings out the windows. This was more to Marie Louise's liking, and she eagerly joined in the fun, sending drawings and rolled canvases after the cushions and pillows he tossed out himself. When the two children left, tired after the long months of work but still pleased with the result as it stood before him, he sat down to make a drawing of the cyclone-struck studio, later presenting it to the little Mlle. Pailleron inscribed "In honor of my reconciliation with the terrible Marie-Louise."

He was honored again at the Salon in 1881, receiving a second-class medal, which relieved him of submitting future works to the jury. His elation is evident in a letter to Ben del Castillo:

> Just a few frantic arabesques to acknowledge the receipt of your pleasant letters and communicate my plans. In the first place I have got a 2ieme medaille at the Salon and am hors concours and a great swell. I accept your congratulations. It is for that portrait of a Chilean lady [Mme. Ramón Subercaseaux] that I was painting last summer Avenue du Bois de Boulogne.

He was definitely climbing the ordinal ladder that one day would find him a Member of the Institute. We can be sure that Carolus, as an important member of the Salon jury, was watching carefully over his protégé, and though his one voice could never have been responsible for this new success, his was the guiding hand that brought honor where he thought it was deserved. Carolus was still young himself, and it was important to him that his cohorts, so closely allied with the revolutionary impressionists still banned from the Salon, became entrenched in officialdom.

The following year, capitalizing on his newly acquired freedom from the jury, and almost as a reaction to the conventional aspects of his canvases the previous year, Sargent sent two striking works. One was *El Jaleo,* a Spanish cabaret scene, which by its daring originality made a strong impression on contemporary opinion. No doubt it was a very spirited performance, though now the somewhat theatrical treatment, intentionally accentuated by knobs on the lower molding of the frame intended to suggest footlights, together with the obvious striving after effect, clearly mark it as a "Salon piece." There is an unfortunate element of contrivance to it that was less noticeable then than now. The second picture was a portrait of a sixteen-year-old girl, Miss Isabelle Vallé, significant for being a digest of the lessons learned from the study of Velásquez and Hals. Present in this work are traces of the manner that in later years would distinguish him: the painting of the hands is particularly strong; and the sympathetic element, the quality of expression, mark the emergence of a maturity that is not technical alone.

El Jaleo was a new departure for Sargent. He had not previously undertaken a large Salon piece, though in 1880 his *Fumée d'Ambre Gris,* a subject drawn from the same Spanish and Moroccan trip, was well received. These paintings, designed for immediate shock, to shout down neighbors on the walls, were an investment in time and money. Many of them were shown by the more successful painters, and we can understand why. They were attractive, caused talk, and were often handsomely reproduced in the press. By this time, with the accrual of a minor fame and the development of a position in the world of honors and awards, he was doubtless chafing at the financial limitations of his practice. For with all the fanfare of 1881 and the notice he received at the Salon, it had actually been a rather lean year for him. In twelve months he had done only two little portraits, and those of Americans. His Parisian practice seemed to have evaporated as suddenly as it began. The *El Jaleo* therefore was a delayed product of sketches made in Spain two years before, painted in time that otherwise was free. Of course, as he had to hire models over an extended period, this became an expensive undertaking, and unless sold the painting would be a big investment to have on his hands. Therefore, when the Salon opened and it received a favorable critical response, he accepted the first offer that came to him, from a New York gallery, Schaus and Co., and arranged for it to go off to America. Doubtless he was hasty.

He remained in Paris through the summer, while the Salon remained open, working in his studio. In the evenings he made his way to Lavenue's on the Boulevard Montparnasse. There, opposite the station, with its hustling crowds, and melee of arriving and departing vehicles, he sat surrounded by a coterie of artists and students. Mlle. Fannie, the cashier, kept an album of drawings she induced her more famous patrons to make for her, and found him most obliging in this respect. Often she produced the book with a request he draw some particular table, or even a guest of his own. It became something of an occasion when Mlle. Fannie walked across the room with her *L'Album Sargent*, as it became known, and he set to work with exaggerated ceremony that pleased the wine-happy bon vivants surrounding him, while eager young aspirants crowded to watch over his shoulders. Carolus' pupils often went to Lavenue's to see this performance, with hope of striking up an acquaintance if they could. They found his English rather British in flavor, scattered through with "I fancy" and "I dare say," and his pronunciation of that favorite word "*curious*" fell with a sound more English than American. Finally, in August, he took himself to Venice, where he was invited to stay with his cousins, the Curtises.

When about 1878 the magnificent fifteenth-century Palazzo Barbaro was divided in two, Daniel Sargent Curtis, cousin to Dr. FitzWilliam, purchased the larger part, installing himself there with his wife and son Ralph, who had graduated from Harvard two years before. Mrs. Curtis, daughter of Admiral Wormeley of the British Navy, presided in her Venetian palace like a doge of old, and soon was tagged the "dogaressa" by her painter guest, who also set about to do a portrait of her. Working with a beauty and precision of outline that might have done credit to Holbein, he gave gentle indication of her simpering mouth, and conferred a considerable distinction.

Cousin Ralph was two years older than John, and nursed artistic ambitions, at which he worked during the winters in Paris, where they met and continued to see a good deal of each other. Ralph appears to have been of a genial sort, possessed of a glib humor that served as a fine foil to Sargent's bantering talk.

Through the late summer Sargent occupied himself with studies of the back alleys and side canals of Venice, rarely picking any large area for his subject, but still interested in bits of walls, and doorways, well heads, and details of ornamentation. Then, as the weather changed, he became more ambitious and developed some small compositions using a hired model wrapped in a shawl against the chill. He also had the girl pose in her shawl for a huge full-length picture, obviously conceived with the Salon in mind.

The city soon was bleak and cold, and he discovered a group of painters down from Paris working wrapped in overcoats. He joined them to do some street sketches, one humorously commenting on their habit of watching young women pass, and the damp chill that lay on the city of the lagoons penetrated into the work he did. Venice was not the sunny bright city he preferred, and, leaving behind the big Salon piece, he went south to Florence, Siena, and Rome in search of a warmer sun.

Madame X

ONLY RARELY in these years was there a troubled note. Sargent was bounding upward with a speed envied by others less fortunate. His success seemed complete and his newly gay exterior, rather different from the quiet appearance he presented in the Duran atelier, confirmed the notion. Yet all the while he felt dissatisfaction inside, where he let no one penetrate. One symptom of this had been the *El Jaleo*, another was the small genre pieces he attempted in Venice, but the most telling was the portrait of Mme. Gautreau.

No definite evidence tells us when Sargent and Mme. Gautreau met. The first mention of her appears in a letter he wrote in 1882, when he was already pressing the question of a portrait. Obviously, then, they had met earlier, most likely in 1880 while Dr. Pozzi was having his portrait done. That distinguished Paris physician was reputed to be her lover, and it is conceivable she might have attended a sitting or was among the crowd who viewed the finished picture in his studio. At any event it is almost a certainty that she first came to Sargent's attention in connection with the Pozzi portrait, and so striking was she, so attuned to his style of painting, that one meeting was certainly enough to fix her in his mind. Ben del Castillo appears to have known her socially, and we may assume that by this means, and his own, he saw her often, the desire to do her portrait growing with each encounter. If there were repeated meetings, as apparently there were, he perhaps hoped she would eventually commission a portrait; and in that event it is easier to understand how he allowed two years to slip by before pressing her to sit.

That Mme. Gautreau had become a conspicuous figure in Paris society was not without design. She dressed with extreme daring, sharing much of her beautifully formed breasts and arms with the world at a time when others were covered tightly to the neck. The lavender powder she used immediately set her apart from other women, who appeared either waxen or leathery beside her tinted complexion and red-toned hair. She was certainly as notorious as she was admired, and seemed conscious of both aspects of her fame. Such a woman attracted many admirers. Her beauty was openly displayed, and of a nature to make itself warmly envied by those less endowed. As was natural, many rose against her from the ranks of shocked propriety. More were motivated by envy, and the knowledge that they could not carry off such paint and adornment without appearing besotted rather than exotic; and their physical attributes, even if *they* dared expose them, could not stand the scrutiny that revealed the perfections of Mme. Gautreau. In Paris during the eighties, every manner of story circulated about her extraordinary ailments; how because of the discoloration of her body she painted herself purple. People were fascinated to watch her bathe at the seashore. On coming out of the water (where she lost much of her make-up), she did not cross the sands or even come to them, but had a mulatto giant throw a huge towel over her, then carry her, completely covered, to a dressing room.

Memories of her are still confused by many of the intentionally malicious fictions circulated, and after the passage of years it is impossible to sort out fact from fancy or decide what sort of person she was. The few reliable facts show her to have been of extraordinary vanity, and like all country-bred people, to have impressed city dwellers as a little lazy. Judith Avegno was born in Louisiana, and brought up among riverboats and plantations in the leisurely life characterizing the ante bellum South. At an early age she saw her father ride off to join his detachment of state militia, and lick the Yankees. Before she was ten she saw the futility of that exploit, when he was carried home from Shiloh mortally wounded. With such unpleasant associations, and certainly not happy in the defeated South, after the war the Avegno family decided on a return to France. It was hoped an advantageous marriage might be made for Judith in Europe, and for that the reputation of a beauty was essential. With her mother's guidance, then, she set about assiduously to cultivate herself, and her marriage to the banker Pierre Gautreau was a satisfactory culmination of strenuous efforts.

From his letter written in 1882 to Ben del Castillo, we learn that Sargent had a "great desire to paint her portrait." His reasons were many. Certainly he was struck by the strange beauty of that peacock woman when they first met. At a later date he wrote of her "beautiful lines," while deprecating the "chlorate of potash lozenge colour" that she used on her skin. More important was that he realized the value of her portrait at the Salon. Few things could attract more attention. The mere fact that his portrait was of Mme. Gautreau would ensure him a greater audience than ever before. All Paris knew her, and would take special pains to see a portrait of her. And, too, he knew she was well suited to his art, for she was the essence of style. He was certain he could produce a portrait of her that would give him the overwhelming Salon triumph that he wanted so dearly. For, despite the acknowledged skill of his work, Parisian society, that backbone of every artist's patronage, continued to ignore his claims, preferring to frequent the studios of their favorites, Bonnat, Cabanel, and Carolus-Duran. He had made numerous efforts to attract them, doing presentation portraits of Mme. Escudier, Mme. Allouard-Jouan, and others that might catch the eye, but always without success. A striking portrait of this woman, who was herself nothing if not striking, he thought would be the blow he needed to penetrate the main stream of patronage, to divert some of its current into his studio, pocketing some of the golden flow of nuggets that tinkled along in it. He knew that thirteen years earlier Carolus, with a similar blow, had established his name and made his fortune. In 1869 his *La Dame au Gant*, in one fell swoop, made him a leader of French art. Perhaps, too, he looked forward with confidence. He would improve on what Carolus did by the addition of important new factors that were within his reach, but had been beyond Carolus'. The model for Carolus' picture was his own wife, unknown to society, and not especially beautiful. Sargent would do his portrait of an acknowledged beauty who was also a woman of importance. His plans were well laid.

But could he get the lady to sit? Chiefly he calculated on her vanity, which he rightly guessed was her most vulnerable point. As expressed to Castillo, he felt he had "reason to think she would allow it and is waiting for someone to propose this homage to her beauty." But it still required a considerable campaign before she agreed to sit. He approached her himself and, uncertain of the result, asked Castillo to tell her "that I am a man of prodigious talent." Possibly he also enlisted the aid of Dr. Pozzi. Whether through the doctor, or Castillo, or by their combined influence together with his own urging, early in 1883 Mme. Gautreau consented to be painted. Only a few drawings were permitted in Paris that winter, however, and she insisted that the work be put off to the summer, when she preferred that he come to stay at Les Chênes, the Gautreau home in Brittany.

At this same time he was approached by Henry White, soon to be American minister at London. White had recently married Margaret Stuyvesant Rutherfurd, of New York, a handsome woman from a handsome family, known for her keen interest in literature and art. She was friendly with Henry James, who, when he frequented Paris in the role of art critic during the eighties, particularly sought her company. Soon after his marriage White thought of having portraits done of himself and his wife. He chose Léon Bonnat, but Mrs. White, who while visiting the Salon particularly admired Sargent's portraits, insisted that her own must be by him.

Probably Sargent first met Henry James, who became a lifelong friend, through Mrs. White. She was posing in his now curiously unkempt studio, its only larger furnishings consisting of a couch and cabinets for his materials. Chairs stood about to receive the visitors who came along to each sitting and the walls were covered with paintings, most of them his own, though interspersed with a pastel of Helleu's, and the Velásquez copies done in Madrid. The corners of the room were crammed with rolled canvases, and from the ceiling hung the long draperies of dull green against which he frequently posed his models. The two possessions he exhibited most proudly were a suit of Japanese armor and his collection of mounted butterflies in their glass case. With great pride he pointed out that each butterfly was in perfect condition, without any defacing pin holes, for he took great care to asphyxiate them with the smoke of his cigars! James, always impressionable, sensitive to people in his own keen way, delighted to find the painter after his own heart, writing to his philosopher brother William: "I have several times seen the gifted Sargent, whose work I admire exceedingly, and who is a remarkable artistic nature and charming fellow."

As a critic and writer of occasional pieces for magazines, James proved an important friend to Sargent, for, impressed by what he saw and always seeking a subject for his comment, he wrote an article which served to introduce him to the English-speaking public. He wrote that Sargent presented the "slightly uncanny spectacle of a talent which on the very threshold of its career has nothing more to learn," a statement which applied to many another talent might have proved more apt than flattering. Sargent, however, for all that he had arrived at a perfection that he might have been content to go on duplicating through the rest of his life, would continue to progress in his art. With remarkable achievements already to his credit, the best of him was still a long way off.

In Brittany the work on Mme. Gautreau, when it was resumed that summer, progressed only slowly. At first Sargent was pleased by his good fortune in obtaining such a model, and a flood of ideas came to him. He proceeded to sketch her in a great number of positions before settling the final pose. One evening at dinner he was struck by the way she leaned forward across the table to propose a toast, and the resultant oil sketch, which greatly pleased her, he inscribed and presented to her mother. It seemed a good omen for the success of his portrait that she was so pleased, a pleasure confirmed when the sketch found its way out of the Gautreau home and into the possession of Dr. Pozzi. This first little picture is one of several evidences to show that he originally thought in terms of a seated composition. He made other pencil drawings of her, one seated more upright in a chair, using watercolor to suggest the proposed colors. By then something about her languor and the way she rested by tumbling haphazardly onto a sofa caught his fancy, and the idea of an upright composition was abandoned in favor of a larger canvas in which she would be decorously seated on a gracefully curved loveseat. This plan was highly attractive and might have seen fruition except that, by the time further thought was given it, other ideas occurred to him. He made two sketches of her standing with her arm in a position that he noticed was peculiar to her. In everything he attempted, the head was turned to show her particularly striking profile: a François Premier nose, small mouth, jutting chin, and retreating forehead, that in sum made a remarkable play of line and rhythm. He began to make careful drawings of this profile, so strange, imperfect, and yet so beautiful, drawing her first precisely as she was, then introducing an element of stylization, which, while not alien to her nature, was perhaps not apparent when one studied her features.

He was taking up a good deal of Mme. Gautreau's time, and was aware that, though he did much work while considering how he ought to paint her, there was still no sign of a portrait, nor even any decision on what sort of portrait it would be. Prodded by a realization of her growing impatience, and without making further preparatory drawings, he determined to paint a standing full-length, with the head turned in profile, though he knew she would not be keen about standing. He ordered a canvas and, when it was delivered to the Gautreau home, commenced to paint. But very soon he was regretting his haste, for he could not settle all the elements of the design. After several sittings, which seemed to go well, with a fast start on the work, the delicate modeling of the head began to look a trifle flat against the umbrous background, and something in the nature of a cameo emerged. He had never seen a modern portrait with such an effect, and as it was the magnificent linear patterns of his model that he was intent upon working with, there was no reason why he could not allow the effect to work its way into the picture, further simplifying the planes of the head until it was almost without modeling. Still, he could not settle the right arm. When he moved it close to the body it seemed to cramp the flow of line, and when moved away it became too prominent. Again and again he shifted it, each time obliged to edge it with background, then lay fresh paint around the entire contour of the figure. By now he had had more than thirty sittings, and was still perplexed by difficulties with no apparent solution. He knew a striking conception was evolving by this painful pragmatic process. He felt on the edge of something, urging, desiring to push on with the work. But Mme. Gautreau had many calls upon her time; there were constant interruptions for social matters, and recurrent days when a servant informed him that Madame could not sit because of more pressing considerations. The weeks were passing, and it seemed his portrait was hardly begun.

Perhaps he was also unsettled by the progress of a love affair about which only little is known. Moving in Parisian literary and musical circles, it was natural that he should gravitate to the inner circles of the Wagnerians, and meet their high priestess, Judith Gautier. Though she consistently reduced her age, Judith Gautier was eleven years older than the young John Sargent, and a woman of considerable experience. Not only had she the distinction of being the daughter of the great Théophile Gautier, in itself a significant qualification, but as a young music critic she had once journeyed to Lucerne, where the master lived in voluntary exile, and there, despite the watchfulness of Cosima, had captivated the great lover that was a part of Wagner's Olympian clay. For years she had periodically been his mistress and the recipient of scores of letters that even now, ninety years after their creation, waft a warm breath to the reader. In this last year before his death, Wagner's relations with her were abruptly terminated. He wrote that Cosima would henceforth obtain all the costly stuffs he habitually asked to be sent him from Paris. There was hardly an adieu, and no further letters. It was a strange ending to an alliance that had lasted nearly fifteen years.

Judith Gautier lived in Paris at 50 Rue des Martyrs, but her real home was not far from the Gautreaus', near St.-Enogat, in Brittany, where she built herself a brick and stone house of square Louis Philippe design, standing on the edge of a twenty-foot cliff immediately above the beach. A stairway with curved stone balustrade led to the sands, and surrounding the house was a garden in which the short and rather bulging figure of its mistress seemed constantly to be overtopped by the plants. "Près des Oiseaux" she named it, with typical poetic fancy, and when Sargent stood at the top of the stair, with the gulls circling over his head in the rising currents from the cliff, their shrill voices filling his ears, he felt it well named. It was a strange experience to swim in the surf at her doorstep and, then, mentally refreshed and filled with physical lassitude, gather up his things and carry them the few steps into a world of ottomans, beadwork hangings, carpeted walls, and pillowed corners. There was an air of haremlike comfort, of quiet and self-indulgence.

That he spent as much time as he could at St.-Enogat while painting Mme. Gautreau at Paramé is easily surmised from the numerous studies done of the house and its mistress. Curiously, there is no formal portrait, as though he did not feel the necessity of employing his fullest talents, nor any desire to set tongues wagging. There are oil sketches though, one of her standing beside the piano that she played less well than he, wearing the loose Oriental kimono she preferred to lounge in, only the crescent in her hair indicating that this was no picture en déshabillé. Many people thought Judith Gautier not especially good-looking; only those with an eye for such things pointed to her nose, flowing straight from the forehead, and said hers was a Grecian profile. Indeed it was, and as she herself felt rather proud of it, we must attribute to it Sargent's indifference to his labors on the piquant nose belonging to Mme. Gautreau. He also found in the two a common impatience. Judith Gautier had refused Lembach when, at the height of his fashionable reputation, he asked her to sit, and this for no better reason than a distaste for holding still. She felt greater need to let Sargent have his way and draw her, standing in the garden, and holding her wide-brimmed hat at the head of the stair, as though in fear it would blow off. He declared himself an admirer of her "beauty," spending the evenings making notes of her by lamplight, even taking the top from a kitchen table to paint on when he had exhausted his available supply of canvases. Soon she learned to fear the appearance of his paints, and the palette being set for another picture. She set him down as tall and strong, young, and capricious enough to be an interesting and a good lover, but she found him tiresome too. The boy was always playing with his paints.

In July, Sargent returned to Paris. Sitting one evening at Lavenue's with Helleu and young Belleroche, a new pupil of Carolus', the festivities of Bastille Day and the accompanying celebration loomed up like a nightmare. He was in no mood for a gay party nor for the mad Frenchmen who stalked the streets. Out of impulse he proposed that they take a three-day trip to Haarlem to see Frans Hals together; they agreed, taking the night train into Holland. The whole lark was indicative of the increasing uneasiness growing from his portrait of Mme. Gautreau and the intricacies of liaison with an artistic woman.

When he returned to the Gautreau home he was discouraged. He realized that his model was unpaintable: the color of her skin, which in the clear light of day was an unholy blue, with purple overtones, had not been taken into consideration when he planned the picture. He began with the hope that, while concentrating on her lines, which he still found wonderful, her color would manage itself, and perhaps in the finished picture not be noticeable at all. These hopes were soon dashed, for her color proved remarkably insistent. The further he progressed the more he saw that the color of Madame's flesh would be a very proper blue, rather than the gentle tint for which he had hoped. The cameo quality of the picture worried him too, for it was a new departure, unlike anything previously seen at the Salon, and he was by no means certain what reactions to it would be. His model, after months of a curious indifference, seemed repelled rather than pleased. She became less co-operative, as much, we may assume, from the exhaustion of her patience as from distaste for what Sargent was doing. He wrote to Vernon Lee: "Your letter has just reached me still in this country house struggling with the unpaintable beauty and hopeless laziness of Madame Gautreau." Clearly both were near the end of their patience.

At what point Mme. Gautreau gave way to wounded petulance is uncertain. But sometime in the middle of October Sargent suddenly returned to Paris with his unfinished picture, and then went off to Italy. On his return, somewhat refreshed, he continued to work on it, slimming the contours of her full skirt, removing some of the bustle formerly visible behind the left hip, painting out pieces of the gown's train that had billowed down from the left hand. When the year 1883 ended, he was still engaged on his task.

Friends who came to call tried but were not able to quiet the
doubts that assailed him. One day he thought the background
unnaturally dark, the forced contrast against the flesh harsh. He
put a thin tone of light rose across it so that something of the
dark glimmered through, then feeling it too pink, added a trifle
of cool green. "Vast improvement!" he thought as he stood back
from it. Turning it upside down on the easel, he went across the
room again to look at it from under his arm. The long sinewy
lines of the figure appeared to much greater advantage, perhaps
even the flesh appeared less purple-blue. Carolus, when next he
swaggered around to view the progress, was impressed. "You
may send it to the Salon with confidence," he said.

Praise from Carolus seems to have settled his worst doubts.
Perhaps the picture was good, though certainly the execution was
not. Compared with his usual manner, this canvas, suffering so
many vicissitudes, was heavy and nerveless in touch. So many
changes had been made, it had so often been covered with a new
coat of paint that the surface was thick and overloaded. The
labor put into it was plain to see, and Sargent, who was known
for a brief dashing execution, became concerned. At length,
though he was now at work on other portraits, he set himself to
paint a replica. It would be easy to copy off his own work. Everything was there before him. The heartrending problems had all
been solved. He could paint it off quickly and easily, and in doing
so he would eradicate the physical signs of anguish. Though time
was short, he got a canvas the same size, mounted the two on
easels side by side, and began. He was at the same time engaged
on a presentation portrait of the wife of a Chilean painter named
Errazuriz and a full-length of an American woman named Moore.
The latter had a remarkable reputation for her malapropisms in
French, and she frightened him half to death while he worked at
her home for fear that when she asked the butler to remove a vase
of flowers she would be misunderstood, and he would be ejected
instead. Possibly as the *Mrs. Moore* developed into a cascade of
stuffs and crockery emitting a tremulous gleam, he flirted with the
hope that, if he could not complete the replica, at least this picture
would be completed by receiving day. If so, he must quickly have
put the idea aside.

The Gautreau portrait had cost him much. It was conceived for the Salon, to shock and delight, to make his name, and he was determined to send it and nothing else. With the many calls on his time, receiving day found the replica only half complete, and the porters who called to take his entry to the Salon were given the original. Most likely because his relations with Mme. Gautreau were no longer of a friendly nature, he made a gesture of concealment with regard to her identity, listing his picture in the Official Catalogue as *"2150 Portrait de Mme. . . . "* It was certainly a futile gesture. The portrait had been in progress more than a year, he was often seen at the Gautreau home, and it was well known that he intended sending it to the Salon.

In anticipation of the thunderous acclaim he expected the *Mme. Gautreau* to bring him at the Salon, he thought to acquire a more fashionable studio in a better part of the city. People did not care to make repeated trips up the dark stairway to his fifth-floor quarters on the Rue Notre-Dame-des-Champs, nor did they like the trip all the way to Montparnasse. Leaving that crowded atmosphere behind, he sought out a location on the Boulevard Berthier, where many of the successful painters were located. He found a small house that was vacant, with its entire second floor a high studio as good as any he had ever seen. Downstairs were a bedroom, library and dining room, with servants' quarters and a dressing room on a little stair just above the studio. It was small and compact, suiting his bachelor requirements to perfection, and the studio was a marvelous place to work! Of course, to take an entire house required courage, for the annual rent was three thousand francs, more than he could afford. But, taking his courage in both hands, he decided he could manage the rent for a few months out of money he already had, and by then his fortune would be made. He took the house, and since he would soon be so rich, he also hired a cook and an Italian servant, so that when the carriages began rolling up to the door and the beautifully dressed ladies and gentlemen made their way across the sidewalk, he would be able to receive them in proper style.

His plans, and the excitement of the next few months, brought him out of the spiritual troubles that had been plaguing him. On his trip to Florence and Rome that winter he met a Miss Popert, who almost seemed to fit his image of womanhood. At the beginning of the year a tome of a letter came up to Paris from her, and it requested, among other things, a picture of him. From his reply we get some idea of his manner at that time, light and charming — that word, normally employed to cover such multitudes of sins, must periodically be reinstated to its own meaning.

Paris, 41, Boulevard Berthier
18 January [1884]

Interesting Mad One —

Your very long letter reached me many days ago. I have finished reading it and I am resting the seventh day. What especially pleased me was the intimation that I would one day have my little Diana. I shall receive her to my bosom.

I have nothing just now worthy of sending to Kofpp, but I shall try to do something nice for him and send it as soon as possible. Please remember me most kindly to him. Also to Capi and Car, whose names I have forgotten, also to Mancinino and Pio.

I hope you now and then draw a little and are aware that sometimes things are beautiful in form and that you are moderate in the use of wine. Copious draughts of Alcartico and Cinzano, even if they result in a momentary appreciation of splendid and exuberant color would always limit you to the fascinating but incomplete art which you revel in, so that if you really want to draw, take fewer fiestas a day.

The most interesting thing in Paris now is Manet's exhibition. It is altogether delightful.

And now God bless you child. I send you a photo of myself from a sketch. It is torn but the only one.

Yours affectionately
John S. Sargent

Another letter written to this same young lady, is equally expressive:

41, Boulevard Berthier
[March 6, 1884]

My dear Friend

You are very good about the [illegible] & I shall wait very patiently for what you will send.

I am working very hard at a portrait or two, and am soon going to England for a while. This summer I shall spend several months there doing portraits in the country.

Mme Gautreau is the only thing I send to the Salon.

I got a letter from an Italian servant whom I kept here for several months, but was obliged to send away on account of his quarrels with the cook. He wants a recommendation to you on the strength of having put my letters to you in the post box and having remembered your name and address, but I refused to give it, and he is not really a good servant and had a tendency to get very drunk and fight the cook . . . So don't receive him if he has the audacity to present himself.

My ideal would be to have a good Italian servant as they are so amusing and steal so pleasantly, and I am very sorry that my experiment did not succeed. Perhaps you will help me to find the ideal when I come back to Rome.

When are you coming to Paris?

Yours sincerely
John S. Sargent

On Sunday, May 1, 1884, the Salon opened. The day was clear and warm, the good weather throughout the spring having brought the chestnut trees lining the Champs-Elysées into early bloom. All Paris turned out in holiday mood to taste the air, laugh a little, and see what the forty judges of the Institute had selected by way of art. By two o'clock some fifteen thousand people had entered the Palais des Champs-Elysées, where the Salon was held, and by closing time at five there had been forty thousand. At least two thousand of these were the artists whose works were represented. Preliminary response to the picture was favorable, especially the Special Salon Supplement of the *Gaulois*, issued a day before the opening. In it Louis de Fourcaud wrote that this was a portrait with a strange refinement, a stunning work, of distinction and rare interest. Had he seen this, Sargent might have gone confidently, but as it happened he only returned to Paris late that evening from one of his trips, arriving at Ralph Curtis's club covered with dust to take his cousin back to the Boulevard Berthier, where they dined. He seemed very nervous, fearing a grand debacle the following day.

No sooner was the Salon opened than the public saw that its established favorites were well represented, and was pleased. The only picture widely criticized and jeered by the public was Sargent's. The identity of his sitter was never for a moment in doubt, and the public condemnation was as much of her personally as of this strange portrait that made an accounting of her every excess. The demonstrations taking place before it were so remarkable that crowds out on the street knew about them before entering, and thus came prepared to roar. Clearly the picture was the storm center of the Salon, as such attracting much greater attention than had it found favor. Crowds pushing into the building asked where it hung in order to go immediately and see for themselves. In the midst of all was Sargent himself, his short nose and troubled eyes clearly visible over the heads of the crowd, obviously hurt, more than usually speechless, bewildered. His cousin, missing sight of his bobbing head over the crowd, found him dodging behind a door to avoid friends with ominous looks. By the back corridors, above the courtyard, Sargent led him to the gallery where it hung. Even Curtis was struck by the color of the flesh, which he thought looked decomposed.

This happy holiday throng was in a mood to laugh. It needed a butt for its humor and found it provided equally by Sargent's picture and the revelations it made of Mme. Gautreau. Women found a much-desired opportunity to indulge their malice at the expense of this doubly painted beauty. They crowded close, hooting at the impropriety of the gown, the obvious employment of cosmetics, all pointed up by the coldly precise treatment. There was nothing to relieve the austerity of the figure itself, which, like a blasphemous thought out of context, laid bare the ungodly element of the lady's charms.

Some dozen artists had arranged to lunch together that afternoon, and Curtis, to get his cousin out of the maelstrom engulfing his painting, took him along. We do not know what transpired, or how well he took his new distinction. After lunch they were both back at the Salon, which now seemed quieter, the first onslaught having subsided. Curtis went with Sargent to his studio, where he stayed while the artist went off to visit the Boits. After he left there was a commotion outside, and Curtis found that Mme. Gautreau had come with her mother to demand the removal of the offending picture from the Salon. There was nothing he could do but explain that his cousin was away. He thought he managed well. When Sargent returned he was followed by Mme. Avegno, who apparently had sent her daughter home and waited for him alone. A fearful scene ensued, Mme. Avegno crying that her daughter was ruined, lost, that all Paris was mocking her. She would die of chagrin, she wailed, in a bath of tears. Coupled with the other events of the day, this was more than Sargent could stand, and his normal quiet diffidence gave way to temper and a heated defense. It is curious that the arguments he used are largely identical with the considered judgments found in the periodicals, when they began to appear. Choking with rage, savagely tugging at his little beard, he told Mère Avegno that he had painted her daughter exactly as she looked, wearing the gown in which she consented to pose. Nothing could be said of the portrait that had not already been said of the sitter, and in print. Once his anger was aroused, he felt more confident. It was against all rules to retire a picture before the end of the exhibition. He would not withdraw it.

Seventeen days later the *Gaulois*, the same paper that had printed Fourcaud's lone bits of praise, launched a savage attack on Sargent by devoting three whole columns on its front page to a scathing indictment of artist and portrait. Under the heading, "Great Beauties of the Past and Their Painters, A propos of the Beautiful Madame Gautreau," they printed fourteen imaginary conversations between the people of famous portraits and their painters, beginning with La Belle Mona Lisa to Leonardo da Vinci and passing on to Mme. de Pompadour and Latour, Mme. Récamier and Baron Gérard, Mme. Moitessier and Ingres, the Empress Eugénie and Winterhalter, the Countess de Pourtalès and Carolus-Duran, ending with Mme. Gautreau addressing Sargent. Whereas the beauties of the ages had heaped praises upon their painters, Mme. Gautreau was given this to say, hers being the only speech put into verse:

THE BEAUTIFUL MADAME GAUTREAU TO
MR. SARGENT

O my dear painter, I swear to you
That I love you with all my heart,
But what a funny countenance!
But what funny coloring!

Veritably, I am ashamed
To see, each day, at the Salon,
My good friends, with pitying mien,
Cutting me up from top to toe.

"Is it really she?" — "No." — "How do I know?"
"It *is* she, look at the little book!"
"But in that case it's a sacrilege!"
"Go on! Of course it's she! It seems!"

It doesn't seem, on the contrary,
And I had, I swear to heaven,
When I got you to do my portrait,
Dreamed of something rather better.

It was a great wrong I'm expiating;
But, never mind! Each day I'll go
Place myself beside my copy . . .
And the harm will be repaired.

                                        Sévigné

It was an unnecessary and rather wanton attack on the young
artist. In his defense a group of American artists in Paris that very
day got up a letter, which they sent to the editor of the *Gaulois*
with a request that it be printed. Sargent wrote too, asking that
the letter be printed, but it never appeared. Fourcaud appears
to have been unable to help, and yet his lone voice in the general
maelstrom had loomed so large to Sargent that he invited the
strange-looking, rather ugly critic to let him do a little portrait
in thanks, which he inscribed, "à Fourcaud témoignage d'amitié."
Though the critics duly noted the public response, their written
comments, when in a few days they began to appear, were far more

kind. The professionals were in no sense led by the public. Whatever they said in defense of the picture was said boldly. Special
criticism was heaped on the qualities one expects would be criticized: the gown was thought immodest, the chains of brilliants
supporting the bodice called suggestive, the flesh invariably calling
forth derision. Some thought the contour treatment too angular,
others came forth to praise it. Henri Houssaye, writing in the
Revue des Deux Mondes, owned and published by the Paillerons,
was particularly venomous, which might not have been the case
had Sargent still been in favor with Judith Gautier and the court
gathered around her, of which Houssaye was a member. They too
were grasping an opportunity to ruin him. Diametrically opposed
was the view held by the critic writing for *L'Art,* who took the
stand that no fault could be found with the painting that was not
properly attributable to Parisian high life. He considered it a
valuable document by which Paris could assess itself, an imputation
that might be extended to include the whole of Sargent's portraiture, fixing as it does the times and manners so well.

In *L'Artiste* we read: "Of all the undressed women exhibited at
the Salon, the most interesting is Sargent's. Interesting for the
ugliness of the profile which recalls Della Francesca, interesting
again for the chainettes of brilliants, which are indecent and give
the impression of a gown which is falling; interesting again for the
pearl blue on the skin, at once cadaverous and clownlike. . . ."

Louis de Fourcaud, writing in the *Gazette des Beaux-Arts,* which
did not come out until June, applied to Sargent for a drawing of
the profile, which he reproduced in the margin at the head of his
column on the Salon. So that none could mistake the identity it
was marked "M.G. . . ." Seen there, it is difficult to understand
what could be objected to in such beautiful pure drawing, which
perhaps was Fourcaud's intention.

It was generally thought that Sargent was so stung by the
reception of his painting that he packed his bags and left Paris.
Nothing could be further from the truth. His letters reveal that
he intended to remain in Paris until the opening of the Salon, then
visit England, to execute the portraits of which he had made
mention in his letter to Miss Popert and see the exhibition at the
Royal Academy, where he was also represented. Though events

at the Salon took an unexpected turn, his trip to England that summer was the result of plans made months before. He did not realize then the extent of the damage done to his reputation by the Gautreau portrait, and his trip was in no sense a rejection of Paris or even a response to recent events. Certainly his later resolve to remain in England was the product of many other factors, most of which were present, if less apparent, long before the Gautreau portrait went to the Salon.

As he crossed to England that summer he fully intended to return to Paris in the fall and pick up where he had left off. Viewed calmly, it appeared that, though something unfortunate had occurred, no great harm was done. The all-important critical response was not so bad as it might have been. The public had been aroused, and the scene with Mme. Avegno had been a nightmare, but that would pass. Taking the long view, he had suddenly gained great prominence, which he could put to account with a good picture the next year. It was a blow to him, but one from which he might recover if he responded to it properly. Fourcaud had been kind to print his little profile in the *Gazette*. It looked rather well on the page, and might give those who thought it ugly at the Salon reason to reconsider on returning home. Perhaps he should have realized that a woman with so many enemies was more a liability than an advantage to him. He made up his mind that in the future he would be careful of beauties.

When he returned to Paris, after Christmas, he still did not realize that there had been any drastic change in his status. He had spent a pleasant summer and autumn in England, doing a surprising number of portraits, though he still had no thought of substituting England for Paris. Paris had been his home for ten years, and it was his chosen battleground. Possibly he first realized that something was terribly wrong when he saw no commissions forthcoming. To keep himself occupied in the big new studio where he had expected to entertain a stream of fashionable sitters, he worked some eighty sittings on a Florentine costume piece for which he induced Albert de Belleroche to pose. It began as a full-length, representing a Florentine gentleman of the fourteenth century holding up a large two-handed sword. Soon he had it cut down to three-quarter length, eventually it became a bust, and finally was put away to be forgotten. This, of course, produced no income, and the reserve from the summer in England was apparently gone; he had no money for the rent, so he asked his good-natured landlord, Paul Poirson, if he would not take a portrait of his little daughter instead. But even to paint this cost money, and he was obliged to buy a cheaper canvas than he normally employed, with a heavier surface broken by nubby thread endings which interfered as he worked on the head. It was a good thing his servant had gone. Now the cook had to go too, and he wrote to ask if his sister Emily could come up after Easter to keep house for him, promising that they would "have a jolly time together in Paris."

He called on his friend Besnard, back from three successful years in England and now carrying out murals for the School of Pharmacy. With time to waste, he posed for a figure in one of the panels. As the season wore on, and he remained idle, some of his friends attempted to ease the disappointment he felt: Ben del Castillo urged his family to sit, and in the spring Louise Burckhardt asked him to do a double portrait of herself and her mother. These few friendly efforts were not able to hide the facts, which were now apparent even to him. For the first time he saw how badly he was hurt, how the very people he attempted to please with his major effort were offended, and so shocked by his revelations of Mme. Gautreau that none of them dared to sit to him. It was a staggering realization.

And then, once again, he could not pay the rent. He asked Poirson now if Mme. Poirson would come for a portrait. This, again, was done on the rougher grade of canvas, and, knowing that this bourgeoise sort of clientele cared chiefly about the likeness, he worked over the head until the shadows threatened to become muddied and the surface enameled. Still, he painted the long loop of her arms with beautiful clarity of draftsmanship, shifting the canvas upward and to the right on the stretcher, the better to balance the long oval loop. All this was done just to remain in this studio, where in a year he had executed only one commission, where the fashionable throngs had never come. In the evening shadows, when perhaps he settled down in the alcove off the studio to view his works from out of the dark, his glance passed over the upright piano for which he had given the maker, M.

Bechstein, two Venetian genre pieces. Had his mind drifted in reverie, he could have seen the six years spent in France since leaving the studio of Carolus-Duran. He had achieved an early acclaim at the Salon, the prospect was bright. For some reason, however, he had missed the next step upward, for those who sought portraits rarely came to him, and that most genuine of all flattery was not his. Though he did numerous portraits, few were commissioned; the larger number were presentation pieces and studies of friends. Of those commissioned, most were of traveling Americans. They came to him because of nationality, through the recommendation of other Americans, or because he was a cheaper version of Carolus. However they came, it was not a patronage with any sort of reliability. It was the Parisian patronage he sought, and there, for all his efforts, he was distinctly a failure.

From the moment he had decided to become an artist, and consent had been wrung from his father's conscience, it was determined that he would be a master. Whether it was his father's ambition or his own was not certain, but he would be one of the important painters of the time, nonetheless. The idea was deeply embedded. From the first he had gone about studying his craft more thoroughly than most, putting all his strength and industry into his work. Now, at twenty-eight, after vainly striving with all his energy and ingenuity for six years, he was nowhere near his goal. Those years had been a waste, gaining nothing, advancing him not a whit. For the first time, faced with obvious failure, he must have fully realized how ambitious he was. He *had* to succeed. He had not worked so hard to be a failure, to be incapable even of paying his rent. In Paris his prospects as a portraitist were gone, and there were those other unpleasant associations. He could continue in Paris and hope that with future paintings sent to the Salon his reputation would again prosper. The public memory was short, and in the face of new honors it would soon forget that it had not liked one picture. He could regain his position, the lauded but unpatronized position he had formerly held in Paris. But even that was no solution; assuming that he did regain that ambiguous distinction, the question remained, would he ever succeed with the Parisian public? He would have to compete with his own master, Carolus-Duran. Carolus would not take that in friendly fashion;

and why, he wondered in the back of his mind, had Carolus urged him to send the Gautreau picture to the Salon? Surely his eye was good enough to see the faults that would bring attack; for years he had scampered across the frothy brew of Parisian taste, surely he knew what would be liked, what jeered. But that must not be thought about. Carolus was his master, to whom he owed everything. And it would be decades before the public forgot he was Carolus' pupil, assumed inferior to him on that count alone.

When he awakened to the fact that Paris had no use for him, many other truths became apparent. He realized that he was ambitious. During the summer in England he could not have missed the response his work received. Of course, it seemed distinctly French, and therefore highly suspect to Victorian-English eyes. The critics were still ready to praise the painted moralities of Millais, so much an advocate of all that was good, fair, and sweet. They were decidedly hostile to the art of Sargent, which sought only its own perfection and made no effort to teach or to preach. Even so, the public seemed rather taken with his portrait of Mrs. Henry White. When the Academy exhibition closed, Mrs. White's picture went home to her new house in Mayfair, where, though reactions to it were mixed, there remained an element of approval; and in the Vickers, for whom he had done portraits over the summer, he appeared to have a patron of means. They asked him to return when he was able to do other pictures for them, and seemed to think he was all that the French had never let him be.

Spring came, and time for the Salon was at hand. The Burckhardt group, the only important work he had undertaken, was not complete. He found it necessary to bring from England a portrait done during the previous summer. Suddenly it became clear to him that he had a better foothold in England than he had ever achieved in Paris!

England — Twilight and Dawn

ENGLAND was not new to Sargent, nor he to it. When he crossed the Channel after the Salon of 1884, he did not come as a complete stranger. He had visited before, and his reputation, with its overtones of notoriety, preceded him to those virtuous Victorian shores. Anyone able to shock wicked Paris was certainly anathema to London, where respectability was in vogue and was cultivated with overwhelming assiduity.

His contacts with England extended back more than twenty years, to childhood visits and later, when his father sailed on lone trips to America, the family crossed to see him off and awaited his return in London. Later still, in 1881, when the family sailed for America, he had chosen to remain in London with Joseph Farquharson, an old friend who many years before had given him lessons in drawing a head. Farquharson was now a member of the Royal Academy, and lived in Porchester Gardens. During that same trip he saw Vernon Lee, temporarily living in England with her family, and among the sketches he did for friends while there was one of her goggled eyes and protruding teeth that was devastating in its frankness. During these earlier trips he was interested to take note of the artistic climate, testing it with reluctant toe, and studying the work of the Pre-Raphaelites, with whom he felt some affinity. Constable and Turner had to be seen too, for Monet had spoken of how closely they were tied into the fabric of impression-ist discovery. He looked through the Royal Academy exhibition, and in 1882, following on his visit of the previous year, sent a por-trait that was accepted and hung, though we do not know how well.

Altogether there was nothing in these rather meager contacts to encourage any belief that England was writ large in his future. More likely it was the fact that two of his friends, Besnard and Natorp, found warm reception in London that attracted him. Albert Besnard had moved across the Channel in 1880, to find a receptive atmosphere awaiting his very Gallic idiom. After Bes-nard's return to Paris, Sargent was naturally exposed to much talk of England. Still, none of what he heard could have much in-terested him until he realized how badly he had been damaged by the Gautreau scandal. Curiously, during the spring of 1884 an Englishwoman had come to sit, Mrs. Wodehouse Legh, and her presence in the studio, for the only commissioned portrait he was ever to do in the Boulevard Berthier, may itself have suggested that he give England a try. Following Henry White's appointment as American minister at London, Sargent was pleased to send his portrait of Mrs. White to the Royal Academy, where he had not been represented for two years; but all this was without special reference, until that summer when he crossed the Channel to find much greater response than he expected. It could not have come at a more propitious moment.

It was through Gustav Natorp that Sargent met the Vickers family. Before he left Paris they had asked him to come out to their summer home at the Lavington Rectory, near Petworth, to paint the first of many portraits. He found the English countryside unfamiliar, and it aroused no enthusiasm in one accustomed to the more gaudy, sun-drenched beauty of Italy. The strange climate of England, where an ever-moving sky shifted over an orderly landscape, inspiring much of Turner and Constable's art, produced no similar feeling in him. The strangeness of even the kitchen gardens impressed him; he was amazed at the rambling growth of the vines. He was asked if perhaps he thought cucumbers grew in slices, and did not deny the inference. Perhaps he was feigning an innocence which his early years with books and his interest in nature seem to belie. He was doing his best to be a pleasant companion during his stay, attempting to shrug off the Gautreau scandal, which returning travelers were carrying to England and which he undoubtedly believed would be short-lived. Perhaps even then it was forgotten across the Channel. Thus in a rather indifferent way he poked about the countryside, exaggerated his surprise at unknown aspects of English life, and filled any momentary silence with whimsy. Perhaps the only sight that struck his imagination was the large white lily that grew in profusion, and he set about doing a garden sketch of the two young Vickers children standing with a watering can before these lilies. Nor was he above seeking favor by doing another sketch of Mr. and Mrs. Vickers at dinner, a picture pointedly demonstrating how he was still working according to tenets of French taste rather than attempting to accustom himself to English, as had Besnard. He was insistent upon his own vision and loose touch, which were thought frankly eccentric in England, as a glance at any of the art journals would have told him. The following June, when this sketch was exhibited at the Galerie Georges-Petit in Paris it brought forth praise: "the last word in definitive painting, the illusion is complete"; but in England such work was queer.

Toward fall he did another portrait, this time of Edith, Lady Playfair, the American wife of Sir Lyon Playfair, a prominent member of the government and former tutor of the Prince of Wales. Then, in November, there occurred one of those revealing episodes that shed so much light on his career and on its inner workings. Charles Fairchild of Boston asked him to do a small portrait of Robert Louis Stevenson. He agreed, and as he and the author were fairly well acquainted since the days at Beckwith's studio, consent was readily forthcoming from that quarter. Sargent appears to have been at low ebb financially, for he asked a loan of five pounds from Fairchild to make the trip to Bournemouth, where Stevenson and his wife, the former Fanny Osbourne, were living. Why he was out of pocket cannot readily be explained, unless he had used the proceeds from the Vickers portraits to pay back rent on the Boulevard Berthier studio. There is no other way to account for the absence of the substantial sums earned that summer. The prolonged stay in England was certainly expensive, but there was a large margin of profit that should have been available. Whatever the exact combination of factors, it seems he had not the necessary five pounds. Another view might also be considered to explain away this unusual circumstance: It is rather unlikely that, having done three important pictures in a few months' time, he would have left himself so entirely without funds, even assuming he made a sizable payment to Poirson, as to be in need of five pounds. He asked four hundred pounds for the group of the three Vickers girls, a considerable fee in those days, and his other works were priced in proportion. Surely he kept money in hand adequate for all small needs, and to borrow five pounds was rather a reflection on himself. It would appear that nothing in the way of earnest money was offered him, and as he would have to travel to Bournemouth to stay with Stevenson, which would entail expense, he no doubt decided that a small loan would insure him against the possibility of loss.

He hopped the train to Bournemouth and on arriving was rather an impressive sight with his big physique cramped into a fly, laden down with equipment, appearing to dominate the commotion about him by sheer mass, and the strength of the smile breaking through his beard. More than six years had passed since they last met in the studio on the Rue Notre-Dame-des-Champs. In the interim Louis had run off to California after Fanny Osbourne, exposure to penury and the severity of the journey turning his illness, already troublesome in Paris, to something more serious. Repeatedly he hovered halfway between life and death, nursed by Fanny, who married him when it seemed he was sufficiently recovered to warrant hope. His friendly game with death was a recurrent episode, and it was while dangling over this precipice that he began to turn out those high-spirited novels that established his literary fame. His energy seemed entirely derived from an extraordinary zest for life, which as he sat posing in a wicker chair for the "charming, simple, clever, honest young man," as he described Sargent, seemed to shine from his dancing eyes. Stevenson wrote of the visit:

"Sargent has come and gone; I repeat what I said to Bob: he represents me as a wierd [sic], very pretty, large-eyed, chicken-boned, slightly contorted poet. He is not pleased; wants to do me again in several positions; walking about and talking is his main notion. We both lost our hearts to him: a person with a kind of exhibition manner and English accent, who proves on examination, simple, bashful, honest, enthusiastic and rude with a perfect (but quite inoffensive) English rudeness. *Pour comble*, he gives himself out to be American."

Soon after Sargent's departure, Stevenson received a letter from Henry James, who was visiting nearby with his ill sister, Alice. Apparently on the basis of Sargent's reports, and his own taste for Stevenson's fine craftsmanship, he had decided that he would like to make acquaintance. The answer was an invitation to visit. James accepted, taking possession of a leather chair, from which he held forth with his usual wordiness, now more fluent than in later years, though he never failed to grope for the proper word, while Louis waited in perpetual breathlessness for the substance of thought to protrude from the maze of verbiage.

To Henry James must go the credit for many of the introductions Sargent had during those first tense years when he sought for any sign of welcome on the English shore. James returned to England a month after Sargent arrived, immediately taking up the London season where he left off in Paris. Very often they were together in the evenings; now as later it seeming one could hardly spy the slightly rotund and bearded pedant without his tall rubicund friend's looming near. After more than ten years in England, James had a widely cultivated acquaintance, which he did not scruple to weed with the aid of his *Red Book* and into which he thought nothing of bringing a friend, such latitude being happily granted him by many a hostess who knew that his discretion could be relied upon. Naturally gregarious, James had the confirmed taste for society, and the truly gargantuan appetite for it, that marked the American abroad; once in a letter to his family he boasted of the number of homes in which he was welcome, recording nearly three hundred evenings on which he had been entertained in one year. Apparently he thought Sargent equally well adapted to the routine of visiting and dining, and took him wherever he went, making introductions with a cryptic reference to "sensation in Paris" designed to inform the host of his friend's celebrity, without causing embarrassment, and failing in both respects. Among the first homes to which he introduced Sargent was the Blandford Square residence of J. Comyns Carr, director of the Grosvenor Gallery, and friend to many of the senior artists and writers, Burne-Jones and Robert Browning particularly. It was a home famous alike for its conversation and the fine food provided by a Bolognese cook. Sargent appeared tall and powerful entering the cluttered Victorian interior that exaggerated his proportions against a sea of bric-a-brac, and the impression of his thick-chested body, now more fleshy than formerly, was emphasized by the hearty grip of his hand.

When introduced to square-faced, hollow-cheeked Mrs. Carr, he immediately noticed the strangeness of her proportions, and notwithstanding otherwise excellent manners, lifted his chin in the painter's way to see more clearly. His gaze became alarmingly frank in its scrutiny, as the three stood just inside the door, Henry James making his interminable explanation lost in its own subtlety. The final cessation of words brought Sargent back to reality; grasping from her dismayed look that he had embarrassed his hostess, he made a flustered attempt to ease the situation, bringing forth a limp "jolly dress," which was his contribution to a strained atmosphere. Mrs. Carr was pleased to recall that it was an ample dress, though rather straight of line for that time, and passed on to greet her other guests. Altogether not an auspicious start. During the evening she became conscious of him again, realizing that he spoke with difficulty, waving his hands before his face when he could not finish a sentence, as a sign for the conversation to go on without him. Still, the halting pace of his speech, plus his general vagueness of manner when pressed, conflicted with the definiteness of his views when at length he did express them; and soon her unfavorable impression vanished before his wholly sympathetic personality. There was a certain similarity notable in the speech of Sargent and James, but it did not run deep, for, while both spoke in halting tones, searching for words with mute, comic results, James's highly ceremonious, even pompous, manner was a perfect foil to Sargent's unpretentiousness, and the way he seemed, considering the extent of his celebrity, to hide his light under a bushel. Comyns Carr had already shown interest in his work; his portrait of Mrs. Wodehouse Legh, done in Paris, had appeared at the Grosvenor Gallery earlier that year. It drew abuse for being "but poorly painted and artificially clever," giving English critics the opportunity, later in the year, to make mention of the Gautreau scandal with an I-told-you-so virtuousness. But Carr was a director whose tastes ran in advance of the time, and he showed no tendency to listen to detractors, making Sargent one of the regulars of the Gallery, despite a steady stream of fire from critics.

When Sargent returned to England for the summer of 1885, after that last depressing winter in Paris, he settled at the Arts Club in Hanover Square, and seems quickly to have struck up a friendship with Edwin A. Abbey, a little Philadelphian with a dry way of saying things that came forth accompanied by a roguish look from behind gleaming spectacles, and a smile that was almost a grin, betraying a sparkle of gold in a tooth. It was Abbey who the previous autumn had suggested Sargent to Charles Fairchild for the picture of Robert Louis Stevenson, explaining that he was a young American just over from Paris with nothing much to do. Abbey himself did illustrations, mostly pen drawings for *Harper's*, which despite their small scale showed considerable skill in line and a certain pregnant understanding of composition. He was also a sports enthusiast and delighted in cricket and rowing on the upper Thames, in which during the autumn he induced his new friend to join him.

The days on the water aroused Sargent's lifelong taste for swimming, and when they reached Pangbourne, with an ill-considered enthusiasm, he climbed up on the weir and dived. His head struck a spike beneath the water with all the force of his jump, and he came to the surface bleeding profusely from a nasty gash. Once he had it attended to, and there were signs of healing, he knocked it a second time, reopening the wound. With his head swathed like the great sheik he became an awesome figure in the English countryside, his towering bulk and natural dignity of carriage topped off with Eastern splendor. Abbey had been heading toward Broadway, a tiny village hidden away in the vale of Evesham, far in the west of England, intending to work there with other artists and illustrators, all of whom had some American background. The chief among them, Frank Millet, Sargent of course knew from St.-Gaudens' studio in Paris, and as he would be able to convalesce in those quiet parts while attracting less notice than in London, it seemed a good suggestion when Abbey asked him along.

Abbey and the Millets were sharing Farnham House, a twin-gabled slate-roofed house of weathered gray stone, standing at the narrow end of the small triangle of grass that served for the village green. When he walked to the Lygon Arms, the town's Tudor and Jacobean coaching inn, where he stayed, Sargent traversed the entire length of the town in his few steps. On the right a single row of Jacobean houses and mullioned windows swung wide around the green, their row of chimneys nestling in cadenced symmetry against the distant hill. To the left were the few buildings that stood in a row before the inn, whose embroidered metalwork sign rose up off the road just past the little segment of grass. Insular and self-possessed, its houses having successfully withstood the onslaughts of time and change, this sequestered vale suddenly was drawn into what must have seemed a minor reign of terror. For it was invaded by an army of cantankerous Americans, who were mad, pixillated, and, as if that were not bad enough, were artists as well. Daily they could be seen painting in some field under the noonday sun, walking the street in cloaks one could not tell from an anarchist's, and playing impossible music half the night. In fact they seemed to prance like school children, and whatever they were up to, the villagers soon resigned themselves to taking no notice. At first they had been much dismayed, but now nothing could scandalize them. When one day Fred Barnard, with an enormous slouch hat coming down over his shoulders, chased another American down the village street, the man being chased screaming all the time and trying to escape up lampposts and down wells, not a villager smiled. Whatever was said or done, worn or sung, the only comment ever heard was, "Them Americans is out again."

Behind Farnham House was a strip of pasturage that by day became the focal point of these artists. Periodically the company was increased by the inclusion of Edmund Gosse and Henry James, the latter coming several times from London at Sargent's invitation to stay a few days. Throughout the summer Sargent continued to study the effects of twilight that he had first made note of the previous year, adding a study of the effects on figures, which seemed to become immersed in the liquid nuance of air during the long English twilight. For a model he used Kate, the five-year-old daughter of Frank and Lily Millet, covering her dark hair with a golden wig borrowed from the props Abbey had at hand for his illustrations.

Through September he had accumulated a number of small oil studies, and now his probing took the form of a canvas seven by five feet. It was at this point that Fred Barnard arrived with his wife and two blond-haired daughters. Sargent looked around and puffed a bit under his beard, "Well, er-um, that is, I think — we should have two children in the picture — yes, two children." Poor little Kate Millet was heartbroken, and the Barnard girls, possessed of the required blond hair, and slightly older, with a consequent increase in patience, took over her duties. The effect he was after lasted each evening from twenty minutes to a half hour between twilight and darkness, when there was a violet glow in the air and outlines were suffused with an unwonted glow of dull luster. It was preceded by a period of excited preparations that became a matter of interest to the whole artist colony. Sargent was, after all, the only full-fledged painter among them; the others were mainly illustrators, some in process of transformation into painters, and they were experiencing the pitfalls inherent in handling oils. Even here at Broadway, where there was not the disingenuousness of studio neighbor relations, there was an awareness of his reputation; indeed, they had all known his works before he appeared off the river like a turbaned wizard. They were aware that he was of modern tendencies, and to see him actually working on what appeared to be a large undertaking was a matter of no small interest.

Everything was placed in readiness: the easel set in position, the canvas brought out from the barn, where it was stored overnight, the little girls dressed in their white pinafores. Then attention was turned to an evening game of lawn tennis, Gosse's particular sport, in which Sargent's lumbering form, skillful at the net but woefully inefficient in back court, made the others appear tiny. In time he would look up. The purple moment had come, and leaving racquets on the court, they all ran to light the lanterns strung through a plot of roses and lilies, while he took his place at a distance from the canvas, trotting forward to place a touch or two, then retreating again, all with a fantastic hustle and bustle that subsided as abruptly as it had commenced when the last flush of purple gave way to another effect. Then they all returned to a last volley of tennis, Sargent joining them after he had attended to his materials, while the young ladies went in to take off their white dresses, to be carefully put away for the following day.

He filled his pockets with candies for the children after they posed, apparently an adequate reward, for like the rest of the company they were essentially interested in this project of which they were a part. These evenings continued until the beginning of November, when the summer dresses were no defense against the growing cold, and the children were equipped with sweaters extending to their ankles, over which the white pinafores were dutifully worn. Winter was coming on, the garden growing desolate and the roses eventually dying, their places taken by other flowers which he wired to the plants, while he himself appeared rigged out in a flat white hat that fitted down over his ears in peculiar Oriental style and a heavy mariner's jacket thrown over his carefully tailored suit. The lilies used for the background of his picture were growing in pots that normally stood on the lawn, and these had to be raised onto chairs to put into perspective for their new use. Thus he worked for those few minutes each evening, surrounded by the dozen or so spectators. Though he was drawing on the endurance of the children, each evening continued to be such an event, preceded by its prolonged preparations and followed by careful examination the following morning in the barn, that they remained sufficiently interested to co-operate as best they could.

He seemed so absorbed by the work on his big garden picture, added to all the sketches he was doing by day, that no one suspected the state he was in all this while, filled with the unhappiness and dissatisfaction continually dogging his steps. Though he had a single patron in the Vickers, the fact was that he saw no real patronage forthcoming to justify permanent haven in England. No one perceived, nor shared with him, the terrible despair that filled him, the awful sense of futility that he did his best to throw off. Never had he felt so alone. He could find no place for himself.

It was as though his gifts, in which he never doubted, were simply not wanted. A letter written that September of 1885 to Edward Russell, who had been one of his friends in the Carolus-Duran atelier and later moved to Australia for his health, gives some insight into his thoughts:

. . . Two years ago I left the old studio and took another one where I am better off, 41 Bd. Berthier, near the Place P . . .

Since the last three or four years I have had more or less ups and down of prosperity. Just now I am rather out of favor as a portraitist in Paris, although my last Salon, two portraits done in England rather retrieved me — I have been coming to England for the last two or three summers and should not wonder if I someday have a studio in London. There is perhaps more chance for me there as a portrait painter, although it might be a long struggle for my painting to be accepted. It is thought beastly french.

By this time I know lots of English painters and have some good friends among them, Wyllie, Abbey, Parsons.

Just now I am in a country village with Abbey and Millet who have cottages here. I am trying to paint a charming thing I saw the other evening. Two little girls in a garden at dusk lighting paper lanterns hung among the flowers from rose-tree to rose-tree. I shall be a long time about it if I don't give up in despair, and at any rate probably two months longer in England — address Arts Club, Hanover Square, London. After that I shall probably go to Italy before returning to Paris, for the Cholera is raging in Spain where I want most to go.

Have you not been able to paint at all all this time?

If there is any change or symptoms of change in French Arts since the last 6 or 8 years it is a tendency towards real painting and a growing indifference for atelier swagger. Bastien Lepage's Joan of Arc had a great influence, and also the work of certain germans, Uhde, and Lieberman. There is no great young talent.

Carolus goes on painting magnificently. I hardly ever see him. I have quite fallen away from him.

Beckwith and Fowler are vegetating in N.Y. Cox and Robinson are I believe pretty flourishing. Eugene Lachaise has much deteriorated. My people are all well and still winter at Nice.

Do write again soon and give a fuller address.

Ever your affectionate
John S. Sargent

It was totally unlike him to speak of his feelings, and yet during walks with Edmund Gosse he again gave momentary expression to his disappointment, an act so unusual as to cause astonishment, and indicating the extreme low ebb to which he had come. He was bursting, he simply had to talk, and one day quietly walking with Gosse he brought himself to the point of mentioning that he was considering giving up art. To Gosse, well aware of his outward success, the achievements and reputation piled up by this still young man, the idea was bewildering. Sargent was so exclusively an artist that one could think of no other occupation for him. "But then," said Gosse, "what will you do?"

"Oh, I shall go into business."

"What kind of business?" asked Gosse, his face proof of surprise.

Here Sargent faltered. Conflict again set in. Undoubtedly he had in mind the various positions his uncles might have got him in Philadelphia. This course may even have been urged on him, perhaps by his father. But to speak of family matters, and the prospect of going to live in Philadelphia, to be a cosmopolitan among provincials, was too revealing of family matters and too painful to discuss.

"Oh, I don't know," he replied; and then, with a wave of the hand to greet the change of subject, added, "or go in for music, don't you know?" He had said too much, and preferred now to talk of other things. There was no satisfaction in telling his troubles either, and he relapsed into tight-jawed silence.

Gosse considered himself intelligently interested in contemporary painting, and even a little proud of his acquaintance with the latest French work. Even so, he was unprepared for the trenchant criticisms he drew from Sargent during their walks, opinions denoting his extreme independence of taste. England then accepted the elegant nudities of Gérôme entirely without reserve, an opinion shared by Americans such as Thomas Eakins who, as one of Gérôme's pupils, entertained a profound respect for his master's work. These, Sargent instructed Gosse, were "all sugar and varnish." More surprising were the liberties he took with the immediate darlings of the French press, Henner and Bastien-Lepage. "Tricks!" he would say, completely disposing of all contrary opinion in the one syllable. Alma-Tadema, then at the height of his fame and, one would expect, enjoying a slight sanctity as Gosse's brother-in-law and a favorite guest of the Millets', left him completely and serenely unappreciative. "I suppose it's clever," he said. "Of course, it *is* clever, like the things you do, don't you know, with a what d'you call, but of course it's not art in any sense whatever!" with which cryptic judgment Gosse was left shaken and awed. Tadema was in many ways the most typically Victorian artist, who by his very perfection in meeting the public taste well deserved his place at the top of public recognition. More important though, in an actual sense, was the way the actors in his canvases, for they were little else, managed to play out some typical bit of homely virtue particularly appealing to the Victorian concepts of home, family, and idealized love. To Sargent, intent upon the artistic side of his work and dismissing the subject matter as inconsequential, he made the mistake of showing he knew too much about the substances painted. His marble and metal were minute renderings of these materials, with no love of the paint employed, no knowledge of the fact that these materials vary in color according to the light playing on them. Sargent held that the painter ought to know nothing at all about the nature of the subject before him. "Ruskin, don't you know, rocks and clouds, silly old thing!" he would interject, with inexplicit reference to the diagrams and formulas by which Ruskin prodded adherence to his own theory of aesthetics. The artist, he went on, should concentrate his faculty upon the appearance, making the picture a consistent vision, reproducing in painterly terms the area taken in by the eye. Of course, he was applying the canons of impressionism to an art devoid of such intentions, and that he did so showed the completeness with which he had been won to it.

His practice that summer was one of improving his own eye by noting the apparent color of all the things around him, training himself to see, in brilliant sunlight, all the subtle variation of color produced by the very dazzle of the light on the eye. Each morning he emerged carrying a large easel, advancing some little way into the open away from the house, then quite suddenly planting himself down nowhere in particular, behind a barn, opposite a wall, in the middle of a field; it made no difference. He was not expecting to paint fine pictures, but wanted to make a study of whatever his eye caught under the particular conditions that he wished to explore. To Gosse, who was often witness to this unexplained performance, it resembled a game of musical chairs, in which he was obliged to stop dead whenever the music in his head ceased playing. His object, of course, was to sharpen his ability to paint whatever his eye met, without any previous selection at all. He was intent on delving deeper into the impressionist practice, and he banished any consideration but pure reproduction of what the impressionist eye saw, caring not at all what those objects were. In that age, when subject matter played so large a part in English painting, becoming largely the distinguishing factor between one mediocrity and another, this was revolutionary, though he was not interested in theory and cared little whether or not he followed the established practice. In a few hours of concentrated work he did a sparkling sketch which dried so rapidly that he was able ruthlessly to paint another over it the next day. He felt no loss in this willful destruction of his work. What he did had no composition; he considered these little bits cribbed from nature hardly worth preserving, though some few were rescued by the Millets. They were studies in the completest sense of the word, something few painters actually make because of an unconscious belief that everything they touch will one day be found a masterpiece.

One noon, during this radiant August of 1885, he was painting in a whitewashed farmyard when Gosse strolled in for his company. As he approached Sargent gave a convulsive plunge in the air with his brush, demanding that Gosse remain glued to the spot, while he reached for another canvas. "Oh, what lovely hair," he gasped. The idea of anyone's thinking his sleek dun-colored hair lovely filled Gosse with mirth. To Sargent, the mousy locks existed only as at that moment, glazed a bright lilac by the cloudless blue sky. "Oh, what lovely hair, no one ever saw such beautiful lilac hair," gasped the painter, while Gosse, confident he knew the true color of it, laughed away, unmindful of the wonderful violet tone it had become, a color which one step into the shade would forever destroy.

In October, Sargent left Broadway for a short time to make a second trip to Bournemouth and Stevenson's ivy-covered brick house. This time he painted a small-scale portrait of Stevenson, pacing the dining room in his pantherlike fashion. He first made several little scratchy charcoal drawings in his sketchbook, to seize his characteristic movement, and this second effort pleased him more. Henry James was now an institution in the Stevenson household, and Sargent and Louis, old acquaintances that they were, found themselves even better able to strike up conversation, not that Louis's droll tongue had ever been still for long. "The hermit of Skerryvore," as he now styled himself, linking his habits with his home, was obliged to strip himself of all the pleasures his life had known, except smoking, and knew in his heart the days of that ought to be over. Seeing the circle of physical impotence closing slowly but inexorably around him, he remained the same debonair, whimsical figure he had been in Paris. "Sargent has been down again," he wrote Will Low, now established in New York, "and painted a portrait of me walking about in my own dining room, in my velveteen jacket [the same he had worn in Paris] and twisting as I go my own mustache; at one corner a glimpse of my wife, in an indian dress, and seated in a chair that once was my grandfather's but since many months goes by the name Henry James's, for it was there the novelist loved to sit — adds a touch of poesy and comicality. It is, I think, excellent, but it is too eccentric to be exhibited. I am at one extreme corner: my wife in this wild dress, and looking like a ghost at the other extreme end: between us an open door exhibits my palatial entrance hall and part of my respected staircase. All this is touched in lovely, with that witty touch of Sargent's: but of course it looks damn queer as a whole." When it was finished the artist presented it to Stevenson, who hung it on the side wall of his dining room, above and to the right of the little "magic" mirror with the gaudy frame presented him by Henry James.

Back at Broadway, Sargent for a while worked on his garden picture, until it was necessary to return to London, when it was stored away for the winter in the Farnham House barn. He was still rather hard up for important work to show at all the exhibitions to which he normally sent his things; in the spring he sent two of his least objectionable portraits to the Royal Academy, *Mrs. Vickers* and *Mrs. Robert Harrison*. Caught for a more typical work to show at the Grosvenor Gallery, he sent the portrait *Mme. and*

Mlle. Burckhardt, seen at the Salon that same year. "Distinguished by a certain eccentricity" was the enlightened verdict of Claude Phillips, writing that July in the *Gazette des Beaux-Arts.* At the same time he forewent showing at the Galerie Georges-Petit in Paris, where he had been part of the group, including both Renoir and his friend Monet, which now held annual exhibitions there. That he did so points to both the lack of important works and his growing despair of seeing any good ever come of Paris, where consistently from the time of the Gautreau portrait he had met rebuff.

The wonderful studio on the Boulevard Berthier, that house spun out of his dreams, was a thorn in his side, for he still held it, though it was beyond his means to retain and served no purpose while he worked in England. It was hard to rid himself of the dream that he could live in that beautifully adapted interior, doing a stream of portraits from fashionable people who drove down the boulevard to his door. Still, eventually he had to come to a decision, and in May of 1886, just two years after the Gautreau scandal, he gave it up, along with every last hope of a career in France. With that decision there came the problem of transporting his things to England, shipping the piano and large canvases like the *Mme. Gautreau,* which had been locked in his studio all this time, and finding space to work in London. The Paris studio was taken by his friend Boldini, for whom the dream became a reality.

Looking around London in the winter, he found he could best locate himself in Chelsea, only a short drive from the fashionable neighborhoods he was nightly frequenting with Henry James. A row of houses on Tite Street running from Royal Hospital Road to Dilke Street, most of them built by Godwin, the architect, alike except for the numbers on the doors, housed a tremendous artistic activity. At the end of the row on the left was a larger structure, called "The Studios," which on renumbering became 33 Tite Street. A year earlier he had taken a lone studio there, just above Whistler's, who was "living next door to myself in this absurd fashion," as the Butterfly chose to put it; for the "White House," designed by Godwin especially for him was next in the row, and since his bankruptcy occupied by the critic, his archenemy and butt, 'Arry Quilter. Whistler had just moved to Fulham Road, and

Sargent now took his former quarters on the ground floor. He soon was made aware that he was well known among his neighbors. His works had been seen by them at both the Salon and the Royal Academy, and he was acknowledged by all, with the natural exception of Whistler, an older man and not one who cared for other people's paintings, as immensely accomplished and skilled far beyond their capacities. Sargent exerted himself to be cordial, though he found the deference paid him plainly embarrassing, pretending not to notice much of the gross flattery that came his way. Some were even a little timid in his presence. Adrian Stokes in particular was frankly awed; and when some years later he mentioned to Jacomb-Hood, who lived across the way in number 26, that he admired a picture by Will Rothenstein, Hood immediately carried him off to Rothenstein's studio, that the praise might be heard from his own lips. Cordial, yet reticent, his neighbors soon decided that there would be none of the easy familiarity with him that existed among numbers of themselves.

The following summer, at Broadway, the Millets moved a few steps down the road from Farnham House to Russell House, which had more extensive grounds for gardens, and Sargent resumed work on the garden picture. Most of the same friends were once again in and around the town, each independently setting up in some inn or cottage, though the Millets' home was still the focal point. Abbey, Parsons, Fred Barnard, Edmund Gosse, and Sargent were reinstalled, joined early in September by Henry James, who came for a short visit. On the grounds of Russell House, some few feet from the kitchen wing, stood an eighteenth-century garden pavilion. Millet had roughly repaired it with window glass in the short frames, erecting an outside stair by which entrance could be made to the crenelated second floor, and this now provided working quarters for the artists and writers present. In the mornings James and Gosse would write on the tiny second floor, while Abbey and Parsons sat at drawing boards just below, with Sargent and Barnard tilting their easels outside. The six of them were in easy shouting distance, and remarkably little serious work was done, for they all conspired to be in towering spirits, making everything the food of laughter.

In all the crowd gathered at Broadway, James seemed the only sedate one, benign and indulgent certainly, but hardly unbending beyond a chuckle, which got for him treatment denoting an involuntary respect. By comparison Sargent mixed very well indeed, living in sympathetic union, partaking of the humor and adding his share. Alfred Parsons in particular had a way with all the children present, and they followed him wherever he went, with many and various calls on "Uncle Alfred." Sargent too was a favorite of sorts, for when later that year Lily Millet gave birth to a son, he was named John Parsons Millet, after his two godfathers, John Sargent and Alfred Parsons. Sargent seems in fact to have been quite able and even willing to put up with children, for somewhere in his nature lurked much tenderness. When his young godson, Jack Millet, aged three or four, one day burnt his finger on the tip of a match, he was pulled up on the huge lap of his Uncle John, who skillfully managed to distract his attention from the stinging finger until cries of "it's worser" were no more.

Early that summer a flower bed was cut in the garden behind Russell House and planted with poppies, which came up in profusion, forming a wild array of color. From the start the intention was to paint these myriad flames in the full light of day, and one by one, often in groups, the artists set about it. Abbey, Parsons, Millet, Sargent, and Edwin Blashfield all made the attempt, some producing better results than others, but all failing abysmally. Sargent meantime scoured the countryside for roses, carnations, and lilies, the flowers with which he had begun his garden picture, and which he needed to resume work. Near Willersey he chanced on half an acre of roses in full bloom, and to the startled proprietor said, "I'll take them all, dig them up and send them along this afternoon." Perhaps it crossed his mind that he was providing a princely housewarming gift for the Millets, and especially raven-eyed Lily Millet, who for the moment seemed to occupy a special place in his mind; but he passed it off as a simple matter of props for his picture. The large canvas was brought out from winter storage, and with the two little Barnard girls the routine of catching an effect of light lasting only a few minutes was resumed. Blashfield noted that when he saw the canvas each morning it appeared to have been scraped down so that all the previous night's work was erased, and still the process continued evening after

evening. Sargent had reduced the canvas by two feet cut from
the left, through dissatisfaction with the lack of concentration in
the composition, leaving it now approximately five feet square, the
grouping immensely tightened. On that piece cut from the left
he started a portrait of Mrs. Barnard in a white dress, her leg of
mutton sleeves billowing out like twin lanterns between which he
framed her head. Originally she was to be holding a cup of tea in
her hands, and the head was well along, all the other parts sketched
in, with a few roses from the garden picture still showing through
the skirt, when he decided to begin it over on a new piece of canvas. Even this was not enough to absorb his energies, for doting
on the approval of the retiring Lily Millet, he began painting her
family, fussing with a portrait of her that never seemed to come
right, meanwhile also making sketches of her son Lawrence and a
portrait of Kate.

One day, seeing her come downstairs to put a letter into the post,
dressed in her petticoats with a blue silk shawl over her shoulders,
he seemed to sense some aspect that he wanted, and walking in
from the dining room asked her to come out to the studio. It was
hardly an appropriate moment at which to catch her, undressed as
she was, and the letter had to be got into the post, but he brushed
that aside; it would get into the second post easily enough. Taking
her by the arm he led the way into the studio, and except for the
gentleness of his touch, it was almost as though he dragged her,
in his earnestness to make use of this suddenly seen aspect before
it disappeared. Frequently his actions toward her had this romantic overtone of moments that must not be lost and inspiration he
dare not waste. The finished picture, done under these circumstances, reinforces such notions, for it is a strange document in his
life; this singularly beautiful picture showing Lily Millet with a
downright coquetry she never possessed. It was by no means the
last time he would thus reveal his own inner life, though whenever
he did it comes as a fresh surprise, so deeply was this part of him
kept hidden by a show of disinterest. Endowed as he was with
obvious personal attractions, it is pitiful to see him reach so desper-
ately for the affection that might easily have been his had he
allowed it to be given. He was attractive to women, and many of
those he knew in his Paris days must have fancied themselves in

love. Romantic notions simmered within him as well, until his interest passed on to another, and still always another. Unconsciously he continued seeking, never certain of what he found and unwilling to take any step from which he could not withdraw, his romantic life residing so much in the imagination that he was capable, as now, of carrying on a vicarious romance of which the object was entirely unaware. For the moment, in that strange way, she filled his heart, he had no thought of others, and it was quite enough.

Now and then, when he had some time away from one of the pictures he was at work upon, Henry James might invite him for a little walk. Generally they were out an hour or more, though they did not progress any great distance, for James, due to the weakness of the back that had kept him out of the Civil War, was inclined to saunter. He also found it easier to utter those long many-headed sentences of his when not obliged constantly to be putting one foot before another, and after all the talk was the thing; if one wished to walk, it was perfectly simple to do so alone. He had preferences for certain roads, in particular he liked level ones, and so they generally headed toward, with little hope of reaching, the ancient gray village of Aston Somerville. He always made the same remark, as though he had never noticed it before, when the first glimpse of the place opened to them, finding that Aston was "so Italian, so Tuscan." How Sargent took the rather sedentary and womanish habits of his friend is not a matter of record, though in later years he was able to give admirable imitations of the novelist's fussy ways. It is easy to understand that he, who had inherited the vitality of his forebears, must have found it necessary to check his natural impatience as they slowly made their way along the level roads, meanwhile seeing every tortoise in England glide past.

Music also played its part in the life of the colony. Alma Strettell, sister to Mrs. Carr, and shortly to become Mrs. L. A. Harrison, joined the ranks that year, and was a Wagnerian. With Sargent she began elaborately to work through the *Ring*, recitatives and all. They played in duet by the hour, each taking all the parts assigned their gender, the painter croaking out Hagen, then soaring into a falsetto Siegfried, while Alma did Brünnhilde, Gu-

trune, Woglinda, Wellgunda, and sent her voice into her boots for
Flosshilda. There were times when to those who were less familiar
with the Wagnerian idiom it did not seem meant for music at all.
"We have music," wrote Abbey, "until the house won't stand it."
The duets seemed interminable, and the perpetrators were dubbed
"comaniacs," an appellation so apt and well earned that it stuck
for years. "We have really had a gay summer," wrote Abbey,
"pretending to work and sometimes working, for there are numerous places with easels in them to hide away in, if you really
want to work, until four, and then tennis until dinner time, and
after dinner dancing and music and various cheering games in the
studio, but mostly dancing." Abbey himself contributed to the
music too, for he was something of a banjo player, and one long
rollicking day spent rowing on the river Avon, there was much
singing while Abbey "obliged" profusely. Henry James, typically,
sat at the prow of his boat like a beneficent deity, a sort of bearded
Buddha, manifestly afraid that some of the happy sprites he sailed
with would tumble into the water.

Sargent left Broadway early in October for a sitting in London
on the fifteenth, probably with the young Mrs. Cecil Wade, who
insisted on being painted in her own home. With him went his
large garden picture, which by then had acquired the name *Carnation Lily, Lily Rose*, a line from one of the songs sung when quieter
music filled the house. It was a fitting title, putting into meter the
flowers figuring so prominently in the composition. Henry James
had come back to London too, where he found Mrs. Isabella
Stewart Gardner, whom he had met in Boston some years before
and to whom he had for two evenings read the whole of one of his
plays: "those two pretty little evenings when I read my play. They
make a charming picture — a perfect picture — in my mind. . . ."
The diminutive, somewhat eccentric wife of a Boston financier,
Isabella Gardner was aware of her unfortunate Continental fame
as a "non beauty," making tireless efforts to surround herself with
things of beauty, the "melodies of your toilet" being James's
oblique reference to her somewhat exaggerated stylishness. When
they met again in London nothing would do but James must
immediately carry her off to Sargent's new studio, where she
might see the notorious portrait of Mme. Gautreau.

The original idea was for Sargent to call on Mrs. Gardner. But now that he had a studio in London he carefully made himself prodigiously busy, becoming involved with a series of sittings that took up almost every daylight hour, and which he pressed the front cover of his sketchbook into service to record. The jolly Tadema was one of those he was painting; Mrs. Boit, over from Paris, was another. Probably the only work he received any money for was the small bust-length portrait he was doing of Dr. Playfair, the third brother of Sir Lyon Playfair, whose wife Sargent had painted in 1884. Some idea of his financial condition at this time can be gleaned from the notation inside the back cover of the same sketchbook: "£ 94. 13.11 for previous deficit. 8th Oct added 176. . ." It would have been well had this Mrs. Gardner chosen to sit for her portrait, as it was devoutly hoped she would, but that, as it turned out, was not her present inclination. She did come to the studio with James, however, for he was eager to serve up to her that most piquant prize, the Gautreau picture, and his expectations were remarkably perspicacious, for as expected she was fascinated by the daring sexuality of the portrayal and its atmosphere of evil.

Looking in one day, Jacomb-Hood, the neighbor from across Tite Street, found him evening the background of the garden picture, from the top of which he had cut another six inches. It is a pity that he still continued to work on it when away from the motif, for a too-obvious blue was creeping in, and he fogged it across the carefully noted values the picture had when it left Broadway. Later in the year, for Lily Millet's birthday, there was a day of great festivity at Russell House, to which he journeyed from London. The house was gaily decorated for the occasion, and so many guests were invited that when the party commenced Tadema was forced to sit in the stove that filled the fireplace, for there was no room at the table. Fred Barnard had got up placecards each bearing on the front a silhouetted image of the guest, while behind he sketched the varied achievements of his life. Thus Frank Millet was pictured sitting on an exploding shell, for he had been a correspondent for an American newspaper at various battlefronts; and one young lady had her regular features drawn on her card, while Sargent contributed a magnificent couplet for the reverse:

A smile for women and a sneer for men,
She wields the brush — thank God it's not the pen.

Sargent's own placecard showed him rather gloriously as a knight
in armor, gonfalon aloft, with "Sergeante atte Armes to ye Broad-
waye Paynteres Guilde" inscribed across the bottom. On the
reverse were two sketches of him, in one seated at his easel with
medals dripping from his pocket and in the other playing the piano,
with waves of music coming forth. Sargent, however, wanted to
do the placecard for Lily Millet, and he made two tiny caricatures
of her portrait, exaggerating the coquettish aspect that suited her
so poorly, labeling this effort "Lily Millet having reached the age
of discretion." Waxing poetic once more, he brought forth a
mongrelized bit of verse, which once more brought into play the
romantic overtone inseparable from his thoughts of her:

Discretion's an age at which man may arrive
For man may grow older in time
But a woman, we know, however she strive
Can never grow older — in rhyme.

Tadema had arranged for this to be a costume party, and the
happy round little Dutchman decreed everyone was to wear a
wreath of flowers round his head, after the style of his Roman
paintings. This levity broke into the solemn dignity of some
present, whose stony brows were decidedly more presentable when
flower decked; Henry James wore his garland with great affability,
but an unnamed New England woman was less pleased, which set
Joe Carr to betting Sargent that he could get her to exchange head-
dresses with him. This was not a wager to be refused, and he
throttled his laughter while Carr, with serious mien, explained that
it was part of the formality of the house for guests to exchange
garlands, winning the bet. After dinner Sargent suggested they
play a game by throwing their shadows on a sheet, scoring the
correct number of identifications each person made. Abbey said
John was proposing a game he was certain of winning, because of
his "diabolical gift of picking out every idiosyncrasy in a face or
figure," and as it happened he proved right. Laura Tadema turned

her head so that her lantern jaw would not be thrown into relief, but Sargent knew the poise of her head and the turn of her shoulder. Abbey himself, short and without neck, proved an easy mark. Mary Anderson, the celebrated actress and beauty, retired from the stage and living at Broadway, would have been difficult to confuse with any of the others. Mrs. Barnard's tip-tilted nose gave her away, and when it was Alice Carr's turn he called, "people with clear-cut profiles oughtn't to play," in diplomatic reference to her meat-cleaver features. Of course had any of the other participants painted as many of those present as Sargent did, they might have stood a better chance; for to date a partial list would have included Tadema, Mrs. Barnard, Lily Millet, her daughter and son, Gosse, and the two Barnard girls, plus drawings of Abbey and Henry James. His familiarity, while it did have something of the portraitist's "diabolical gift" to it, also came from the fact that he had studied the features of them all rather well.

The Harrison family, into which Alma Strettell soon married, were soon Sargent's friends as well, and a portrait of Mrs. Robert Harrison appeared at the Royal Academy in 1886, creating something of a stir. The following summer he went to stay with that branch of the family at their country home near Henley on Thames, where in an exceptionally hot and dry August he made a little floating studio of a punt on the river. Still affecting Parisian modes, he was clad in white flannel shirt and trousers, with a silk scarf around the waist, a straw hat with colored ribbon on his head, as he worked on impressionistic sketches of the heat-seared foliage. As he explained in a letter to Claude Monet, his equipment was already packed for a trip he was about to make, and while his application was constant, he felt hampered by a lack of materials.

George Henschel, recently returned to England from Boston, where he had gone to form the Boston Symphony Orchestra, was another guest of the Harrisons', and attracted to Sargent by his skill at the piano and understanding of music. It was inevitable that Henschel and Sargent should eventually be thrown together, for the list of guarantors of the newly formed London Symphony, Henschel's second organization, read like an honor roll of Sargent's friends in England: Mrs. L. A. Harrison (Alma Strettell), Henry James, Gustav Natorp, Dr. Playfair, Albert Vickers, and Henry

White were all present and accounted for; Sargent's absence from the list indicating once again his lack of fortune at the time.

By the early part of 1887, had Sargent taken stock he would surely have concluded that the outlook in England was not bright. He had arrived preceded by his Continental fame, which spared him the anxiety of being unknown. Many doors were open to him, people obviously looked on him with respect and accepted him, though the influence of Henry James was partly responsible for that. At the Academy, where he was considered an example of extreme modernism, suspected for the Gallic idiom employed in his work, he was not hung without some internal wrangling, and the attitude of the viewing public only added to his discouragement. True, there was a small element who understood and appreciated his work. The portrait of Mrs. Henry White hung in the dining room of her house in Grosvenor Crescent, where it performed a missionary and educational function. As the center of a constant discussion, not always well informed but usually dogmatic, it made his name familiar to many. The assurance that flowed from the complete acceptance of Mrs. White, plus the proselytizing zeal that marked her relations with members of her society, reassured even more, though it is doubtful if through the early years this produced even a single commission. At the same time the group of the three *Misses Vickers*, after being hung at the Salon, was at first rejected by the jury of the Royal Academy, and finally accepted only through the threat of Hubert von Herkomer that otherwise he would resign. When the *Pall Mall Gazette* polled a plebiscite of public opinion on the Academy of 1886, Sargent's entry won handily as the worst picture of the year.

He was simply too far from the established mode of English painting to find critical acceptance. In France his pictures had figured in the more advanced categories, but in England he found less flexibility of academic rule, though surely France had little enough. He was drawing closer to impressionist principles in his practice, and it seemed that consequently his chances of public approval grew more slight. There was no denying a certain chic to his work. It had the fine sense of style present in all the great classic portraits, a quality running more to the heart of great painting than was realized. Those who saw portraits of persons familiar to them were amazed at the likeness and at the sensitivity with which he was able to catch the very atmosphere in which the person moved. Still, he was no better off in England than he had been in France. There too he had occupied himself painting portraits of friends.

He was not alone in his predicament, for at this time many French-trained artists were returning to England with the new breath of fresh air in their works. Their young and uninhibited minds were quick to grasp elements of impressionism, which they added to the already formidable array of academic training. Often these youngsters found themselves excluded from the Royal Academy exhibitions at Burlington House, then the legitimate goal of all aspiring artists; and even the Grosvenor Gallery, where under the patronage of Sir Coutts Lindsay, Joe Comyns Carr displayed a mixture of eccentric and academic, was not always open to them, for the Grosvenor counted on assembling an array of imposing names. The only solution was for these young artists to band together and exhibit their works without attempting to acquire the imprint of official sanction that was then so important; and to their first exhibition in 1886 they invited Sargent, to whom they looked as a new canon of excellence. He sent two canvases to their exhibition at the Marlborough Gallery: a small outdoor study, clearly impressionistic in its nature, and his equally impressionistic portrait of Mrs. Barnard. It was from the New English Art Club, as the group dubbed itself, that Sargent drew his friends among English painters, some of those intimate in later years, such as Wilson Steer and Adrian Stokes, being members at the start. For many years the New English Art Club was the most forward-looking group in England, among whom Sargent was clearly the most advanced, and it was to the New English that he transferred the place previously occupied by the Galerie Georges-Petit, to which from this time forward he no longer sent his works.

It was while still deeply discouraged, perplexed, and exasperated by his repeated failure to catch on that the remarkable events of 1887 began to unfold. With one quick catapulting motion he seemed to rise from the depths to which he had fallen. Whatever the disillusionment he experienced in those years, few had any notion of what he felt, and even to those who had some indication, like Gosse, it remained a mystery why he felt as he did. Disinterested onlookers still viewed his life as a triumphal progress, and through those trying years it was a view he was careful not to contradict, though it took all his strength to keep up appearances.

Ever faithful to his own beliefs, in 1887 he sent to the Royal Academy his most ambitious work of the two preceding years, *Carnation Lily, Lily Rose,* which he fully expected would arouse an even more violent storm of abuse than had greeted his previous contributions. As an antidote he sent with it his rather highly polished portrait of Mrs. William Playfair; then awaited the sound of exploding academicians from the direction of Piccadilly. Strange to say, the garden picture was greeted by a surge of approval. It was even considered poetic rather than merely brutal, as much of his previous work had been called. London was enchanted by this poetic vision of two little girls lighting lanterns at twilight; the two children in pinafores transformed into Botticellian angels lighting the shrine of an invisible madonna, whose presence seemed implied by the roses and lilies and the fading summer afternoon. All the poetry of this remarkable vision he no doubt justified on the score of "effects," a reservation we need not trouble over but take as intended. For though to him it was purely the painting of an effect of fading evening light, with the warm glow of lanterns in the semidarkness, to us it is evident that the poetry of the piece is all the more sincere for being unintentional and that it is filled with the brooding melancholy of his own troubled soul. The pure artistry of his perceptive faculty, able to select such a scene on the score of "effects," translating it into a thing of extraordinary beauty, is itself worthy of admiration. The picture was selected by the Academy for purchase under the terms of the Chantrey Bequest, and the price was set at seven hundred pounds, money that came to him as a gift bestowed.

Soon it was whispered about London that he was really not so much eccentric as the product of a new school, new thinking, that he was a harbinger of forces that one day would be important. There was a considerable rejoicing among the younger men that one of them had been honored in so telling a fashion. Though he himself was the last to assume any guise of leadership, for he had

none of the drive necessary to organize, or to carry others with him
in his convictions, his good fortune was assuredly breaking the way
for them all. He had opened a breach through which they would
all pass. But this was an opinion by no means common, as a certain
George Bernard Shaw, then donning the first of his many disguises,
this time as art critic, made certain in the *World* of April 13:

> These gentlemen are painting shortsightedly in more senses than
> one. The trick of drawing and colouring badly as if you did it
> on purpose is easily acquired; and the market will be swamped
> with "new English art", and the public tired of it, in a year or two.
> Then there will be a vain lamenting over lost ground to recover,
> bad habits to correct, and association with unsaleability to be lived
> down. The "new" fashion may be capital fun for Mr. Whistler,
> Mr. Sargent, and a few others who can swim on any tide; but for
> the feebler folk it means at best a short life and a merry one.

And then, lightning struck a second time, and from America,
where it was least expected. Several of his works had gone there
on the huge wave of collecting even then beginning, which eventually made the United States the greatest repository of the riches
Europe could no longer support. During the eighties it was still
contemporary collecting that was in vogue, and the masters most
popular at the Salon and the Royal Academy year by year saw an
increasing part of their produce streaming across the Atlantic.
Some early sketches of Sargent's reached America with returning
students late in the seventies, while the greater part of his commissioned portraits done in Paris were destined for American walls
as well. In 1882 Schaus & Co., to whom he had sold his *El Jaleo*,
exhibited it in New York, where it was hailed as "the most important work by an American artist abroad that has yet been brought
to this country." The picture was sold to Mr. Coolidge of Boston,
a gentleman who as American minister at Paris had become familiar
with the prevailing trends in Europe. The portrait of Miss Vallé
after it appeared at the Salon of 1882, was shown at the National
Academy in New York the same year, while the *El Jaleo*, which
now reached Boston, excited admiration there. Perhaps it was even
seen by Charles Fairchild, who two years later commissioned the
little portrait of Stevenson, which when brought back to the

United States early in 1885 was yet another example of his work on this side of the ocean. There were sufficient examples in America now to produce interest, and early in 1887 he received a letter from Henry G. Marquand, inviting him to name a price for coming to Newport to paint his wife.

This was an unheard-of occurrence, one that filled him with misgivings. Were the expedition to prove worth the time expended, he was willing. He was certainly not so busy in England that he could not leave. He was conscious though of dealing with an unknown across a wide ocean, and there were elements of doubt in his mind. To be absent any length of time could mean the loss of work which, had he remained in England, might have come his way. He was doubtful. A few people of substance had been sitting to him of late. Must he always be seeking new fields? After ten years France had proved a barren land, and he moved to England. He was in England barely two years, faced by a strangeness with people and customs, beginning again where he had started in France a decade before. Was it practical always to be moving to new lands? Would England not serve? In his reply to Marquand he named a price of three thousand dollars, three times what he was receiving in England. If the Marquands accepted at that figure, he would undertake the voyage and consider it profitable, the time well spent. But probably he also knew so stiff a price would serve to deter acceptance, which would thus rid him of his own indecision. He did not honestly believe there was much chance the order would be confirmed: but it was!

One important provision had to be made before he took ship. In a letter to Claude Monet, written shortly before his departure, he took care to see that his friend shared his good fortune. After telling him of his intended trip, and making humorous reference to painting on the Thames when his materials were already packed away, he added, "If you have difficulties . . . the bankers Drexel, Harjes et Cie, 31 Boulevard Haussmann recognize my signature."

America — The Discovery of Gold

A T NEWPORT the railroad barons and the emperors of finance competed with the consuls-for-life of copper and steel, pitting marble palace against granite-turreted castle in their quest for splendor. Nothing could be too elaborate in this seaside community that lived but three months a year, where money was a common possession, spoken of in terms of pride and admiration, and culture served as the defense of ladies bored with mundane discussion. The season was already waning when Sargent arrived by taxi from Providence. Loaded with baggage and equipment, glistening with perspiration, he rode out to the Torpedo Station, where Admiral Goodrich, one of the officers his father had collected at Florence, had asked him to stay. On his way he passed through the troops of ladies out for drives, the regular afternoon diversion at Newport. Leaning back in victoria and barouche, they drove the length of Bellevue Avenue past the most fashionable villas, then around the Ocean Drive skirting the rocky region between Narragansett Bay and the Atlantic. They were dressed as though on their way to a race meet at Auteuil or Ascot: all brocaded and whaleboned, in satin-striped dresses, with flower-trimmed bonnets tied by a length of tulle under the chin. They eyed each other passing on the avenue, now and then with a grave bow of the head, blocking traffic by drawing carriages side by side at intersections for a chat. His own ruddy and bearded face was receiving a considerable scrutiny too, and considering that the ladies were only making a circuit between wilderness and waves, he thought the regalia of dotted-tulle veils, fringed silk and velvet sunshades, with elaborately carved and jointed handles, was remarkably ostentatious. It told him much about Newport.

He arrived at the Torpedo Station huge and dominant, smiling and eager. It was years since he had seen the Goodriches, and since those peaceful days at Florence his Sunday-school teacher had borne a son, doubtless one day to enter the Navy, and a daughter, both of whom he would meet. It was pleasant to find friends in a strange place: Admiral Goodrich, who still spoke of the sea and ships as Dr. Sargent had, and Mrs. Goodrich, who had taught him when young. He gritted his teeth though when he called on his model, for Mrs. Marquand proved to be a plain matronly woman, with a long nose and no particular distinction. She would have been difficult to paint amid Parisian frippery, but even that was not granted him, for she was a drear woman, drear in wardrobe, drear in expression. If he could not have a beauty, he preferred someone at least of a more cultivated appearance for his first work in a new land. Meanwhile he prepared to do his best with the mature dignity and benign appearance she presented. When she brought a plumed fan to pose with, he could not help contrasting the elegance of that poor object with its owner, and kept it closed. Propping her in a chair with a pillow to get the best of her bearing, directing her to turn her head a trifle to allow the mellow afterglow of contentment to shine from her face, he set to work.

He had sailed from England on September 17, sad at the prospect of a long sea trip, for he was always a bad sailor and filled with dread of the seasickness he experienced on the Channel. He had only little notion what awaited in America: an unseen model to be painted under doubtful conditions, reunion with a few friends perhaps, and whatever, if anything, fortune brought. He was careful to propose the visit for after the summer, so that he would not miss the English season, and he was certain to return before it began again the following Easter. If opportunity offered, he would wander afield in America, get an idea of what the scene there held for him, and return to London without having missed anything.

The break in his work would easily be made up by the large fee pocketed for this single America picture. He no longer had close relations in America. His grandfather had died while he was studying in Paris, and no one of real importance was left to him, though there were sundry cousins, and some uncles in Philadelphia, whom he felt no obligation to visit.

As a proper send-off for his friend, Henry James revised and brought up to date the article he had written four years before, introducing Sargent to England, and arranged for it to appear in the October number of *Harper's* Magazine. Appearing just as Sargent was first becoming noticed on his daily trips to and from the Marquand house, it was a conspicuous example of good planning. Its romanticized account of his Florentine birth, years in France, and worship of Velásquez in Madrid (typical Jamesian hyperbole) added a touch of glamour to his already dashing appearance. The flair for self-publicizing that Sargent himself lacked was more than made up for by a master hand whose words wove a spell about his name. A sweet perfume of distant romance was breathed on the name "Sargent," its aroma lingering like a mystic enchantment. James had been sparing of facts, and the discriminating reader might indeed have wondered precisely what he was saying; for the entire article was only a maze of suggestion, of nebulous beauties floating by, presenting no clear image other than an astonishment that so young a man had achieved so much. What was the achievement? James seemed reticent, only saying that he was not unjustified "in writing almost prematurely of a career which is not yet half unfolded." James, in fact, seemed unwilling to state the achievements that were obvious: the medals, the reviews, the excitement created by his works at the Salon and the Royal Academy. Even the question of whether he could be considered an American, which was to follow Sargent throughout his career, James boldly proposes and then timidly refuses to answer. He did, however, achieve the effect he sought, producing in the sheer magic of words an image of youthful achievement and brilliance, and creating the impression at Newport that artistic success was accompanied also by more worldly considerations. In the breezes of Bellevue Avenue, he seemed borne along by limpid atmospheres of sweet European approval; an air of prosperity surrounded him;

and Newport, having read of him, and seen him pass on the Avenue, was anxious to make his acquaintance.

There was no difficulty meeting Sargent at Newport either, for the regular afternoon ritual involved *calling* on the way to the Ocean Drive. It seemed impossible to see any woman without her card case in her hand, and calling was a formidable affair, although the younger women already had emancipated themselves from the rigors of it, merely driving from house to house depositing cards, all duly turned down at the upper left-hand corner, to the indignation of hostesses who considered it lack of courtesy when they "did not ask." Even so, the number who did ask was great, so that work must frequently have been interrupted by the inevitable footman coming through, each time to usher another whaleboned lady for a half-hour visit in the dim, shaded drawing room or on the veranda.

More striking than the dowagers' parade was that of the young ladies, married and single, who as guests at Newport villas expected by right of decorum to be taken for the afternoon drive by the master of the house or one of his sons. Fashionable young men did their duty at the reins of a four-wheeled conveyance drawn by a stepper; older men drove handsome phaetons, with a showy pair, an impressive cross-armed groom seated in the rumble. Carriages, horses, harnesses, and grooms were all of the latest, most irreproachable cut, the double line of glittering vehicles and horses parading between lawns and scarlet geranium borders making Bellevue Avenue a pretty scene out of a period pageant, strangely resembling in fact, as it did in inspiration, a living tableau based on some painting by Frith. It was a comedy of manners, material for Henry James, Sargent might have thought when he was properly dressed to join the parade and visit the Fairchilds, with whom Louis Stevenson was now staying; ill after his ocean crossing with a cargo of monkeys and horses, the stallions "protrud [ing] their noses in an unmannerly way between the passengers and the dinner." It was good he decided to call too, for Fairchild, now that his family had Louis in the bony flesh, wanted a portrait painted of an illustrious brother — General Lucius Fairchild, who had lost an arm in the Civil War, and now, elected commander of the G.A.R., was coming east in November to be painted by a Boston artist.

Perhaps it was at the Marquands', where he was working mornings, or while going the rounds in answer to courtesies, that he met Stanford White, that infernal architect with blazing brush-cut hair and a mustache the color and shape of a frankfurter. His firm, McKim, Mead and White, had built a number of the newer villas, as well as the Newport Casino, all of which made him a well-known figure about the resort. When introduced, he was able to tell Sargent that he had heard much of him from mutual friends. White had been associated with Frank Millet early in the decade, during the building of Trinity Church on Copley Square in Boston. Doubtless Millet had mentioned White out at Broadway, for they remained in communication, as did Augustus St.-Gaudens, who surely had told him in Paris during the seventies that it was White who was designing the pedestal for his statue of Farragut.

The bluff energetic architect and the reticent but equally energetic painter found they got along well. Newport was emptying by this time, and White suggested a visit to his home in New York, when Sargent should come to town. Just when that would be was uncertain for a time, for his plans were unsettled. In a note he said, "Just now I am working on time . . . but in a couple of weeks or three I shall be going to Boston to paint a portrait and shall be there a good part of November." Nonetheless, when he did get ready to leave, he headed for New York.

The ride took only four hours by train, and he arrived feeling more buoyant than when he had passed through to Newport. Beckwith was expecting him, and together they went on a tour of studios, trying to find one where Sargent could do two little children's pictures that had been asked of him before he left Newport; probably the reason he had come to New York. People were forever trying him out with children. They were pleasant enough to do when they sat well, but they so rarely did. He had had to paint too many children when he was in France, where people wanted to see the results of a harmless experiment before risking their own portraits. It happened again in England; and now in America he was once again faced by a passel of "brats."

The day's search over, the two men had dinner at the Parker House, then went on to the Metropolitan Opera House where *Tristan and Isolde* was having its American première. It surprised

Sargent that Beckwith, who had sat through the interminable rehearsals of Berlioz' *Damnation of Faust,* at Carolus' behest, found the Wagner too heavy. Sargent's own enthusiasm knew no bounds, but then, Beckwith somehow seemed so stodgy altogether. It was something he had not noticed during their Paris years together, though of course that was almost ten years past.

Apparently he was in touch with Stanford White immediately after his arrival too, for the very next night, November 3, White arranged a dinner in his honor, to which Beckwith was invited. In the following week White received a letter from Frank Millet in England, who seemed to have a similar tribute in mind:

> I had a letter from Sargent yesterday saying he had seen you at Newport. He seems to be very prosperous. I am glad he is. He deserves it. I want to propose him for the Tile Club. All here vote for him, Boughton, Abbey, Parsons, and Millet. Try him on when he comes to New York.

There had been no need for the recommendation, for White and Sargent were on friendly terms long before Millet's pat on the back arrived. Doubtless White was pleased to know of the wholehearted way his friends among the artists had accepted Sargent, a latecomer to a group already bound by ties of mutual friendship. His dinner, tendered fully a week before the arrival of this letter, is adequate testimony that it was his own idea. By now it was less the possession of mutual friends than the energetic nature of the two that formed the basis of their friendship. They had a certain temperamental likeness and their interests ran in parallel lines. White habitually dabbled in the decoration of the houses he designed, adding paintings to the interiors when he could interest clients in them. He developed friendships in New York with men like Curran and Dewing, for whom he sought commissions, sometimes even employing his own splendid draftsmanship to design their frames. He was certainly aware that Sargent, to whom Millet and St.-Gaudens paid special deference, was of rather extraordinary capacities, and might also be a profitable enterprise. Soon he had him in touch with one of the two partners in his firm, Charles Follen McKim. "Blarney Charles," or "Charles the Charmer," as he was so aptly called by St.-Gaudens, was more than simply the social member of the firm, but he could charm the birds off the trees when it needed to be done and he, too, quickly realized that in Sargent there lay an opportunity.

Other wheels were turning, too. Late that Sunday evening Sargent went charging into Beckwith's apartment carrying two Venetian landscapes. They had just arrived from England, sent by Abbey, to whom he had left the use of his Tite Street studio, for an exhibition already being planned for Boston. He offered Beckwith his choice, as a wedding present, apologizing for coming so late in the evening and saying that the canvases had just been unpacked and he wanted to make amends immediately. This breathless atmosphere which seemed constantly to surround his friend left Beckwith a trifle dazed, but after some indecision he chose the larger, *Venetian Bead Stringers*, a group of figures that had been composed in the hall of the Rezzonico.

To all who knew Sargent in New York his movements at this time were lightning-like. He would disappear into a studio for long hours, then emerge with calls to make, people to see, complex discussions of business to carry on. Then, as suddenly as he had appeared in the city, he was gone, like an apparition dissolving into formlessness once more: off to Boston, it was said.

In Boston he began work on the portrait of General Lucius Fairchild, which had been commissioned at Newport. He took a studio overlooking the river, and by Christmas he had another full-length portrait to do also. His sitter was the strange little woman whom Henry James had once brought to Tite Street to see the *Mme. Gautreau* — the woman with the odd tight little mouth and exaggerated clothes, who seemed so overpowering and full of chatter — Mrs. Gardner. He had soon forgotten her, along with so many of the people James brought around. But when he arrived at Newport she wrote to him, asking him to come visit if he came to Boston, and the result had been this portrait. He was getting along poorly with her, and perhaps it is well to remember that he was under strain. There were two sitters a day to cope with, the individual quirks that annoyed him now coming in double doses. The bewildering succession of people that flowed before him had to be remembered if possible, invitations were always waiting for replies, messengers' shuffling feet were getting on his nerves. Through it all it was important that he maintain his equanimity, replying with lightness to questions that should not have been asked. All that anyone had a right to know about him was contained in the *Harper's* article. He did not propose to say more, probably for no better reason than a constitutional distaste for being asked questions. Answer one and another was fired at you, and how in the world did one reply to the inane, "How do you like America, Mr. Sargent?"

Mrs. Gardner, it seemed to him, after being a vivacious hostess, had become a model intent on irritating him from the start. She believed herself some sort of Venus, standing with her dress open to reveal a narrow slice of flat white chest between her breasts. She made an impossible sitter, breezily watching ships on the river instead of holding her pose. She repeatedly said she wanted an extraordinary picture, clearly implying that she meant something shocking, while Sargent felt that she would have nothing at all if she continued to answer his pleas for co-operation with the silly naughtiness of a little girl.

She brought young Dennis Miller Bunker to her sittings. He had studied in Paris with Gérôme, as had Helleu. Possibly the two had met there, though it is questionable at best. Bunker was a pleasant little fellow, with odd flat brows that made his eyes look like thin slits in their shadows. He had picked up the Parisian nonchalance, had a gay manner, and cluttered the air with jests. Sometimes he had a tendency to sulk, though, which made him less attractive. He had himself painted portraits of various members of the Gardner family, his style reflecting every influence blowing past Boston. Sargent seemed to see Bunker as a youngster whose talent needed guidance, and the two painters got on well.

Mrs. Gardner's relationship with Bunker somewhat confused Sargent, for Bunker treated this woman nearing fifty with the offhand camaraderie he might show for a bouncing lass his own age, and they were constantly seen around the city together. Had he been interested he might have heard that. Mrs. Gardner was, as it happened, in the midst of a warm dalliance with the author F. Marion Crawford, whom he had known many years before in Rome. Mrs. Gardner in fact was inclined to let the painter know of her wickedness, so that he might get that certain air into his portrait. For his part, he considered all this no business of the artist. It was distasteful, and he shrank from the blatancy of it, the whole business striking him as stupid rather than evil. To top all that, each of the successive heads he produced on the canvas displeased her, none having the wanton look she desired. He was always scraping off, so that for all the difficulty there was no progress, and no end of the uncomfortable sittings in sight. One evening at dinner he unburdened himself to friends, so exasperated that he reproduced all the spluttering moments in the studio with marvelous fidelity, answering his own pleas with an imitation of her sweet-sixteen manner. His hilarious performance was greeted with roars of laughter and he was advised that Mrs. Gardner was attempting to break her contract without obligating herself. She wanted to irritate him, he was told, to the point where he would give up the work.

Seething with a hatred he could but ill conceal, he told her at the next sitting that he was all for abandoning the painting. Surprisingly, she did not want to, insisting that he complete the portrait. Feeling perhaps a trifle guilty over his suspicions, he settled down to do as workmanlike a job as he could on a canvas now wearying him, and Mrs. Gardner, also somewhat contrite, became more helpful. She was still outspoken in demanding a picture with the air of sex and wickedness that her quick but shallow mind saw as the only distinction of the *Mme. Gautreau.* He attempted to fit her into as decorative a composition as her short heavy-boned figure allowed, though she was too broad of shoulder, too wide of hip, for any lineal flights, her arms striking him as the only supple parts of her body. These he decided to make use of by looping them before her, somewhat in the manner he had done with Mme. Poirson two years before. Once he had thought out the design, she exaggerated the pose set for her, throwing back her shoulders artificially to stress the contours of her breasts. When she demanded that he narrow her waist beyond what was realistic, he knew it would make her appear to be standing with her posterior thrust out as no modest woman would stand, but he allowed the effect to remain as a small measure of revenge. All the while the picture was in progress he hovered between hate and contrition, urgently desiring to have done with the impossible conditions he worked under. Toward the end, with a final vindictiveness, he added highlights deep into the bosom accentuating her immodesty. So much for Mrs. Gardner, thought he.

By this time it was getting closer to the date set for the exhibition at the St. Botolph Club. There were innumerable letters to write, collecting his few important pictures in America, importuning unhappy owners, issuing shipping instructions; then receiving complaints from all parties.

He could not avoid Mrs. Gardner either, for she was everywhere in Boston. Though something of an outcast, she managed frequently to turn up at the same places to which he was invited. She was still pleasant enough socially, and did not at all disguise her pleasure with the finished portrait. Though he could never look at her without some little wave of revulsion creeping over him, she had such interesting friends, gave such pleasant dinners, and in every way tried to make herself so pleasant that he soon realized she was succeeding. Of course, it was embarrassing to have her boast throughout Boston that he had done his finest portrait of her — a claim she could make with impunity since she had seen so few. Nonetheless, she was frequently his hostess now and he found her friendship useful.

He attended the Boston Symphony concerts, interested to see what sort of orchestra his friend Henschel had put together. At the performance he was particularly pleased by the solo work of a young violinist named Charles Martin Loeffler, who was heard in the Lalo *Symphonie Espagnole.* He went around to the artist's room to congratulate him after the performance, and finding that Loeffler was acquainted with Mrs. Gardner, said he would arrange that they should meet again at her home on Beacon Street. When they did, they were soon playing the *Symphonie* through for the other guests. Loeffler, watching the way Sargent played through the third movement, with its rather complicated rhythms, was considerably impressed by the verve and spirit of his execution. Next Sargent suggested they try Gabriel Fauré's sonata, and sailed easily through his piano part; if he did not play all the notes, as Loeffler perceived, he played all that were necessary. They both seemed to enjoy the evening, and when, soon after, Mrs. Gardner asked Loeffler his fee for having played at dinner, he wrote: "You don't owe me anything at all and you *must* accept my having played for you as homage to you and Mr. Sargent."

Meantime Sargent's portrait of Mrs. Marquand was brought down to the Marquand home in New York, where Beckwith and St.-Gaudens joined the people flocking to see it. There was a general agreement that nothing like this had previously been seen in America. It was in fact a remarkably sympathetic rendering, nothing in the style obscuring the simple traits of this elderly gray personality. The dark harmony of color and simple stateliness of arrangement were singularly suited to the subject, and forced those who thought of Sargent as a painter of brittle flamboyance to realize his extraordinary flexibility. Delicacy of perception was projected without hint of sentimentality. Perfect satisfaction was expressed on all sides, apparently only the painter being aware of a certain lack of balance in the characterization, for when Edwin Blashfield praised it he replied, "Don't you think it's more an éloge than a portrait?"

On January 30 the St. Botolph Club exhibition opened with a bang. The famous Mrs. James Fields poured tea, with the help of Sarah Orne Jewett, and thirteen hundred people crowded in. Some twenty pictures were hung, including six portraits done since he had arrived in October, the *El Jaleo*, and some Venetian landscapes. Virtually all the pictures Henry James had specifically named in the *Harper* piece were there, inspiring the boast made in the Boston newspapers that this exhibition "would have made a sensation in New York, or Paris, or London." His European fame was fully exploited. A certain pride was felt that Boston had been able to attract him, as though he paid the city a compliment by choosing it to show his wares. Some of the subjects of his portraits were seen in person among the crowds attending, providing that comparison of portrait with model which never failed to excite interest. "It is to be recorded that nearly always neither the subject nor the portrait suffered in this juxtaposition," wrote the *Art Amateur*, which also reproduced two pen drawings he had especially made of Venetian landscapes in the exhibition. Perhaps the only adverse criticism was of his portrait of Mrs. Gardner, which appeared shockingly immodest. But the plaudits flowing to him from the exhibition found him gone — off to New York.

In Boston, Mrs. Gardner was disturbed to receive a letter from a friend calling her attention to the immodesty of the portrait and the newspaper reactions to it. She sent it on to him in New York, and his response was typical of his attitude toward gossip:

Clarendon Hotel
Friday

Dear Mrs. Gardner

. . .

Many thanks for the friend's letter which I return. The newspapers do not disturb me. I have only seen one or two at any rate. Do you bear up?

I have not yet managed anything about Loeffler and fear it will be impossible — also have not yet written him about dining and opera Wednesday evening. Have lost his address. Extraordinary!

Sincerely yours
John S. Sargent

The day after the opening of the St. Botolph Club exhibition he appeared for a dinner arranged in his honor at Stanford White's house in Gramercy Park. Talk centered about the wonderful show being held in Boston, where all the fine canvases noted by Henry James were brought together, with the addition of landscapes and, amazingly, six portraits executed since his arrival, but not including two that he had been unable to borrow from unwilling owners. He had done a spectacular amount of work in three months, and the flow of it appeared to be continuous. It is not known whether any members of Colonel Elliott Shepard's family were present that night to meet the artist, though a dinner given in his honor seems to imply introductions in a city where he was still unknown, and McKim, Mead and White had work in hand for the Shepards. However White managed it, the introduction was made, and Sargent was soon at work on a portrait of Mrs. Shepard. Once again now he found a studio in New York, where this daughter of W. K. Vanderbilt came for a portrait in a brilliant scarlet dressing gown. He began to paint her against a background of glazed brown the rich color of dark walnut, which seemed to be an infinite space out of which she had come. On the floor was a fuzzy tan-yellow rug. Everything seemed right, and still he experienced great difficulty. The sittings grew more and more numerous, and were enlivened by visits from Mrs. Shepard's fourteen-year-old daughter Alice, a charming youngster who spoke to him in French and recited poetry and made him want to paint her. Perhaps he was feeling badly about the way the picture of Mrs. Shepard was coming and thought such an idea would hold the interest of the family. Whatever the reason, he asked if he might do a portrait of Alice too; and the answer was "No." She had fallen from a tree not very long before, her back was weak, and her mother said she certainly could not pose forty times or more, as she herself was doing. He persisted, promising it would be done in a few short sessions, and eventually, when Mrs. Shepard came to sit, he made some quick attempts at getting a picture of Alice done too. She was a lovely child, with high coloring, lustrous dark hair done in a long braid down her back, and large coal-black eyes. It was a pleasure to paint her. He set about it with gusto, laying on a thick impasto not hitherto employed during this American trip. He produced a beautiful study of the child, employing the snowy tone of her white-lined jacket to set off her complexion. The charm of the thing had instantaneous effect, and soon her mother's portrait was making progress too. For all the trouble that went into it, this picture is painted with greater broadness than he ever had before essayed. It illustrates that this quality in his work was by no means the product of a lack of effort. Quite the contrary, it frequently indicated a painstaking simplification through many sittings. Here he juxtaposed brilliant flesh with startling shadows, reduced the eyes to almost nothing, left the mouth hardly indicated — and makes one conscious of fingers which, on closer inspection, completely lack definition. The entire canvas is glazed over with a sweeping brush, more delicately in the flesh, where tones of blue and green are employed against the scarlet of the gown. Amazingly it all falls so into place as intensely alive and is one of his most realistic canvases, even down to the round table, with decorative metal terminals and railing, which was added as an afterthought. The extent to which he employed glazes also is a surprising feature; apparently when faced with the blazing scarlet his mind went back to the *Dr. Pozzi*, done seven years before in

Paris, which had made similar demands in terms of color and pro-
cured its effects through the use of glaze. His technical knowledge
was so complete that he had no inhibitions about employing means
that in other hands implied a certain dullness, producing a brilliant
portrait.

Curiously, at the same time he was also doing Mrs. Adrian Iselin,
working with restrained color, brushing it in in a monotone of
black, with ochers and flesh adding the only accents. He seems not
to have enjoyed this picture, his bluff-faced model, with large ugly
ears, apparently demanding the elimination of too many wrinkles
and lines to suit him. He shows her as she stood, looking at him
in a rather uncompromising way, decidedly on her guard and ready
to admonish him for any unnecessary liberty taken with her features.

He had expected this American venture would be short, and
now that March was drawing to a close, marking six months in
America, there was still work in hand. His social obligations had
grown enormously, occupying him every moment he dared spare
from his easel, even carrying him in flying leaps to Boston, for
dinners at Mrs. Gardner's, and back to New York in the morning.
In this breathless whirl Beckwith lost sight of his friend, writing
a little ruefully in his diary: "John Sargent I hear much of about
town being entertained very much and painting Mrs. Vanderbilt
and others." Bunker, too, marveled at his success, early in April
writing Mrs. Gardner: "J.S.S. is still in N.Y. I hear of his princely
life occasionally — Il mène une existence de roi — c'est un homme
étonnant." With Bunker he was planning to return to England to
paint once more on the upper Thames, but events kept shifting
their plans. Finally, though it was now really too late to be in
London for the opening of the Academy, to which he had shipped
the portrait of Mrs. Marquand from New York, he purchased a
ticket to return May 19, writing Mrs. Gardner: "I am working like
mad to be through by the 19th & it is hotter than parliamentary
language can express. I hope I shall see you somewhere on my
way to Italy." Quite probably it was on an invitation tendered
through Sargent that Mrs. Gardner stayed with the Curtises at
Venice that summer, apparently in the upper apartment of their
palazzo which Henry James had occupied the year before. Indeed,

cousin Ralph Curtis and Mrs. Gardner seemed to get on well. Several times Curtis acted as agent for her in the purchase of furniture, steering her to Venetian dealers with whom he had an understanding and finally, culmination of all his efforts, guiding her in the purchase of a Vermeer in Paris.

For the first time Sargent had reaped the harvest of his intensive application. For the first time he had found more substantial rewards than those of purely artistic approval. During the early years, artists had provided most of his admirers, and, though from the age of twenty-one he was an acknowledged master of his art, considered among the leading figures of the younger generation, patronage was not his to any great extent, and it was with difficulty that he earned his keep. He did better in England than in Paris and had lately found some little patronage of a substantial sort, though not enough for him to be assured he could make England his home. Always in the back of his mind he carried memories of the years in France when the smooth progress of his career filled others with anxiety over their own slow progress, but actuality had not justified the brilliant outward appearance. With all his efforts to sell his works, to do portraiture, small genre, or even large Salon pictures, he still failed to make his way. He altered his attack, varied his strategy, imitated the methods of Carolus as well as he could, making a place for himself in French society. But there remained the fear that he would be obliged to turn to other pursuits or the small open purse of his mother. Even the critical approval he had won was dissipated in the catastrophic scandal of the Gautreau portrait. He had planned this work as the foundation on which a self-sustaining career might be fashioned, a hope that was shattered in France, though the resulting notoriety counted for much when he arrived in England, and was a still more important stroke in America, where they had few other yardsticks by which to measure. The New York newspapers, in fact, in reporting that disaster blamed it on an excess of *realism*, which had a favorable ring to American ears.

Only the year before, when he turned thirty, it had seemed he was no better off than he had been at twenty. Youth was slipping away, and with that gone he would settle back into the pattern of typical middle-aged mediocrity, and be shoved aside by the younger generation. His consciousness of this was plainly shown in the letter he sent Russell from Broadway, mentioning with rather too much emphasis, "There is no great young talent." That was a specter he did not care to face. Then suddenly at Newport all changed. He wrote to Frank Millet soon after his arrival, and in a tone that conveyed his prosperity, though he would never say outright that he was doing well except to mention that he was painting more than the one portrait for which he had come. It was the first time in his life that he was trading toil for reward, and it was a pleasant feeling to know it could be done. Suddenly the appearances he had maintained through the long years of disappointment became real. The pattern he had cut out for his life was coming alive, coming true. The exhibition of his works in Boston was clearly the most impressive the city had seen. Its fame followed him to New York, and was vigorously discussed. After one eight months' visit to America he had as many portraits spread about the walls there as he had managed to do in ten years of Paris. Then too, meeting Stanford White had special significance. With his tremendous energy and strong opinions White would remain an ally for years, while McKim would be largely responsible for the heights he would reach in the upward swing he was now embarked upon. McKim was a firm believer in the efficacy of a dinner for transacting his business. At table his quiet unassuming manner, through which rang a tone of urgent conviction, was most effective. It was the practice of this remarkable firm of architects to enter fully into the lives of their clients, giving expression to their desires and directing their tastes, often, it is true, after considerable persuasion. McKim was the efficient member of the firm in this respect, his personal enlistment on behalf of Sargent thus assuming great importance. As the years passed, he would show himself consistently able to draw sitters from among the architectural clients of his office, doing so in a manner pleasant to all involved and possibly unknown to many. It was this connection in America that Sargent built upon, for he had few of his own, and the numerous sitters who would cross the ocean to him in the next two decades, by and large, were sent by McKim.

Newport, then, was the turning point of his career. He had been able to start in America at the very top, as he had not done in France or England. Even the large price he quoted the Marquands was fortunate, saving the necessity of raising fees while in midstream, as it were, and giving prospective sitters that added respect for his work which arose from knowing it came high. He had come into port at last, under full sail, with flags flying and a cheering crowd on the wharf to greet him. At last he could consider himself a success.

English Interlude

THE PORTRAITIST must always keep occupied. When there are no sitters knocking at his door he must still be producing. There are exhibitions at which his work is expected but he has no stock to draw upon, for his completed pictures have gone to their owners. If he wishes to exhibit, he must have new work and new sitters, and thus the necessity of forever working is on him. Equally important to Sargent was the fact that a portrait sent to the Royal Academy, or the Grosvenor Gallery, remained on view only a few weeks or months, while those hung in homes were seen the year round. The more work a portraitist spread about the walls of the city the greater his chance of being seen, noticed, and liked. Sargent often proved capable of attracting new sitters from among the people who accompanied a model, to *assist*, as he liked to put it, by talking to keep alive the expression while the painter gave his work undivided attention. A chance remark, some trifle of flattery dropped not within hearing of the individual but to another who would report it back, might confirm a desire to sit, and was a device he consistently employed. When his studio remained empty, however, no such artifice was of service. Moreover, when he was producing nothing to shock or to delight at exhibitions, he could not speak, while dining out, of the persons he was painting, and so direct attention not to his painting — that would be too obvious — but to their sitting, speaking of them and not the picture.

The drawing power of names that were well publicized was important too, for interest among gallery-goers was intense when they came to a portrait of someone well known. To paint such people was to achieve an instantaneous audience. The demimonde in particular had a fascination for the public, the tinsel of their lives even then attracting as much interest as was bestowed generally on people of more substantial repute. Musician, actor, actress, there was magic in their names. Thus when Sargent was not busy, as he was not busy on his return to England, the painting of demimondaines was all to his advantage.

George Henschel, whom Sargent had met again in Boston, was a well-known figure in London life, where before winning honor as a conductor, he had sung for the *at homes* then so popular, making a reputation as a singer almost entirely without reference to the concert halls. Sargent and Henschel often met at the Lewises, in Portland Place, a house where the fashionable world had opened its doors wide, not only to writers and painters, but to actors and actresses as well. When approached, Henschel was flattered and willing, but was able to sit only Sunday mornings. During these sittings, Henschel sang as Sargent worked, mostly from *Tristan and Isolde.* Both men looked forward to Sunday, for when Henschel was not singing they engaged in long rambling conversations about music, spiced by Sargent's typical explanation — *"a certain sort of something,"* often the closest he came to definitive expression. There were rare moments of quiet too, as when the mouth was being painted, and much that was said had to be illustrated by reference to the upright piano. One morning in February, the last sitting over, the painter carefully fitted the still wet painting into the frame, and artist, model, and picture went by hansom to Henschel's house in Bedford Gardens, where they were expected for lunch. Other guests were waiting for them, including a woman of particular beauty who had been invited in hopes of pleasing Sargent. Good German stock that they were, it bothered the Henschels that anyone so eligible should remain a bachelor into his thirties. The two men made an entrance, the picture in Sargent's hand. He presented it to Mrs. Henschel: "I made this for you, Mrs. Henschel." She put it down to look, then exclaimed, "How beautiful! It's George, having arrived in heaven!"

Alice Comyns Carr was at this time designing costumes for her friend Ellen Terry to wear in the forthcoming production of *Macbeth*, which Henry Irving was mounting for his Lyceum Theatre. Like all Irving's productions, *Macbeth* was being done with thought to its visual effect, for his name had been made by spectacles. Shortly before the opening on December 29, Sargent was invited by Joe Comyns Carr to share his box on opening night, and was glad to accept, explaining, however, to Mrs. Carr that he only did so "in order to support your fainting form into the fresh air at the critical moment," an ill-omened thought that nearly turned prophetic in respect of the play. Irving's lavish production was uneven, and in the early parts the audience's lack of enthusiasm was particularly apparent. Until Miss Terry's first entrance, the play was coldly received. A new interest was kindled, however, the moment she tore onto the dull gaslit stage, her velvet cloak in heather tones floating behind a long gown of green silk and blue tinsel, the whole effect so overwhelming that it reached Sargent, who let a lingering "I say" escape from him, audible through the length of the dim box. Pictorially, Lady Macbeth was superb, the desire to paint her as she made that grand entrance instantaneous. At the reception following the performance he found she was willing to sit, for her own early marriage to Watts had left her a dedicated model but, as the reception of the play was uncertain, she hesitated before posing as Lady Macbeth.

Three days later, he wrote to Mrs. Gardner: "Miss Terry has just come out in Lady Macbeth and looks magnificent in it, but she has not yet made up her mind to let me paint her in one of the dresses until she is quite convinced she is a success. From the pictorial point of view there can be no doubt about it — magenta hair!" The play met with divided criticism, but finally settled down for a run of one hundred fifty nights. It was still playing to capacity when the season, then strictly upheld, ended on June 29.

It was typical London weather, foggy and dark, when Ellen Terry first came for her sittings. Oscar Wilde was looking from his window across the street, when to his surprise the mystic vision of Lady Macbeth, in full regalia, swept from a carriage. "Where else in the world could one see Lady Macbeth step down from a

carriage in broad daylight?" said Oscar, looking around for someone to whom he could repeat the remark. In truth, there was so
little daylight that the sittings frequently resolved into sittings by
the fire, or at the piano by lamplight.

The scene of Duncan's arrival at Macbeth's castle had been
singularly impressive in the theater. The effect was of deepest
night, with Duncan welcomed by torchlight and Ellen Terry
sweeping from the castle in her first entrance between rows of
bowing ladies. The torchlight, the "effect," appealed to Sargent's
pictorial taste for the artificial light he had periodically painted
over the past seven years. He liked the swirl of drapery and the
women bowed down on both sides. To make an initial sketch he
had Miss Terry walk up and down the studio until she complained
that she was ready to drop from exhaustion in her heavy costume;
while he, unmindful of the physical exertions, shouted "That's it,
that's it!" and, excitement suddenly mounting, bounded across the
room to indicate in paint the swirling he had finally seen. He
worked feverishly for short periods, his enthusiasm infecting the
actress, then relaxed at the piano, bringing forth peals of music
from the poor instrument, which looked as though it had never
been played softly. Up he jumped again, replacing the palette on
his left hand, thrusting brushes into the palm, and begging her to
pace once more. As the little sketch progressed, he became more
interested in Miss Terry herself. She was certainly not pretty,
though her face and manner were stamped with charm; decidedly
she was a striking woman. Looking over his sketch, he decided that
it would become too large and too complicated with figures to
show well, and abandoned it for a more concentrated blend of
Miss Terry with the part she was playing. The costume itself had
great pictorial possibilities, as he had realized in the theater, and the
trappings of the stage settings and supernumeraries suddenly became superfluous. He tried simplifying the design to some single
gesture typical of Lady Macbeth, through which Ellen Terry, too,
would shine, and arrived at the idea of having the actress stand
with upraised crown, as though about to place it upon her own
head. The obviously theatrical quality of the gesture conveyed
with great impressiveness both an essence of the play and the part
being played. And something typical of Ellen Terry shone

through, as it had on the stage. While studying the part, she had written in the margin of an essay giving the great Mrs. Siddons's views of Lady Macbeth's character: "Play to the best of one's powers — one's own possibilities. Adapt the part to my own personality with the knowledge that sometimes nature *does* freak and put an honest eye into a villain's head." Sargent created one of the great theatrical portraits by similar means, by realizing Ellen Terry was a personality herself in the guise of the woman of Inverness. He did so in terms of pictorial invention, producing a canvas that grips and holds attention by the magnificence and boldness of its characterization.

"What a saint!" he remarked to Ellen Terry, after Henry Irving first came around to Tite Street. She thought it boded well that Sargent saw that side of Irving immediately, for too often he appeared the stiff inflexible theater manager he was, lacking in human qualities when off the stage. She never left off asking Irving to sit for the portrait Sargent implied he would like to do, and several times, calmly nurturing his project, when Irving became the subject of conversation he remarked, "What a head!" It is true that Irving was impressive. He had schooled himself so thoroughly to be an actor that he made every change of mood perceptible through all the rows of the Lyceum. All the same, he was no saint in appearance, but a martinet. Sargent's comment clearly implied that Miss Terry had betrayed her own sympathies, for Irving's pale, sunken face spoke more of illness than ascetic fervor, except to those few who knew of his devotion to the theater. When at last Irving did come to sit, Sargent's too-true eye seemed at each attempt to grasp the mechanical aspects of his personality, and his wan smile, thought beatific by some, left the artist expecting to see it shut off. The smile was in fact hardly more than a facial exercise, and one that Sargent, who felt it necessary to remain in sympathy with Miss Terry, thought it indelicate to indicate; finally he said that it baffled him, and turned to a serious expression.

Sargent's studio was still only one large room, with narrow halls leading to a bedroom and a dining room, on the ground floor of 33 Tite Street. In the middle of the day, or in the evening, he was often seen eating at the Chelsea Arts Club, only a short distance away, where in a studio that served as messroom he would meet the

Dr. FitzWilliam Sargent

Violet, at seven

Vernon Lee

Henri Lefort

Paul Helleu

Auguste Rodin

Mme. Buloz

Mme. Allouard-Jouan

Judith Gautier

Mrs. Jules Vallé

Louis de Fourcaud

Three sketches of
Mme. Gautreau

Mme. Gautreau

Sir Edmund Gosse

Mrs. John Joseph Townsend

Flora Priestley

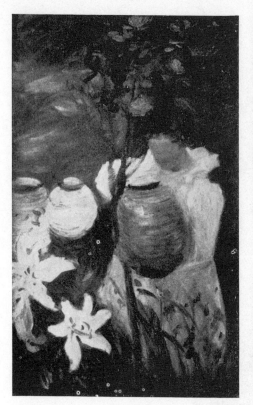

Two sketches for "Carnation Lily, Lily Rose"

Sargent painting "Carnation Lily, Lily Rose"

Gabriel Fauré

St. Martin's Summer

Carmencita

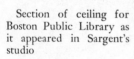

Section of ceiling for Boston Public Library as it appeared in Sargent's studio

Elsie Swinton

Mrs. Charles Hunter

Asher Wertheimer

Theodore Roosevelt

Mrs. Joseph E. Widener

Three sketches
presented to Mrs. Hunter

Charcoal drawing of Mrs. Hunter

A Scene in Venice

Landscape near Frascati

Gourds

Cypresses

Val d'Aosta, A Stream over Rocks

Val d'Aosta,
Stepping
Stones

The Cashmere Shawl

The Pink Dress

Corner of the Church of St. Staë,
Venice

Courtyard, Tetuan

Lady Cholmondeley

Henry James

John D. Rockefeller

Gondolier (Nicola D'Inverno)

Gondolier

Daniel J. Nolan

Two charcoal studies for murals

Figure study

other painters frequenting the district. The family-style service, waiters carrying dishes of vegetables around the single long table at which all sat, produced a singularly pleasant atmosphere. It was a friendly place at which he could relax, eating the table d'hôte dinner with a liter of wine while the chef prepared an additional steak for him. Upstairs in the then very modest quarters of the club was a room for newspapers which he never read, tables for the chess he particularly enjoyed, and a general sociability. He was a jovial companion at the club, spreading good cheer and considered rather lightheaded by those unfamiliar with his brand of idle banter. Often, too, he dined out, with the Playfairs, George Lewises, Harrisons, or Comyns Carrs. He was still seeing his gouty friend Natorp, who managed to have his works exhibited at the Royal Academy by means of influence and ghosting and who had for some months been struggling with a medallion of Robert Browning, finally allowing a ghost to complete it.

Early in March 1889, Sargent chanced to sit next to Browning during dinner at Boughton's, an Academician who was a friend of Abbey's and a frequenter of Broadway. The poet showed himself perfectly familiar with his work, speaking to him of his own son, living at Venice, where he owned the Rezzonico. "What, all of it?" asked Sargent, amazed to hear that the huge barracks-like house in which he had rented a room for ten francs was again a private home. He began to explain his familiarity with the place, but Browning knew about that too, explaining he had seen his "autograph and scratch of a drawing on the wall," which, he went on, his son intended to leave uneffaced. This reference to a youthful prank, one he had probably forgotten, amused and pleased Sargent. It told him in what respect his work was held by Browning and his son. Here then, he thought, was someone ripe for the plucking. Browning was not poor, and his dealing with Natorp demonstrated no aversion to having his image set down; in fact his carefully tended hair and beard implied a rather vain fellow, which put Sargent in a hopeful frame of mind. Between forkfuls he tossed off the remark that he was painting Ellen Terry in the role of Lady Macbeth. His hint was fairly obvious, though Browning missed it, apparently willing to take it at face value. He was sufficiently interested by meeting Sargent to write an account to his son wherein, after having the matter in mind for several days, he still shows no glimmering of penetration into the painter's motives. Unfortunately, it seems the two did not meet again, and the possibility of a fine portrait of the poet was lost. Browning did take special notice of Sargent's works at the next Royal Academy exhibition, troubling to write praises to his family in Venice.

Henry Irving's portrait continued to give trouble, for even when the artist had become sufficiently annoyed with the smile to try a serious countenance, the question arose, just which one? Irving had many stored away, he delighted to spring new ones and the multiplicity became dismaying. Ellen Terry thought the picture looked a little mean about the chin at first, but soon after put in her diary:

> Everyone hates Sargent's head of Henry. Henry, also. I like it, but not altogether. I think it perfectly wonderfully painted and like him, only not at his best by any means. There sat Henry, and there by his side the picture, and I could scarce tell one from t'other. Henry looked white, with tired eyes, and holes in his cheeks and bored to death! And there was the picture with white face, tired eyes, holes in the cheeks and boredom in every line.

And Burne-Jones, who came to see how Sargent was getting on with the picture of Lady Macbeth, went off raving about it, having suggested slight alterations of color that were immediately adopted.

When finished, *Ellen Terry as Lady Macbeth* was sent off to be exhibited at the New Gallery, apparently through a wish not to raise the ire of the Academy. Nothing could have been less academic, the picture creating a sensation even at the *New*, where standards were progressive. Opinions about it varied as much as they had over Miss Terry's playing of the role. Dense crowds clustered before it, and though doubt was expressed at the daring of the artist, no one could doubt the beauty of the picture itself. Soon Henry Irving purchased it for the Beefsteak Room of the Lyceum Theatre, where it hung in an alcove, and under it on many occasions during the following decade the artist was to sup with Miss Terry and Alice Carr, commenting once, "You and I ought to have signed that together, Alice, I couldn't have done it if you hadn't invented the dress." Henry Irving visited a less kind fate on his own portrait. When it was returned from the Academy, where Mr. Punch called it *"Hedley Irvil wi' such a bad cold id is 'ead,"* he hid it in a cupboard in his Grafton Street house, never allowing it to be seen or exhibited. Eventually he destroyed it.

Three different exhibitions in London showed Sargent's work that year: the Royal Academy, where the portrait of Henschel was a particular success; the New Gallery, where the *Lady Macbeth* drew huge crowds; and the New English Art Club, where his modernism continued to lead the pack. "We must confess to finding them somewhat unpleasant in color, but we acknowledge their veracity and the infinite cleverness, and they scintillate with sunlight," wrote the *Magazine of Art*. Even his contributions to the Royal Academy were anarchic to the contemporary eye, and though he sent his least objectionable works there, he was still considered "the most brilliant, the most defiantly original."

During these years of struggle his relations with his family had become less close, although his mother's affectionate, domineering nature never ceased to overflow in his direction as well as all others, and he did continue the visits to them, wherever they might be, that had begun ten years before when he was a student in Paris. Once he had returned from the United States, however, all clouds of misunderstanding passed, for it was now abundantly clear that his career was on a new, more substantial, footing, which the fanfare greeting every appearance of his pictures gave ample evidence of sustaining. The American trip had proved the practicality of his ambitions. He would be able to provide for his own needs through the agency of his art, without recourse to outside income. This had been an important consideration to a family without fortune of their own and from whom a grown son would need help unless he could provide for himself. Sargent's earnings, from the American trip alone, were considerable, and his father, with New England thrift, must surely have pointed out that the capital accumulated on that venture was equal to that they had all lived on for so long. His puritan conscience must have rested more easy. He could continue to express pride in his son, whom he seems always to have considered remarkable. His restrained nature had to be understood before his feelings became clear. Even so, it was good to know that his quiet approval was added to the affectionate pride of the mother. The good news flowing from America had been received at Nice, where they were wintering, as they had for many years past. Welcome as it was, it was rather dimmed by the fact that FitzWilliam Sargent, now sixty-eight years old, had suffered a stroke which left him partially paralyzed and an invalid. His memory was affected, and he was able to move only with difficulty. At this crisis they all turned to John, for it was decided to bring the gravely ill doctor to England, which it now appeared would be the permanent home of the son he wanted so much to be near.

Arriving in England at the end of May, John's first task was to find a home for his family, preferably in the country, and in three weeks' time he discovered a suitable place at Calcot, out near Reading. It was on the branch of a river, with willow trees, boats, and all the pleasant inducements of the English countryside. His family moved out there, and after seeing the Boits, who were in London, and getting things back into order at Tite Street, he went off with Bunker to join them. Bunker, it seems, felt uneasy at first about eighteen-year-old Violet, writing back to Boston: "The youngest Miss Sargent is awfully pretty — charming. What if I should fall in love with her? dreadful thought, but I'm sure to — I see it coming — "

Plans remained indefinite. Dr. Sargent seemed somewhat improved, yet, though Sargent talked of a visit to Paris, he did not want to wander far, and so spent the summer close at hand, watching his father with a tender solicitude few would have attributed to him. Staying close to the house, he and Bunker meanwhile contrived to make use of the glistening sunlight. Sargent continued to experiment in impressionism, demonstrating to Bunker its great potential. The things he was doing show an almost complete acceptance of its tenets, departing from them only in the greater attention still paid to drawing and form, and the feeling he continued to have for paint itself as a medium of beauty not to be tortured by the staccato piling up of crumbled and broken bits. Impressionism as it existed across the Channel had already grown into a formula which with his own intuitive strength he rejected, taking only its nuances and effects to be applied in his own manner.

Then, the day's work over, John would take his father's arm, and with quiet care lead him from the dinner table, to talk until time for bed. "I am going to sit and smoke," the old man repeated night after night, "with my son John," an obvious pride in his weak voice never failing in the repetition. The life of empty expatriation had been a bitter pill, leaving him silent and broken; the fiercest emotion he still could muster was pride in his son, his sacrifice of principle having at length been rewarded. At the beginning of September, Bunker wrote: "Mr. Sargent père is a bit better than he was . . . but is far from being well — in fact I don't think he will ever be any better. Sargent fils is working away at all sorts of things and making experiments without number — He makes them look awfully well — the experiments I mean — and is altogether a wonderful being . . . but I'm afraid you'd think it dull here — there is nothing to do — we are off on the river all day painting — or else saying bad things about the weather . . . We have been known to play poker — but very sleepily — and with beans. The people are awfully kind — I mean the Sargents . . . "

The following winter a house was taken at Bournemouth, a short distance from the one Louis Stevenson had formerly occupied, and throughout the winter months Sargent came down from London often, his sense of duty and the new depths of his emotions calling him to the side of his father. And it was there on April 25 that FitzWilliam Sargent died, his years of expatriation ended at last.

The elements of emotionalism that had play in Sargent's life during this time were reflected in his paintings, for his work was unerringly responsive to his every feeling. The gratification of complete understanding with his family, followed so closely by the illness and death of his father, a serious loss for that close-knit group to sustain, brought forth a tenderness that had not previously appeared, though it is a maternal inheritance without which his nature is unfathomable. He was loath to have it seen and was aware that few people "give me credit for insides." The increased emotionalism of this period found expression in a new emphasis upon mood, the feeling of the countryside, the wholehearted human sympathy with which a figure in sunlight is invested. There is a quality of charm, of warmth and human feeling in everything he did during

1888 and 1889, while his invalid father made call on his heart, and later, during the grief of loss. Surrounded by his family for the first time since childhood, there appears a note of intimacy in his sketches, of an emotional vision, that cannot be explained on technical grounds.

It was in June that he finally made the trip to Paris that he had spoken of the previous summer, in time for the International Exhibition, to which he sent six portraits, exhibited in the United States section, for which he was awarded a medal and made Chevalier of the Legion of Honor. It was a curious thing for him to be receiving honors from La Belle France now — France, where after the debacle of 1884 his works rarely received notice. He had felt so little hope that he sent nothing to the Salon of 1887, as a gesture of contempt. Why should he bother to ship anything from London? At that date he could find derision near at hand and had no need to look for it again across the Channel. Strange, too, that he was honored as an American at the International Exhibition, a distinction much greater than were he honored at the Salon, yet how much less it meant coming now, when he was finding himself established elsewhere, than if it had been given him when France was his home, and the honor something he was striving for.

He remained several weeks in Paris. Wading through the pavilions of the Exhibition, he found his way to the Allée des Etrangers, which clung to the edge of the Champ-de-Mars, on the banks of the Seine, like a dust ruffle. Variegated tents flanked his way and perspiring barkers importuned the crowds. As he sauntered along in the hot July sun, his ear caught a twang of guitar and castanets, breaking through a tent flap. From the platform out front came cries of "Carmencita, the renowned dancer," and yielding to persuasion, he paid the fifty centimes admission. Inside the musty tent, alone on a crude stage that threatened to collapse, was a tigress of a young girl, who when he peered close seemed to have a certain barbaric beauty. From her features and costume, and the ragamuffin, cutthroat aspect of the guitarist whose strumming followed the beat of her castanets, he judged that she was gypsy. She moved with grace, and the few customers in the tent joined in a desultory applause when she bowed. The tent was unbearably hot, and Sargent was glad to get out and continue on his way. Farther along he came on a group of Javanese dancers who did their muscular, spastic dances in an improvised island hut. Their Eastern exoticism was new to his experience. The strange movements and tinkling music, without recognizable rhythm, had immediate attraction, and he attempted to make drawings of them on the inside of the cover of his sketchbook, simultaneously noting the indeterminate progressions of their accompaniment. The results were not enlightening. He got only a blurred scratchy drawing, and was unable to read back his musical notations; but, his interest aroused, he set about getting a studio in Paris, then arranged for two of the dancers to pose for him. His ambitious *Lady Macbeth,* and the pleasure it had given him, called forth a desire to do something of the sort from these strangely articulating automatons, in their bizarre costumes, with ornamented helmets, and knives stuck into their scanty coverage. His imagination was set in flights that soon had him preparing full-length canvases. He also did one smaller unfinished sketch of a female dancer painting her face and filled a sketchbook with pencil notations of hands, feet, and heads. These Javanese, with their round Oriental faces made even smoother by an application of decorative masklike make-up, called forth all his love of the exotic. They, too, were done with the impressionist touch, the paint thinly applied in a running application of nuance and color.

He also did a small portrait of Gabriel Fauré. Probably they were acquainted earlier, for their friendship was a long one, though it cannot be documented earlier than this year, when they were together during the International Exhibition, and Fauré posed for the portrait. Like all Sargent's noncommissioned works, this head of Fauré is distinguished by freedom from the conventions of portraiture. The raised head and the incisive lines thus formed make a pattern of beauty, one that does not attempt to hide the high-bridged nose that was Fauré's most obvious characteristic. The pose is striking, the result of a study the artist made of his model. The position is that of a short man playing the piano, head thrown back, eyes cast down to the keyboard, the particular high-chinned posture so characteristic of Fauré himself. Undoubtedly, therefore, the inventive quality and the compositional fertility shown in this portrait are products of the artist's acute observation. He had eyes, he could see; he could pick out what was characteristic in his model, and if it is upon first sight arresting to those viewing his works, it is never that alone. It is rather the product of his capacity to see clearly; choosing intelligently from among the impressions received by his eyes, he found projections of his imagination.

When Monet came to Paris to see the Exhibition, he was greeted by the strange phenomenon of "second generation" impressionists, like Sargent, receiving honors, while the pioneers of pure impressionism were still banned. With the curious instinct for convention that marked himself and his brethren, Monet thought an art like impressionism, essentially a revolution against an older academism, should itself be made an institution. He wanted badly to find recognition for the masterpieces produced by the original impressionists, which to date had been refused them even though the ideas they set forth had been mined by both older and younger generations. The world seemed to be passing this gallant band without thanks or reward. He proposed to Sargent that they organize a movement to purchase Manet's *Olympia* and present it to the Louvre. There were humanitarian motives as well, for the painting then belonged to Manet's widow, to whom the sale and the subsequent prestige would be of inestimable value. In all the panoply of his new honors, therefore, Sargent began the weary task of calling on friends in Paris to explain the project and to solicit contributions for the purchase of the *Olympia*, which Mme. Manet agreed to sell them for twenty thousand francs. The reaction was mixed. Some, who were willing to oblige him out of friendship, though they had no great enthusiasm for the project, gave what amounted to token donations of a hundred francs. Roger-Jourdain, on whom he possibly counted for more, did so, and even Carolus-Duran, who had been a friend of Manet's, would give only two hundred. But he induced the dealer Theodore Duret to give a thousand, the Academician Roll five hundred, and even got one hundred from his former neighbor Duez. Boldini, happily installed in the heartbreak house on the Boulevard Berthier, with his usual flamboyance promised a thousand, finally giving two hundred. Other friends, many of whom could not afford to give even so much, eked out fifty francs (Helleu), twenty-five (Rodin), or a hundred (Besnard). Monet and Sargent each swelled the total by a thousand, finally amassing 19,415 francs, which Mme. Manet agreed to accept, writing to Monet, "It is with profound emotion that I read your letter announcing that you, M. Sargent, and some friends . . . ."

During this summer, too, Sargent went to Giverny, where Monet was now settled, and where the two friends for a while worked side by side in mutual dedication to the gods of sunlight and nuance. Sargent, standing before his canvas and constantly having to move back to view his efforts from a distance, differed from Monet, who sat placidly before his easel, working with apparent ease. Sargent has left a slight oil of Monet as he sat working, Mme. Monet off to one side in a little copse where she was shaded. In this sketch is implicit all the difference in the temperaments of the two men. Sargent never got closer to the petit point of doctrinaire impressionism than at this time when he was suppressing his own technique to adopt the methods of his friend. Even then it was not complete acceptance, for every canvas was still stamped with his own individual touch and a flavoring of his thought, which differed so vastly from that of Monet. Though the influence of Monet is obvious in these works, Sargent was actually experimenting in Monet's method to see how far it was applicable to his own vision and pictorial taste.

The Javanese dancers had pointed once again to an essential difference between Sargent and his friend Monet, already apparent in the comparison of their working methods. Sargent was the cosmopolitan, worldly in viewpoint, fascinated by the bizarre, willing to borrow from various cultures. Impressionism, as such, could be a passion to him — indeed he had suffered for his convictions in favor of it in England — but he was aware of other horizons and other processes, more intellectual and imaginative than the placid color notation that excluded all other elements of interest and was the preoccupation of Monet. He also sensed that impressionism was approaching a dead end through the continued lessening of defined forms, as in the work of Monet, who insisted on overwhelming the objects he painted with a piling on of pigment in the vain effort to catch every shadow, every sparkle, every tone. Sargent's was still a selective art, and even the painting of nuance was practiced with a discretion which did not allow the total effect to be overwhelmed by the predominance of parts or by the sea of pigment that Monet permitted to hide the very nuance he attempted to catch. One could no longer see what Monet was painting, though his whole intention was to paint it more truthfully than the next fellow. The strength of his earlier work, the rock-ribbed roads and stanchly standing trees, was giving way to a watery shimmer that proceeded from a tangled unassimilated paint surface. All this still won Sargent's admiration. He knew Monet was a tremendous painter, but he also realized there were other beauties than those of color that Monet was systematically abandoning. His own personality was too well balanced to be caught in the meshes of any formula, and seeing the way impressionism was heading, he drew back. He accepted all that he found of real value in impressionism, while maintaining the equilibrium that distinguished his nature from the Frenchman's. When he had finished his studies of the Javanese dancers, if he gave them any thought aside from the pleasant days spent painting interesting models, he must have wondered why he had done them, for surely the results, in Louis Stevenson's words, were "damn queer as a whole." But he knew they held some of his best work.

That August he returned to Worcestershire, joining his family at the Fladbury Rectory, a tiny spot not far from Broadway. The entire locality was hardly more than a church and a post office nestled low beside the village green, and the town proper, if there was one, must have been the string of odd-shaped cottages that rambled here and there beside the road from Evesham. The church had a nice square old Norman-looking tower, and a graveyard walled in red brick, to the right of which was the rectory itself. Though only a few feet from the road, this high oblong building of red brick actually faced the river, for both church and rectory were set on the high bank of the Avon, the house towering over three steep terraces, at the foot of which was a miniature dock and young willows edging the deep little stream. At the level of the terraces, these young trees screened the countryside from view, except for the sparkling ripples and muted images that broke through. From the upper windows of the house a short expanse of river was visible, while on the other side lay wide water meadows on which cattle grazed. Far off the village of Wood Norton lay partially concealed behind indistinct clumps of green.

This large house needed filling, and what with Broadway only twelve miles distant, there was no difficulty about that. Vernon Lee, who had visited with them the previous summer, during Dr. Sargent's illness, was now back again at Emily's invitation, this time accompanied by Caroline Anstruther-Thomson, another high-blown, intellectualized woman, who suited Vernon well and whom she tried to transform into an expert on art, as she did all her friends, eventually making her a collaborator in the aesthetically, philosophically, tantalizingly frothy essays she wrote. Kit Anstruther-Thomson, in fact, was simply a nice strapping handsome girl who went well to hounds but seemed to lose something of her individuality when in company with her author friend. For Vernon, who had no life of her own, took delight in manipulating others. Every afternoon, under her auspices, a symposium raged, in which by immutable right she was endowed with final powers of settlement, awarding the laurel to contending parties and chiming in with her own high unpleasant voice whenever it pleased her to illuminate, elucidate, and illustriously obfuscate the question. Most of the talk was utter rubbish, and Sargent was happy to be out sketching during symposium time, in fact avoiding Vernon as much as he could, that being the unwritten agreement by which they avoided catastrophe. There was something essentially irritating and unattractive about this girl, who was all bones and art. However, Emily seemed to like her, and it was as her guest that Vernon remained. John brought Alfred Parsons over from Broadway to stay as his own companion. Flora Priestley was Emily's choice this time. Then the tall lean Helleu arrived on his honeymoon trip, with a beautiful sixteen-year-old bride. One of Dr. Playfair's daughters stayed as companion to Violet, and the Roller boys, new friends of Abbey's, were nearby, where Sargent often joined them in attempts to ride.

The little English trains could be heard chugging miles away in the countryside, and each one that eventually wound its way through the low-lying clumps of trees, breaking through borders of green to cross the river just below the church, seemed to bring more friends to visit. The Fairchilds, who were staying at the Lygon Arms in Broadway, came over as well, while their daughter Sally, just Violet's age, spent her days getting the coachman at the inn to teach her to drive a tandem pair, the trick being to keep control of the forward horse. The very number of people underfoot, which might have seemed an impediment to work, actually provided Sargent with a choice of models, and everything became the excuse for a painting or a drawing. In September Abbey came over from Broadway and was amazed at his friend's application, writing to his intended wife, "John thinks of just nothing at all else and is always trying and working at something."

Paul Helleu accompanied Sargent when he set out with easel and paints in a canoe across the Avon, and the two worked together on the edge of the water meadows opposite the rectory, frequently accompanied by the young Mme. Helleu, though it was dull for her. Even so, her red hair and doe-like beauty were irresistible, and she was soon added to Sargent's summer gallery, sitting dreamily in idleness behind her husband, as he painted the overcast afternoon. Seldom had he seen more beautiful coloring than her delicately tinted complexion, shaded by a festooned straw hat, the soft glow of river and meadow mingling with her own radiance. Both of the Helleus figure in sketches made that summer. Lying in the bottom of a canoe, one foot extended to hold the weir, tall Helleu seems all carefree nonchalance. Both painted young Mme. Helleu lying in a canoe on the rippling stream, while Sargent's sketch portrait, done in the rectory, gives a more comprehensive view of her beauty. Vernon Lee figures in a drawing, which was given her, and in an acid caricature, which she was not shown. Kit Anstruther-Thomson was done in full length against the garden wall, standing with head thrown back and arms akimbo, the finished canvas a grotesquely vigorous portrayal of her "hounds" aspect, leaving her profundity to Vernon Lee.

Sargent was expending enormous energy that came from a bottomless reservoir, in five months completing seven full-length canvases, with strength left over for many smaller oils, landscapes, drawings, and at least eight smaller portraits. Nor, for all Abbey wrote, does this actually take into account all that he did: there were also the continuing efforts, lasting until November, to collect funds for the *Olympia;* the time necessarily spent entertaining his guests; the rainy days when "Auld Robin Gray" and "Kathleen Mavourneen" were sung around the piano; the riding and the tumbling with the Rollers; and the arguments with Vernon Lee, for he could not always escape her, and she earnestly desired to be of help to him in his work. Abbey needed aid in the handling of oils and found help in suggestion and example, for Sargent was not good at explaining. Another letter of Abbey's from Fladbury is expressive of their friendship at this time:

> Tuesday, September 24
>
> . . . Last night we — John and I — talked about what we ought to do until away in the small hours — talked and talked — and I am always refreshed by him . . . He may paint a nude in New York, if he can find any good figure, and thinks I ought to do the same — that it would widen me out to paint — rather over life size — a large, pale, fattish, nude woman with no particular drawing in her. I never painted from the nude at all — think of that!

Abbey was now occupying a particular place in his friend's affections, just as Bunker had, because he was someone to whom he could be of aid. They differed enough in their ideas to argue interestedly, not enough to disagree absolutely, acting in that sense as broadening influences and stimulation. This was especially noted in Abbey, who under Sargent's guidance was growing to be the complete artist that his younger but more experienced friend had seen he could become.

With the coming of autumn Sargent began packing his equipment for a journey down to Kent, where the Comyns Carrs and the Harrisons were encamped as guests of the American General Palmer. Carr, in his capacity as manager of the Grosvenor Gallery, had arranged a portrait of the general's daughter Elsie. General Palmer, now proprietor of the sixteenth-century Ightham Mote House, had been the owner of the Garden of the Gods, in Colorado, from which he had amassed a fortune, and just as good Americans went to heaven, so wealthy Americans went to England. The visit seems to have lasted several weeks, beginning with an attempt at a full-length standing portrait of the fourteen-year-old girl, with long hair. This apparently did not get far before Sargent had made a sketch of his model seated against the cherry wood paneling of the ancient house. This was a more appealing idea, and the larger canvas was abandoned in favor of this seated composition. Bit by bit the house was turned into a studio as he progressed, for with the portrait under way he was also working in the garden, where he made Alice Carr pose. "No, no, you can't go yet," he told her when lunch was ready. "You're a lovely green and orange, and the light will have changed later." Nor did he waste the evenings, for lamplight was another *effect* by which to try portraits. He never before had done any in life size by it, though he had tried smaller figure pieces for a decade. His sister Violet and Miss Priestley had been pressed into service in this connection at Fladbury, and now, in his evenings at the Mote House, he was ready, when complete darkness had fallen after ten o'clock, to pose Alice Carr and then to goad her to inane chatter just to keep her eyes open. She ran through the complete inventory of her husband's rude comments on their mutual friends, while he threw in just enough words of his own to maintain the flow. But this was not enough and late during one of these sittings she awakened to hear him mutter, "Well, we won't have large dark eyes. Anyone can have fine eyes."

As the portrait of Miss Palmer advanced inside the house, there appears to have been a definite change in the weather outside, which now was chilly and rather gray. Here was a new effect. As the only canvas Sargent now had at hand was the abandoned full-length, he took it outside and painted over it a picture in which the house figures as the principal interest, and all his friends, wrapped against the cold, play a game of bowls on the lawn.

Abbey's letter of that September shows that he and Sargent were planning a trip to New York together, most likely in response to urging from the firm of McKim, Mead and White. The first sentence, "Last night we — John and I — talked about what we ought to do . . ." refers to the problems presented by the trip, which naturally implied certain hazards to artists who felt it necessary to remain constantly employed. Only a few days later Stanford White and his wife arrived at Fladbury, in time for dinner. He was full of roaring talk about the Library that his firm was building in Boston. The Whites stayed over, and the next day Abbey walked with them through the village, pointing out everything of interest, before they all took the train to London, where Henry Irving was opening that night at the Lyceum in *The Dead Heart.*

Another Whack at America

SARGENT and his sister Violet arrived in New York that December after a smooth passage. Violet had arranged to go off to stay with the Fairchilds in Boston, while John lodged in New York with a friend of Abbey's, the banker Thomas Lincoln Manson, at 325 Madison Avenue. These arrangements had barely been completed when the first sitter, Mrs. Richard H. Derby, made her pencil-slim appearance. Her husband was a friend of Stanford White's, and McKim rented the Derby house at 9 West 35th Street. With one portrait in hand, and others likely, one by one introductions were made to the people for whom McKim, Mead and White were building: the Goelets and Hamilton Mc-Kown Twombly.

A succession of dinners consumed the first weeks, the Sundays being reserved for the afternoon smoking concerts held in St.-Gaudens' studio, where a quartet regularly played Mozart, Schubert, and Beethoven. In brief intervals unclaimed by the maneuverings of White and McKim, Sargent ran up to Fifty-seventh Street to look with jaundiced eye on the quiet humdrum existence into which Beckwith was settled. Though he was slowly becoming known, Beckwith himself must by this time have realized he was not cut out to be any tremendous figure in the arts, though the affection showered on him by a doting wife seemed to compensate somewhat for the disappointment of his career. That his more eminent friend still valued his company was obvious. Sargent dropped in at odd hours, inviting Beckwith out to parties and the opera. Once they were together, all the old intimacy was present, and Sargent was full of the boyish humor so unlike the austere impression he made on those he knew less well.

It was just so one Wednesday evening toward the end of December, when Sargent stopped at Beckwith's apartment. The portrait of Mrs. Derby was nearing completion, and as they sat talking, he told Beckwith of having received a letter from Richard A. C. McCurdy, president of the Mutual Life Insurance Co., asking him to call "concerning a portrait." Though he said nothing, the news came as a personal blow to Beckwith, who had painted Mrs. McCurdy and believed he had an understanding with McCurdy himself. Too loyal to betray his chagrin, he wished his friend good luck. On the following Saturday evening Sargent mentioned that McCurdy had confirmed the order at three thousand dollars. The suddenness of events was startling to Beckwith, and he was equally dismayed by the price Sargent was able to get. His portrait had not brought half so much.

Beckwith seemed to occupy the only quiet nook in New York. Anywhere else Sargent went he was certain to fall over Stanford White, that redheaded demon of an architect who was busily putting up and pulling down buildings all over the city. In Washington Square he was erecting a huge arch; his Madison Square Garden was going up close by Sargent's studio at 115 East Twenty-third Street. At Thirty-second Street and Broadway he was just completing a hotel, for which Abbey, when he arrived from England, was given a mural commission. To begin this work, Abbey took a studio for himself four flights up on the corner of Sixteenth Street and Fifth Avenue, White supplying him with lavish furnishings chosen from the wealth of decorative materials that he held in storage. Another smaller project of White's was an alteration to Edwin Booth's house, which stood directly across Gramercy Park from his own, and was in the midst of transition from a private residence to a club for actors, soon to be known as The Players. Before the building was properly accommodated to its new purpose, a larger dining room had to be knocked together and partitions shifted to provide more adequate kitchen facilities for the increased demand in that department. Hearing of the scheme,

White with his usual buoyant enthusiasm volunteered to draw the plans. Soon he learned that the Committee was at the same time considering the presentation of a portrait of Booth to the club, in honor of his generosity in giving his house. White naturally applauded the gesture, letting it be known that the only man to undertake the work was his good friend John Sargent. Opinion from White was an important recommendation to the Committee; he had great personal influence, and was known to be friendly with many eminent painters, including La Farge, Dewing, Chase, and others. His indication of Sargent demanded earnest consideration.

The hectic scramble of activities continued through Christmas week, when Sargent's days were filled by McCurdy's morning sittings, the labor of working up the full-length canvas keeping him in the studio until the afternoon gloom fell. Friday night he was at one of Stanford White's fortuitous dinners, at which we must assume he met members of the Committee from The Players. To mask the dinner's purpose, and give his talk freer flow, he had arranged for Beckwith to be present too. In the meantime Edwin Booth, who had appeared in London with Henry Irving and Ellen Terry and was aware of Sargent's recent activities in those quarters, heard rumor of the Committee's plans. He intimated to his daughter and, likewise, to the gentlemen of the Committee that, little as he liked posing, since this was "the only opportunity of having so distinguished an artist" paint him, he would yield to the annoyance. Word was sent to Sargent, and next day, smoking his after-lunch cigar, he came round to Booth's house in Gramercy Park.

The bare little park, possessed of few trees and a bedraggled fountain based on some unhappy European example, looked tarnished in winter, divested of its green. From the north, where he entered the square, he could glance across to the south where the actor's house stood, a cab waiting before the door. Inside number 16 Booth was dressed for traveling, his luggage already dispatched to the station. The message Sargent brought caused a sudden alteration in Booth's plans: he proposed that the work begin at once; he would pose the following morning and give every possible moment until Saturday. He would even pose Saturday morning and take the three o'clock train in the afternoon. He had his bags brought back from the station, and his apparent interest was a fine note on which to start. The two men stood warming themselves before the fire in the dim drawing room, the artist looking down into the actor's pasty face, where he saw the same dull opacity that characterized Irving's. Off stage, denied the advantage of make-up, he saw no hint of color, no expression to enliven rather apathetic features. Pleased as Booth was, voluntarily putting off his journey without notice, animation was missing, and an emotional exhaustion seemed to grip him. He was a strange, spiritless ghost, projecting a well-modulated voice, difficult to distinguish from the prevailing gloom of the room.

When that evening Thomas Bailey Aldrich called on Booth, he brought some rather succinct advice. As a friend of Mrs. Gardner, he remembered the ruckus her portrait created at the St. Botolph Club a year before, when its less pleasant qualities were taken as revelations of the model, rather than expression of the painter's contempt. He advised Booth that if he intended to sit to such a merciless judge of humanity he ought first to lock himself in a dark room and sandpaper his soul. Otherwise the pitiless painter would betray every secret sin. It is curious what impressions were current at a time when he was so much sought after for his work.

Next morning Sargent had a large canvas ready when Booth drove up from Gramercy Park, cloppering over the cobblestones to Twenty-third Street. He proved a limp model, as had been feared, expressionless and without color, "as though he'd been fished up from the bottom of the sea." A sense of personal tragedy haunted his face, making it unpleasant to look upon. Sargent tried searching for some pleasanter look, something that would not repel, an indication of soberness rather than morbidity, but abandoned the attempt after a few sittings. There was no help for it, and he set about painting Booth as he stood, limp, dull, his thumbs thrust into his pockets in a gesture expressive of futility and morbid musings. Quickly a separate sketch was made on a small canvas to question if the habitual expression of the man would pass muster with the Committee, as luckily it did. During frequent rests, he sat down at the piano and, with hope of some response from Booth, played the most spirited strains that occurred to him, the (Liszt) "Ràcòczy March." His stubby hands and short lean fingers pounded the keys energetically, and though Booth seemed pleased, once again pleasure failed to lighten his expression. Back on the model stand he was as stolid as ever.

By the second week in February the portrait of Booth was finished. No one among those who came to the studio to see it could entertain any doubt — it was Edwin Booth, standing as though in life. It was Booth as his friends knew him; not the great actor, but rather the man off stage, aging and pale, with great dark hollows for eyes, reflecting all the pathos of his life. The stalking of an insanity that took off his father and the shame of a brother who killed Lincoln were in every line of it; the haunting sadness of his life and the fears brought with it were clearly spelled out. It was impossible not to accept the picture with feelings identical to those one had for the man, for no difference could be seen, and the portrait was immediately hailed a great success, though Booth, seeing himself betrayed as Aldrich had jokingly prophesied, was not certain. The pose spoke of casual informality, a raggedness of posture that he was not certain exactly expressed himself. Had he struck that pose, he wondered, or had Sargent placed him in it? He asked, and Sargent pointed out that even as he spoke he stood exactly as in the portrait. It was true, then. Again, on stage in *Hamlet,* he noticed himself taking the same stance and realized that Sargent's powers of observation had produced more knowledge of his habits than he had himself.

As a background for the figure Sargent had painted the mantel in The Players, inscribing the picture with the paraphrase of Shakespeare's epitaph which Booth had placed over that fireplace in bronze letters:

GOOD FRENDE FOR FRENDSHIPS SAKE FORBEAR
TO UTTER WHAT IS GOSSIPT HERE
IN SOCIAL CHAT LEST UNAWARES
THY TONGE OFFEND THY FELLOW PLAIERS

a warning in gentle irony to those who viewed the portrait as well.

The Legion of Honor awarded to Sargent that summer was still undelivered. It was sent to England and then followed him to America, where the New York consulate was unable to locate him.

Officials were familiar with Beckwith, though, and forwarded notice of its arrival to him. With the simple anxiety to please that was among his most appealing qualities, Beckwith quietly picked up his friend's pin, and the next evening, at dinner, allowed Bertha the honor of putting it on his coat, presumably with the appropriate kiss on each cheek. After they had eaten in holiday mood, Sargent suggested they all go to Koster & Bial's music hall on Fourteenth Street, where the Spanish dancer he had seen in the Alleé des Etrangers, off the Champ-de-Mars, was appearing. She had joined the bill a week before, quickly rousing audiences to fever pitch. The preliminary acts were tedious to sit through, but at the very end, amidst tremendous applause, Carmencita appeared on stage. For a moment she appeared poised on one foot, then catching her silken scarf in the fingers of one hand, she whirled across the stage in fluttering grace. A little guitar orchestra sat behind her, led by the same piratical-looking guitarist who had been her only accompanist in Paris. Moving energetically about the stage, Carmencita showed what a superb creature she was, tall, full bosomed, slim at the waist, dancing with long bare arms to accentuate every movement of her body. The cheering audience were enthralled by the untamed quality of her performance, an appreciation shared by the crowds that every evening jammed into Koster & Bial's, willing to sit through a poor show to see her dance. Even Henry Adams, that most irritating and respectable friend of Henry James's, came to see Carmencita.

Before he reached home on Fifty-seventh Street that night, Beckwith bethought himself to give a party in his studio for which he would hire Carmencita. His wife's birthday was coming along in two weeks and could be made a splendid affair if Carmencita would dance. Several times during the next few days he called backstage at the music hall before he saw her, and when she consented he was extremely proud of his plan. On the evening of February 27 the Beckwiths, Frank and Lily Millet, Sargent, and a large party went to see *The Gondoliers* at the Park Theatre. Afterward, as though it was a sudden happy thought, Beckwith asked them all up to his studio, where they found supper laid out, and near midnight Carmencita arrived with the dozen men making up her troupe. She danced, and danced wildly, until nearly three in the morning, when, in a surprise gesture, Sargent took her home. Perhaps the entire party was no more a surprise than Sargent's leaving with this strange dancer at three in the morning.

Riding through the silent streets, lit with globes of flickering gas and echoing the clop of each hoof, he found Carmencita, notwithstanding the rigor of her two performances, something of a chatterbox. Her English was poor and heavily accented and she was pleased to slip into a French more attuned to her conversational needs. She was rather youthful, only twenty-two in fact, and had the soft smooth complexion of a young girl. Her dancing eyes had a tendency to ogle when she lowered her chin in a coy gesture that lacked subtlety, but he was able to see how well her features were formed, the large dark eyes with heavy lids, soft full lips, a straight nose a trifle heavy at the base, fine contours to her cheeks, and a beauty spot on the side of the chin. She would be fine to paint, he thought, and he recalled that he had intended to do a nude when he came to New York. She still talked volubly, pleased to give her criticisms of America, where she was constantly given *"eye-water*. The nasty stuff, I'm sure if you took a bath in it it would kill you. To drink it, pah!" She was more approving of the hot baths, which she found wonderful, the large tubs making them pleasant, though her sprinkling of Americanisms still caused trouble. "Every morning," she ventured, "I take a sokker." An admirable model, he thought, even then aware that the imaginary erotic life he had known through the last years was in danger of abandonment. His experience in the Parisian ateliers had taught him that a woman with considerably less figure than this dancer painted better, and was preferable. His judgment having abdicated, his professional perspicacity did not function either, and he was being swayed by considerations of an entirely different nature. When he told her what he had in mind she understood too well, consenting to pose as a dancer, in costume, a condition he found himself accepting as they reached Twenty-seventh Street and she disappeared up the brownstone steps, leaving him doused by the sweet odor of violets.

Soon Sargent was suggesting to Beckwith that they all go to Koster & Bail's again to see Carmencita. Though he had no love for "that villainous" music hall, Beckwith doubtless would have been willing to see Carmencita dance even if his curiosity had not been aroused by Sargent's overwhelming interest in her. An enterprising reporter from the *World*, newly purchased by the St. Louis newspaper tycoon, Joseph Pulitzer, learned through an interview with Carmencita that she was posing for Mr. Sargent, and the news was published to all New York.

When Carmencita began to pose, Sargent spent several hundred dollars on trinkets for her, selecting with his own fine taste thin gold bracelets that she could wear six at a time on her cameo-tone wrist. As the sittings progressed and their relationship grew more established, the painting of the picture became more difficult and expensive. She was a sullen and childish young woman when asked to hold still, and when not paid the desired attention had no scruples about walking off the platform, leaving her cavalier to fume. The flat Moorish upper lip, smiling so gracefully against the soft and sensual lower, easily thinned into a sarcastic smirk, the trick of raising her left eyebrow independently completing a mask of contempt. One moment radiantly angelic, her soft and beguiling expression bespeaking a warm heart and deep affection, in a twinkling she was a brazen wanton or a shrieking hellkite. There were violent scenes begetting little work at each of the many sittings that he wrung from the time that should have been given to others. Though not a child, she exhibited a child's indifference to the painter's task. Once, attempting to break a spell of sullenness, he began to eat his cigar. His pained expression caused more laughter than intended, as she taunted him to finish down to the ash. The stunt was too great a success, for it became a ritual, demanded whenever she entered the studio. And her love of jewelry was insatiable. No longer content to have presents given her, she demanded to choose them herself, selecting a five-tiered pearl choker, with twenty-four strands of pearls hanging pendant, and another double-tiered choker from which ten looped strands hung onto her bosom. One Sunday afternoon, as the interminable wrangle of their sittings proceeded, Beckwith called at the studio, and attempting to hold her attention while his friend worked, he asked her price for dancing at a party. Her reply was one hundred dollars, considerably more than he had paid her only a short time before.

For all the difficulty of its creation, the picture on the easel excited Beckwith's admiration. It was an aggressive concept, clearly typical of the dancer's verve and energy. She stood with hands on hips, as though just having stopped dancing, skirts still swirling about, and on her face the arch, boastful smile typical of her stage presence. If it did not do justice to the charm of the girl herself when she cared to be quiet and beautiful in her dark pensive way, it was characteristic of Carmencita the dancer, as everyone knew her. Sargent was painting her as he found her, confident of her powers, displaying herself before him with contempt, the attitude grown from the wholesale gifts of jewelry she extracted by employing her wiles. A quality of unwholesome flaunting and a too-evident sensuality in her intentions were apparent in the picture.

One wonders how much of the drama he witnessed was evident to Beckwith, who was more interested in the half-completed canvases ranged around the room. He knew some of the people, recognizing them at sight: Old Vanderbilt's son-in-law, Benjamin Kissam, was one. His sister-in-law, Mrs. Hamilton McKown Twombly, was sitting for her portrait in an elaborate Louis Quinze interior setting at her Fifth Avenue home. Blarney Charles McKim's introductions were responsible for these, as well as for the little *Beatrice Goelet*, two years old and evidently uneasy in her brocaded floor-length skirt, whose picture stood on another easel. Still another easel held a three-quarter-length of a shy-looking young woman holding an orchid. No wonder he found it necessary to work Sundays on the *Carmencita*, and remarkable that even that time was free. Every hour of daylight was crowded with sittings at the studio, a routine broken only by those at Mrs. Twombly's home. He was much in demand socially, and heavily obligated to accept the invitations tendered him — which required elaborate plotting for a man with a lady love. Often he was at the opera, sharing the boxes of his sitters, even managing to bring Beckwith to hear *Die Götterdämmerung*, and taking Bertha when Beckwith was unable to go.

In later years he admitted spending in excess of three thousand dollars for "bracelets and things" during the few months that Carmencita upset his habitual balance and restraint. The situation was immensely complicated at the time, not only by the fact that Carmencita danced nightly until midnight and spent her mornings giving dancing lessons to the daughters of the four hundred, nor merely because of his own frantic schedule in the studio and the various drawing rooms that demanded his presence, but because he was staying at the Mansons' and was aware that his activities would not bear too close an examination. The most immediate solution was to move out, which he soon did. It was not an unwarranted act, for Abbey was now staying with them, too, and excuses of consideration could be made to stick. He established himself at the Hotel Clarendon, at Fourth Avenue and Twentieth Street, where he had stayed two years before. It was a convenient location, near to the studio, close by Stanford White in Gramercy Park, and The Players, where he had privileges. The added assurance that his hours now went unnoticed made the move even more expedient. He was departing far from the habits of a solitary existence. This entire episode, so thoroughly out of keeping with his former behavior, indicated that the first flush of prosperity had gone to his head. It is curious to examine the reaction he had to the loss of so large a sum as the money he spent on Carmencita. His conscience was disturbed and he seems to have decided he would consider the whole thing an investment, to be recovered with the sale of the picture. He was being foolish and knew it, but was not of a nature to admit foolishness even to himself. He would have to sell the picture immediately to stand quits with that little ass Cupid, and he made frantic efforts to do so.

His first thought was of Mrs. Gardner. Since the time of her own portrait she had been pressing T. Jefferson Coolidge, who purchased the *El Jaleo* when it appeared in New York, to let her buy it from him. He agreed that one day he would sell, but no definite transaction was consummated. Might not Mrs. Gardner be interested in another equally arresting Spanish dance subject? With her desire to purchase the *El Jaleo* she seemed a perfect buyer for the *Carmencita*, if only he could arrange for her to see it. That was rendered difficult by the fact that Mrs. Gardner rarely came to New York, though recently, with the death of her father, she had been left a house on Fifth Avenue. Busy as he was, his time further occupied with the dancer herself, he could not see his way

clear to taking the picture to Boston purely on speculation, nor
could he do so without ruining appearances. Again, he could not
ask Mrs. Gardner to come down simply to see his painting, but —
and here was a thought — he could certainly ask her to come to
see a sensational dancer! Perhaps she would like to arrange a party
similar to the one Beckwith had given, inviting her own friends for
the performance. That way his stone would have a flock of pigeons
for its mark. He was about to propose it to her when, in curious
coincidence, she wrote that she would like to see Carmencita. He
hardly stopped to praise his luck, but answered immediately:

Dear Mrs Gardner
  You are up to the mark as is your wont! Only day before
yesterday I was sending you a message through Dixey to tell you
by hook or by crook, here or in Boston, you must see the Carmencita. I will be delighted to make the arrangements for you
and there will be no difficulty excepting the place. I should have
wished you to come and see her in my studio long before this if
there were any means of lighting it at night and if the floor were
tolerable, but it is not. Could you have her at your house in Fifth
Avenue? If so might I go and see if the floor or carpet would be
good, or whether there is a chandelier against which she would
have to break her head. It would have to be about twelve o'clock
at night after her performance.
  Just a line to say whether it can be at your house or whether
you had rather it were somewhere else.
                                            Yours sincerely
                                            John S. Sargent

Mrs. Gardner did not wish her house to be used, and the difficulty
he foresaw, "the place," became rather hard to settle. Probably at
this impasse Beckwith suggested the studio of his friend William
Chase, who taught with him at the Art Students' League. Chase
had met Sargent five years before in London and was on friendly
terms with Beckwith, who as early as 1880 had lent him the little
Cancale study presented to him by Sargent in Paris. With more
haste than grammar Sargent wrote:

My dear Chase
  Mrs Jack Gardner whom I daresay you know, writes me that
she must see the Carmencita and asks me to write her to dance

for her some day next week and she will come down from Boston, but my studio is impossible. The gas man tells me he cannot bring more light into the studio than the two little jets that are there.

Would you be willing to lend your studio for the purpose and be our host for Tuesday night or Thursday of next week? We would each of us invite some friends and Mrs Gardner would provide the Carmencita and I the supper and whatever other expenses there might be. I only venture to propose this as I think there is some chance of your enjoying the idea and because your studio would be such a stunning place. If you don't like the idea or if it would be a great inconvenience speak up and pardon my cheek! Send me an answer by bearer if you can, if not to the Clarendon soon, as I must write to Mrs Gardner.

Yours sincerely
John S. Sargent

Chase agreed, and the following went off to Mrs. Gardner:

Dear Mrs Gardner

It is all right for Tuesday April 1" (eleven thirty or twelve o'clock at night) at Chase's studio 10" Street, a capital big place. I will contribute wine, and supper, and the Carmencita with two guitars will cost you $150, which is her price *en ville*.

May Chase and I ask a few people? Chase says he only cares to invite two or three, and I dare say you and I would think of the same people, the Chapmans, Miss Dunham, Miss Lockwood — and I should like besides to ask Mrs Derby, Mrs Cleveland, the Laffans, Millets, Mansons, Wister.

Please let me know how many people you think of asking, from the point of view of sandwiches.

There was no having it in my studio, the gas man could not arrange any more light.

Yours sincerely
John S. Sargent

Considering that only two weeks before, when he visited the studio, Carmencita asked Beckwith one hundred dollars, which probably included her entire troupe of twelve guitars, and he thought that figure high, it becomes clear that this was a padded price Sargent quoted Mrs. Gardner. It is not unlikely that without being aware of it she underwrote supper as well. But she accepted

Carmencita's fee without demur, replying to his letter with one of her own inviting him to dinner at Delmonico's and requesting that he forward the notes of invitation that she enclosed. The most important matter was still to be settled though, and in reply he got it off as inconspicuously as he could in the last line: she must see the painting of Carmencita, the reason he had gone to all this trouble!

Dear Mrs Gardner

I accept with pleasure for Delmonico's and have forwarded your notes. I will ask *very few people* and must keep extremely dark about it, as hundreds would want to come. You must come to the studio on Tuesday at any time, and see the figure I am doing of the bewilderingly superb creature.

In haste.

Yours sincerely
John S. Sargent

Despite the pains he took to arrange it, the evening did not go well from the start. He felt he had a select company, but should have realized that bringing together people from Boston and New York was not wise, nor did the sprinkling of artists and Chase's students add to the homogeneity of a party that included the President's wife. The guests were largely unknown to one another, and proved stiffish company. Carmencita herself, when she arrived from Koster & Bial's late in the evening, was wearing her hair in a new frizzled manner which had to be changed lest it make her look unlike her portrait. He could not allow her to ruin the association of individual and painting that he was so carefully building. Taking her aside, he smoothed the hair with a wet brush, even wiping off some of the overgenerous layer of cosmetics she wore. Though necessary, this was carrying the prerogatives of friendship too far, nor was Carmencita one to be easily reasoned with. By the time she began to dance, every guest could see that she was in a fierce temper, glaring at him where he had gone to sit on the floor half hidden in the deep shadows. Before she had gone many steps her humor changed, however, and she threw him the rose from behind her ear, which he picked up from the floor and placed in his button-hole, to ratify a peace certain to be short-lived.

To make the impact on Mrs. Gardner as great as possible, Chase's long high studio was arranged similarly to the scene portrayed in *El Jaleo*. The heavy-framed paintings lining the walls, mixed with shields and parasols, and ferns in copper pots, and fans and drums and porcelainware, were all lost in the darkness, as a light played on Carmencita from below, lending emphasis to her serpentine movements and a dramatic quality to the spectacle. By turns she strutted and writhed to the insistent accompaniment of the shadowy guitarists sitting behind, presenting to the dim recesses of the studio a brilliant display of color and movement, unfortunately appreciated only by the artists present. Mrs. Gardner was not a woman to appreciate another woman's beauty, especially one younger, nor could she fail to see the currents passing between dancer and painter. The breath-taking spectacle was not sufficient to melt the mood of frigidity gripping the party, and there were no inquiries about the picture.

Sargent had erred in his strategy by allowing the picture to remain incomplete at the time of the party. He was counting on its dynamic quality to override reservations created by its still-sketchy state, believing that the wonderfully arrested motion of the dancer, so well contained within the compositional limits of the frame, was an element strong enough to overcome other objections. What he had not properly assessed was the effect of age that his picture gave to a woman still notably fresh and blooming. Suffering from the small amount of work that had gone into it, the portrait seemed to be of a middle-aged woman. The head was by no means finished, the hands only indicated in the first sketching, but the effect was decidedly unflattering to the dancer. She herself no doubt made the matter clear to him, his guests at the party making their own comparisons with the youthful and vivacious dancer, by no means so lacking in the flush and bloom of youth as his picture indicated. The only positive result of the evening was that Chase expressed a wish to paint Carmencita too.

Soon after, Sargent gave another party at Chase's studio, when once again Carmencita danced. This one, too, was held through a desire to bring people who might care for his picture into closer contact with the dancer who had inspired it. We have no list of the guests this time. At the end of the evening he asked Carmencita to sing, drawing on knowledge gained in private. Whatever she might do when alone with him, she had no intention of singing in public and made that adequately clear in a few words. She was not a singer, she said, and adamantly refused until taunted by his asking what sort of Spaniard she was who could not sing and knew no songs of Spain. Oddly, when at length she obliged, the soft chanting of the songs left a deeper impression than her dance. She had little voice; it was the songs themselves, the quiet manner of their presentation, so different from her dancing, that impressed the guests. The results of this party were the same, though, and when Sargent returned to England the picture went with him.

By the early part of May this attachment begun in February had run its course. The exact quality of relationship existing between two such opposed personalities can only be guessed at. Carmencita's ability to extract so much from Sargent in the way of valuable gifts serves to indicate the scheming venality of the dancer and is frank admission that he was not functioning with any sort of logic. Carmencita doubtless appealed to a particular facet of his taste, she was "strange, weird, fantastic," those words he employed so frequently because they were applicable to qualities that delighted him. His individual predilections often ran to the exotic; the bizarre quality of relationship that could have existed between his superrefined nature and her more elementary character may itself have pleased him. But it could not have been long before his natural fastidiousness, the other half of his taste, revived. His nature was not attuned to feminine requirements. All his life he was unable to express emotion or give vent to the depth of feeling that frequently arose and threatened to choke him. He urgently wanted affection, yet shrank from it when it came his way, experiencing an embarrassment greater than the accompanying gratification. Not incapable of an erotic mood, finding particular stimulation with this dancer, he was incapable of giving it vocal expression, and in this she was well suited to his needs, for she was not demanding of the delicacies another might have missed, in her primitive way knowing all that he could not give voice to. Unequipped to deal with a complicated nature, she was pleased with her conquest, and while completely absorbed in self, left him at an ease he had never before known with women. For a short while it was a mutually satisfactory arrangement, from which both derived benefit. But in time he could not help becoming critical of her gypsy habits, and her tasteless, overdecorated manner of dress. It was not a relationship conceived to last long, and soon it ceased to exist because of the very elements that had made it successful.

Leaving the portrait still incomplete, Carmencita consented to pose for Chase. He prepared a large canvas, expecting to compete with Sargent. In no time she discovered that this artist, who had a rapidly expanding family, would give her none of the presents to which she was accustomed, and probably after no more than one or two sessions she failed to return. Unwilling to abandon what he had begun, Chase went to Sarony the photographer, on Union Square, where he selected several photographs of Carmencita at ten cents each, and painted his picture from them. A trifle hurt by the way he had been treated, he allowed himself one little jab in allusion to Sargent — at the bottom of his picture, beside a bouquet of flowers, he painted a bracelet rolling toward the dancer, as though in tribute from an admirer.

Life Was Good

A UGUSTUS ST.-GAUDENS and his brother Louis were
working on the ornamentation of the Boston Public Library, the largest undertaking to date of the firm of
McKim, Mead and White. As envisioned by the architects, the
building required the casting of Renaissance fittings and fixtures,
work only a sculptor could do. Through Stanford White and
Charles McKim, Abbey, Sargent, and St.-Gaudens were meeting
often.

Sargent admired St.-Gaudens for his gruff and breezy manner
and the coarse wit he used to embellish his conversation. His
personality was pronounced for what it was, he made no bones
about it, letting himself go in caricatures of himself and friends
that were clever bits of observation. For his part the sculptor was
much amused by Sargent's earnest efforts to get him to undertake
work based on unlovely models raised to a status of beauty only
by being well done. He felt it good for the artist, whether painter
or sculptor, not always to work with beauties, and comically urged
St.-Gaudens forward by reference to Booth: "Don't be afraid.
I've got a sitter down in my studio who looks as though he's been
fished up from the bottom of the sea." In return for a plaque of
Violet that St.-Gaudens was doing, Sargent invited Mrs. St.-Gau-
dens to bring her son Homer down to the Twenty-third Street
studio to be painted. The ten-year-old boy found posing only just
bearable, obliging his mother to read to him from the adventure

books of Louis Stevenson. The St.-Gaudenses were particularly fond of this only child, dressing him in outfits of great elegance, with lace collars or flowing cravats, of the sort he wore for his sittings. His long black-stockinged legs were a particular delight to paint, and were done with superb draftsmanship, while the head was worked with a fat and juicy pigment, fused into a magnificent complexion, subtly modeled, the form flowing back and forth through shadow and reflection a single unbroken mass. Undertaken as a fast portrait, the work is an amazing tour de force. It has purity of color rarely seen, a dark harmony of umber and navy that glow against each other as perfect foil to the flesh. One day, to her surprise, Mrs. St.-Gaudens saw that, out of sudden impulse, she had been rapidly painted into the picture as she sat reading, a warm human touch offsetting her son's delicately conveyed expression of repressed boredom.

By this time it was becoming evident to even the least discerning that something was in the wind. Abbey, though recently married and eager to be off on his wedding trip to Italy, was marking time in New York, McKim ran down from Boston with more regularity than was demanded by purely personal considerations, and all of them were going from one studio to another, gathering regularly at St.-Gaudens' for long discussions of an undivulged nature. Something was being negotiated with great earnestness, ringed with secrecy. McKim, Mead and White, that firm of mountainous energy, never still, always filled with new ideas, wanted something done. They were completing their new Library in Boston, which if not a profitable undertaking, was exceedingly rich in point of prestige. They were intent on adorning it by every means possible. Certainly it ought to have murals!

In the fall of the previous year, while in England, White had spoken of the possibility to Abbey and Sargent, pointedly admonishing them that the project still required a most solicitous nurturing. There was no certainty that it could be arranged, but he urged that they would be helping the plan, if they were interested, by being in America and near at hand when the question was raised with the Trustees. In the early winter White returned to New York, followed shortly by Sargent. Abbey, who arrived in January, was the last conspirator to come on the scene. White and

McKim were aware that they could not expect these two painters to tarry long in New York without employment. In their long midnight discussion at Fladbury the two had threshed that out themselves, and the architects were careful to arrange what they could: the little hotel mural for Abbey, and a succession of portraits for Sargent, which he managed to increase by additions of his own. That he was able to do so was largely good fortune, for he committed himself to remain on the spot until the mural scheme came to fruition or failed. The great difficulty lay in the fact that no money was immediately available, the building so far exceeding original appropriations that none could be asked from the city or the Trustees. It was thus necessary to find assurances of private funds before bringing the plan before the Trustees. Conscious of the success Sargent had made of his first Boston visit, of his accumulated fame, and of his family connections with that city, the architects felt it imperative to have him associated with their venture. Perhaps the earnestness of Blarney Charlie McKim, plus the willingness of these eminent men to undertake the work, would elicit the necessary assurances of funds. While Sargent and Abbey labored in New York, McKim canvassed Boston with their names. To associate the two further with the enterprise, he proposed a reception to introduce them to the people he found interested, and others who had already made contributions to the building.

Rather hastily, then, the firm had invitations printed and sent to a list of leading Bostonians drawn up by McKim, inviting them, in the name of the firm, to attend a reception at the Library. The date set was April 25, 1890, and the time 10:00 P.M. When the Mayor of Boston received his invitation, it appeared for a moment that the reception would be called off. To whom, asked his honor, does the Library belong? Has it been constructed out of public funds or is it the property of the architects, and theirs to give parties in? Finally, in explanation, a formula was contrived to fit the situation: as the reception was planned for ten in the evening, past normal business hours, the architects were not encroaching on the proper uses of the still-unfinished building. They might, therefore, as a mark of esteem, make use of the building for their reception. With that prodigious bit of juggling out of the way, proper Boston arrived to meet the two painters from New York, and the Boston Tea Party was under way. It was an apparent success, for within a week McKim had assurances of almost forty-five thousand dollars with which to do his murals. Final decisions had to be made before presenting the scheme to the Trustees, and a meeting was arranged at The Players to bring Abbey, Sargent, and St.-Gaudens together with McKim, Mead, and White.

The club was a convenient place to meet, lying in the rough geographic center of all their separate activities, and for Sargent it was a pleasant place as well. Two of his portraits hung there now, the picture of Booth's second lead, Lawrence Barrett, commissioned by Booth, joining the other on the wall of the sitting room. One night before the proposed meeting Beckwith was invited to the Mansons', where not a word was said about the murals nor the meeting. At seven the following evening Sargent and the others met over dinner. The initial plan of the Library called for dividing the books into separate collections grouped according to subject. Abbey, who had carefully examined the building while in Boston, was chiefly interested in the Shakespeare Collection, presenting as it did wonderful opportunities for him to work against the English countryside he loved. Sargent, at that date still interested in all things Spanish, dancers and the like, expressed an interest in trying something from Spanish literature. As they spun out their plans after dinner, Abbey, overcome with his own enthusiasm, seized the wrapping-paper that plans and photos had come in to sketch out allegorical figures. The party was amazed at the extent of his enthusiasm, voiced in an unsuppressed Philadelphia twang, as he drew and talked, explaining his scratches in words and his words in line, as though they were one joint function. The next day he did an oil sketch in his Sixteenth Street studio, which McKim went to see. The whole thing was developing so favorably that McKim sat down that same week to write a long account to the Trustees. He proposed that the group all return to Boston, make their arrangements with the Trustees, and begin the work.

The following Wednesday, McKim hired a private railway car to carry them up from New York, then found Sargent less than eager to go along and be exposed a second time to the embarrassment of crowds and a possibly ridiculous attempt at a speech. Living precariously as he did in the role he had imagined for himself, anything that might publicly break the image was an abhorrence to him. This was a hard nut for McKim to crack, for he was depending on the effect of Sargent's presence. Saying that it would be a "black eye" if any of the New York contingent did not arrive, he persuaded the artist to make the trip.

After the dinner it fell to Sargent and Abbey, as key figures, to orate to the Trustees of their ideas and intentions. One can hardly think of anything more difficult for Sargent to do. In later years, on the few occasions that he was ever seen to rise to his feet, he hung onto the edge of the table rather spectacularly, and with frantic gasps for air, finally subsided into his chair amidst roars of laughter and applause without having said a word. He seems to have done better at this juncture, when so much was at stake, though we can assume that what he managed to say was brief and that the effort wounded his vanity to the extent of chilling him to further attempts.

At his suggestion it was agreed that Puvis de Chavannes and Whistler would be invited to join in the decorations. Sargent himself would undertake the large vaulted corridor at the head of the principal staircase, a location that appealed to him because it was completely dissociated by its position from the efforts of others, leaving him solely responsible for the effect achieved. Abbey would decorate the distribution room, on the floor below Sargent's corridor. The weight of Sargent's reputation was a large factor in bringing about the realization of the murals, and the naming of Chavannes and Whistler, both virtually unknown in America at that period, stands as ample indication of his influence. Still, his own reputation for modernism seems to have troubled the Trustees. The murals might be *impressionistic* or *eccentric*. In a letter to McKim, written aboard ship on his way to Italy, Abbey tried to calm such apprehensions:

I went into his studio a day or two before I sailed and saw stacks of sketches of nude people — Saints, I dare say, most of them, although from my cursory observation of them they seemed a bit earthy. You will surely get a great thing from him, he can do *anything*, and don't know himself what he can do. He is latent with all manner of possibilities, and the Boston people need not be afraid that he will be eccentric or impressionistic, or anything that is not perfectly serious and non-experimental when it comes to work of this kind.

Abbey's intention in writing was certainly to quiet any doubt McKim might feel, but the tone of his letter implies that he was at the same time bolstering his own hopes. He did not realize that Sargent was incapable of doing anything commonplace when presented with an opportunity of this magnitude, and the nonexperimental work that Abbey guaranteed was not at all in his mind.

Back in New York Sargent was still knee deep in portraits, completing those Beckwith had seen in his studio and replacing them with others. Joseph Jefferson, who had crossed the ocean many years before with Dr. Sargent, was at this time appearing in his famous role of Dr. Pangloss, and after seeing him at The Players, Sargent made three characteristic and whimsical sketches of him, once again successfully blending the personality of the actor with the part played He was doing so much painting that he was working more rapidly, feeling completely free to handle the paint in whatever manner seemed most natural. In the haste of these crammed weeks his style was developing into a new richness, and the last vestiges of Carolus-Duran fell away. Painting became an even more natural function, the results fuller in texture, simpler and broader in concept. If one must choose a point at which the mature artist definitely emerges, to remain consistent to the end, it is during these months, when working under pressure he allowed his natural bent and his accumulated experience a free rein.

Particularly in the portrait of the little St.-Gaudens boy, or the *Lawrence Barrett*, we find a new Sargent. These are the courageous products of a man with complete control of his means, who needs give it no thought, since the painting is done by instinct rather than by contrivance. More than any other portrait of the period the picture of young Homer St.-Gaudens is a triumph of visual painting, the eye of the painter raising all it encompassed to new heights of richness and poetry. As the little boy sat in the cool studio on Twenty-third Street, it is impossible that there existed anything like the wonderful contrast of his cheek against the back of the chair. The flush of complexion, the tone of the hands, would not bear comparison with the actual cheek and hands, no doubt cooler and grayer than he saw them. One doubts that the blues were actually so blue, the background so limitless and warm, the flowing cravat so spanking white. Sargent translated the world into a better realm, carried away by the innate poetry of his vision, the poetry that created *Carnation Lily, Lily Rose,* produced by the functioning of eyes that as they grew older saw more beauty everywhere, a beauty that to a large extent they themselves created. The man himself continued to paint objectively, as he had from the first, for his artistry was a deeper matter than any crossing his conscious mind.

As the spring ripened, New York began to empty out, his friends one by one leaving for their homes on Long Island and at Newport, St.-Gaudens for his studio in Cornish, New Hampshire. Only Stanford White remained in town, bustling about in that distracted fashion of his with preparations for the opening of his Madison Square Garden, June 16. It would be a tremendous event, and he had gone so far as to import ballet costumes from Europe, which at the instigation of patriotic American groups were seized in customs at the pier. Whenever he came into the studio, which he did frequently now, he was the grand panjandrum, arriving as though shot from a cannon, expressing absurd opinions, and leaving as suddenly as he had come. It was best to stand back and let the tornado blow itself out. One thing that he mentioned was curious though: he had wanted to hire Carmencita for the opening, offering her two hundred fifty dollars a week to dance with the ballet, and she refused, rudely replying that she had many such offers. Bunker was still in town, for New York was his headquarters now, and he was preparing to be married, meanwhile sketching out murals for the Whitelaw Reid house that was being built on Madison Avenue by McKim, Mead and White. This commission was no doubt Sargent's handiwork, and the best wedding present any young painter ever received. In August, Sargent gave up his studio. News of the mural commissions had stirred his admirers in Boston, and a flurry of requests reached him in New York. America was a bewildering place; money flowed so freely, he had never seen anything like it. Of course, he wished he was more certain how much money all these sums represented, for he was translating all the dollars everyone spoke of into pounds and the pounds had to be translated again into francs so that he could gauge their worth. The computations were becoming more and more complicated, and people must have wondered why he stared vacantly at the checks he held in his hands.

First there was an invitation to join Violet, at Nahant, where the Fairchilds had a house for the summer. He readily accepted in the hope of a short break in his work. It was a lovely frame house, with rooms that wandered about the edge of the cliffs on several levels. One room, lower than the rest and virtually over the edge of the cliff into which it was set, became his, and there he kept all the paraphernalia of an artist. The neighbor right across the beach was a new congressman from Massachusetts, Henry Cabot Lodge, who was an intimate not only of Charles Fairchild but also of Henry James and Henry Adams. Through mutual friends and accidental proximity, a portrait was obvious, so Sargent walked daily over the sands to the Lodges' place, where he painted the representative who was soon to be senator. The Fairchilds left him to do as he pleased and he was never idle. There was never a wasted moment nor a quiet one, and when for darkness or visual fatigue he stopped painting for the moment, it was only to throw himself down at the piano and bang away with all his might. He experimented with watercolors on the cliffs, and brought Sally Fairchild down there to paint her wrapped in a blue veil against the shadow of the stone. He had a passion for magenta that had grown on him ever since the portrait of Dr. Pozzi, and he taught them all to think it beautiful, though they were never sure why. So long as he was there they were all caught up in the breathless whirl of his presence.

By September he began a new campaign in Boston, launching it with members of the Loring family, and painting Mrs. Hemenway, a lustrous-eyed, dark-haired woman, who somewhat resembled Lily Millet. In gentle reference to her pregnancy, and almost to Mrs. Millet as well, he painted a water lily in her hands, adding a charming note of color and a delicacy of sentiment few would have suspected in him. He had as a sitter, in Salem, the 86-year-old George Peabody, whose massive determination shone through a body quivering with age, and whose eye, though slightly puzzled, spoke frankly. It is remarkable the extent to which all the portrayals of this time are individualized, revealing not a note of formularization, no sign of haste, but a complete acceptance of the person before him as an individual, a new problem, to be wrestled with separately. Throughout his life it seems as though it was in such moments when it was necessary to be done quickly, and the very pressure of all he was doing distracted him, that his keenest bits of personality analysis were done, as though they came forth not through any conscious desire but because he was not preventing them. In Worcester he did a full-length of Mrs. Edward Livingston Davis standing with her white-clad sailor-suited son, and here he also did a quick portrait of Miss Katherine Pratt.

Later in October he was out at West Medford, where he did a somewhat complicated composition of Mrs. Peter Chardon Brooks, seated among columns and hangings, draped and holding a small figure of Mercury. The example of so many works by Copley seen throughout New England had not been missed, and this is the first example in which he employed the standard devices of column and drape so long and intimately connected with portraiture. He also did a bust of Peter Chardon Brooks, son of the man of the same name who had done business with his family's shipping firm in the years before its failure. This he executed with a return to the impressionistic touch that he had not employed since leaving England, feeling it less suited to formal portraiture; painting with a running stroke, smoothing the impasto of the forehead into a highlight with his fingers. He did a large picture of the Brooks daughter as well, and to fill the time between sittings on these three portraits he tried his hand at landscape, dashing off in one afternoon a quick sketch of the fields outside their home.

The last act in the life of young Bunker was about to unfold at that point, and on October 2 Sargent attended the young man's wedding, at the Emmanuel Church in Boston. It was in keeping with Bunker's own breezy ways, an informal sort of affair, where the guests had been invited by word of mouth. Mrs. Gardner shortly left Boston, and Bunker's letters followed her: "Mr. Sargent, who is still with us, and whom I am expecting to see shortly, is always a well of joy and a rock of strength . . . He . . . has done a hundred portraits since you went away — and grows daily in strength and power and all manner of good qualities and likewise

in the esteem of D.B. in his corner with the other mice. . . . " Less
than three months later this charming, talented young man, only
twenty-nine years old, was tragically dead of pneumonia.

Though all this time Sargent was moving about continually and
doing "a hundred portraits," he was turning over in his mind the
structure of the Library vault he would decorate, using his frequent visits to Boston to decide what sort of treatment and what
exact subject matter would best suit the space. He found that the
crepuscular vaulted pile of masonry he had selected in that Renaissance structure had a distinctly medieval mood. It was a high, gray,
and solemn space, almost oppressive in its stillness, having none of
the serene beauty that he associated with the true Renaissance
buildings he had known from earliest youth. The mood of the
place went further back into an era untouched by the modern
tastes of the Renaissance. These were the dark and damp surroundings in which the ancient church had been born out of the chaos
of tottering empires. It was Biblical! And there was a splendid
subject. Abbey's choice of Shakespeare was fitting to a Library,
but the Bible was a greater classic, telling a story touching far more
of humanity, having greater influence than any purely literary
work. It was essentially the story of man himself, the diary of his
increasing understanding when faced by the perplexities of a uni-
verse containing unknown forces that he felt influencing his destiny. It was the story of man's growth from belief in idols to the
love of a single omnipotent God. Such a subject presented infinite
possibilities. Michelangelo had chosen incidents from the Bible,
spelling them out as stories across the great ceiling of the Sistine
Chapel: here the creation, there the flood, all around them the
prophets. His three-dimensional forms tore into the ceiling and
walls creating a turbulent new world tottering from the top of the
chapel. Michelangelo, entranced with his own vision, forgot that
his mission was to decorate walls and ceiling — he completely an-
nihilated them. The possibility that a like subject could be treated
by other means in this much smaller room was immediately apparent to Sargent. A mural must decorate. It must lie flat and add
something to a space, without becoming distracting to those who
would enter the apartment with their own thoughts and purposes.
Could the message of the Bible be transmitted without telling a

multitude of stories in anecdotal manner, the spaces be filled instead with symbols that remained unrelated except in the larger framework of religious thought itself? Was it not possible by this symbolism, and a careful weaving of his decoration, to contain all that need be said in a well-mannered design that would not transfix the poor innccent who cared to pass through the room without taking notice of the emblazoning of the walls? There was a challenge to occupy him as portraiture never had, for no portrait entailed the complexity of thought and design that he would throw across this vault and four walls. The vastness, the scope of the undertaking seized his imagination.

This was the most extended of his early visits to America, lasting altogether nearly a year. He had begun to feel at home in the New World, where he found himself more wanted than had ever been the case in Europe. The satisfaction that came of this cannot be stressed too much, for events of the preceding years in Europe had wounded him to an extent from which he never fully recovered. Still, at the end of his stay, without apparent thought, simply out of naturalness, he picked himself up to return abroad. Looking back it appears that he was making a definite choice in favor of Europe when, with continuous employment in America, he could very well have settled down to execute his murals. Yet it was the only natural thing to do; his family awaited him, he had always intended to return, delighted only that success obliged him to tarry so long on the foreign shore. Europe was the atmosphere in which he worked, the site of all he knew; he went back to it as naturally and thoughtlessly as a child returns to its mother.

With this second batch of portraits he continued to add to his rolls the leading families of America, and for years to come the golden ladies, all tiaras and influence, would think of him alone when they thought of portraiture. It was strange that they would, for he betrayed them unmercifully, giving lasting expression to his own contempt for their useless lives and wasted mentalities, but doing so in such brilliant style that when he had finished they were pleased to find themselves more interesting than they had thought. He was able to outperform other European visitors completely. His unerring grasp of personal peculiarity, his portrayal of fundamental character traits, was hailed for the smartness of appearance he was able to give his work and the completeness of the realistic illusion he contrived to achieve by a combination of fine values and impressionistic color.

Not all his portraits were unflattering. In those instances where he felt sympathetic toward his model we are immediately aware of the fact. These, however, are exceptions among the cold and incisive estimates to which he was more accustomed. His reactions, if not warm, are yet broadly human, responsive to many sorts of mood and character. The youthful awkwardness, altogether sympathetic, of the young lady with the orchid, the sarcastic hauteur, the sophistication, of Mrs. Manson, are cases in point. He did not, like Goya, force all his sitters into one contemptuous pattern or attempt to fit them into *any* mold, but portrayed them honestly as they were, with a warmth of understanding or a harsh depiction of their failings that made for truth in the work. Above all, it was *truth* that he sought. And it was truth, the same truth their ancestors had expected of Copley, that his sitters desired from him, swallowing new ideas of composition, impressionistic color, modernistic brushing, and all the newfangled equipment of this most advanced European painter, because they saw truth more precisely grasped in the final product. Other European painters — even Carolus-Duran — would profit by his example and journey to America to make short tours and return to Europe with their pockets lined. The industriousness of their short visits did them credit, but none ever rivaled Sargent, nor achieved a position even approaching the supreme dominance he maintained. None had his knowledge of Americans, none supplied the authentically American, Copley-like feeling of Sargent, and plainly none was his equal as an executant.

His success was gratifying after the failure he had known before his first American trip. The continued good fortune of this second American venture solidified his position until it became impregnable. After the years when he had to ask people to sit for him, there was tremendous satisfaction in having them come to him and pay large sums for the privilege. There was a feeling akin to revenge in the sweet confirmation of his talents and ambitions that America provided. Even more gratifying were the murals, which he saw leading to wider fields in which to try himself. Since the time, twelve years before, when he worked with Beckwith on Carolus' large ceiling for the Luxembourg Palace, he had wanted work of that sort for his own — large compositions of an imaginative nature in which he might express substantial ideas without being dependent on a model. Portraiture was an exacting craft with much to recommend it; there was a pleasure in doing a fine portrait that never ceased to excite him. But portraits were things he knew he could do, and he wanted further challenge.

Sargent was still filled with the ambition to be all that Carolus was, to have the public commissions Carolus executed, to lead the life he led, to win the esteem, the position his master had in those days when as a young aspirant he was invited to Carolus' own studio and saw the treasures and admiring throngs crowding it. One by one all his desires had been realized: first, the general esteem his work was granted in France; then acceptance and the purchase of his *Carnation Lily, Lily Rose* in England. The financial success that had so long eluded him was finally found in America, and now he had murals too. Everything he had sought and longed for was coming to him, it seemed he had all the things he admired when they belonged to Carolus. Life was good, it had treated him well, and best of all, with all his achievement, he was still only thirty-four.

The Siege of London

IT WAS typical that Sargent should throw himself into his mural project with all his enthusiasm. Leaving New York, he sailed direct to Marseilles with his sister Violet, there to be joined by his mother and his sister Emily. The Holy Lands of the Bible were his goal, to steep himself in the lands, the places, and the ancient cultures that gave rise to the book he would interpret. His first stop would be Egypt, land of the Pharaohs, for he would first tackle the origin of monotheism, and the struggle of the first monotheistic people against the multiple gods of their oppressors. He wanted to study the Egyptian arts of decoration, and the Assyrian, which came later, perhaps as an afterthought. When he took ship at Marseilles he planned to investigate Egyptian ornamentation and symbolism so that he could make accurate use of it, but more important, though no doubt this was not planned, it would be a stylistic source too, for in his first large lunette he synthesized ancient arts with his own modern manner. It was a startling idea, and fortunately the Trustees were not yet aware of it. This was before the era when it was considered natural to study primitive expression for style, and the combination of these forms into modern work was still unheard of. Probably it was only when he saw the strange markings and configurations of Egyptian monuments that any idea that it *could* be done settled into his conscious mind, the ancient art making an immediate appeal and the attempt to use it intriguing him.

Sargent was not the first European to travel in the East, nor was he the first artist to seek inspiration in the cultures of the desert. Many had done so before him. His very choice of Egypt as a primary goal would seem to reflect the preoccupation with that land present in contemporary French literature. He was, however, the first Western painter to see the desert cultures with eyes not blinded by the conventions of Western art, not forcing them to conform with his own training, but realizing that they were unique. He was the first to realize that he was seeing something that could be made use of, not as subject matter, but as a refinement in Western methods and a new reservoir of design and style. The Japanese print had invaded Europe in the early sixties, soon becoming a new religion in the arts, a tremendous influence on painting, especially in the French and French-dominated schools. With the passage of years its fundamentals were completely assimilated, its influence no longer a separate strand, so thinly was it spread through all the fabric. It had provided a much-needed enlivenment, and new ideas drawn from it became firmly established within the larger endemic culture of France. Until the time, thirty years later, when Sargent had his eyes opened to the overwhelming potential of the ancient Egyptian arts, there was no new comparable stylistic source carried into European thought. In a sense he was the discoverer of a new culture, which, like the Japanese, had been known but ignored. He was the first to realize its potential and that it might have a profound influence, especially in the field of mural work, where, in a form that was consistent with its own flatness, it could be employed to enrich the capacities of European design.

Political conditions were tense in Egypt before Christmas, when the four travelers arrived in Alexandria. Sargent himself had no idea of conditions in the country — the restive natives, the dervish hordes, the death of General Gordon, the local governments straining to maintain order, were all beyond his view. His immunity stemmed from a deep-seated ignorance of political systems; he read few newspapers, comment passed over him unawares. His splendid isolation from the grim realities of the situation allowed him to apply himself with wonderful concentration and with a bravery of which he was unaware.

First he intended to make studies of Egyptian types, perhaps heads and costumes, that might be welded to figures when his composition was further along. He had made only a few such studies when the magnificence of the ancient arts themselves struck him, and any thought of expressing the Israelite struggle in terms of contemporary convention was quickly abandoned. In Cairo he ran across Mrs. Farquharson and her stepson, living in a home of Egyptian style. All together, then, this band of six — the Sargents and the Farquharsons — boarded a river steamer sailing up the Nile, and visited the ancient sites then known and excavated. Sargent drew everything, from architectural detailings to statues and hieroglyphics. This only whetted his appetite, and he started inland over the desert in areas not assuredly safe, with a native dragoman guiding him to Fayoum. In the desert he came on the rigid art of a vanished people, which confirmed his taste for pure Egyptian forms unadorned with Westernisms. An experience he never forgot was the sight of ancient mummy cases being lifted out of tombs, colors brilliant and clear, accompanied by the slight acrid odor that characterized them. Then he saw the colors fade before his eyes, their clarity passing in a few minutes into dusty tones and taking on the look of ages. In fifteen minutes the colors were gone. He added this sight to the piece of porphyry in the Via Tornabuoni as one of the two most beautiful things he had ever seen.

The thought of being in places where ancient lives were lived, where people had slaved over huge monuments or had sought answers to the secrets of incomprehensible nature — all the fierce power and vigor of this vanished civilization — pressed deeply into his consciousness. The conviction grew that the awesome story of the Bible could only be expressed in terms of the grotesque forms associated with the Biblical era in Egypt. The character of the terrible Egyptian gods could never be expressed except as they were visualized by their charges; the sheer terror of them could never be summoned up better than by seeing the Pharaoh of the upper kingdom advancing upon the Israelites, under the aegis of his protecting deity. Sargent came away with packages of sketches bundled up with cord; studies of statues, paintings, weapons, gods, helmets, decorative apparel; studies of such minutiae as wing tips in the ancient manner, the way a Pharaoh grasped the hair of a fallen foe before decapitating him, and the weapon he used to do so.

His myriad impressions would later be sifted and sorted in the quiet of London; meanwhile he would store up more material for the next step in his scheme. For this purpose, in April, he and his mother and sisters crossed the Mediterranean to Greece. There, seeking works of ancient art expressive of the gods of that land, he set out for Olympus and Delphi. His activity was intense. At four in the morning he was in the saddle, scouring the Greek valleys, carpeted with wild flowers, where ancient monuments were revealed betwixt the new blooms. However, his purpose in Greece quickly became more purely pictorial, as he soon realized that Greek deities of the classic periods would have little place in his scheme for expressing continuity of Biblical thought. He did some watercolors of the ruined Acropolis, produced many sketches, but found less material useful to his purpose than in Egypt.

From Athens, still with his mother and sisters, he crossed to Constantinople, seat of the Byzantine Church and of the empire that once bestrode the center of the world. He found only disappointment in the fact that the medieval forms he sought were not well revealed on the site of their principal development, for he remembered wonders at Ravenna and had hoped to see them surpassed.

By June he returned alone to London, then recrossed to France, where his sister Violet was about to be married. While in Paris for the ceremony, fortune caught up with him again, in the form of a commission for a portrait of Thomas B. Reed, the Republican Speaker of the House of Representatives. The portrait seems to have been suggested by Henry Cabot Lodge, and was brought to fruition by the fact both men were then in Paris. The money, once again, seems to have been supplied by Charles Fairchild. Sargent borrowed a studio from Albert de Belleroche and got to work on what proved to be a difficult task. Reed's huge bulging figure was not acutely pictorial. For all his fluent language and remarkable urbanity, he seemed more an image of an overstuffed porker than a Speaker of the House. As day by day he stood in the studio, the artist fancied he saw the red apple protruding from his lips. Sargent was aware that he was by no means doing justice to the personality of his sitter. The result was later summarized in a letter he wrote Mr. Fairchild: "I found him awfully hard and this is the result of a second attempt different in view and character from the first, which I destroyed. His exterior does not somehow correspond with his spirit and what is a painter to do? I am afraid you and your friends will be disappointed and that I could have made a better picture with a less remarkable man. He has been delightful." Reed's own views are equally interesting. "That portrait has given me a queer experience in life. All my friends are hurt, and the Democracy seem to think that all my sins must be expiated by the treatment I have received therein. As for me, I like it. I am under the dreadful thrall under which I am told all Mr. Sargent's subjects are, and I am not in the least moved by the criticism of so many, except perhaps I am willing to admit the picture is not so good looking as the original . . . *I* like it." When the portrait appeared in the Speaker's Lobby of the House of Representatives, during the special session of 1891, one irreverent critic summed it up this way, "He is supposed to be in the act of counting a quorum but in fact has just been inveigled into biting a green persimmon, a distinctly rebel and Democratic fruit, tabooed, unclean, and anathema maranatha to all loyal Republicans born north of the fortieth parallel."

While Sargent was thus engaged, McKim arrived on the scene with Samuel Abbott, chairman of the Trustees of the Boston Public Library. McKim was naturally aware of the rather casual friendship existing between Sargent and Whistler (who was then also living in Paris), and wanted to make use of Sargent's presence in the city to explore the possibilities of Whistler's executing decorations for the Library. The relationship between Whistler and Sargent, while never close, was easygoing. When he was in London, "Jimmy" would burst into the studio, eagerly beginning a monologue with "Well, John, what do you know about — " and proceeding to tell the story of his most recent encounter with refractory mankind. In Sargent's words, he was "a scream," and was encouraged to call as often as he liked. However, even in London, where their studios were not far apart, they met infrequently, except in the convivial atmosphere of the Chelsea Arts Club.

Something of the largeness of Sargent's nature was obvious even

to Whistler when they came together, and he described the suggestion of his name to the Boston Trustees as "an act of rare and
noble camaraderie." McKim asked Sargent to arrange a dinner at
Foyot's, over which the four — Whistler, Sargent, McKim, and
Abbott — might meet to discuss the project. When Whistler accepted, Sargent felt it best to caution McKim that the unfathomable Butterfly might still arrive in a wasplike mood. "Now," he said,
"one of three things will happen, and I don't know which. Either
he will be as silent as the grave, or outrageously vituperative, or the
most charming dinner companion you've ever met." As it happened, Whistler arrived in good humor, flattered by the deference
paid him, anxious to learn what location he would be offered. The
dinner was a great success, though the men enjoyed themselves so
much that nothing of any definite nature was arrived at, making
it necessary to arrange a second evening at Foyot's. When the
table was cleared Whistler was positively bubbling with enthusiasm, drawing on the white tablecloth a tentative idea for a great
peacock fifteen feet high. His companions watched, and departed
in the greatest good spirits. Then the tablecloth went into the
wash, and nothing further ever came of the mural, the order for
which was eventually withdrawn.

Early in the fall Sargent returned to England, where he tore into
the work he had laid out for himself. In the interval, Abbey had
cast about for a spot where he could execute his designs with complete attention, in an atmosphere at once congenial and isolated.
With these qualifications in mind, he found the village of Fairford,
near Cambridge, and in it a house called Morgan Hall, which was
all that he and his wife dreamed of. On its grounds, at the edge of
the village common, he erected a large studio of corrugated iron,
in the barnlike proportions suitable to mural work. He got busy
and, pleased with himself, soon was inviting Sargent to visit, then
suggesting that, as they were really working on the same project,
they ought to share the studio. The idea met with Sargent's grateful approval, for he was eager to separate the Boston work from the
routine of portraiture carried on in Tite Street.

In November, as he was about to go to Fairford, Sargent left
a portfolio of Helleu's portrait etchings with Jacomb-Hood, a
member of the Royal Society of Painter-Etchers. As Sargent in-

tended, Hood was impressed with them and wrote directly to Helleu with the suggestion that he allow himself to be proposed for membership in the Society. He also prepared an article on Helleu with reproductions for the *Studio* magazine, which was the first step toward making Helleu the fashionable success he soon became. Out at Fairford, Sargent installed himself in the east end of the large studio, while Abbey worked in the west. Together they labored over long days rather happily, and many were the meals Sargent was content to miss while concentrating on what he was doing. To vary his activities, and to keep down his increasing weight, he kept a horse nearby and, poor rider though he was, once a week rode with the local hunt. One evening, after Sargent went to his room to remove his boots, Abbey heard his voice sharp and clear: "Terrible! *Terrible!*" Abbey was alarmed, and rushing to his friend's aid, found him seated comfortably on the edge of the bed staring at his dirtied, bashed-in hat.

"What's wrong, John?" Surprised at Abbey's anxiety, Sargent explained that he was just thinking how he had fallen from his horse during a jump and lost his hat. The horse came down on the hat with all the force of its hind legs, "and can you imagine if my head had been in that hat? Terrible! TERRIBLE!"

Before Christmas of that year, as he rode back to Morgan Hall one evening through the early twilight, he chanced to cross a field of winter wheat. It would never have occurred to him there was such a thing, and he was all ignorance and innocence when the farmer advanced on him with a torrent of abuse. It was so unexpected and inexplicable that he was taken completely aback and, not certain what the difficulty was, dismounted. As the man drew closer, he tried to apologize, offering to make good any damage he had done. The farmer, however, was not to be appeased and continued his flow of abuse, until in an attempt to draw him up short Sargent cautioned him that that was no way to talk to a gentleman. He knew profanity too, were he of the mind, but he was aware that he was in error and, having caused damage, preferred to make reparation. The farmer replied that he was no gentleman, and this in particular was taken as an unbecoming statement. Sargent was too sensible to let the matter go further, though. Maintaining a firm hold on his rising temper, he remounted and rode away. He arrived at Morgan Hall obviously much agitated, and recounted the whole affair to the Abbeys. Not satisfied with telling them once, he returned to it at intervals, unable to get his mind into other channels. For two days he did no work in the studio, appearing moody and lost in thought. Then, late on the third day, he went for a walk. Only a few minutes later, Mrs. Abbey, returning home past the house of the surly farmer, saw a large figure walk down the path toward her in the dark. "I've done it," he said, when she recognized him. He had decided, he explained, that the only thing to do was to settle the matter personally. Therefore, he had called on the farmer and told him to come outside and defend himself. Urging his household to witness the assault, the farmer stepped out into the evening, where Sargent carried out his plan in fine style.

Now, suddenly, he was relieved of all anxiety. He returned to work. His mind was untroubled, and likely not another thought of the matter entered his head. The farmer, however, did not intend to leave the assault unavenged, as might have been realized when he called on his family to witness. There followed an interval when Sargent's friends were uncertain whether the farmer would proceed by summons before a magistrate or, what was more likely, as he no doubt wished to make of it as good a thing as possible, sue by civil action for damages. Poor Henry James was worried beyond endurance for his friend, in his agitation confiding to the skeptical Henry Adams all his fears that Sargent would find himself in jail for what he had done. Adams's strange mind saw the whole thing as a matter of humor: "Sargent . . . after riding up and down his field of spring wheat, had been wrought to such a frenzy by being called no gentleman, that he went to the farmer's house, called him out, and pounded him; for which our artist-genius in America would surely get some months of gaol, and may get it even here, which much distresses Henry [James] who has a sympathetic heart. This too was confided to me, and has not yet got into the newspapers. As Sargent does not seem to distress himself, I see no reason why James should do so . . ." Placing the matter in the hands of his frequent host, Sir George Lewis, one of the most trusted men of law in England, Sargent worked peacefully on his frieze of the Hebrew Prophets, with whom he felt a new companionship, for on reading the Testament he discovered that they, too, knew something of personal honor and vengeance. On January 21, Sir George informed him by letter that the farmer had issued a writ for damages, advising payment into court of fifty pounds. The sum was considered adequate, it was accepted by the farmer, and the episode was ended.

Seven days after he received Sir George's letter, while perspiration was still being mopped from Henry James' brow, he was writing to McKim from Fairford:

> The work is getting on steadily but slowly. I shall soon be wanting absolute figures, as I cannot trust to the little models. I wonder whether you are near carrying out on the wall those details of the divisions of my surfaces we talked over. One item I should propose an amendment to. I complained that the width of the space for my row of prophets was very small and begged for more inches. There again I am willing, I think, to give up the idea of separations in the plinth running under the feet of my prophets, all except the center trio, which must have an actual relief.
>
> I want to know definitely whether you admit of this treble thing in real relief. You can reduce the relief a little if you think proper, but not the breadth of the panels, as I cannot squeeze a life-size figure into a narrower space than twenty one inches and ½ . . . I shall be entirely at sea with my prophets if you object to this proposition . . . These are the questions about which write what you can do for a fellow — the character of the cornice within the limits of my painting, the parrelleled projections for Moses & Co., and the question of the top of the wainscot and the width of the band for prophets — 6 feet 9 or 7 ft.
>
> The large lunette is in a fair way of being done very soon and the large scale of it suits the kind of thing well. The Israelites, the pharoah and the Assyrians are arranged just like the first sketch. Jehovah and the rest quite different and much better.

In the summer of 1892 McKim again came on a visit, with Abbott, traveling to Fairford, where the two found Sargent and Abbey deeply involved with their decorative work. In a letter of thanks to Mrs. Abbey, McKim wrote:

The more I think about it all, the more I like to, and the more confident I grow of the verdict when the "Abbey Room", as it is henceforth to be called, is finally completed . . . And Sargent (in another way), what an undertaking, and what an achievement, his splendid "machine" painted with the "blood of empty stomachs" is! . . . I thought I knew something about struggle till I reached Fairford, but the attitude of these two men towards their work has been a *revelation* to me.

The nature of the work Sargent was doing seemed a trifle doubtful to another guest at Fairford — Carroll Beckwith, who visited during the summer of 1893, on proceeds from his work done for McKim at the Chicago World's Fair, for which he had doubtless been suggested by Sargent. At the time of this visit Sargent was taken up with making casts which he intended to apply to the painted surfaces of his murals, in the Byzantine manner. The idea interested him, and as he experimented with it at Fairford, applying casts to different parts of his large canvas, he felt that the relief and the splendid way the gold shone achieved an unmatched richness of texture. He had early decided that portions of the work would be in actual sculptured relief, as the letter written McKim a year earlier reveals, and he therefore saw no reason why he could not consistently employ casts on his painted surfaces — except that for seven hundred years it had not been done, which he did not consider a valid objection. Beckwith questioned the propriety of the thing, for without a background of study in Eastern and Byzantine art, it seemed to him to be nothing more than cheating on the relief that ought to be obtained by strong modeling while painting. Beckwith spent a few weeks in England, during which time he lunched at the Tite Street studio and saw the *Mme. Gautreau* for the first time.

He also saw his friend mentioned in the newspapers as a possible selection as associate of the Royal Academy, which Sargent himself did not think possible. The Academy was still too much the center of older painters who would oppose the election of anyone so nonacademic. The following day Beckwith lunched at the studio again, and there found the Stanford Whites, the Abbeys, Alfred Parsons, and Lily Millet all crowded into the little dining room.

Despite Sargent's views, the Royal Academy had not been able to ignore his claim to a place in that body. His prestige and the obviousness of his achievement were so positive that the Academy was reluctant to leave him outside with such rowdy fellows as those at the New English Art Club, and the rumors that Beckwith had read were foreshadowing what became a fact in January 1894, when he was elected an associate member. The *New York Times* of January 21, 1894, reflected the general incredulity at this development: "The Royal Academy has been passing over painters of the orthodox Academic routine to elect revolutionaries like John S. Sargent . . . In their present fit they may be quite capable of electing even J. M. Whistler if they did not feel certain he would laugh at them."

Sargent's own feelings after his election were rather mixed, as when he journeyed back to London from Fairford to make the customary courtesy calls on older Academicians, he reflected that it was curious, after years of hating a man's work, to meet him and find he was an altogether delightful fellow. He was almost troubled lest there be more likeness between himself and the Academy than he had heretofore suspected, a phenomenon which in the following years became nothing less than startling, as the Academy covered its walls with a host of painters following in his wake. His position in England had altered radically since his arrival just ten years before, even since his return from America in 1888, when he had found himself becalmed in the home port. His reputation was great; the way he had broken into the Academy, taken it by storm, was apparent to every observer, to whom it was also immediately apparent that he had no intention of trimming his sails once inside that body.

Portraiture had never actually been neglected; it was too large a part of his life to fall victim to other enthusiasms. Of course, during the first two years of work on his mural, Sargent had not especially sought portrait commissions in England, finding his time already sufficiently occupied. And when, in June of 1894, he was reminded by the National Academy of Design in New York, to which he had been elected a member, that he had not presented a portrait to their collection, as was required upon his selection, he replied that he had not complied with the rule because he had "for two years been exclusively occupied with a mural decoration." It was a reasonable inference, though not strictly true; he had done portraits, but none he was at liberty to present to the Academy. By 1894 he was once again as engaged in portraiture as he had been formerly, once more giving more liberal time to this branch of art. As early as June of 1892 he had journeyed back from Fairford to paint Miss Chanler, who with her sister had previously purchased his *A Street in Venice* from the St. Botolph Club exhibition and presented it to the Stanford Whites. The three Misses Dunham, one of whom had been invited to the first party at Chase's studio, were all painted about that time. And since he was occupied with portraits, that summer he also invited Lady Lewis to sit, apparently in gratitude for Sir George's tactful handling of the late agricolan unpleasantness. Early in 1894 there was a request from W. Graham Robertson, another of the guests of the Lewises, that he undertake a full-length of his mother. At the same moment an order came from a Mrs. George Whitin, of Whitinsville, Massachusetts, for a portrait of Ada Rehan, the actress, then appearing in London with Daly's theatrical troupe. By chance Mrs. Whitin's letter reached him in London, where he was making his calls on the Academicians. He replied:

> Jan. 27, 1894
> Morgan Hall
> Fairford Gloucestershire

Dear Mrs Whitin

Before receiving your letter I had a note from Miss Rehan who informed me that you had cabled to her and invited me to call which, as I was in London, I did at once. I am glad that you incline to a portrait *not* in character, as both she and I feel the same way. This is all we could decide at the time, but when I go up to town again she is coming to my studio with several dresses to choose from, and there in the proper light, I will be able to come to a conclusion about the proper treatment of the picture. I think that it ought to be a full length in spite of the fact it will have to stand on the ground or very nearly.

The price that I asked you for painting Miss Rehan ($2500) is below my usual price and you would do me a favor by not mentioning it, as I have several orders to fulfill in America at a higher figure.

I think the whole impression, and the upper part of Miss Rehan's face is very fine, and I hope I shall satisfy your ambition for the portrait.

We expect to accomplish it in the months of March and April. Believe me

Yours truly
John S. Sargent

Mrs. Robertson and Ada Rehan began to sit at the same time, in the spring, when he returned to London from his winter's work at Morgan Hall. Mrs. Robertson proved rather a frozen, timid sitter, very loath, as she expressed it, to "sit still and be stared at." She required the reassurance of her son's presence, who naturally could not attend without his dog. Luckily the animal proved toothless, for it had neurotic urges, taking an immediate dislike to Sargent and invariably starting the day's work with a bite from his leg. "He's bitten me now, so we can go ahead" was the painter's laconic comment every morning.

Graham Robertson was a theater habitué, and friendly with some of the stars, later serving as channel of correspondence in the famous paper romance between Ellen Terry and George Bernard Shaw. What with the painter's own interest in things theatrical, this common taste proved a good conversational gambit, especially as Ada Rehan, whose unfinished portrait stood in the studio, was a friend of Robertson's. The two large canvases progressed apace. Soon the fan of white ostrich plumes that Mrs. Robertson had brought for her own picture was borrowed to figure more prominently in the portrait of the actress, where it flames out of the white satin of her gown. It also appears in a third portrait Sargent did during this time, of Mrs. Ernest Hills.

The rhythmic name of the woman commissioning Miss Rehan's portrait was rather fascinating to Sargent's musical ear, and it ran through his mind as he worked in the studio. Now and again it became audible, as he broke into a low, almost liturgic, chant: "Mrs. Whitin, of Whitinsville, *Mass.*" the "Mass." coming in the deepest tones, like a final great Amen, in which he was reverently joined by Robertson.

Miss Rehan's vehicle for that season was to be *Twelfth Night,* and when the play went into rehearsal, sittings on her portrait were interrupted. Robertson went to the opening with J. J. Shannon, then nearest among the younger men as a rival portraitist, though hardly a threat, and the two men were amazed when a note from the star was delivered to Robertson during an entr'acte:

> I have something particular to tell you about Sargent — something he said of you — you must hear it and, I hope, act on it. Shall I tell you before your friend? — you must bring him. This evening is so nice — it has unnerved me a little.
>
> Affectionately,
Ada Rehan

Unable to imagine what it was Sargent had said of him, except perhaps that his dog ought to be shot, Robertson was surprised when the actress told him that Sargent had said he was extremely paintable in the long overcoat he wore, and that he would like to paint him. When Robertson, recovering, asked precisely what Sargent had said, Miss Rehan admitted she was not certain, for doubtless the painter's thought was so cut up by his searching for words that it was completely disjointed in her memory. From what she did get across, Robertson realized that the overcoat more than himself was in demand, but urged on by the actress, he decided to be painted. As the year rolled into June, then, Sargent had three full-length canvases lined up in his studio. It was warm summer weather, and Robertson rather feebly rebelled against the heavy overcoat he was asked to wear.

"But the coat is the picture, you must wear it."

"Then I can't wear anything else!" he cried in despair. With the sacrifice of most of his apparel beneath the coat he became thinner and thinner, much to the satisfaction of the artist, who pulled and dragged the coat more and more closely around the skinny young man until it might have been draping a lamppost.

Sarah Bernhardt was appearing in London that summer, and was curious enough about Sargent to want to come with Robertson for one of his sittings. No one could imagine Sally B, as Ellen Terry called her, sitting still while another person was painted. It was unlike her not to share a little in the limelight, and that little, thought Robertson, might be enough to unnerve the painter.

"But it will bore you," he ventured.

"No," said Mme. Sarah. "I want to see the picture and I am going. You must call for me and take me with you." If the sun had risen in the west that morning it would have surprised Robertson less than to see Sarah Bernhardt standing ready and waiting, at an early hour, in a neat, businesslike walking dress and a small black hat. Sargent watched her out of the corner of his eye all the while she was in the studio. And once, when she leaned forward to see the portrait in a little hanging mirror high up on the wall, her head thrown back and profile in delicate relief against the black-lacquer screen filling one end of the room, he whispered, "I never saw that she was beautiful before. Look at her now," a sentiment in which Robertson joined.

In the midst of this stream of portraits, while he was still anxious to return to Fairford, where the frieze of the Prophets was not yet completed, news arrived that Mrs. Gardner would be in Europe the end of June. Taking a break of a few days, he went over to Paris. He introduced her to Besnard, from whom she purchased a pastel head, and they visited the Salons — there were two of them now. At the New Salon, the Salon of the more adventurous painters, Whistler's portrait of the Count de Montesquiou made Sargent uneasy, for it seemed to bear some relationship in composition and dandified stance to the portrait he was doing of Robertson. Returning to London, he was worried that a charge of filching would be leveled against him. Whistler had shown his picture first, and though it had not been seen prior to that showing and indeed was painted secretly (the mystery of doing so had appealed to both Montesquiou and Whistler), Sargent feared comment when his own picture was shown. His originality was a matter of importance to him. His uneasiness was based on only the very slightest parallelism in the two works, but he was uneasy. Yet when the picture was shown, no mention was made of the Whistler, to which it bore almost no resemblance.

During the moments of free time that still were his, one of Sargent's pleasures was to look through the curio shops of London for furnishings with which to enrich his studios. Curio shops, in fact, were rather a specialty of his and he often sought them out on the Continent. They had some special and potent charm, and it was not an impractical hobby, for fine fittings were an essential part of his craft. In one shop he came across a rug that suggested a tack that Cousin Ralph Curtis seems to have used more consistently. When Mrs. Gardner arrived in London a short time later, he wrote her:

> Would you like to see or buy a magnificent Persian rug of the finest design and period, worth all the pictures ever painted? It belongs to a little Turk whose shop is too small to unroll it, and who is going to send it to my studio to show one of my sitters on Tuesday the 17″ at five o'clock. He wants between three and four hundred pounds for it and it is worth the money. O that I were not so practical and full of forethought — I would buy it myself.

The example of his cousin bore fruit, for by the twenty-third he consummated the sale to Mrs. Gardner, on that date sending her the Turk's receipt for three hundred fifty pounds, which he had presumably paid out of his pocket in her behalf. The full nature of his dealings with the Turk is a mystery beyond what we know from his rendering of the receipt to Mrs. Gardner. "So practical and full of forethought," as he described himself, and as we know him to have been, we must doubt that he had thus troubled himself without expectation of return. All the same, he did have an honest interest in the carpet, begging Mrs. Gardner to allow him the use of it, as long as it was in his studio, for the portrait of Ada Rehan. Careful examination of that picture does show beneath the present surface a pattern bearing comparison with the rug now at Fenway Court in Boston. The explanation for his failure to make it part of the final picture was written to Mrs. Gardner in October:

> The picture of the carpet never came off. Whenever I put my model on it, she covered up something infinitely more beautiful than herself, so I gave it up and merely did a sort of a map of the carpet for the pattern.

In another letter he wrote:

Miss Rehan became a mere understudy and the carpet played the principal part, so it had to be taken out. But I simply must paint it and I beseech you to let me keep it a little longer.

Neither letter is without a certain subtle flattery to Mrs. Gardner, who, after the experience with Carmencita in New York, he knew would take pleasure in the belittling of an actress.

Curiously, Carmencita herself was then in London, dancing in one of the large music halls, where she was popular though no longer the sensation she had been in New York. Sargent had managed to dispose of her portrait three years before, at a considerable loss, by selling it to the Luxembourg Gallery. Her arrival served to remind him of that fact, the price still being an irksome matter. Then, in a strange melancholy desire to relive something of the magic of those days in New York, he decided to give one more party at which she would dance. Graham Robertson found him bent over a long list of guests, many of them apparently not very much desired.

"I suppose I must ask . . ." he said dismally.

"Why should you?" demanded Robertson.

"Oh, well, you know — I suppose — I ought to."

"But do you want to?"

"No," he said, with unusual frankness.

"Then don't."

"All right," he said firmly, scratching out the name. "I won't. I'm — I'm damned if I do!"

Robertson, who it seems was equally particular, decreed a sweeping series of proscriptions to which Sargent gave hearty endorsement. It was a merry hanging. Nevertheless, when Robertson arrived the night of the party, he met every "noxious humbug" formerly stricken from the list. The originals of many portraits were there, prowling around each other suspiciously, paying false tribute to rival charms, each with the certainty he or she was the sole possessor of that "certain sort of something" Sargent had ascribed to them during their sittings.

Carmencita's wildness, which was authentic in New York, seems to have abated with the years. Her Spanishness now became more the hip-wiggling, ogling, French variety. At first short-

skirted and decked with tinsel, she changed after her first dance
to a dress of dead white falling to her feet and having a heavy train.
She sang the wild crooning "Paloma," circling with splendid arm
movements, her feet hardly moving, the white train sweeping and
swinging about her. Sargent whispered a request. She looked
angry, then sullen, shaking her head in a violent "No." He persisted and, going to a cupboard built into the dark studio paneling,
held out a beautiful white cashmere shawl with long fringe. She
snatched it and threw it over her shoulders, flicking its fringes into
his face, then slowly sank down on a stool, her face quiet and
grave, her hands in her lap. A low strumming came like a whisper
from the guitars, and she sang mournful folk songs, clapping her
hands gently and swaying with the rhythm.

The party was a success and the dancer must have been happy,
if only because she pocketed a fee. Thrift was one of her virtues,
her plunge at being painted resulting in larger returns than she
could have believed possible. Jacomb-Hood, who asked her to
dance for a charity concert, was appalled by the single room he
found her occupying with Señor Eschapara, the piratical leader of
her guitar orchestra, who was now styled her "husband." Sargent
must have further realized what a fool he had been when Hood
relayed this last bit of information!

Though initially his reserve may have exceeded the cordiality
he wished to convey, as time passed Sargent's confreres in Tite
Street found him more friendly than any of them had expected.
His neighbors in the studio building, Robert Brough, Wilson Steer,
and Charles Furse, became particularly close, and he watched over
their progress with a mildly avuncular eye that delighted them.
Furse in turn was his warmest admirer, in time becoming the closest
of that group clustered in Tite Street. Small though his quarters
were, Sargent liked playing host to his intimates. Will Rothenstein was often one of those in the early days:

Dear Rothenstein
    I have been in Paris for a week, and am only just returned —
I left Abbey in Paris — Hotel de Lille et d'Albion, rue St. Honoré
on his way south. Do come any day — if you will take pot luck

at lunch at one o'clock. Hood told me that he had told you certain views of mine about the danger of going in for portraits. I hope you do not think me impertinent.

Yours sincerely,
John S. Sargent

The friendly solicitude of this short note appeared in all his relations with his Tite Street friends, as when he invited Rothenstein, who suffered through lack of good early training, to join him in painting a nude. It was valuable experience for Rothenstein to watch him work out a full-length canvas, and to make comparisons with his own faulty procedures. Writing in his memoirs, Rothenstein said, "Sargent's reticence prevented him from telling me how bad my painting was, and I was too stupid and conceited to see that here was a chance of acquiring the constructive practice I lacked, and above all, a scientific method of work." But neither the conceit, which was apparent, nor the stupidity, which was not, prevented Sargent from attempting to aid the young artist if he could.

When infrequently Albert de Belleroche was in London, he was besieged with questions about old Paris friends, though oddly, Paris itself, where Sargent had been rebuffed, lost its interest for him. The two friends went next door to see Steer, whose pictures Sargent described as fine in color. Once they drove the short distance to Kings Road to see Augustus John's drawings. Belleroche, like Rothenstein, had become interested in lithography. "Do you know Will Rothenstein? He studied in Paris. I promised to go see him; he wants to show me some prints. Come and see him with me." What Rothenstein had to show were doubtless prints he had made of the portrait of Sargent, as part of a series of prominent people undertaken for a publisher. He had been a poor model. Unable to abide the idleness of holding still, he puffed away at his cigarette with an explosive effect that each few minutes obscured him like Zeus behind clouds of smoke. He was amused to see how little Rothenstein tied himself into knots to rest his chest against the low drawing board, draping his feet over a succession of chairs, and he insisted on turning the tables by drawing Rothenstein in that distorted position as soon as his own stint was over.

Sometimes, too, he managed to join Rothenstein for a ride in the early morning hours, the increasing bulk of his body causing concern for his health. He was still a poor horseman, saying he not only looked like a sack of potatoes but felt like one. And his horse, when he lent it to Henschel, disclosed a dangerous tendency to go through plate-glass windows. More often he rode in Hyde Park with Jacomb-Hood, Henschel, and Shakespeare, the singer. When he chanced riding to the hunt, as he still did occasionally, he was fearless across country, though it was not unusual for him to fall off jumping into a field and then fall off again jumping out. It seemed that he might have done rather better without the horse. Carolus-Duran had no competitor in this respect, though it was in imitation of his skillful master that all Sargent's dives off horses began. Joseph Farquharson suggested lessons at the Kensington Riding School, but this did not appreciably reduce the trouble. Jacomb-Hood suggested they try bicycles instead, the danger being less, and one day they went some twenty miles into the country on a visit. But Sargent was so tired on arriving that he could only lie on the couch throughout the afternoon, and in the evening they returned to London by train, the bicycles checked in the baggage car. It was only rarely he came to the Chelsea Arts Club now, complaining he could not get enough to eat there, though his steak and liter of wine, added to the regular table d'hôte dinner, left his confreres staring. More often now he was at the Hans Crescent Hotel, where he could better satisfy his gargantuan appetite. When near the Academy, he ate at the Café Royal, where he was pleased to characterize his fare as "a chop and a glass of beer," though it consisted of considerably more.

On January 5, Henry James's play, *Guy Domville*, was produced at the St. James Theatre. Sargent and Robertson, who had sympathized with his problems over the summer, were invited to the opening night. When they entered the stalls, they found themselves surrounded by a host of James's literary friends, including Gosse, Shaw, and H. G. Wells. James himself was too much on edge to stand the strain of the opening performance, so he took himself across the square to the Haymarket Theatre and sat through a performance of Oscar Wilde's *An Ideal Husband*. His own audience was charmed by the sets Abbey had designed but showed considerable annoyance with the play. Only the stalls, choked with his literary claque, responded kindly. When at the end of the last act James entered by the stage door, he was greeted by the spectacle of the stalls loyally trying to drown out the tumult raised by an unhappy gallery. Alexander, the actor-manager of the production, who had been sanguine of success, brought him on stage almost by the scruff of the neck, where for a few moments he was forced helplessly to stand before a house that let loose a crescendo of boos, the stalls furiously redoubling their applause. It was clear who the dominant party was, and James, who had not witnessed the response of the audience during the play itself, expected a triumph when he was thus led on stage. To him it was the most terrible moment of a long life.

All the way home with Robertson, as the hansom clattered through cobbled streets, Sargent expressed his indignation in the most violent terms, letting forth a molten, devil-scalding stream of profanity. Possessing the poet's love of language, Robertson had never before heard such a magnificent flow of sullied verbs, nouns, and adjectives, entirely without repetition, boiling on and on from the rapidly moving mouth of his usually silent friend. Sargent was now livid with rage, spitting forth endless foul verbiage, displaying a mastery of expression that had never been suspected. Here indeed was a lord of the language!

The Emergent Colossus

THE FIRST phase of Sargent's decorations for the Boston Public Library was completed late in 1894. Two of the panels, a large end-wall lunette and the ceiling it adjoined were got together on the proper barrel-shaped support and sent to the Royal Academy in May, where, installed in the most suitable position just under the skylight of a room, they caused a sensation. The frieze of the Prophets was finally completed in the winter of that year, when he induced Coventry Patmore, the poet of whom he was doing a portrait through September, to pose for Ezekiel. The letter he had written to McKim in January 1892, by which date the conception of the frieze was already in the form of sketches, illustrates with what prolonged care the final free execution was prepared. It was a product of nearly three years' study, during which time Sargent plotted the drapery in both charcoal and oil, requiring a succession of models before he was satisfied with the effect.

Angelo Colarossi was the first model engaged by Abbey for his work, and Sargent also used him at Fairford. Colarossi was among the most famous of the London model hierarchy, most of them Italians, who had been found to possess in greater degree than the English the feeling for classic stance required by the art of the period. He figured in many of Leighton's classic wonders, even posing for the much-admired *Athlete and Python*, his famous piece of sculpture. At Fairford, as a very gentle, older man, he showed anxious concern when Sargent was absent on the hunt: "Sometimes he not come off the horse at all," remarked Colarossi, not without a certain pride. When the need of a younger model was felt, another of the London Italians, a man named D'Inverno, was brought down. One evening returning from London, he brought along his younger brother, Nicola. The slim boy of nineteen looked quite lithe and muscular, and Sargent found him to be precisely what he needed and engaged him for the following Saturday. As finally done, the frieze contains faces of Colarossi, Nicola D'Inverno, George Roller as Hosea, Nahum and Isaiah, and Coventry Patmore as Ezekiel.

Early the following year Sargent wrote to Mrs. Whitin:

> March 22nd, 1895
> 33, Tite Street,
> Chelsea, S.W.

Dear Mrs Whitin

I have just received your letter from Alexandria, and am glad to know your whereabouts as I was just about to write to you to America.

Miss Rehan's portrait has only lately been finished, as all winter long I have been unable to work on anything but my Boston decoration for which I have been much pressed by the Trustees of the Library. Hence the reason of my not having been able to send the picture to New York.

The picture has now a background of tapestry which improves it very much. I have found a charming old frame for it which I hope you will approve of . . . I think it had better go to the New Gallery where you saw Mrs Hammond's [Hammersley's] portrait, and where it will have a first rate place. I am leaving for Boston next week. My address is Tavern Club, Boylston Place.

Believe me

> Yours sincerely
> John S. Sargent

In company with Abbey and his wife, who also brought over completed murals, Sargent arrived in Boston early that April, staying at the Tavern Club while the two Abbeys became guests of the Charles Fairchilds on Commonwealth Avenue. Then began the process of superintending the installation of the murals, done by a method called marouflage. The top of each canvas was tacked along the upper edge of the intended wall space, then it was rolled up to the tacking. Beneath, the wall was given a thick coat of white lead and the canvas, already prepared with red lead on its reverse side, was allowed to roll down like so much wallpaper. When dry it became as solidly fixed as though part of the wall. This worked well enough for Sargent, though he was troubled to see Abbey hit a snag. The many pin holes where that drawing had been fixed to the canvas oozed white paint, and the workmen's hands, covered with it, smeared the pictures. These extrusions had to be removed, and where that was not possible, repainting became necessary. Abbey also came to see the wisdom of his friend's relief work and casts, for where Sargent wanted to see gold it shone with metallic luster. Abbey's golden halos in his large *Holy Grail* panel, placed high up on the canvas where there was a minimum of light, showed black. He was heartbroken, and after consultations with Stanford White, elected to follow Sargent's lead, building up the halos in relief. Once they were regilded, he had the pleasure of seeing the golden glow he intended.

McKim arranged another of his Boston Socials to greet the unveiling of the murals, and sent invitations to more than two hundred people in New York, Philadelphia, and Washington, as well as Boston. When he came up from New York himself he brought a large party along by rail, and called upon Sargent for one of his melancholy attempts at a speech, which always had particularly deleterious effects on the artist's inner self. At the height of Sargent's discomfort during the reception, at which he and Abbey were naturally the guests of honor, he was addressed by a stern-visaged, elderly lady: "I believe you are Mr. Sargent. Will you be kind enough to tell me in a few words what all this means?" In a few words! For someone else it would have taken hours. For Sargent it was impossible!

Once unveiled, the decorations had an electrifying effect on the city. Abbey's were praised for their many beauties, but Sargent's were something entirely new — the blend of Egyptian and Assyrian styles, with Byzantine casts applied to the surface, combined with the very contemporary treatment of the frieze, made a lasting impression. Nothing like the haunting intensity of the Pharaoh and the Assyrian monarch, standing in regal splendor, had ever been seen on a wall; nor was his vision of the Phoenician seductress, *Astarte,* on the ceiling likely to be matched. Boston was not satisfied with the murals alone; while they had Sargent with them they demanded portraits as well. Probably some of those he mentioned in his first letter to Mrs. Whitin were executed now, and the time he could take from the installations at the Library was applied to the routine of portraiture.

On May 18, Abbey wrote to Alma-Tadema from New York: "We had a great time in Boston. I wish you could see the things in place — John's looks stunning. You see it from a great distance below, and he has gilded the whole interior of the space and lighted it all by strong reflected light; it gains tremendously and as a composition is for the first time complete. We both suffered, as I have said, fearfully from the heat, working on scaffolds under the ceiling."

Sargent passed through New York with Abbey, where Stanford White spoke of a portrait of his eight-year-old son, Lawrence, who previously had put his finger on a wet canvas in Tite Street. That never materialized. Instead, George Vanderbilt commandeered him with an invitation to his estate in the Carolinas, there to do portraits of Richard Morris Hunt, the architect, and Frederick Law Olmsted, the landscape architect, who were responsible for his magnificent establishment. Henry James, on a later visit to the estate, described it as "the extraordinary colossal French Chateau of George Vanderbilt in the said N.C. mountains — the house 2500 feet in the air, and a thing of the high Rotheschild manner, but of a size to contain two or three Mentmores and Waddesdons."

Invited for May 15, Sargent was soon at work on two huge full-lengths, which he elected to do outdoors. The finished paintings were so striking that Vanderbilt had a three-quarter-length portrait of himself done as well. On the completion of his work in North Carolina, Sargent was bound for Spain.

At the end of August he was back from his Spanish excursion, to find that Mrs. Whitin, whose name had been ringing in his ears for good reason, required another letter.

33, Tite Street
Chelsea, S.W.
August 22, [1895]

Dear Mrs Whitin

I have just returned to London and put Miss Rehan's portrait in my studio and looking very well I think. As I wrote to you on leaving New York I have in mind your suggestions, and will do some slight work to the background. I have by the way not received any letter from you since then, in case you may have written.

. . .

Believe me   Yours faithfully
                               John S. Sargent

He immediately returned to work. "We went to Sargent yesterday afternoon," wrote Mrs. Abbey in a letter, "saw the sketches and Gothic stuffs he brought back with him from Spain — all very fine. He is working at the design for the second ceiling, as yet only on paper in charcoal, but he has decided to paint it in London. There are so many figures in it, and he will need such a variety of models, and will want to look up things in the National Gallery and the British Museum that he thinks it will hamper him to be at Fairford, so he will probably not be with us this year at all. He expects to do the lunette at Fairford, but that will probably not be for a long time, for he will probably not begin it until the ceiling is well advanced." In London, however, there was a problem of space. The Tite Street studio simply could not accommodate his complicated work on the mural panels in addition to the portrait work. As a consequence, he found a studio off Fulham Road, only a few blocks away in Chelsea, where, past an inner court and down a long dark corridor, there was room enough for the large panels required by his Boston work.

In a strange despairing way both Henry James and Sargent had always been fond of society, though why Sargent, who often appeared ill at ease and whose conversation dried up completely when he was not with intimates, should night after night have "gone everywhere" was often something of a puzzle to those observing him. Soon after his return from America he met Mrs.

Charlie Hunter, wife of a coal magnate who was amassing a tremendous fortune. She once commented to her sister, the composer Ethel Smyth, "I consider it my *sacred duty* to spend every penny I can of Charlie's money," a pious resolve she in time accomplished, though it took tremendous doing and most of England to help her. Each year Mrs. Hunter took one or another of the large houses in London, and made herself one of the fashionable hostesses of the period by giving the huge house parties and crushes associated with the gilded age. Her husband, who had not the strength to deny her anything she really wanted, shared in her comprehensive sort of hospitality. The golden waves of prosperity were rolling higher and higher about her when she met Sargent. Possessed of a very appealing personal charm, Mary Hunter added to it many of the devices a hostess in her position found indispensable — the dangling of a name to attract other guests, the ability to pick up knowledge by listening, and the intuitive ability to distinguish who was the right person to listen to. When Sargent became her guest, she was delighted to invite others of his circle who would attract him and keep his talk flowing, for he could be an easy and really good conversationalist with his cronies.

There developed in time a warm reciprocal friendship between them, which many people thought might have been more. For though from the time he first reached maturity many women had attracted him, seeming for a short time perhaps to fit the pattern of human relationships he dreamed of, so that he temporarily became dependent upon their admiration and approval, none had ever so successfully supplied the assurance he needed as did Mrs. Hunter. For her the image of the artist and the man he had sought to make of himself was complete. She saw him precisely in that special light, and to her his kindness flowed forth as it never had before. The portrait he painted of her in 1898 shows a large, robust woman, of matronly proportion, invested with a dazzling charm that is plainly seductive. Her photographs do not show half the radiance or the beguiling look of her that Sargent saw, and it must be admitted that this is another special portrait suggesting that the stone heart of the painter had melted. There was something a trifle exotic about Mrs. Hunter, if we may judge from the portrait, and the exotic still exercised as potent a charm over him as ever. Her photographs, however, do not show this quality; suggesting that it was one with which he invested her. It is a portrait that patently says the painter was appreciative of her feminine charm and, whether consciously or not, was viewing his sitter with a purely masculine eye. What their relations were has been a matter debated almost from the moment they met.

Of late years he did not seem ordinarily to seek society, for often he was content when left alone to do his work. His conscience doubtless chafed if he was too long away from his easel. At the same time, people *did* interest him, the pleasure of really congenial company was never lost on him. Mrs. Hunter provided a home where he could bring friends, for he soon found that the heart within her ample bosom had warmth enough for all, and her purse was rarely closed to anyone bearing the seal of his approval. There he brought Claude Monet, when that artist had as yet no public in England and needed introduction to potential collectors. He urged the works of Monet with all his own reputation behind his judgment. There too he brought Rodin to do a bust of Mrs. Hunter, and the Italian, Mancini, whom he met in Rome one summer. At Mrs. Hunter's too, in later years, he introduced the woman painter Mrs. Annie Swynnerton, whom he called the greatest painter of children's portraits. A picture of Mrs. Hunter's grandchildren riding a horse later hung in her house as an example, and he sometimes urged her work with the very direct "You ought to have her paint your children." His position was so supreme that even so direct an attack only served to enhance the fame of Mrs. Swynnerton, or Mancini, or Rodin, or whoever's work he was now suggesting. Through the nineties Monet's paintings began to sell in England largely through Sargent's efforts, and Mancini became established as a portraitist.

Mary Hunter's sister, Ethel Smyth, as musician and composer, brought musical friends who were equally of interest to Sargent. Dame Ethel, as she later became, was soon his friend too, for music remained his second passion, only a little behind painting. Over dinner one evening, Mary Hunter explained to him that Ethel no longer smoked. Ethel sat next to him at the table, and thought he looked particularly cross. "What's this nonsense about your giving up smoking?" he finally spat out. She explained that she was unable to limit herself to any sort of moderation, and decided that it was time to quit. His own conscience must have been bothering him on that score, and he had not liked the way Mary Hunter used mention of Ethel to rebuke him. He would not grant the point, growing hot, finally ending the argument with "Well, I should never have thought you were so weak-minded!" pronounced with the utmost disgust. It was an unexpected retort to the headstrong musical sister who wrote opera despite severe male prejudice, even managing at times to conduct her own works. Sargent's own incessant smoking, begun long before in Paris, had become a problem, and doubtless he was fighting advice to give it up. The solution he arrived at, some years later, was a handmade Turkish cigarette bought in bulk by the thousands from the tobacconist next to his studio on Fulham Road, "*H. Lord's Turkish No. 3*," which the sweet-faced Mrs. Lord made in the rear of the shop. He claimed the cigarettes were so weak that they had no effect at all, and smoked them with a profusion signifying his own complete acceptance of the idea.

His interest in Ethel Smyth, who was sharp-tongued, odd-looking, and heavily opinionated (she was jailed as a militant suffragette for heaving a brick through the Home Secretary's window), stemmed entirely from musical sources rather than from any personal pleasure he found in her company. He was even ready to put up with primitive conditions when he was invited to Miss Smyth's home, "One Oak," happy to accept the invitation of that Caesar's wife, even though he knew it meant having to sleep crosswise, northeast by southwest, in the skimpy bed that was all her guest room offered. He found the musical atmosphere of the place sufficiently rewarding to suffer also the inconvenience of the well, from which at times unlikely objects were fished (it was lower than the cesspool), and the lack of a bell on the door, for which a hunting horn was substituted. Mercifully the cook was good, for he was more sensitive to the pangs of an empty stomach than the ache of his back, and while such needs were adequately met, and music filled the air, he was content. Harry Brewster, the librettist of her operas, was a frequent guest as well, and his "sombre, magnificent" verse — "unlike any poetry I know," as Sargent wrote Miss Smyth — was an equal pleasure. Brewster wrote chiefly in French, a particular recommendation to Sargent, who was "soaked in the French poets" and had been considered something of a judge ever since he first astonished Edouard Pailleron twenty years before. The careful finish of French letters made strong call on his appreciative faculties, and he preferred French and Italian literature to English, with which he was never able to make much headway. The modern French novels of the time were generally among his favorites, Daudet, Flaubert, and Gautier being listed as classics; but he was unable to become interested in Dickens, who he thought was too journalistic and of whom he had unflattering opinions.

The musician cherished above all was Gabriel Fauré, who was invited to stay at the studio in Tite Street. There Sargent gave musical parties at which Fauré's works were often heard for the first time in England. The studio, now filled with rare furnishings, carved Flemish panels, Brussels tapestries, and all the curious and beautiful objects picked up in his travels and prowling the shops of London, made a unique background for music. He arranged performances by Léon Delafosse, Percy Grainger, and other distinguished pianists, and was indefatigable in introducing Fauré to those who might arrange performances of his larger works. He had only to announce approval of a musician in his spluttering style to have London hostesses engage these protégés in the hope that this would assure his own much-coveted presence, which generally it did. Perhaps his own early years had borne in on him the value of help when one is young, for his aid was a boon to many struggling young musicians, as well as painters, highly beneficial from a practical viewpoint, but also comforting on purely artistic grounds. He had a tenacious memory for the highly specialized points of workmanship that were usually lost on the listener, and Percy Grainger considered few as balanced in musical criticism as Sargent.

The remarkable inscrutability that he managed to maintain, even at a time when he was on exhibition as continuously as any of his paintings, continued to be a byword in London, and his extreme reticence concerning anything he considered his private life made him something of a mystery. The fact that such a socially desirable individual remained unmarried so late in life (for by 1897 he was forty-one), was looked upon by more than one matron as a grave fault. It was difficult enough for their daughters to find likely husbands, men were not to be countenanced who refrained from marriage — that was not playing the game. In London there were many, especially among those with artistic interests and pretensions, who remained unmarried, and generally it was understood that they had good reasons. But it was impossible to associate Sargent with any particular cause, and his single state remained a puzzle. He was a large and strong man, with, if one knew him at all, enough indications of virility not to be taken for an example of the intellectualized homosexuality notable among the artists of London. He impressed everyone as possessing a supercharged vitality, a tremendous energy that was evidenced in everything he did, certainly in his work, which was always expressive of the subtler nuances of his nature. Surely he could not say, as his friend Henry James did, that he was "not a marrying man." It was only natural, therefore, that talk about him would be heard in a society like London's, where conversation was cultivated. On the one hand, there was talk of his closeness with Mary Hunter and, on the other, that the young musicians who trailed him everywhere were thought effeminate. He had some strange friends, some of whom appeared to have relationships among themselves of which society, though aware in an oblique way, did not openly approve. It seemed a reflection on him that he was seen in such company, yet it was impossible to believe that this huge robust individual, with such healthy tastes and none of the petty preciousness displayed among oversophisticated intellects, could be anything but the vigorously masculine individual he seemed. Perhaps the most obvious measure of his relations with these protégés was the fact that they, too, complained that he remained completely inscrutable.

What, then, of his relations with Mary Hunter? Later in life she thought it advisable to destroy the letters he had written her during the early years of their friendship. This detail is in itself suggestive, as is even the warmth of what he wrote her later. For it was to Mary Hunter alone that he could pour out his feelings, talk in words of compassion, and through the years, speak in the terms of human feeling that his correspondence otherwise lacks entirely. She alone was the confidante of his heart and of his strongly restrained but highly emotional nature. Consistently, when writing those later letters that are preserved, he used no salutation, as though signifying that something was omitted. They start out of nowhere, with a conspicuously easier tone than he, achieved with others. Yet, except for these few indications, there is nothing, for if there were indiscretions they were of the most discreet sort and nothing but outward marks of esteem can now be invoked to prove what was thought a very close relationship. The watercolors he presented to her, until it seemed her house was overflowing; the two huge columns he marbled for her when later she lived in Essex, working like an ordinary housepainter to do the thing as he thought it ought to be done — all these speak of the warm nature of their friendship. None say more. Much the same pattern of behavior runs through all his friendships, the same extreme kindness that was expressed in favors, when he could do them without a hint of the sentimentality he possessed in so large a degree. If Mrs. Hunter seemed more consistently the recipient of these favors, she also dispensed her kindness more consistently to him and to the many friends he introduced to her hospitality and her purse. The only distinction she had was that she seemed to be his only friend from among the beau monde to share the hospitality he dispensed at his mother's table in Chelsea.

As he climbed into a position that soon completely dominated the artistic world, becoming the uniquely social and artistic lion that he was, his family more and more ceased to accompany him. Only his closest friends had any notion that he had any family in England. The days when he took his sister Violet along with him ended with her marriage and, strangely, even on those occasions when one expected to see his family, if he had any, such as the private views of the Royal Academy, they were absent. Except for the music parties in his studio, it was thought he did no entertaining, and no one expected him to return the invitations lavished upon him. Henry James, of course, saw the family regularly when in London and in later years, when he lived only a few steps from Emily, he dined with the Sargents twice a week;

he had known them long and well. The artist friends with whom Sargent was particularly at ease were taken there too, for a dinner and a quiet game of chess; and at these functions he was decidedly a good talker, the same interesting conversationalist he had been at Broadway and Fairford. If this was a distinction Mary Hunter had, then it was a small one, and probably only the result of the ease he felt in her company. It is hardly the basis upon which to build a romance. Still, the Empress Eugénie, who lived so long in England, once asked her, "Is your husband jealous?"

"Not at all," came the reply. "English husbands never are!"

"No!" said the Empress. "They always think it's all right . . . *but it generally isn't.*"

Sargent's inscrutability, if carefully examined, was actually a strangely hollow beast, for the point appears to be that, while he invited no inquiries, there was actually little about which inquiry could be made. True, he guarded the facts of his relationship with Mary Hunter through all his life. But aside from that, his existence was roughly divided between easels at Tite Street and Fulham Road, his thought primarily of his work. Of personal life, the hidden quality so wondered at and so protected, he appears to have had little. We hold an advantage over his contemporaries in our knowledge of his youthful romances, none of which seems to have been particularly happy. If there was more, it is not of great importance, for after the episode with Carmencita he seems to have realized that his was not a nature to be soothed by such sordid relationships. It was his silence that exaggerated to remarkable proportions the few moments a day that were his, spent in directing his household, doing his shopping, and answering his mail. His family probably had predilections of its own for not being seen: Mrs. Sargent was now over seventy and Emily, conscious of her malproportioned body, was periodically overtaken with fits of tears that came on for no reason, punctuating the brave and happy personality she had built for herself. Violet and her family sometimes accompanied him to Mrs. Hunter's and he did Emily and his mother the compliment of bringing a select company to them, which to a large extent was all he could do.

Surveying his cool exterior, it was obvious that no personal questions would be tolerated. The assumption became general that there was something he preferred not to make known. Even his social moods were marked by periods when he seemed to wish he had not accepted the invitation he was honoring, when his mind drifted, and he stalked up and down rooms like a caged lion, adopting this perambulatory method presumably to forestall conversation. He looked formidable then, tall and sullen, his quick roving eyes seeming to say, "I want to be alone, respect my mood." Once, after sitting next to Mrs. Patrick Campbell at dinner, he rose from the table in such a mood. Her malicious coquetry had been revolting, as when, unable to get response, she put her hands together in an attitude of prayer, begging, "Oh, Mr. Sargent, *do* paint my portrait." He looked up from his plate only to stare her straight in the eye as he replied, "I cannot paint beautiful women." He was irritated and took to pacing for solitude. The art critic C. Lewis Hind caught sight of him and, taking in the situation, began to walk alongside, talking about a convicted murderer who had that afternoon fallen asleep while hearing sentence from the black-capped judge. Sargent listened with increasing attention, then dropped into a chair and motioned to a seat by his side: "Asleep? Extraordinary! Give me more details." It was humanity in the large that interested him, not vain beauties nor the peculiarities of supersophisticates.

As a sudden and unexpected stroke, on January 14, 1897, the Royal Academy elected Sargent a full member. It had been generally expected that he would have to wait a few years more, as others generally waited, and the press confidently expected the election of B. W. Leader. In fact, on the first ballot Leader received ten votes, but when the trend began to appear, many shifted to Sargent, who finally won with thirty-two votes against twenty for Leader. The amazing manner in which he carried the last citadel within the stronghold startled many, though the London *Daily News* wrote: "The Academy has done admirably and has manifested its intention to invest the expression 'Academician' with a more honorable significance than usually attaches to it in an artistic sense."

By sheer strength Sargent was pushing all before him. His paintings were the great attraction at the exhibitions, and though he was still considered a gross innovator, a weird modern, few failed to see how his portraits, which lived and breathed and practically spoke, made all the others look like pale paper cutouts. The boldness, the virility, of his work was its most telling quality, by the brute strength of which he was taking London by storm. No one could compete with him, no one could feel comfortable hung by his side, and that greatest of all compliments, imitation, was widely practiced. At one blow he swept away all the ingrown conventions of the Victorian era — the sweet sentimental portraits of young girls, the pompousness that passed for dignity, the grossness masquerading as taste. He was revivifying English portraiture, which since the death of Lawrence, sixty years before, had remained without a painter of stature. In his very first year as an Academician he again startled the throngs with his portraits. No less a critic than the perpetually damning Henry Adams, he of the bitter gall and spleen, who had no love for Sargent, wrote:

> Sunday, May 2, 1897
> ... But just now we all go to the Royal Academy to see Sargent's portrait of Mrs Meyer and her two children. Mrs Meyer is a sprightly Jewess, who did us the favor to stand under her portrait on the private opening day to show that she is as good as her picture. Decidedly, this time, Sargent has done it. The art of portrait-painting of Jewesses and their children may be varied but cannot further be perfected. Nothing better was ever done, or can be done. Yet he has also a little girl in black — Laura Lister — which is in one respect even finer, at least to me, because it seems almost *felt;* a quality in painting and generally in art which not only has ceased to exist, but has ceased to be missed in the universal solvent of money evaluations. These two works put Sargent quite by himself. I am really pleased for once to admire without qualification, and say so as loudly as I can.

During the early spring of 1897, Sargent met his recent sitter, Mrs. Meyer, in Rome, where she told him of sitting for an Austrian sculptor named Emil Fuchs. She was so pleased with the work that she induced him to accompany her to the studio. He liked the bust well enough, even praising some drawings he saw on the wall, though after Fuchs himself drew attention to the fact that

they were a little crabbed in style, he agreed. Before he left Rome
he stopped at the studio a second time, offering Fuchs the use of
his London studio that fall when he came to England to finish the
bust. He repeated the invitation when Fuchs arrived, though the
sculptor, knowing better than Sargent the effect of marble dust
on wet paintings, wisely refrained from accepting. Instead, he
made a counterproposal, asking if he might make some oil studies
in the studio, that Sargent would oversee or criticize. The startling plan he outlined was that he would begin at five-thirty in the
morning and clear out by ten, when Sargent expected his own
sitter. Several times Sargent got up at an early hour to see what
Fuchs was doing, and how he went about it. He rarely said much,
for, as with Rothenstein, he was hampered by an inability to hurt
anyone he knew was making a serious effort, and the pungent
criticisms Fuchs might have valued never came forth. Sargent
offered the use of all his materials, the brushes, paints, and palettes
that lay about in profusion, and which to other painters are sacred
objects for their own use alone. Now and then, saying little, he
came in and helped with the painting of a passage that Fuchs found
difficult. "Color," he remarked one morning, "is an inborn gift,
but appreciation of value is merely training of the eye which
everyone ought to be able to acquire." He invited Fuchs to come
with a friend to lunch one day and, when they arrived, told them
he had accepted an invitation for them all from a sitter, whose
rather shrewd face was mocking them from the easel in the studio.
Off they went to the New Bond Street art gallery of Asher
Wertheimer, where he particularly admired one piece of china
and then was unable to dissuade Wertheimer from having it
wrapped and sent to Tite Street.

When the Royal Academy exhibition opened the following
year, Wertheimer peered down from the walls. For sheer probity
his picture surpassed anything else seen in those august rooms.
With remarkable fidelity and intensity of expression it conveyed
a wealth of knowledge about the individual, his Jewish background, and the source of his apparent wealth. It spoke of a certain craftiness of which the owner himself was aware, and with
which he seemed to be quite satisfied, a self-admitted keenness that
was not unmixed with realistic perception of its limitations. Here

was a man who would be a hard one at making a bargain, but no Shylock either, for there was pathos and humor in the face too, enough humor certainly to see himself for what he was. The figure had a natural dignity that was not put there by a trick of the painter, but accompanied his transference to the canvas. And, finally, it was obvious that Sargent, seeing him in this frank way, tendered him a grudging respect. For with all that it says of the man, curiously enough, the canvas is not unsympathetic. Instead, it leaves the spectator with a sensation that Wertheimer is rather a good soul, with a warm heart inside. Henry Adams had seen the picture at Tite Street the previous November: "Sargent has just completed another Jew," he wrote. "Wertheimer, a worse crucifixion than history tells of." He completely missed the scope of characterization given the work, grasping only the immediate and obvious aspect and missing all the admiration with which the portrayal is imbued.

Wertheimer lived on a large scale in Connaught Place, surrounded by antique treasures and many children. It was a happy household, one in which Sargent was pleased to be a frequent guest. His attendance there was so regular and happy that it was rumored for a time that he was a suitor to Wertheimer's daughter Ena, who doubtless was his favorite, though such gossip momentarily angered him as well as her actual prospective groom, Robert Mathias. Strangely enough, the friendship with Wertheimer was very real, and though originally based on considerations of business, grew in personal warmth throughout the decade that followed.

It was in 1896, or early 1897, the two had become acquainted, probably on one of those expeditions when Sargent was engaged in seeking furnishings for his studio. It would appear that Wertheimer was just the shrewd dealer he seemed, with an eye for merchandise that necessitated a wholesome respect for Sargent and his art. It was no coincidence that from the time of their acquaintance a new type of sitter became discernible at Tite Street, the thin-nosed and strong-chinned English types that had predominated now being joined by people of obvious, almost too obvious, wealth and of wholly or faintly Semitic appearance. As it happened, they were eminently paintable and, swelling the ranks of his applicants as they did, helped to produce the bidding of money against money that was raising his prices. By the late nineties it was well known in London that Sargent took a thousand guineas for a portrait, and that he had a list of applicants.

The full extent of Wertheimer's influence is difficult to assess. There is little more to go on than the stream of portraits of his own family that year by year issued from Tite Street. The portrait of Asher Wertheimer himself was done in 1897. At the Academy in 1898 it was accompanied by a companion piece of his wife in white gown and pearls. Two daughters seem to have been done in rapid succession, and in 1901 there appeared a double portrait of two more, followed the next year by portraits of Alfred and Almina Wertheimer; then two groups, each with three children. In 1904 Mrs. Wertheimer was done a second time, followed in 1905 by a portrait of Ena, the second time she was done if the group in which she also appears is considered. All together twelve canvases, three of them large groups, were done of the Wertheimer family, more even than that wealthy cynic could have paid for.

It seems clear that the Wertheimer portraits were done, each of them, in response to some volume of business sent Sargent by the dealer. They do in fact occur during his most prosperous, busiest years, and Wertheimer appears to have been more successful as an agent than even the two American architects. Business relations with these various people sometimes resulted in events that Sargent did not himself know the meaning of, as witness a letter written to Stanford White at this time:

> October 14, 1898
> 33, Tite Street,
> Chelsea, S.W.

My dear Stanford

A box has arrived from Allard who writes me that it is sent to my care at your command, and that I must unpack it to see if it is all right. It is — a Velasquez head of an Infanta, in perfect condition, delicious in color. Meanwhile I have screwed it up again in its case, renewed my fire insurance and hired a policeman to watch my house — until I hear from you what is to be done with it. My abode is not proof against fire or burglar, and I must turn into a dragoon and sit on this treasure.

Where are you and when are you coming over? If you do,

come to Fulham Road. Great developments. Same message to
McKim — and love to you both.

Yours
John S. Sargent

That a certain mutual relation existed with them all is further
revealed by another letter, written two weeks later:

Oct. 27th [1898]
33, Tite Street,
Chelsea, S.W.

Dear Mrs Gardner

I find myself, in the same breath, giving notes to you to two
very different kinds of people — one of them is Ian Malcolm, a
charming fellow . . .

The other presentation is to you in some character as a collector
of old pictures. Mr Asher Wertheimer has asked me to give his
son Edward a line to you and I have succumbed in judicious
language. This son is taking over to America a good collection of
Dutch pictures that his father bought last year, the Hope collection,
and some English last century things, among which you may find
some new toys.

I am sorry to hear Mr Gardner has been ill lately & hope he is
better.

It seems a long time since we have seen you over here.

Yours sincerely
John S. Sargent

In February 1899 a comprehensive exhibition of Sargent's work
was opened at Copley Hall in Boston. In an age when the "one-
man" show was still a rarity, if not entirely unknown, Boston had
never seen an exhibition of this size and scope. The catalogue listed
ninety-four portraits and landscapes, many of them borrowed from
English collections, plus an assortment of thirteen drawings, including sketches of George Meredith and Gabriel Fauré. Sargent's
reputation, already firmly established by the St. Botolph Club
exhibition of 1888, the murals unveiled in 1895, and the numerous
portraits, now sprang to new heights. Boston experienced trans-
ports of delight over a man they could consider one of themselves,

and the show was so well greeted that it was shortly demanded en bloc by the Museum of Fine Arts in Philadelphia. Because of the complicated consents to be obtained from owners, this was impossible to negotiate. In the midst of this excitement a report circulated in America that the artist had died. The report, of course, was greatly exaggerated but was not retracted until many enterprising newspapers had run glowing obituaries. In Tite Street, Sargent was bombarded with expressions of remorse, sympathetic telephone calls, and even a few inquiries from someone who wished to rent the studio. When, the following evening, a representative of the New York *Sun* called, Sargent was amused to see the newspaper accounts, which he looked over with laughter, explaining he had been working all day and until six that evening at Fulham Road, where he was modeling a *Crucifixion* for the Boston Library. He admitted being vexed by the calls that broke into his work all day, and seemed to bear particular resentment toward the way the report was carried, a reference to his having died at the home of a son seeming indelicate in the obituary of a bachelor; had he died *anywhere*, he insisted, it would *not* have been at the home of a son. Finally he set about answering telegrams, Mrs. Gardner in Boston rating only three words: *Alive and kicking, Sargent.*

The crucifix he was working on that day was of particular interest to Sargent, for it was the most ambitious piece of sculpture he had yet undertaken, far more complex than the *Moses* he had made for the Hebraic end of the vault. When it was completed in small scale he went over to Paris with it, to ask St.-Gaudens' advice about the enlargement to full size. A short time after his visit St.-Gaudens wrote:

April 12, 1899

Sargent has been here recently, and I saw a good deal of him during his visit as he came to see me about the enlargement of his crucifix for the Boston Library. It is in sculpture and is to go directly opposite the Moses. He has done a masterpiece. He is a big fellow and what is, I'm inclined to think, a great deal more, a good fellow. . . .

A letter written by Henry James a few months later contains a parallel of thought that is interesting to note, as both men were apparently impressed by the increased avoirdupois of a friend they recalled as a slim youth:

Nov. 12, 1899

Sargent grows in weight, honour and interest — to *my* view. He does one fine thing after another — and his crucifixion (that is the big Crucifie with Adam and Eve under each arm of the cross catching drops of blood) for the Boston Library is a most noble, grave and admirable thing.

A third description of him dates from that same year. During February, just as the exhibition opened in Boston, he had begun work on a large group portrait of the three daughters of the Honorable Percy Wyndham, which, contrary to his usual practice and insistence, he consented to do in the drawing room of the Wyndham home at 44 Belgrave Square. Stepping through the little marble hood over the doorstep after one of the sittings, he chanced to pass a cousin of the Wyndhams' arriving for lunch, who noted in his diary:

March 9, 1899

I met him on the doorstep as he was going out, a rather good looking fellow in a pot hat, whom at my first sight I took to be a superior mechanic.

It was true enough that he never looked like an artist in the outward way adopted by many of his confreres, and since the early days, when something of his natural fastidiousness gave way to the flannels and silk scarf in which he sketched on the Thames, he became a typical Londoner, whose calling was in no wise apparent in his dress. He struck people generally as having the look of a professional man, a lawyer perhaps or a businessman, perhaps a banker, certainly not an artist, and few had the cheek of Wyndham's cousin to think him a "superior mechanic." His appearance denoted careful barbering and a good tailor, though he had none of the patent leather shine, the overdressed look, associated with Henry James, which made the author something like an actor dressed for a part. He was the typical Londoner of his circumstances, well off, well brushed, not overdone. His winged collar seemed tight about his neck, and people liked to attribute his rubicund complexion to it, though it showed considerable clearance beneath his beard when he stood. He wore fine dark ties, often with tiny designs dancing over them, and a stickpin thrust through the knot. Across his front hung the gold watch chain that had been his father's, and he carried a gold-headed stick. On visits to Temple, the Wertheimer estate, his straw hat added a further touch of jauntiness, which he liked to exaggerate with a rosebud in his lapel and a sporting air. Still, he was never more than smartly correct, without in any way being conspicuous.

He was increasingly busy as the old century ran toward its end. The murals increasingly were a pleasure pushed into the background by the daily call of portraiture. The portrait of Asher Wertheimer was calling forth a considerable admiration at Philadelphia, where it was sent alone in place of the Copley Hall exhibition, and he was at work on the *Wyndham Sisters*, the largest portrait he had yet undertaken. The drawing room at Belgrave Square was large enough for him to work comfortably, and in that respect it was well he had acceded to request, for with this large canvas and other pictures in hand he might have felt cramped in Tite Street. The commodious furnishings and the portrait of Mrs. Wyndham by Watts, considered one of that painter's best, all proved fine additions to his own composition. Early in March he had all three sisters sketched in, and had already been told that he was not to consider himself free to use the magentas and mauves he loved. His answer to that, as to all such suggestions, was a gentle acceptance which did not imply that he would alter his vision one iota. The success of this huge work was complete when at the private view of the next Academy the Prince of Wales called it "The Three Graces."

The death of Queen Victoria and the planned coronation of King Edward gave added stimulus to demands for portraits, which were now reaching undreamed-of proportions. He was still living in the studio at 33 Tite Street, but the quarters were now cramped, the one studio insufficient for all the works he had in hand. When the small building next door, at number 31, became vacant, he took that too. A thick common wall stood between the studio apartment he rented on the ground floor of number 33 and the new house next door. He had a little archway knocked through, making these two odd domiciles into one. The entire second floor of the new house was made into a studio, which now became strikingly like the old one on the Boulevard Berthier, with a rear window that looked out over the green of his back garden and the larger garden attached to the Royal Hospital next door. Nicola, the model who had been with him at Fairford, for seven years had been his valet as well, and now two maids were added to complete the household in its larger quarters.

There was no longer any question as to who wanted to be painted by Sargent, but rather whom he would find time to paint. McKim was still busy over in America, and suggested a portrait to Henry Lee Higginson, with whom he was associated in the building of the Boston Symphony Hall, and other projects out at Harvard. During the summer of 1901 Higginson went abroad, spoke to Sargent, and reported back to McKim:

> July 18, 1901
> . . . I talked with Sargent, who was far too busy to take me up —
> tho' ready to try — and so we may get at it in September. . . .

September proved futile, and for a while it lay fallow, while he wrestled with the things already begun in the studio; Lord Ribblesdale, whose wife (an Astor) was an annoyance, and had to be asked not to come; the pink-complexioned Lord Cromer, looking like a business executive; the Duke of Devonshire's three daughters in a group, and their brother's wife on a separate canvas; and finally two groups of the Wertheimers, which gave him "an extreme case of Wertheimerism." He had gone to spend a month at Welbeck Abbey, estate of the Duke of Portland, where he did the Duke and Duchess, posing the Duke with his two collies in one of the queer underground chambers built by a previous and crazy duke. The Duchess's portrait was not a success at first, and after working over it too long he slashed it across the middle. She burst into tears, overcome with the disappointment and the fatigue. He felt called upon to reassure her: "I know you so well by now, if you will let me try again I am sure I can paint something alive, which will be a credit to me, and satisfactory to you and your family; so pray forgive me . . . " That was the worst of dealing with emotional women and nobility: the silly way one had to treat them! And those dogs of the Duke's! No sooner had he painted one, than the other, without a moment's hesitation, saluted it "in the way dogs usually do when they wish to pay a compliment, or recognize a friend." "Well!" he burst out in amazement. "That's either the greatest insult, or the greatest compliment, an artist has ever been paid!"

And on the completion of his work he left behind at Welbeck a mound of the rapidly made sketches he constantly made, which the Duke carefully preserved, together with happy memories of many piano duets.

In the midst of all this he found time for his friends. When a move was afoot to give a dinner to Wilson Steer, Rothenstein was delegated to ask him to act as chairman, knowing full well the value of his presence. He replied:

> 31, Tite Street,
> Chelsea, S.W.
> Dec. 6th (1901)
>
> My Dear Rothenstein
>   I will be delighted to join you in doing honor to Steer, and I note the 21st — let me know where the dinner is to be and at what time.
>   My only misgiving is that if there are to be speeches (& I scent them in the air) one might be expected from me, and I am utterly incapable of saying a word. I dare say that this is a recognized fact by this time and I need not fear being asked.
>
> Yours sincerely
> John S. Sargent
>
> I should very much like to show you my decorations but this is my month at the R.A. schools, morning and evening, and I rarely get to Fulham Road. Later on I would be glad to give you your choice of time for coming.

At the dinner he was asked for a toast, the very request appearing to paralyze him. Rising, bug-eyed and purple, he clutched the edge of the table rather prodigiously, and in explosive little bursts, amidst much throat clearing and an embarrassed silence, one word at a time came forth. It never approached any sort of syntax nor sense, and each piece was greeted by wild roars of approval and applause. In the general tumult the nature of the toast was lost, though Will Rothenstein recorded it as "I rise to propose the health of our guest."

In May of the following year another dinner was given in London, this time for Rodin, and it was presided over by George Wyndham, the eminent politician, and brother to the three Wyndham sisters painted two years earlier. Wyndham, D. S. MacColl, the critic, and the French ambassador all made their speeches before Rodin arose to read a dear little schoolboy effusion from half sheets of note paper pinned together, constantly losing his place. With the dinner over, another more intimate gathering awaited at the Arts Club. Rodin, coming out of the café to enter a cab, found boys from the Slade School and South Kensington unhitching the horses. They hauled him through the streets while Sargent replaced the driver on the box and handled the whip and reins. Hardly more than twenty persons were at the club, including Alma-Tadema, and Abbey, Wyndham, and Sydney Cockerell. It was the sort of small rollicking party among intimates that Sargent enjoyed, and he provided magnums of champagne while Tadema spoke in a happy vein. Next came Abbey, quite at his ease, who ended on a saucy note: "I will say no more, as my friend Mr. Sargent is anxious to talk to you." This, as they all knew, was precisely what Sargent was anxious to avoid, but he was forced to his feet amid much applause, to struggle through a few sentences that never quite found their meaning. Rodin had always been one of his staunchest admirers, and making the rounds of the Royal Academy Galleries after the dinner, he halted for quite some time before the group of Mrs. Hunter's daughters. "Here is the Van Dyck of our times!" was his flattering comment. "Sargent has never done anything better than that. It is a bouquet of flowers! It is a masterly composition, without effort."

Abbey had become a famous muralist in the years since he was first assisted by Sargent in the handling of oils, and now he was chosen by King Edward to paint the official coronation picture, an onerous task few liked to undertake and for which he had been chosen over the entire ranks of British painters. Once selected for the job, there was no refusing, however. During sittings with the Prince of Wales, the future King George V, Abbey was amazed to have the Prince question him about Sargent's income. Apparently it was much discussed in London, and the Prince supposed that a close friend of the artist might know the answer. Abbey replied, with truth, that he did not know. He might have had means of estimating his friend's wealth, but Sargent had never told anyone the amount of his income. The Prince saw that his intention was to evade and prodded him with "Do you suppose it's ten thousand pounds?"

"More likely twenty thousand," Abbey answered.

"My God! I wish I had twenty thousand pounds a year," said the heir to an empire.

William Chase also was in London during that summer of 1902. A group of his students planned to present a portrait of him to the Metropolitan Museum, and they proposed that Sargent do the picture first and then allow it to be shown at Knoedler's in New York, where money for its purchase might be raised from those viewing it. He accepted these terms at a time when he was putting off other applicants, and writing syrupy letters to do so:

Dear Mrs Horner
    Many thanks for your kind letter . . .
    I have been thinking ever since those pleasant days at Mells of those four beautiful faces that I mean to do — and of how to do them. If it were not for other pictures I should propose posting straight back, and starting at once. As it is I suppose next spring and in my studio — if that suits everyone.
    . . .

                                                    Yours sincerely
                                                    John S. Sargent

But the loss of time and the uncertainty of payment were not the only inconveniences consequent on painting Chase, as his letter home shows:

. . . Sargent's portrait of me is now finished. He did it in six sittings, and I think you will like it. My friends here say it is perfection . . . He has done me as a painter and they say he has caught my animation — whatever that means . . . I shall be glad to get away now that the picture is done as every American I meet (and there are many of them) wants to go to Sargent's to see me on canvas. I am afraid it will prove a nuisance.

Sargent will most likely go to America next winter. We have arranged to paint one another when he is in New York again. Sargent exhibition at the Academy is *magnificent*.

Despite all the rush and anxiety of these months, nothing disturbed the close personal relationship with Wertheimer, who regularly walked across the Park on Sunday mornings to Tite Street. The two men found it a good time to discuss their business together, and of late Wertheimer, who was an exceedingly warm-hearted parent and was much disturbed by the dissipated habits of his son Alfred, found it soothing to bare his troubled soul to the sympathetic artist. A strange union bound them at these moments, when the artist's great but carefully hidden reservoirs of compassion were touched. Wertheimer's grief seemed to become his own, he was so unhappy with the grief of this father over a son. He would have done anything to spare his friend this pain and, unknown to the father, wrote inviting young Alfred to lunch at Monico's one Thursday. The question at issue was some money Alfred had taken from his father and which, now that the loss was discovered, he was unable to explain or replace. Very hotly he claimed that he had lent it to someone and would say no more. At luncheon, too, he proved to view the matter with a hot-tempered irascibility, declaring that he was prepared to go on the stage as a means of earning the money to repay his father. This obviously was no solution, for Sargent realized that it would only upset Asher further were his son to embark on the uncertainties of such a life. He returned home still deep in thought, and sat down to write to the young man again:

Thursday night
31, Tite Street,
Chelsea, S.W.

My dear Wertheimer
Your news of an hour ago took my breath away I have ruminated it all the way home; and I cannot refrain from writing to you that

I think you are entering a very critical stage and one which may make your brouille with your father much worse, for the simple reason that it makes a public eclat of what is really a private matter, easily patched up.

Let me propose to you, if I may do so with safety to my life, for you have a celebrated temper, and no doubt wear a revolver somewhere behind, that I should be the man you lent the money to, return it tomorrow, and you take it back to your father and the incident is closed.

There would be the advantage of ending a false situation, and of not touching the stage with a pair of tongs —

Yours sincerely
John S. Sargent

Whether or not young Wertheimer accepted the offer is not known, and the only further fact that can be deduced is that the two men parted on good terms. Soon after this Alfred Wertheimer seems to have asked for a picture of Sargent, and was given a copy of the lithograph Rothenstein had made, suitably inscribed: "To my friend Alfred, John S. Sargent." But later that same year the father's hand came down strongly, whether for this or other sins is not known, and he was sent off to South Africa, where he died.

The Better Mousetrap

THE CALL of Boston was becoming more urgent. One can well imagine that, much as the Trustees wished the new panels to have proper gestation, the continued delay was not sitting well with them, nor with McKim. Hence, as early as December 1896, or some eighteen months after the installation of the first phase, McKim thought a second installation should have been ready:

December 19, 1896

My dear Sargent:

I am not a famous letter writer, as you know, — but then neither are you; but I none the less wonder constantly about your work, both for the library and otherwise, and delight in your achievements, as we all do in talking about them. The people who went on to Boston the last time to see the result of the first canvases are eager to go again . . . It will be too much to hope that Mrs. Jack [Gardner] will be absent the next time, so make up your mind to another speech!

. . . and if you will send me a page of the history of your work up to date and the outlook for its instalation, I shall be much obliged, as they ask me when I expect your work.

Hoping that you are in robust health — notwithstanding your exhausting study of architectural panels — and that the work advances, and with messages to Mrs Harry White when you see her.

Yours faithfully
Charles F. McKim

P.S. I had a letter from Ned Abbey the other day saying that he had forwarded his 'Fiametta', but we have not seen it, and I don't know whether it has gone to the bottom of the ocean or not. My client expected it last summer. If it doesn't come pretty soon I don't know what chance I shall have of disposing of it for him.

In his subtle way, McKim managed to cram into the body of this letter three passages urging haste in the completion of the second portion of the murals, and the postscript, with its talk of Abbey, clearly implied that work delivered late is difficult for him to handle. Probably it would not have been written to Sargent, concerning Abbey as it does, had it not been intended as a warning. Thus it is apparent that by the end of 1896 McKim seemed to think the next section of the murals should soon be brought to completion, urging Sargent by every means short of outright exhortation to get it ready. Despite this letter, with the solemn resolution that typified him, Sargent continued to work at the pace he felt best, finally requiring the six years that followed the receipt of this letter.

McKim, of course, was the first to be made aware that the long-awaited panels were finally to be shipped and installed, and after sending a stream of portrait applicants across the ocean, he was now able to work more effectively at home. Major Higginson must have breathed a sigh of relief to know that he would finally be painted without the necessity of another trip abroad. Others were also being gently stirred in the inimitable manner of Charles the Charmer. McKim was then at work on the reconstruction of the White House, with which he had been entrusted by the new President, Theodore Roosevelt. It was a mean job, necessarily carried out on a limited appropriation and within a time limit imposed by the impatient young Chief Executive. Mrs. Roosevelt was consulting McKim on matters not strictly architectural, though they fell into that wide range which McKim, Mead and White liked to assume as their responsibility. She wrote a full letter that spring from Oyster Bay dealing with pictures, their placement and manner of hanging. From there it was a simple matter to mention that there was need for a portrait of the President as well. Early in May, Henry White sent a letter over to Tite Street from the American Embassy, which, as it happened, had an enclosure:

May 13, 1902

Dear Mr. Sargent

I must send you a line to say how greatly I am pleased at the good news that you will paint my portrait for the White House. Disregarding entirely my personal feelings, it seems to me eminently fitting that an American President should have *you* paint his picture. I cordially thank you.

Sincerely yours
Theodore Roosevelt

McKim was also in contact with Secretary of State John Hay with reference to the plans to build the Lincoln Memorial, at a suitable moment no doubt mentioning Sargent's trip and the portrait of Roosevelt. It was a good starting point. During the summer of 1902 an official announcement was made that Sargent would arrive in December to supervise the installation of his new works in the Boston Library, and also, while in America, would paint a portrait of the President.

Sargent, returning from a short trip to Norway, found sitters besieging his door, their numbers swelled by the coronation fever that gripped London. They kept him so occupied throughout the fall that he despaired of leaving in December, for he refused to quicken the pace of his work or reduce the number of sittings, which not infrequently reached twenty-five for a single portrait. McKim was uneasy about Sargent's arrangements awaiting in America, the Trustees were restless, and he finally announced that he would sail in January.

On the morning of January 17, Carroll Beckwith kept a lookout for the liner *Lucania*, which was reported delayed and whose exact time of arrival was uncertain. The next morning he was up early and down at the dock again, where he stood in the Siberian weather, shuffling his feet to keep warm, until the ship was nudged into the pier. This time Sargent could not quietly slip into town as he had before. Reporters were questioning Beckwith on the pier. They turned to meet Sargent as he made his way down the gangplank, puffing frost through his beard. There was a barrage of questions, which he answered as best he could, the reporters noting his deliberation, his evident feeling of embarrassment, and the modesty of his tone that was remarked on by them all.

"I shall stay in New York only two days," he said quietly, "and then go on to Boston to complete another part of the decoration in the Boston Library. The work for the second part is due to arrive on a steamer in Boston in two days."

He was being very deliberate, and despite the cold and the winds off the river, against which he raised his collar, he chose his words carefully, shifting his face around whenever a camera was raised, so as not to be photographed.

"I may not be permitted to speak of its character, but it is a sequence of what is already in place . . . Its central idea is that in the teachings of Christ to his followers the religious thought of the world found its culmination. The portion now in the Library depicts the development of Christianity in the history of the chosen people. I cannot say how long the work of placing the second part [on the walls] will take me, but I shall be in this country two or three months. There is a third part to be put up in the Boston Library, but I cannot say how long it will be before it is ready, or when it will be placed. Each part will be in sequence of the preceding."

There was greater interest in his plans to paint the President, a point on which he was prodded.

"From Boston I shall return to New York and also visit Philadelphia and Washington. I expect to paint the portrait of President Roosevelt in the historical series of the Presidents of the United States. It is the official portrait."

Eventually Beckwith was able to get his friend away from the press and go with him to Herbert Satterlee's house for lunch. It was typical of McKim's close planning to take Sargent from the dock directly off to lunch at Satterlee's, though it is apparent that he had not figured on the presence of Beckwith. For years McKim had been associated with Satterlee's father-in-law, J. P. Morgan, in connection with the American Academy in Rome, in which Frank Millet also was active. Morgan eventually asked McKim to undertake the building of a library for him in New York, together with a residence for his daughter, Mrs. Satterlee. McKim apparently felt that the matter of a portrait hung on a personal interview between Sargent and Satterlee, but Beckwith's presence made the proper discussion impossible. Two days later Sargent was in Boston, where a freighter deposited the deal-wood crates containing his decorations. It was still necessary to keep his plans fluid to accommodate the wishes of the President, whenever he chose to express them, but, as no word was awaiting him, he began sittings on the first portrait planned for Boston — Mrs. W. C. Endicott, Jr.

This commission followed on the portrait of Mrs. Endicott, Sr., done the year before in Tite Street, by all odds one of Sargent's finest achievements. Apparently preferring not to take a studio for the still-undetermined period before he would leave for Washington, he undertook it in the Endicotts' Marlborough Street house. In the drawing room the light did not come from a good direction, and he was told of an empty bedroom on top the house that might suit his needs.

He went back there for dinner the night before the work was to begin, and found Mrs. Endicott wearing a Worth gown made specially for the portrait. "No, that won't do at all," was his comment, after which fiat he was shown a party dress, which he thought equally inappropriate. "Haven't you got something black and white?" The result was an old flowered muslin dress, in which the picture was begun the next morning.

The top floor of the house could be reached by a little open-grilled lift. The room itself was regular in shape, except for the rounded projection of four windows, behind his back and toward his left as he stood before the easel. He had no model stand, so he placed Mrs. Endicott just beyond the last window, where the light hit her well and she was against a shadowed section of the wall. It was not a perfect light, halftones hovering over the face, tones that were a nuisance and difficult to blend into the value scale. He got the hang of it, though, and proceeded to make use of this unfortunate feature to give the picture a delicacy of tone that brings an intimacy generally lacking in the more impersonal studio lighting. When he stepped back fifteen feet from the easel his back was pressed against the window casements, and that too limited him, for he did not want to place strong accents without seeing their effect from a greater distance. As always, he allowed himself to be guided by the circumstances, turning the difficulties of the situation into strengths, replacing his more accustomed boldness with delicacy, his strong accents with subtle halftones.

Sargent's days were thus being divided between sittings, on Marlborough Street, and supervising the installation of the murals at Copley Square. It was necessary, of course, and important to see Mrs. Gardner, on whom he depended for the proper introduction to society of Mary Hunter and Ethel Smyth, who had come to Boston to attend the performance of Miss Smyth's opera.

He found Mrs. Gardner deeply involved in her newly completed house on Frederick Law Olmsted's "Fenway," a house which seemed to have grown from a demented fancy. Cousin Ralph Curtis, who at a profit had supplied much of the materials, must have told him of this latest extravaganza of Mrs. Jack's. Now he could see it for himself — centered on a great glass-roofed court, where flowers could be grown the year round, it was in that respect an expression of her delight in the visits made to Italy. All the rooms and passages of the house opened onto this great inner courtyard so that the whole, when heated in winter, presented the appearance of an oversized greenhouse, but the strangest greenhouse ever. For, largely inspired by the Palazzo Barbaro, the house was laid out in a jumble of Gothic passages, erratically placed steps, and doorless chambers, and had then been filled with the spoils of Mrs. Gardner's travels abroad: purchases made through Bernard Berenson and Ralph Curtis, not to mention the Persian rug "of the finest design and period" acquired in London. There was no longer any Jack Gardner to restrain her fancies, which now were expressed with fantastic liberality.

Mrs. Jack had a notion to have Mrs. Fiske Warren painted in her house, and Sargent thought it a possibility, even finding himself willing to increase his burdens by alternating sittings between the Fenway and Marlborough Street. Some of the properties of the house — the statuette candlesticks, busts, elaborately carved chairs with gilded terminals — would lend themselves to a portrait, and since something might result from the attempt, he was willing to humor Mrs. Gardner.

Not only was Sargent working every daylight minute of those short winter days, but his evenings too were obligated, for he was attending a round of entertainments, many of them apparently in his honor. One evening, at Mrs. Sears', he chanced to sit behind the little doll-like Mrs. Fiske Warren, whose tiny proportions and highly colored cheeks made her the living facsimile of a Meissenware figurine, the likeness stressed by a dress of green velvet, evidently worn for his approval and for the picture. The green exaggerated her color; the beautiful glazed quality of her cheeks, with their youthful bloom, made him fearful that the coloring in his portrait of her might be ascribed to cosmetics. It stirred vague memories, and he thought it best to attack directly.

"I hope that isn't the dress for the picture."

"Yes," came the frank reply. Probably she was intimidated, as most people were, though she asked rather sweetly, "Do you like green?"

"No," he shot back. "You must wear pink."

His thought was that the similarity of tone would prevent her complexion from appearing artificial: the pink would absorb much of the red of her own coloring. Completely taken up with his solution of the artistic problem, he had perhaps been harsh and appeared to miss the dither in which his ruling left Mrs. Warren. She did not have a pink dress.

He chose the Gothic Room in Mrs. Gardner's palace, on the second tier of passages, for this portrait. He carefully arranged the easel and model stand in the farthest corner, so that he would be able to walk back across the tiled floor and through the passage to see his work from a distance of nearly forty feet. At his order a large piece of cloth was fitted over the small rose window high up on the wall behind the model stand, and propped in place by long poles that rested against the floor. Mrs. Warren arrived in a makeshift answer to his orders, for all Boston had set to work hunting up a pink dress for her tiny form, no one finding one that fitted. The best belonged to her sister-in-law, and it was much too long and full, wrapping around her feet when she attempted to take a step. Nor was there any dress for her twelve-year-old daughter, without whom she would not consent to pose for fear of the boredom that might come over her. The girl was seated behind her mother, her body partly hidden to conceal the formlessness of the plain piece of pink cloth in which she was wrapped. The stand itself received the full glow of daylight streaming through the twin Italian windows behind the easel.

All this was a boon to Mrs. Gardner. She was pleased to think of her house being the site of important work. It was a further boon to have Sargent about for her luncheons, and on the occasions when he was too occupied to leave his work, she brought the ladies up to watch him before his easel. In fact, Mrs. Sears brought her camera along, and snapped him as he dashed about during a sitting: his hip-length smock hanging open over his imposing vest and watch chain; his humorous look as he held a brush in his teeth while his hands were busy; his full-armed vigor as he mixed the colors on his palette.

Between sittings, the murals, and social obligations, he probably did not see an editorial in the *New York Times,* congratulating him on his return to the United States and on the fact that he would paint the President. Finally, on February 1, a letter arrived from Washington:

January 29, 1903

Dear Mr. Sargent

Will you give Mrs. Roosevelt and myself the pleasure of staying at the White House during the time you are occupied in painting the portrait? Come any time after next Monday during the month of February. How long will you take?

We look forward to seeing you.

Sincerely yours,

Theodore Roosevelt

In answer he explained that he was unable to get away from Boston for another week, that the work would probably occupy a week if prosecuted directly, and that he would require a day to look over the White House for a place with proper light, fitting windows with blinds if necessary. Roosevelt replied:

February 3, 1903

Dear Mr. Sargent

Good! We shall expect you on the 10th or 11th, and shall look forward to a visit of at least a week from you. Your room will be

all ready the evening of the 10th; then we can settle where you
are going to paint.
                Sincerely yours,
                                        Theodore Roosevelt

This arrangement left time to conclude the work in hand, rather
than to have to pick it up later, as he had feared might be necessary.

The picture of Mrs. Endicott was coming along well. He
broke the tragedy of painting her hair gray by saying, "I'll put
some gray in your hair, because it will get gray"; successful in
that little ruse, he next determined to add a stylized landscape
background, doing it in tones of warm ocher and umber, carrying through the rich hues of the figure. It was entirely different
from his usual product, more intimate, with a most engaging
friendly warmth. The hands and draperies were left as improvisations, a flower and a fan were merely indicated for their
color, without being brought into focus or making important
additions to the composition. In sum it was a large sketch, with
all the best of Sargent, in a warm and mellow mood. Mrs.
Warren's picture, on the other hand, was more along the lines
he had previously employed, though it, too, had a greater intimacy
than was present in the mass of works that issued from Tite
Street. In fact, it was a remarkably successful essay, technically
one of his finest achievements, its chromatic range extended by a
richness of ornamentation that shimmers and looms through the
dimness behind the figures, producing an awareness of beauties
lent by the presence of objects only half seen, but felt in an
extraordinary way, adding an emotional enchantment to all the
armory of his pictorial improvisation. Mrs. Warren was of too
active a temperament to sit still and be stared at by the bevy of
personalities who watched her sessions in the Gothic Room, including the Boston artists who made a demonstration of Sargent's
technique out of the progress of her portrait. The boredom that
stole over her features could not be eradicated; in the completed
portrait she wears an unfortunate air of smugness which mars
the picture badly. Perhaps because through a number of sittings,
after her daughter had a bad fall and turned up with a swollen
nose and eye, Mrs. Warren had to sit alone, she does not suggest

maternity in her upright posture, which in itself gives no indication of another human presence. Teamed with this, the tender
portrayal of the daughter is a jarring note, especially as she nestles
against her mother and rests her chin precariously on one shoulder.
The softly lit Italian terra-cotta Madonna that shines through
an upper corner of the canvas, instead of enforcing the sympathetic
union of mother and daughter, seems almost to wave a castigating
finger, and though intended to reflect the relationship portrayed,
serves actually to point to something false. The many beauties
of the painting itself, the extraordinary and unmatched display
of values, the magnificent projection of light into the darks, are
all overlooked in the immediate distaste for the attitudes of the
models that is aroused in the observer.

Now Sargent turned to Washington. The President was being
gracious in inviting him to stay at the White House, an honor that
raised not only his personal status but also that of his profession,
which many still considered somewhat doubtful socially. Painters
were honored here and there. It was an age when even an actor
could be knighted, so far had these previously scorned callings
been elevated by the example of a few fine men. Nonetheless,
a portraitist, though he might be the guest of a duke while working for him, hardly expected the courtesies normally reserved for
the heads of states. We must realize that Roosevelt was motivated
not only by consideration of Sargent's position in his profession,
but by the personal esteem of so many mutual friends, men like
Henry White, Joseph Hodges Choate, and John Hay, who considered him a wise and a good man.

On the way to Washington Sargent stopped off in New York to
see a Tintoretto that was offered Mrs. Gardner. It was a fine
one and, as he had admired Tintoretto since as a boy he filled
letters with descriptions of that artist's work, he recommended
the purchase, writing that he was happy to have a hand in swelling
her wonderful collection.

The White House did not seem a propitious place to work that
first day when he went prowling with the President, looking for
a good light and a good pose. First they went to the South Portico,
but he objected to that. Then they went into the Blue Room, and
he did not like that either. Roosevelt began exhibiting signs of

irritation as they made their way upstairs, calling back over his shoulder, "The trouble with you, Sargent, is that you don't know what you want."

"No. The trouble, Mr. President, is that you don't know what a pose means." Roosevelt had reached the landing halfway up the stairs, and grasping the glass-topped newel post, he swung around sharply, shouting, "Don't I!"

"Don't move an inch. You've got it now," said the cool painter. The stance was acutely pictorial, showing Roosevelt in all his arrogant, strutting nature. It would typify him nicely and, by giving him something to hold onto, help anchor him to the spot.

Roosevelt, that advocate of the strenuous life, seemed intent on making Sargent's life strenuous while he was in the White House. For the first few days, immediately after lunch, he would issue from the executive wing carrying a batch of papers and walk quickly to the living quarters where Sargent awaited him on the stairs. A few blinds over the nearby windows gave what approximated a studio light in its steadiness and single direction. The President arrived a trifle breathless, urging him to work immediately, as he had only little time "today." It was the part of the day when he normally fenced with General Leonard Wood, his professional adviser in the Rough Rider days. Roosevelt's entire retinue was present during his sessions of posing, and he was rarely still, turning away, twisting about, bellowing to everyone in sight, often completely forgetting himself in his energetic gestures. Posing was not to his liking. He had never been able to hold still, and the fact that only a week earlier he had given Chartran sittings for a portrait, one that he did not like, added to his pent-up feelings of pressure. Soon, his patience spent, he was off again into the executive wing, his retinue at his heels. For Sargent the problem was to discover some single aspect that was entirely typical, thus simplifying his problems. The President had settled that the first day when he turned on him on the stair landing. Roosevelt's very marked characteristics were entirely clear in that pose, his athletic propensities were stamped on his very stance, his squint and pince-nez with trailing ribbon were typical, and the overstressed muscularity of his hand on the newel was evidence of his vigor. Vigor certainly would be the key to any portrayal of

Roosevelt, the painter realizing that if the thickset body was silhouetted in the position he assumed it would carry an essence of the man. It would not be a subtle character study, there would be few overtones, little room for expressive nuance. Were the President a better sitter, finer work could be done of him, but an official portrait was not the place for soul searching.

The White House was a dull place for a painter to be guest. Except for meals he was left pretty much alone, devoting his mornings to work on little landscapes of the grounds, which he presented to Mrs. Roosevelt, who sent them on to Sagamore Hill. He had many friends in common with the President, who unfortunately took conversation into his own hands. Instead of learning, like others, to talk with Sargent about music, books, or criminology, Roosevelt made the natural mistake of turning the conversation to art, and found his guest equally pleased to turn it away. Sargent disliked vapid generalities, and hated even more to talk about his own work. In contemporary fields it was impossible for him to say anything that was critical, for he knew full well that every comment was taken as defense, a phenomenon that he brought to the attention of Mary Hunter when he said, "Do persuade your sister to *pretend* she likes Elgar's music, for when she says she doesn't, people think it's jealousy." Literature or the peeves of Henry Adams, who particularly annoyed him, would doubtless have filled their talk with much thought and humor. But Roosevelt was always impatient to get the best out of everyone he talked with, and with Sargent it was art. Then, too, it was a house full of children, to whom a bachelor would not be expected to respond, and the "White House gang," that brood of outrageous juveniles the President was nurturing, thought it sport to shine mirrors on the roof of the Senate Chamber and to bring their ponies upstairs in McKim's new elevator. Boxes of paints and brushes were not safe with them about. Sargent was to be counted lucky if they did not attend their father's sittings on horseback.

In his eagerness the President made no difficulty about sittings at first, granting him the period after lunch each afternoon, then hurrying off just as it seemed some work was about to be accomplished. But soon he complained that it was becoming more difficult to give him even that, what there was of it, and Sargent considered beginning his other works while still in residence at the White House. He had hopes of getting back to Boston with reasonable speed, at least in time to check the murals before their unveiling, even though Roosevelt's prancing habits were making this uncertain. When the sittings carried over into a second week, and were no longer being held every day anyhow, he decided it would be best to begin on the portrait of John Hay, which McKim, with his usual deftness, had arranged. Hay was, of course, a natural subject for a Sargent portrait, sharing both friends and literary interests with the painter. The wonder of it was that he was not painted during the years he had been ambassador to the Court of St. James's, when the two were so often thrown together socially. Hay was close to Roosevelt, who regularly dropped by at his home after church on Sundays for a chat.

It was a busy week. Above the routine of his work and the disappointments attendant on Roosevelt, he would have to leave early Thursday morning for Philadelphia, where he expected to receive on Friday an honorary degree from the University of Pennsylvania. Monday and Tuesday he seems to have had sittings with Hay, in his house on H Street. All this was very secret, only Henry Adams completely savoring the secrecy, having wormed the story out of Mrs. Hay. Adams urged her to sit also, but in that was unsuccessful. Then on Wednesday, Roosevelt decided to sit, and a note was dispatched to Hay:

[Wednesday, Feb. 19, 1903]

Dear Mr Hay

The President has decided to sit this afternoon, so I am obliged to ask you to excuse me — I am leaving for Philadelphia tomorrow morning, with the intention of returning on Saturday night — Can you give me a sitting on Monday morning at 10 or so? Or Sunday afternoon? Or, if not Sunday, Monday? . . .

That afternoon Roosevelt's portrait was completed. He dictated a typical note to his son Kermit, who was at Harvard: "This afternoon I had my last sitting with Mr. Sargent. I like his picture enormously. I am going to play single-stick with General Wood."

To Sargent the whole experience was a singularly vexing one.

He would not forget it for years. He "felt like a rabbit in the presence of a boa constrictor," and his vexation was expressed in an interview with the press. He estimated that he had sittings of approximately half an hour in length, an intentional misstatement expressive of his petulance. He seemed to feel that he might have done well had he been less harassed, had the President been more co-operative. With a morbid, brittle humor not apparent to those interviewing him, he explained that the President's characteristics were so well defined that *he needed no time for study*, an obvious absurdity to anyone who knew him and was aware that he never happily competed with God in the rapidity of his creation. He was feeling sour when he said there were five sittings, each of a half hour's duration, immediately after luncheon: the President was very busy, and his impatience added to his speed. It was not funny; it was a personal joke he was enjoying in public, mocking himself before the crowds. It had been a galling experience. Actually Roosevelt had spent more time with him than he said, though doubtless not the length he had specified he required. The actual operative time he had Roosevelt's attention and could paint was, he thought, hardly half an hour a day. After five sessions he cried quits. What he produced was hardly more than a sketch, the blocking and modeling occupying his attention more than the features. The President's eyes would have come later, and were never actually done. Out of disgust he placed some finishing highlights, an indication of the pince-nez, the silk lapels of the frock coat, the key chain, and declared himself done. He would never again allow himself to be used so ill.

The following morning he made his way through the snow to catch a train to Philadelphia. The commencement exercises were being held there in the Academy of Music. Would not his father have been proud? Old FitzWilliam had been troubled by the latent unrespectability of the painter's life, the socially doubtful aspects of his condition. Now his own school, the University of Pennsylvania, where he had earned both his Bachelor's and Medical degrees, was honoring his son with an LL.D. During the ceremony Sargent noticed that General Wood, of whom he had heard in the White House but had never met, also was receiving a degree — decidedly a good-looking man. After the ceremony, he men-

tioned to Wood's aide, "He has a magnificent head, and I was painting his picture in my mind's eye. Do you think he would want me
to paint him?"

Oddly enough, another recipient of the Doctor of Laws degree
that day was a lean professor of political science at Princeton,
whose Cassius-like head he failed to notice, though one day he
would paint that too — Woodrow Wilson.

Back at Washington, he continued the sittings on H Street.
Hay also had clearly marked characteristics, and a well-defined
badgerlike look, but Sargent stomached a sufficiency of heads
that needed no study. With a certain revulsion for what he had
produced of Roosevelt, he was unwilling to allow surface elements
to dominate this study. The badger look was not avoided, but
the penetration of gaze and the clarity of mind were what he
made dominant. He manipulated his tools with a certain brute
energy, loading on pigment, using his fingers in the rich impasto;
the white beard looking bright in the light reflected from the snow
outside, telling against the shimmer of red lip, but all remaining
subordinate to the slight squint of the eyes that speaks more than
all his biographies of the inner life of the man.

In the meantime General Wood was pleased by the opportunity
to be painted by him. He had Sargent call to look over the house
on Connecticut Avenue in which he was living, and at length
the little trunk room in the attic was chosen to work in. The first
sitting was on February 23. "Sargent is a nervous man," Wood
noted in his diary. "Very intense, and working rapidly . . . with
tremendous concentration." The second day he was surprised to
see all the work of the previous day scraped out, and what appeared to be a new start made. For short periods the two talked
casually, the painter smoking furiously and apparently as much
concerned with the conversation as with his work. Then suddenly,
amid puffs even more volcanic, he would stride to the easel, forced
almost to turn his back on Wood because of the very tight quarters,
and paint as furiously as he smoked. Wood tried to interest
him in the Philippine Islands, which he described as a fine subject
matter with brilliant light, highly decorative flora, and beautifully
built Igorot natives. Probably realizing that tropic lands without
a classic heritage of the European sort were outside the scope of

his art, Sargent was not much interested; besides, the sea trip alone was enough to dissuade him. "Nothing but ban*a*nas, ban*a*nas," he said, pronouncing the words with a broad British *a*, "and besides, Winslow Homer has already done them." To McCoy, the general's aide, he spoke again of Wood's magnificent head. "It looks," he said, "as though it had been hacked out of granite with an ax." A note of sincerity rings through this comment on Wood's head, for it did have a fine sculptural quality, and he was not speaking pleasantries now, nor business formulas, but honest conviction. After sittings every morning the picture was finished on February 26, and looking it over, he seemed quite pleased with the finished work.

Henry Adams, John Hay's boon companion and next-door neighbor, who annoyed Sargent by the superficial and pleasantly maiden way he went about damning everything, came in to look at the finished picture of his friend. It was obvious to Hay that Adams liked the picture, although he said mischievously that it would take him a few years to see what meanness he had not recognized in their forty years' intimacy. It seemed a proper gesture for Sargent to call on Adams before leaving Washington, and though he had no enthusiasm for it, he did call, and was received in the upstairs library. Adams at the moment was a trifle put out that he had not been allowed to see the picture done of his friend Theodore, which had been sent off to the framer with strict instructions that it was not to be seen by anyone, critical gentlemen with beards included, until the public view on March 28. The two men spoke to each other somewhat cautiously, reserving their opinions.

March 3, 1903

At last the man I sought, the corruscating lime-light of enthusiasm, John Sargent. Holy Virgin, how useless civility is when you have an artist to handle. Still, I did my little phrase book, and he looked as irresponsive as ever, and so he soared to heaven . . . Sargent is stodgy!

He came in to see me before he left for Boston, and was pleased to say that Washington seemed pleasanter than New York. I can understand how an American catches English manners; and how they do catch English minds! Especially how they do keep such in these days when the English mind is no longer good form even in England. The generation of Harry James and John Sargent is already as fossil as the buffalo. The British middle class must be exterminated without remorse. . . .

The interview must have made a scene of comedy: the two men sitting in the quiet of Adams's library, inwardly glaring, Sargent commenting on the pleasantness of Washington, hopelessly comparing it with New York, which he had examined for the excruciating length of two days; Adams replying with gravity to remarks that tickled Sargent's ribs. He never penetrated to the contempt for him that Sargent concealed, the complete boredom his company produced on the painter. It did not even occur to Adams that the purpose of the call was to give him the opportunity to speak up if he wanted to be painted too, now that his friends Roosevelt and Hay were both done. Adams's curiosity was nonetheless piqued. Within a week he had wheedled permission somewhere, troubling himself to go to the framer, where he could see the *Roosevelt*. His verdict ran this way:

March 8, 1903

The portrait is good Sargent and not very bad Roosevelt. It is not Theodore, but a young intellectual idealist with a taste for athletics, which I take to be Theodore's idea of himself. It is for once less brutal than its subject, and will only murder everything in the White House. Of course we all approve it. Indeed it offers nothing to criticize except Sargent.

That last sentence — after all, there *had* to be criticism — must have caused Adams some effort, the criticism at best being weak, if in fact it means anything. Had the picture actually conveyed as much as Adams saw in it, Sargent would have been exceedingly pleased. Actually it presented only the one aspect that the painter saw clearly, as epitomized in the stance taken that first morning: the tremendous *will* of Theodore Roosevelt, the most telling of all his qualities, quickly singled out by the painter's instinctive perception.

Back in Boston the first week of March, he was in time to inspect the final work on the installations in the Library and be present for the unveiling. In the press his huge Byzantine panel of the Redemption was criticized for obscurity and for the liberties he had taken in changing the seven archangels to eight for the sake of symmetry. The excitement caused by this second installment was reassuring, however. His friends, the Sargent cult that was flourishing in Boston, took added vigor from it. In the midst of everything there was always business to be taken care of, too. John Lambert, from whom he would borrow a studio to work in Philadelphia, wrote asking prices, perhaps with something in mind. An answer was dashed off:

March 6 —

Dear Mr Lambert
My price for a 25 by 30 is $4000 — and for a ¾ length $5000 —
In haste
Yrs truly
John S. Sargent

He had expected that Mrs. Gardner would take responsibility for introducing Mary Hunter and Miss Smyth through Boston, which she did, though not without dismaying results. For the two sisters soon became aware that Mrs. Gardner suspected some intimate connection between *her* painter and the wealthy, rather handsome Englishwoman now borne so triumphantly on the wave of the Sargent cult. It was ill-becoming for a friend of the painter to do so, leaving one to wonder what sort of friendship it was in which she could spread rumor of that sort. Certainly she knew that anything said about what he considered his personal life was anathema, which may in itself explain her actions. To penetrate his vast façade of inscrutability doubtless appealed to Mrs. Gardner. She found pleasure in seeing him faced with rumor and gossip. She had borne much of it during her lifetime, though generally there was substance to reports of her romances, and she set to work spreading the word throughout Boston and New York. Perhaps she also gained an aura of credence from the splendidly carried, beautifully dressed Mrs. Hunter, who radiated a sense of enjoying life to the utmost. Mary Hunter, for her part, was not at all disturbed by the tales that came to her ears. She found it rather delightful to be talked about, and the impressions being spread were possibly encouraged by some of her thoughtless actions. She did seem to float about the country in his wake, arriving after he left but seeing the same people, who were not slow to connect their names. Sargent himself was not cognizant of the extent of the game until he returned to Boston.

He was greeted by an atmosphere of expectancy mixed with festivity, what with the presence of Ethel Smyth, the fanfare of her opera, and the presence of Mrs. Hunter. He had work to do. Although Mrs. Gardner engaged him with luncheons and dinners at which she displayed the two sisters, Mary Hunter taking a definite precedence in the interest she stirred, he gave the core of each day to the portraits he had to do. Worst of all, to Mrs. Gardner's thinking, was that he borrowed a studio from Frederick P. Vinton, the venerable old Boston painter, and seemed hardly to emerge from it, though he was much in demand. McKim arranged definite sittings with Major Higginson for the end of April, and the others — Mrs. Rotch, William Caleb Loring, and Mrs. Curtis — had to be spaced around Higginson's appointments. With his usual devotion to work he was not sufficiently the impressive presence at Fenway Court, he was more the impressive unseen. But that difficulty was overcome when, after staying a short time with the Sears on Arlington Street, he moved into Fenway Court to stay as Mrs. Gardner's house guest. He wrote one morning from the Sears':

> 12 Arlington Street
> Tuesday
>
> Dear Mrs Gardner
>   This is to break it gently to you that I am arriving before lunch this morning, preceded by trains of baggage.
>
> Yours sincerely
> John S. Sargent

There would be no escaping the role assigned him now!

For two months he worked on in Boston, keeping daily sittings in Vinton's studio. He managed to see Loeffler now and again; Mrs. Gardner invited the musician to rehearse an orchestra for

concerts in the music room at Fenway Court. Taking advantage
of Loeffler's presence, Sargent did a quick portrait, in his best vein
of characterization and impressionistic values for all the speed of
its execution; this, on Mrs. Gardner's birthday, he presented to
her.

It is typical of his enormous powers of concentration that even
under such strained circumstances as were present all the while he
worked in Boston he was able to turn out some of his best work.
Mrs. Rotch was a sitter of striking nervousness, in its way typical
of the lack of repose found in modern times. There was a fluttering
quality about her, a muscular tenseness while she sat, and, rather
than attempt to smooth these into the blandness seen in most portraits, Sargent made them the motif of his picture. The tense neck
and fidgeting hands are notable elements of the painting, as is the
way he did the draperies in Greco-like patterns that betray the
further restlessness he felt within the sitter. The portrait is remarkably dynamic in quality, and fine artist that he was, he contrived
to build it on a monumental composition, not allowing the expressive nature of the work to ruin the natural dignity of the sitter,
or the compactness of his design. It is an outstanding example of
modern temperament in portraiture, a fine reading of the life we
still see about us, but which our contemporary portraitists prefer
to ignore. Sargent would not ignore it, and was artist enough to
carry it off without making the picture obvious, or laughable. He
could show the traits of his sitter without in any way reducing the
attractiveness of her rather handsome person, thus rendering unto
both Caesar and the Muses, which is essentially what was required
of him.

His grasp of character was never stronger than in the *Higginson*,
nor were his remarkable powers of invention better put to use than
in this large canvas, where the figure, which seems to reach hardly
halfway up through the mass of dark, dominates with a sureness
that immediately indicates an artist in complete control of his
resources. Probably there was never a portrait of this size wherein
the painter elected to fill so large a part with darkness, one almost
thinks uninteresting darkness, for such is the first response. Only
gradually is it realized that the entirety has been carefully planned
and the darkness weighed to set off the very intensity of the subject,

whose forceful nature is projected with unsurpassed strength. Few men have been fixed so absolutely as is Higginson in this portrait. The shortcomings of the *Roosevelt* immediately become apparent on comparison with this, the completely projected personality. Like all Sargent's finer portraits, it is remarkably uncompromising. Perhaps the single softening note lies in the understanding one feels between artist and sitter, Sargent's coolness of eye in this instance being matched by the understanding of his heart. He sees Higginson impassively: his impatience, self-esteem, and irascibility are clear to him, but in his heart he knows the founder and benefactor of the Boston Symphony is good and his personal judgment is restrained by sympathetic understanding of the ideals on which a life has been built. He may have no feelings of friendship for Higginson while they are together in Vinton's studio, he may place his strokes without compassion, he betrays the difficult nature of the man, and all the while his admiration of larger traits builds an atmosphere of peace and harmony, of good conscience, that robes the figure in grace. If perhaps here the Muses have been served more than Caesar, it is man who has benefited.

During the first days of May he settled with Vinton for the use of the studio, and as an added, more personal, measure of thanks did a dynamic sketch of him, painted with remarkable boldness, quite the boldest and wildest sketch he was ever to make, extraordinary as an example of the swift vision with which he saw the flash of momentary expression crossing Vinton's rough-hewn countenance. His next stop was Philadelphia, where he moved in with Dr. J. William White, with whom Abbey had stayed only the year before, when he brought his own second installation of murals to Boston. He saw little of his hosts, for immediately he was at work on portraits of the Wideners. When Dr. White asked whom he would like to meet in Philadelphia, he set him guessing by replying "Thomas Eakins." Dr. White had forgotten that many years before he had posed to this artist as a part of the "Agnew Clinic." Sargent spelled out the name while a hunt was made through the city directory for the address, and they went off to see that painter of intense, if somewhat photographic and dull, realism. It seemed to Sargent that Dr. White represented an answer to all of Eakins's problems. A successful portrait of him, it seemed, would certainly bring other, more lucrative, commissions. But how to manage it? The simplest solution, at the moment, was praise. Lauding Eakins to the skies, he offered to make an exchange of portraits with him. Yes, he and Eakins would paint each other — that was it! They would do it their first moment and then, of course, Dr. White would sit to Eakins also, wouldn't he? Well, he would. Not happily though, and without enthusiasm. But he would, in the spring of the following year.

Chase came down to Philadelphia one or two days a week to teach a class, and one afternoon, with an hour's free time after his sittings, Sargent was off to find him, his arrival in the classroom creating a flurry of excitement. "Sargent is in the building!" had preceded him down the hall and now, as he stood off near the wall waiting for Chase, he was watched by dozens of eyes. To one favorite pupil Chase commented, "If you have any intelligent question, I'm sure he'd answer it."

He seemed formidable to approach as he moodily scanned the room, withdrawn and mute. Still, it was too wonderful an opportunity to miss. The chance to speak with Sargent might not come again, and the young man approached. "Is there anything that you have trouble with?" he asked. This was the intelligent question.

It sounded rather foolish to Sargent. He was a little uncertain how to answer. As he cast about, the same mordant humor he had used with the reporters in Washington arose, and after the moment's hesitation he replied, "The nose always baffles me." This met a responsive note, the youngster's eyes brightening to see the clay feet of the idol. Perhaps *he* was not baffled by noses. "Does it, Mr. Sargent?" He was giving himself away, showing too great an eagerness to know more. His desire to delve into another's difficulties, rather than seek advice, was contrary to Sargent's ideas of conventional manners and the things proper for a youngster to ask an older, more experienced man. He would never have put such questions to Carolus.

"Oh, yes," he went on, suddenly amused as the story began to string itself out in his mind. "I always have to make a *photograph* of the nose with my smallest brushes, then go over it with larger ones when I have it right." There must have been a twinkle in his eye. This was pure invention, but it made the youngster very happy.

As with so many of the people he did on this trip, the Wideners were being painted at home. Working in homes, he discovered once more, was a mixed blessing. However, properties were sometimes available that made a setting that would have been impossible to arrange in the studio, and it made up for certain inconveniences. Mrs. Widener, for instance, posed in beautiful surroundings. She sat on a fine Louis Quinze chair, its gold shining with the dim luster of things grown gracefully old. Behind her was a Boucher tapestry, rich in the restrained glow of crimson, ocher, and gold. From her wardrobe he selected a brilliant turquoise gown, hung with pearls, the arms overlaid by a cascade of smoky tulle. The low raking light of the windows became an added strength in his hands, producing an unrestrained singing of flesh, a glow of shoulder and bosom, a sparkle of rosy lip amplified by the heavy dark shadow of the nose thrown on the cheek, and the lustrous black hair. Here was study in sensual beguilement. Her attractions were not those of the classic proportion and exquisite chiseling to which he was accustomed, but of glowing and robust vitality. The portrait he made is strikingly sensuous, the work of a man lost in admiration of the richness of texture and color. This puritan painter, this cool, shy gentleman, betrays his own self, painting as if drunk with the beauties he beheld. Technically it is one of his supreme examples of spontaneity, the surface, once covered, left undisturbed, the technical resources exactly suited to the work done. Throughout it is a remarkable example of pictorial integrity, product of a man who for years has worked strictly to the rule, schooling himself in discipline, suddenly working in the heat of intense inspiration, unbounded by any convention other than his own eye as unerring guide.

By the twelfth of May he had finished the Wideners and switched to the studio borrowed from John Lambert, where Dr. Silas Weir Mitchell and James Whitcomb Riley became his subjects. Riley, with his thin voice, Hoosier dialect, and nasal twang, must have made a special impression, for he was made to pose five hours the first day, while Sargent unerringly set down his characteristics. There was also a portrait of Alexander J. Cassatt, president of the

Pennsylvania Railroad, and brother of Mary Cassatt, the artist. Though Cassatt was a close friend to Winthrop Sargent, one of the few remaining relatives in Philadelphia, one sees here, too, the fine hand of McKim, who had only recently been working on the new Pennsylvania Station in New York.

Then, with all this finished, the Sunday before he left Phila-delphia he insisted on doing an oil sketch of Mrs. White. With due consideration his offer was declined, and the refusal was brushed aside in his airy manner. Of course he would paint her, and their contrariness vanished. "He *insisted* on doing it, and we had not the self-denial to refuse, though we tried to do so," wrote Dr. White. She sat two hours that morning, with a break for lunch, and two hours in the afternoon. "It doesn't flatter her, or make her seem younger than she is; it is not a photographic likeness; but it has something I am not skilled enough to describe, and that represents Sargent at his best." Thomas Eakins thought it the best thing he did while in Philadelphia.

Summer was coming on now, and it was difficult to remember that he had been caught by a blizzard in Washington only three months before, for now he was noting that the thermometer daily hovered above the ninety mark, and *that* in the shade. Mercifully, his work was concluding. He would allow a few days in New York, and then be off. Like Boston, New York always made social demands, people apparently not realizing that his rare American trips were arduous. He was sailing on the twenty-third for Spain, where in the bright sun and clear light he would paint watercolors and enjoy his "nervous prostration." He tried to see Beckwith before leaving, but had only a telephone conversation in which he answered the query as to how many portraits he had done by saying between twelve and sixteen. Actually it was nineteen.

On the day he was to depart he managed to do a sketch of little Kate Haven, the five-year-old daughter of Mrs. J. Woodward Haven, known to him through the Crams. Rushed as he was, in three hours he had a rather nice head — not a bad study, he must have thought as he looked it over. The ear too big and out of drawing, but the modeling large and simple. Taking the back of the brush, he scratched into the wet paint, "To my friend Mrs. Haven, John S. Sargent 1903." With goodbyes, instructions about letting it dry and putting a little varnish over it, he was off to the boat.

The trip had been a success, once again. It was his fourth, and well worth the strain and difficulties. McKim made use of his presence to consummate commissions that might not otherwise have fructified. His last two trips — those of 1895 and 1903 — were filled with as much work as he could carry out, certainly more than he would have tackled in a like period in Tite Street. There he preferred to take things more slowly, using an extended checking process as each canvas progressed. On the average he did good work in America. He could not have bettered much of it in London, and some few things undeniably gained an added spontaneity that put them beyond his normal production. Still, it did not please him to work in this way, and the results, while happily they were good, left him uneasy. He did not like to press his luck too far. His was not the temperament of those painters who made it a practice to swoop down periodically on America and execute a stream of portraits in a fantastic whirl. He crowded a lot into the ninety-eight days of his visit and was indebted to his powerful physique for the mass of work produced under such circumstances. It was a strain even on his constitution to keep up with such a jumble of events: sleeping in Pullmans, eating bad meals in worse company. It was not pleasant. America had still a strange atmosphere, not one he willingly suffered for any length of time. It did not really interest him. He came across the Atlantic only when it was unavoidable, did the work awaiting him, and then took his leave.

From the purely financial point of view, this last venture was probably the most successful he had made on these shores. His winter's work had earned him somewhere in the neighborhood of sixty thousand dollars. Though unspecified amounts of this went in commissions, and naturally he had substantial expenses, it was still a goodly sum. He was aware of the embarrassing devotion he inspired in Boston, a remarkable phenomenon, and very uncomfortable to have surrounding him, though of course it had comforting aspects too. To be sure, his murals were criticized this time, almost as though the same critics who had stood open-mouthed before the first installment had recovered now and were intent upon making themselves heard. Anything said about his murals hurt him more than similar criticism leveled against a portrait, as they represented thought of a larger, more pervasive kind. He realized that at best the criticism was petty — of course the panels were obscure. Did anyone expect that work of that sort, on the subject he selected, could be otherwise? He was sane enough to realize that the criticism did not touch the heart of what he did, and was willing to let it pass, though somewhere inside every little barb was stored away to rankle.

Sittings

TITE STREET had a small and quiet look at ten in the morning, when the first sitter made his progress down from the north end. Neither the complete lack of trees nor the discoloration of the buildings nestling beside their little strips of pavement suggested London. It appeared more typical of some little provincial corner tucked away in the quieter part of an industrial town, the sudden appearance of a Chelsea pensioner in scarlet livery making his way slowly past forming the only enlivenment to the drab scene. On the right were the rows of Godwin's houses, mostly studios, their fronts protruding like the vests of so many paunchy gentlemen. The left was blocked out by the long front of two adjoining hospital buildings.

Just beyond this unbroken façade stood number 31, and as one approached it, near the end of the street, it was easy to catch a glimpse of the Embankment, only half a street beyond. It was a small house, with a big studio window on the upper floor, looking rather crowded by its larger neighbors from which there was little to distinguish it. The acute might notice the nicety of the circular window beside the door or the bottle glass with which the upper parts of the three casements were filled. They seemed an indication of some more tasteful hand, but it was only when the carriage halted and the wiry little Nicola, with his mustache and shock of black hair, bowed open the door that the impression was confirmed. Inside was a little vestibule, where a second circular window echoed

the first, decorated by figured crimson curtains and ormolu hold-
ers, with a dwarf silk blind. At right, up a few steps done in crimson
carpet, was a landing, where the eye rested on an Italian majolica
bust and a Portuguese settee with canework seat. Nicola led the
way up the stair again, this time around behind the echoing window
to the studio door on the second floor. There stood the smiling
painter in his blue serge, immersed in the smells of oils and turpentine peculiar to that room, his hand outstretched in greeting.

Nicola had arrived at seven, letting himself in through the
adjoining door to number 33, and immediately going to wake the
master in his bedroom on the ground floor. The morning schedule
was strict. Breakfast had to be ready at eight in the little dining
room over the garden, and breakfast was an imposing meal like all
the others. Then, while the table was cleared and the mail arrived,
Sargent took his bath, returning fully dressed to sit at the high
roll-top desk that filled an entire wall of the dining room, where
for an hour he did his correspondence. He always seemed in good
humor as he filled the four sides of his printed letter sheets with
impossible lines and scratches that were his code communication
with the world. If the recipients were particularly clever they
could fathom what had prompted him to write this time; if they
were not, it was no matter. They could puzzle over it. Prominent
on his desk was a rubber stamp he had recently acquired, which
when impulsively inked on the pad always near to hand, printed
a large and legible DAMN anywhere his exasperation led him to
desire it. Finally he made lists of those he wanted to invite to lunch,
and while Nicola got on the telephone with his formula, "Mr.
Sargent's compliments: he wants to know if you can come to
lunch today," he climbed the carpeted round stairway to the studio.
Shortly he heard the crunch of carriage wheels on the street below,
and knew the bell was about to ring. Soft footsteps on the stairs
preceded the appearance of the sitter. The day's work had begun.

Regardless of what his portraits show, for they are responsive to
his innermost sensations while faced with the people who took
their places on the stand, the fact remains that he seemed able to
strike up acquaintance of a genuine felicity with them all. There
was always that certain uneasiness at first with those he did not
know, the tendency to quip somewhat self-consciously about things

in general until the sitter began to respond. Once that was past, though, his idle banter and his strange wordings and queer phrases for things brought about a harmonious atmosphere.

The person on the stand of course had his difficulties too, fears that had to be dispelled and a consciousness of being looked at that did not contribute to ease. In later years when he did a charcoal drawing of the young bride of the Duke of York, later to become queen, he remarked that she was the only "completely unconscious" sitter he had ever had. Some, like Jenkinson, the librarian of Cambridge, who shared his interests in music, could be lulled with recordings of Spanish music, and put under Sargent's spell by reflections on the rhythms. Joseph Pulitzer had begun by asking what his methods were, suggesting that he would probably just "study me by talking, conversing, and generally summing up my character," during the first sitting. "No," Sargent smiled in reply. "I paint what I see. Sometimes it makes a good portrait; so much the better for the sitter. Sometimes it does not; so much the worse for the both of us. But I don't dig beneath the surface for things that don't appear before my eyes." Lady Speyer was another with whom he could share music as a bond, and as he knew her in friendly fashion long before the portrait was begun, he was able to make of her one of his most sensitive portrayals.

It was to the Speyer home in Grosvenor Square that he often went to dinner with Henry James, who was a favorite in that household, and where he brought his young musicians, particularly Percy Grainger and Cyril Scott. At the Speyers' he met Grieg, and heard Mme. Grieg sing her husband's songs, with unashamed tears rolling into his beard and growing angry when another of the guests commented that her voice was not good. "What has that to do with it?" he roared. "It's beautiful music!"

The young musicians were glad he could bring them to Speyer's table, for Sir Edgar was the head of the syndicate that ran Queen's Hall and the Queen's Hall Orchestra. The conductor, Henry Wood, was Speyer's personal choice for the position and his warm friend. Through this contact Percy Grainger was able to get solo engagements with the orchestra while Cyril Scott had performances of his early symphonies. Grieg seemed particularly interested in Grainger's skill, undisturbed by the marked eccentricities the pianist exhibited, though Lady Speyer had dubbed him "the village idiot," explaining, "Percy, every town has one, and you're London's." He was a nice boy withal, a fine pianist, and Grieg invited him to his home in Norway to be coached on the concerto for a Grieg festival that was planned.

Debussy was another musician to be met at the Speyers' table; and Sir Edgar's special friend, Richard Strauss, who dedicated his Opera *Salomé*, just being premiered on the Continent, to *My Friend Edgar Speyer*. Strauss was a more frequent guest than the others, one who made suggestions about the household, as when he proposed that a wild-looking band wandering the streets of London playing Spanish music ought to be hidden in the garden during dinner. It was done, and Sargent, when the music first sounded, jumped up to look out the window. The lure of food was strong too, and he went back to the table; but again indecision set in, as he ran to the window. These barbaric strains had him enthralled. Though Sargent did not do his accustomed justice to the food, Strauss was pleased with his idea and Lady Speyer knew her dinner, even uneaten, was more successful than usual.

She had been a violin pupil of Ysaye's, and before her marriage had appeared at Queen's Hall, where her performance brought down the house. Henry Wood was not surprised, for she had come well recommended by her teacher, and to Sargent her musical gifts were of far greater importance than the fact that she was now one of the most distinguished hostesses of London. He decided to paint her as a violinist, in itself rather an unusual procedure for a portrait of one of the "London ladies." He wanted no false note to spoil the musical motif of the picture. She had come the first morning with a large selection of her costliest gowns, all of which he found unsuitable, though he kept her popping into the dressing room off the studio with her maid, trying on one after another. Eventually the maid was sent scurrying back to Grosvenor Square for more outfits. She returned with an armful of clothes.

"What's that?" he asked. It was only a white underslip over which a gold brocaded tea gown was worn, but he wanted her to try it. The tea gown itself he discarded the moment he saw it. No, the underslip was what he wanted, simple, unpretentious; it would not destroy the sound of the music.

"Haven't you a painted harpsichord in the music room?" he asked next, as the composition took shape in his mind. The instrument arrived another day, when she was already posed against a tapestry that hung at one end of the upstairs studio, standing so that its central medallion framed her head like a halo. She was never on the stand for long. He motioned to her that it was enough, and had her walk about the studio, playing her violin all the while.

"Now, will you get on the platform for a few minutes," he would call out, and after some further work, which never seemed like much for the pleasantness of it, he would excuse her.

"Play that thing by Bach," he called over his shoulder.

"But, Mr. Sargent, it will sound awful alone. You accompany me on the piano."

"No, no. It will be all right," he motioned with a slight impatience, and when she had finished he asked for something else. He was listening to the music, which served also to prevent her from talking while he wrestled with his problems. Laying out a portrait — and this one required much organization — was a trying operation, and so she played, he enjoyed listening, and when necessary she mounted the platform again so that he could refer to her movements. It worked wonderfully.

He painted her head, then took it off with the palette knife, and began to do it a second time. By her next sitting it had been scraped off again, and when she left it was allowed to dry, only to be scraped before she returned. This was his way of building the forms, refining the drawing and the color. Each time he scraped the canvas a thin smooth layer of paint was left. Over this he could work again without the paint becoming too thick or any brushings beneath interfering with the freshness of the new surface. He seemed to dislike making small corrections. Once, when he began to worry the mouth, he muttered, "Stop niggling," and took it all off to be done again. Frequently all this was a mystery to the sitter, and he was content to leave it that way, for the explanation of technical procedures to a layman was something like talking to a Chinese on the telephone; he preferred not to chance it. Lady Speyer remarked, after she had seen her head done a dozen times, "Mr. Sargent, you keep taking it off, and it always comes back the same."

"Is that so?" he replied. "Well, then, we'll leave it this time," and apparently because he had come to a point beyond which he felt he could not further refine the drawing, he did, humoring her without interfering with the work. But eventually he came to enjoy the playing more than the painting. He had her return to the studio some twenty-five times before the summer was over. When the picture had progressed sufficiently he asked that Sir Edgar come to see it. There was only a single reservation when he did: "My wife's neck is not green."

The painter looked at the neck. He looked at the model, then began a scarcely audible muttering. "The neck, the neck," he was saying. "The neck. Something *is* wrong with the neck."

He was lost in thought, as though forgetting their presence in the studio. Suddenly he jerked out, "I know! Not enough green in it!" and charged forward to lay more onto the canvas. Sir Edgar remained silent, and there was no further talk of the neck.

Perhaps, had he not been so taken up with the music, the portrait might have been completed in those twenty-five sittings that summer; but it was not, and in the winter, when he wanted to ready it for the Academy, Lady Speyer's sister came to model the dress, the skirt of which still needed some little work. Now there was no music, and none of the fascination of personality. Consequently, the dress did not go well. When he saw the picture after it went home he did not like the look of the skirt's weak conical mass. "Always keep something in front of the sugar loaf," he told Lady Speyer, and she always has.

Ten years earlier he had been equally enchanted to have Elsie Swinton pose for her portrait. She was a singer of remarkable beauty, with an incomparable warmth of tone in her voice. She, too, enjoyed his company, for he played the piano for her and there was music to the exclusion of the work in hand. Mrs. Swinton was a beautiful woman with a hint of the delicate sensuality apparent in his picture of her. The accentuation of her full lips, and the pliant painting of her décolletage are striking to anyone who looks at the portrait. That these effects were no accident is made clear by the fact that in two charcoal drawings of her, made ten years later, the mouth, which was full in nature, assumes the opulent quality that it had in the previous portrait, and in one of the drawings the

eyes look askance in a way to mark further a very masculine reaction to her beauty.

Though Sargent got on swimmingly in these few instances, there
were people with whom he found little in common except a mutual
shyness. When that was the case there was none of the ease of
conversation that has been noted. His portrait of Mrs. Ernest
Franklin gives the impression of a woman of withdrawn nature,
with a certain innocent charm. The fact was that she and the
painter were so shy of each other while in the studio that
neither of them spoke.

Names sometimes came to him with difficulty, and he did not
care to be troubled with them. When, in 1905, Miss Elizabeth
Garrett, the founder of Johns Hopkins Medical School, sent over
her four best doctors for a group portrait, they were very famous
men indeed — Drs. Welch, Halsted, Osler and Kelly. Dr. Welch
was soon complaining that he called them all "Kelly" with remarkable lack of discrimination. However eminent they were in their
fields of medicine, to Sargent they were no great beauties. He
worried over posing them, and when Dr. Osler asked if he might
wear his red Oxford gown he set off an oration.

"No, I can't paint you in that. It won't do. I know all about that
red. You know, they gave me a degree down there, and I've got
one of those robes." His words were coming forth with that
well-known muffled mutter: "I've left it on the roof in the rain.
I've buried it in the garden. It's no use. The red is as red as ever.
The stuff is too good. It won't fade."

Then for a moment it seemed that a bright idea had struck him,
and he went on in better spirit. "Now, if you could get a Dublin
degree? The red robes are made of different stuff and if you wash
them they come down to a beautiful pink." But that thought was
submerged in the reality before him, and his spirit sank again.

"No," he went on slowly, "I couldn't paint you in that Oxford
red! Why, do you know, they say the women who work on the
red coats worn by the British soldiers had all sorts of troubles with
their eyes."

The doctors came to sit sometimes in groups of two or three,
but more frequently, while sitting for the heads, alone. As usual he
talked to them constantly while at work, smoked innumerable

cigarettes, and walked to and fro, attracting the particular attention of Welch, who mentioned it. With a laugh Sargent explained he had once computed that he walked four miles a day in his studio. Just as everything seemed to go well, and the models were elated over the progress of the picture, he grew discouraged. One day he paused, knitted his brows, and lifting his hands with a gesture of bewilderment, said, "It won't do. It isn't a picture." For a while he stood thinking it over, his eyes on the canvas. Presently the clouds seemed to pass. He asked if there would be anything incongruous about the introduction of an old Venetian globe into the background. It was in his Fulham Road studio, he would have it brought around. For the next session all four doctors were assembled and put into position before the fireplace of the downstairs studio, with his recently purchased El Greco shining in the light over their heads. They were surprised at the condition of the doorway when they entered — it had been chopped away to allow entrance of the globe. Seating them all before it, he studied the composition with a rather anxious air, then dashed forward and swiftly drew the outline of the globe on the canvas.

"We've got our picture," he said.

Still, the portrait of Dr. Osler did not seem a success, and after the others left London, he stayed on to be done again. When he had first walked into the studio, Sargent threw up his hands in delight, pointing to his face and saying that, though he had never before painted a man with an olive-green complexion, it would be a great pleasure. Osler himself was not co-operative on this score, for during the course of the sittings he grew less green, much to the disgust of the painter. When the group was completed, it was carted from Tite Street to Fulham Road, where strips were added to the left and the top, which could not have been accommodated at Tite Street.

Though his attitude varied with the sitter, as he responded to each personality, from the moment the door was opened and the studio entered there was never any doubt as to whose domain this was. The certain resinous, painty smell that filled the room was a constant reminder that this was unlike other rooms and that the master of it was absolute master. The rather short, grunted replies he made when his mind was elsewhere were indicative of an underlying attitude of gruffness, which became more noticeable as time went on. He was kindly and talkative, and his stories, with the frequent accompaniment of mimicry, were likely to bring laughter, but he was also mindful that this entertainment was a side issue, and he kept at work. He refused to repeat himself, he disliked lengthy explanations, and when misunderstood was frankly explosive. His tone with most sitters was domineering. They had come to be painted. He would tell them what to do, he would put his knowledge, abilities, and experience at their disposal. If they could be friendly, so much the better; he made the effort. But they had no rights otherwise. It was their place to accept what he gave them as a portrait. He reserved decision about the way the picture was to be done. He alone was the judge of the setting, and the furniture used in it was his, unless he specifically asked that some piece be brought to the studio. The color and composition were his decisions, and he rarely acceded to requests for changes, though he bitterly complained of the frequency with which he received them. He would fuss and fume, call on his daemons, and explain away what he had done if he could. He knew that the reason he had done a thing was because he wanted it that way, and no argument could effect his resolve. A letter in reply to such a request is illustrative of his attitude:

> . . . the point on which we differ is one which a long experience of portrait painting has made me perfectly familiar — I have very often been reproached with giving a hard expression to ladies portraits, especially when I have retained some look of intelligence in a face . . .
>
> The expression . . . in the portrait is kind and indulgent, with over and above this, a hint at a sense of humor. If I take this out, it will become as soft as anyone can desire. But as a matter of fact nothing will make me, much as I regret not meeting your wishes.

Obviously he did not like to leave room for ambiguity.

At the very end, with the picture nearly finished, there often was a final flourish and gesture to conclude the sittings. When the sitter arrived he saw the portrait on the easel as it had been, but thought it looked remarkably better, then noticed around it a frame from Sargent's collection. This was a surprise, and the simple good-natured way he did it, hoping to please them, was extremely winning. But he did not always do this; in fact, when people exhibited even a modicum of taste he did not bother. It was just that he was fearful of what might happen once his works left the studio to be at the mercy of the sitter for a frame. It was a nice gesture, and it prevented the perpetration of a horror.

Five o'clock was the signal for all work to cease. His second sitter, if he had one that day, had left after three, and for the last two hours he had been alone in the studio, working on the furnishings and accessories that went into the pictures. Now Nicola took over the materials, to clean palettes and brushes, while Sargent walked down the stairs. It was the hour he usually set for the many people who wanted to call — Americans who sent around notes of introduction, friends with whom he might be going somewhere. Timothy Cole arrived one day just as Chase was expected to arrive with a class to look over the studio. He greeted Cole and was beginning to explain about the imminent descent of Chase and his horde when the bell rang. Nicola went to open it. In stepped Chase, all pomposity and inflation, preceded by his proudly held paunch. Behind him marched the class. One by one he brought them up the few steps to the landing, where he made introductions. It was all first names. "This is Mary, and this is Louis, and this is Edward," he continued, and it was amusing to note that he carefully made these introductions worthless by withholding the last names. This ritual past, Chase himself led the way up the stairs, and Sargent covered his face with both hands, shaking it back and forth. "I won't be able to stand this much longer," he mumbled.

At the top of the stairs the Marlborough group was in progress, the Duchess appearing to be completed, the Duke sketched in charcoal, and the children roughly indicated in the first washes of paint. On a second easel stood the *Countess of Warwick and her Son*, while still another held the *Duchess of Sutherland*. After naming the subjects of the pictures, Chase continued to hold the floor, centering all attention on himself. His compliments were many and vociferous, leaving his host obviously embarrassed. Down the stairs again they all trailed, through the dining room, into the little library, and through the small passageway that opened into

the other studio, with its dark wood paneling. A fantastic portrait
of Ena Wertheimer was in progress there. She was wrapped in a
cloak, flashing a smile, and wearing a plumed hat, just as she had
arrived one day, late but radiant, like a ship *in full sail* (A Vele
Gonfie) as the picture has always been called. He borrowed Marlborough's Garter robes, which were left upstairs between the
Duke's sittings, to provide the little bit of braided collar he wanted
jutting out of her cloak, an ingenious bit of improvisation that the
Duke probably would not have fancied had he known.

"Wonderful, my dear fellow. Marvelous!" exclaimed Chase.
"You couldn't do better!" and indicating the plume, "You mustn't
touch it!"

"I'm going to scrape it out in the morning," was the almost in-
audible reply.

At the far end of the studio, on the floor, was a rack, and in it
numerous small canvases, most of them studies of heads. Chase
wanted them shown to his students, and one by one Sargent pulled
them forth, throwing them flat on the floor.

"Wonderful!" said Chase. "Marvelous!" with the next. Each
time Sargent gave reply with a pitiful little, "Do you think so?"

"Wonderful!"

"Do you think so?"

"Marvelous, my dear fellow; marvelous!" as the next hit the
floor.

"Do you think so?"

Chase's showmanlike air was certainly embarrassing Sargent, and
he was quietly shrinking into himself. Chase, on the contrary, was
in his glory, and then came the finale. He stopped short, drawing
himself up to full height, before exclaiming, "I want you all to remember this moment. You are in the presence of the greatest living
painter!"

It was too much. Sargent grabbed the little Chase around the
waist and whirled him into a jig step or two. They both broke into
laughter, and the anxious moment after Chase's words, when the
students had stared at him like a guaranteed genuine Egyptian
mummy, was nicely bridged. He had not had to bear it in shy
silence.

On another occasion, when Chase came calling alone, he was

shown the large, still-unfinished portrait of the Countess of Warwick with her son. Sargent seemed particularly to hate that canvas,
in a fit of pique declaiming, "I've simply got to finish that damn
thing. The boy keeps getting older and the woman keeps getting
younger." When another visitor asked if he would sell some of his
earlier things, he refused. "I need to keep them around to console
me for the rotten stuff I am doing."

Miss Popert, the "interesting mad one" of thirty years before,
came to London, and by way of inviting her to his studio he gave
her a dose of his portrait-hardened personality:

> 31, Tite Street,
> Chelsea, S.W.
> April 7, 1908

Dear Miss Popert

I have received your cannonade and I answer it for myself
alone, as my sister is abroad in Ireland. I am sorry that you have
felt crushed at my not looking you up when I was in Rome, but if
you knew what a profoundly unsociable old crank I have become in the last thirty years you could not take it as a personal
matter. My hatred of my fellow creatures extends to the entire
race, or to the entire white race and when I escape from London
to a foreign country, my principle object is to fly from the species.
To call on a Caucasian when abroad is a thing I never do. I am
not proud of this, but neither am I of a bald head and other
changes that you will notice if you do me the pleasure of coming
to see me in London. I keep up an appearance of politeness well
into May.

If you will propose a day, you will be astonished at the cordiality
of my welcome, especially if you will come to lunch.

> Yours truly
> John S. Sargent

P.S. Falchetti is no more a count than I am — merely a bore.

Lady Speyer, certainly not the kind to be a troublesome sitter,
was a trifle worried over something in her picture. She was wearing her magnificent string of pearls, which hung to her waist as she
stood playing her violin. There was no other jewelry in the picture: not a ring, nor a brooch, nor any of the scattered bits of

sparkling mineral matters sitters liked to bedeck themselves with. This was to be a musical portrait. There must be no distraction, no parading of stones, for Sargent was painting an artist. He even minimized that fortune in pearls, indicating them, as he always did, with a long narrow sweep of a round brush that put in the carefully noted halftone, then dotting the row of highlights. But this time he carefully kept the highlights dull, producing what is almost a *notation* of pearls; a message that said yes, there are pearls here, but I, Sargent, choose to do no more about them. Returning to Grosvenor Square in her car, Lady Speyer wondered if she had the courage to tell him she was unhappy over the pearls. Finally, one day when the chance came she did say so, and he stood up straight, sticking out his stomach and intoning in deep notes, "Those are very good pearls." Not another word was said. At first he exaggerated the length of her index finger as it rose high off the wood. This she called to his attention also, and he dodged the question.

"That finger touches heaven," was the evasive reply, though eventually he saw the error himself and, bringing a bit of background across the tip of it, lopped off half an inch.

"That's what comes of painting too many taper fingers," he muttered.

Lady Speyer was one of the good ones. At the same time he was painting Lady Sassoon, and one day when Lady Speyer arrived for her sitting she found Sargent terribly agitated, in fact, in a rage. The picture of Lady Sassoon was nearly complete now, and he ran through a list of some six or eight relatives who had just been in to see it, interposing a weighty *and* between the names, making the list a metered intoning of doom. He tugged at his collar, his normal redness now an apoplectic purple, as he unburdened himself. At the end, for this was what he had been bringing himself to say, he stood up to announce with sententious emphasis: "It seems there is a little something wrong with the mouth. OF COURSE THERE IS SOMETHING WRONG WITH THE MOUTH! *A POR- TRAIT IS A PAINTING WITH A LITTLE SOMETHING WRONG ABOUT THE MOUTH!*" And he asked her to play her violin, which in time calmed him until he could think of working again. It was astonishing how deeply he was hurt, how much to heart he took the criticism that the usual professional in time learns to pass off as part of the game. Lady Sassoon was back on another occasion, as is shown by a letter written by Mrs. Endicott during her husband's sittings that year:

> London
> May 9, 1907
>
> . . . Just before we left, Lady Sassoon walked in and we were able to see how much her portrait was like her. She is about 50, slight and refined & was spontaneous & in this caustic to Mr. S about her picture & mightily pleased with it we thought. We were told later she did not like it — She certainly acted quite the opposite when we saw her —

To Americans like the Endicotts, who made the trip abroad for their portraits, it was a somewhat different experience. They had arrived from Boston at the end of April that year, staying at the Berkeley Hotel, where their expenses were just over thirty dollars a day. They sent a note to Tite Street announcing their arrival, and inquiring what attire Mr. Endicott should wear for the sitting. The reply did not seem enthusiastic.

> Monday [April 29, 1907]
> 31, Tite Street,
> Chelsea, S.W.
>
> Dear Mr. Endicott
> It had better be a frock coat I suppose.
> Kindest regards to Mrs Endicott — tell her I have received her letter.
>
> Yours truly
> John S. Sargent
>
> Will expect you Saturday at 3

After the first sitting, there was a telegram:

> Will expect you tomorrow at eleven
> Sargent

The laws of the Medes and the Persians! The result, and something of the experience of sitting, is conveyed in a letter Endicott wrote home the next day:

Berkeley Hotel
May 8, 1907

. . . We saw Mr. Morgan yesterday here who was anxious that we should come and see him today at eleven; which we agreed to do with great pleasure as neither of us have ever seen his pictures. In the afternoon a telegram from Sargent came saying he wanted a sitting today at eleven so we had to write & say we could not go to him. I am sorry for I suppose he will think we ought to have given up Sargent. That seems to be his way if one can believe all one hears. Yesterday was a tremendous (downpour) all the morning, clearing in the afternoon, so the sitting did not amount to much and Mr. S said today he should rub out all he had done . . . He showed us his portrait of Eliot — a dignified ascetic rather sad and contained figure standing — where do you think? — on the steps of a Roman Villa . . . A balustrade with posts surmounted with stone balls — a building at the top of the steps — a blue and gray sky — and a tree. The scheme is very harmonious and charming but is it appropriate for the head of a New England College [?] — I doubt it. And I doubt very much what they will all say and think about it in Cambridge. He has had "an awful" time with it for two months and has been by no means idle. He tried Sanders Theatre with its "handsome" light yellow gothic woodwork" . . . then another & etc. and this is the only thing possible, taken from a sketch he made in Rome. There is no left hand which must now be painted from someone else. How queer people are not to wait and see a portrait finished! and then poor Sargent is bitterly blamed. Mr. Eliot did not bring his robe and yet he wanted to be painted in it . . . Sargent says his hands are handsome, and yet how little this will look like his hands if painted from someone else . . .

Sargent had always encouraged visitors to come by while he was at work, in the early days for reasons of business, and even now he usually asked that some friend or member of the family be brought to "assist" and keep the expression alive. This took the weight of conversation off him, allowing him to pay fuller attention to his work, and if conversation became of interest, he was able to throw in a word at the proper time. One such visit was the occasion of round two with Mrs. Patrick Campbell. The sitter was young Cynthia Charteris, who had come for a charcoal drawing. A redheaded girl with a broad, somewhat flat-featured face, Miss Charteris was rather shy, and Sargent himself was feeling shy in her presence. When the witty, enthralling, fascinating Mrs. Patrick Campbell walked in, the most famous actress of the day and at that time quietly working into her romance with George Bernard Shaw, she seemed precisely the person to ease the situation.

"Oh, you are trying to draw my golden frog!" she warbled, in her husky dramatic voice. "Isn't she Batrachian? Mind you, get the preposterous width between her green eyes. They're so far apart that if a fly wanted to go from one to the other he would have to take a fly — I mean a cab."

Miss Charteris giggled, and Sargent was not amused by this talk of his model, which was contrary to the rules of studio courtesy. It was not an auspicious start. Another guest volunteered that she was not like a frog; "more like a cat — not a hearth rug pussy, larger and semi-wild, but definitely feline."

It was no use. The center of the stage was definitely in the expert hands of Mrs. Campbell. "No, no, no! She-is-the-great-frog-of-the-western-world," she trilled in her lower octaves, her throat rippling up and down.

Sargent's expression conveyed that, though Mrs. Campbell might be fine on a stage, she had decidedly less value in a studio. Must she upset everything? But this was only the start. She next went fumbling into her cascading sleeves and brought forth — a tiny dog, previously concealed in her voluminous draperies. It was not a pleasing object somehow: hardly a dog, but too canine to be a mouse, and rather a cross between an undergrown weasel and an oversized potato.

She held it forth with something akin to triumph, until it was practically in his face: "Wouldn't you like to draw my Pinky-Ponky-Poo? Isn't he be-yoo-ti-ful? He's got Wemyss's whiskers, Balfour's nose, and Marjorie Manners' eyes."

He scanned the thing with obvious distaste. "I like *big* dogs," was all he said.

"If you were a real artist, you would draw my lovely Pinky-Ponky-Poo instead of that plump, pale frog," she sang.

He grunted and drew out his watch. This was intended as a signal to her, but she returned to the attack.

"But, my dear man, you mustn't make my golden frog's hair *black*. Can't you see it's the color of the best marmalade?"

"Dae*mons!* Dae*mons!* Dae*mons!*" he spluttered. "Since the er—um *medium* in which I am *trying* to work is black and white, how can I make Miss Charteris' hair look er—um fairer, without making it er—um appear to be *white*."

His only trump card at such a time was Nicola, who led the prima donna gently off stage. The drawing was finished another day.

It was the portrait of Elsie Swinton that attracted to him one of his greatest misfortunes in the selection of sitters, the Sitwells. They had been around to most of his friends: Tonks had done Sir George; Richmond, Lady Ida; and MacColl had been approached for advice on who could paint an eighteenth-century conversation piece, to match a Copley. Sargent must have known what to expect, and thought he was ready. Yet how could he be prepared for the fact that Sir George thought it a duty to mortify the artist at every opportunity, to goad him into a display of his "temperament"? He exhibited remarkable self-control, even though Sitwell offered an opinion on every matter, whether of taste or feeling or technique, with an air of absolute and final authority, only immediately to distract him again by swiftly abandoning it or, alternately, by behaving as though it had been Sargent's theory and not his own at all just as the artist had agreed to accept it. At moments that became steadily more frequent while the work progressed, he tried to play a strong hand, and it was only the fact that Sargent, too, sometimes elected to express himself that allowed the picture to make progress. His sudden bull-like rushes to the canvas, the shouting that accompanied them, played their part also. There was quite a scene on one occasion, and Sir George triumphed by obliging him to paint out a table with some still life on it. He had been loath to lose it, and had not hesitated to state his own views plainly on the painter-patron relationship. Again, Sir George pointed out that his daughter's nose deviated slightly from the perpendicular, directing that this flaw be emphasized. The request incensed Sargent, and he plainly showed that he did not think that was the way to speak before a supersensitive child of eleven. The result was that he made her nose straight and Sir George's crooked and absolutely refused to alter either of them. The fascination of watching him at work wore off rather quickly for the two-year-old Sacheverell, who became restless almost immediately on entering the studio. Then there was the problem of holding his attention, which Sargent managed by a display of whistling through his teeth, the strange sound rooting the child to the spot. When that no longer worked, he could recite, again and again, a limerick:

> There was a young lady of Spain
> Who often was sick on a train,
>   Not once and again,
>   But again and again,
> And again and again and again.

This brought forth a look of rapt amazement, and little Sacheverell seemed to listen as long as the artist could stand repeating it. Of course, even this failed eventually, and he fidgeted until as a last resort Sargent had a doll made, exactly his size and coloring, which took over the job of posing when the child became impossible.

"Picture Sunday" was a tradition that was necessarily carried on for fear of being the first to break it. Each artist lined up in his studio the works he had selected to send to the Academy, and when they were portraits the models, their families, and all of fashionable and intellectual London knew they were welcome to call on that day. This ritual took place generally on the first Sunday in April, and Tite Street was filled with Hunters, Edens, Asquiths, and the other notables of the day, whose carriages and motorcars crowded the little street. Lady Randolph Churchill was one of those who came by, and Henry James was sure to be there "though I loath the general practice." It was a harrowing experience for the artist — praised, on the one hand, and victim of sarcastic comment, on the other, he was caught between two fires, with no place to hide. Rival beauties took opportunity to cast aspersions on their opposite numbers, rival sitters wailed because they had, or had not, worn the other outfit, and everything that had made his life a misery for the last year was all at once cast up to haunt him again. When, as sometimes happened, a picture was not finished in time for the Academy or was not chosen to be among those sent, there was a special show day too, for the aunts had to pass on every work that issued from the studio and everyone had an aunt with a critical eye and a scornful mouth.

Sir George Sitwell had naturally desired such an occasion for his various relatives living in London, and the request, a normal one, was granted. They came, with the intention of giving the artist the benefit of their informed advice. Sir George, of course, wanted no more than to be congratulated on his taste and the fine bargain he had made, so there was a certain misunderstanding to begin with. But more, these were Lady Sitwell's relations, and they were not entirely sympathetic to Sir George's eccentricities, which they came prepared to find out and inform him of. Thus Lady Ida's mother, Lady Conyngham, and her maiden sister, Lady Geraldine Somerset, this latter replete with elaborately flounced and pleated ear trumpet, came into the studio, surrounded by an eager group of younger relatives, all concentrating on the picture. Poor picture! It was only so much carrion to be picked apart and decapitated. The clothing, especially selected by Sir George, seemed to attract them first.

"Why riding things and an evening dress?"

"Why an evening dress and a hat?" they demanded of each other, quite rhetorically, for they allowed no answers.

"Why?"

"Why d'you suppose?"

"And why not go to an *ordinary* painter?" Here the younger relatives came into play, taking up and echoing the refrain like a Greek chorus. "Why do you suppose?"

"Why go to an American?" (Chorus: "Why do you suppose?") Soon came the swelling crescendo, after which, with all the haste allowed by good manners, they were politely shown out.

When the last portraits Sargent sent to the Royal Academy are compared with the first he submitted to the Salon, it immediately becomes obvious that somewhere in the intervening years he radically altered his technical means. It is also apparent that the end was implicit in the beginning, and the alteration was one of strength, scope, and degree, rather than method. From thin, smooth, charming school pieces in the manner of Carolus-Duran,

such as the portraits of Miss Watts, the Pailleron children, and even
the slightly later study of Louise Burckhardt, he went on to produce work of a distinctive power, endowed with tremendous vigor
and with a restless energy that had never previously appeared in
formal portraiture.

Of course, the qualifying admission must be made that even such
early works as the *Boit Children* and *El Jaleo* would never have been
envisioned by Carolus-Duran. They were a distinct expression of
a totally new artistic personality; but the innovation was limited to
composition, for the means by which these pictures were accomplished, except for certain characteristically courageous bits of improvisation, are the same as those employed by Carolus. Thus we
see that Sargent's artistic mind, though able so early to strike out
into new paths and to achieve distinct victories by the employment
of an inherent empiricism when it did, was nonetheless limited by
the technical processes he had been taught. Before his full potential
could be realized his technical equipment required an expansion
to match his intellectual agility. However, a young man gifted by
nature, with a fine teacher, and with an abundant technical equipment is not likely to know that he will want to alter those means.
His subsequent development will not necessarily be the bold step
forward, but rather a laborious expansion of means, in each instance caused by some present and pressing problem. Thus Sargent's advance was slow, scarcely perceptible except when the later
product is compared with the earlier. But then, how startling!

This was the problem that confronted the restless spirit of the
young artist, but its existence as a problem was certainly hidden
from him, and every step forward was instinctive rather than a
conscious attempt to solve the larger intellectual equation.
Through the process of solving this personal problem he became
the most important individual innovator that portraiture had seen
since Frans Hals first liberated it from the tyranny of ancient techniques. Still, at each step he no more than solved a present problem.
For he was not consciously aware of his destiny nor anxious about
his mission. He continued to paint the best portrait he knew how
to produce, to that end employing new methods he had seen developed on all sides. Cumulatively he was adding that huge energy
and drive which slowly brought the technique of Carolus-Duran

from the thin, charming manner it was in those hands to the massive, powerfully fused heads and dynamic portraits later sent to the Royal Academy.

The very process of painting a head, as taught by Carolus, was an essentially empiric process, in which one learned to accommodate the means to the necessities, judging the results by standards that altered with each model. The student exposed to such methods will either master them, or, as was more commonly the case, evolve one method and follow it ever after. Sargent was the single example, among Carolus' pupils, of a student able to master the empiricism of the process, and he carried it further than ever intended by the master. For, having a complete understanding of this shifting standard, he was admirably equipped to work with shifting means as well. He was able to judge his work however the means might be applied. This intellectual agility lies at the foundation of any innovator's practice. Recalling the methods by which the portrait of Mme. Gautreau was developed, the processes of his empirical mind become more obvious. He had before him a woman of striking linear beauty, whose very physical being required the use of more linear means than he normally employed. From the beginning he had tried to pose his subject in a manner best calculated to emphasize her particular qualities, instinctively placing her full length with her head turned in profile. He did not turn the entire body to face in the direction of the profile, as any less inventive painter would have done, but realizing the greater beauty of her lines when the body stood in contrapuntal position, he accepted this challenge. Thus he was already exhibiting a certain courage when he began to sketch the portrait and required more when he grasped that, as the masses of the picture were disposed, further simplification would produce a cameo effect. The lines began to flow with tense lilting rhythms, which was a gratifying vindication of his actions. Nonetheless, it required great tact to prevent these vastly simplified planes of the head and figure from becoming like cardboard cutouts. Here was a further challenge that he accepted too, or was at least willing to chance as he struggled, successfully, to keep the figure a three-dimensional solid, immersed in its atmosphere.

Thus we see that whenever he came upon an opportunity to

produce a work of greater beauty, he grasped it. Every departure added to the difficulties inherent in finishing the portrait. The mounting problems were enough to have ruined it entirely. His months of toil are an index of the difficulty he experienced, and the way he overcame details gives exposition of his methods in small. Mme. Gautreau's right arm, from the start, was twisted on its own axis, and placed with the hand holding the leading edge of the table behind her. Somehow it never seemed to come right. He moved it closer to the body, only to find that the angle of the elbow fitted too well into the angle of the waist, as though he had distorted these parts to fit like the pieces of a puzzle. It was a disturbing effect. His lines looked too cramped when they came together so closely, the spacing was not right, and the free flow of the linear pattern was affected. Obviously the arm had to be moved farther from the body. But how far? His first efforts left the figure awkward, the arm too dissociated and threatening to become a center of interest in itself. To solve what was becoming a major problem, his first idea was to move the table, so that the hand now leaning on the near edge would appear to be on the far side. This was hazardous. The change in the table's position heightened the perspective of the figure, causing it to rocket into the air. But it also brought the linear patterns into sharper relief, by freeing them from distracting collision with solid objects. Thus, by that purely pragmatic scale, it was a good move, and with slight alterations in the perspective of the table top to suit the altered perspective of the figure, he allowed it to remain. The arm still had to be settled, and as he moved it a little this way, then edged it a trifle back, he found that it came right more easily because of the less-cramped relationships now existing in that part of the composition.

It was in this way, by use of pure painter's logic freely applied in every case, that the picture, certainly the masterpiece among his early products, was done. Preconceptions were not a factor at any point. Had he run afoul of any firmly held principles, they would certainly have been discarded. It was the result that counted. Nothing else. It is one of the curiosities of history that a painter who all his life worked by such principles should have been acquainted with William James, the philosopher pioneer of pragmatism. The principles of pragmatism, as they were eventually set forth by James in 1907, parallel with remarkable fidelity the empiric working methods that Sargent had adopted instinctively more than three decades earlier. The pragmatic idea — that truth is relative to result, and any means producing a proper result is therefore proper means — finds a parallel in the total lack of doctrinaire devotion to method in Sargent's work, and his total lack of interest in the means as such. His fundamental concern was with the result, and this curious workman's philosophy, based upon the craftsman's belief in his own skill, the ability of his hands to meet the problem, is the pragmatic philosophy applied to art, pure and simple. It hardly needs saying that he was himself no philosopher, except in the simple way that every craftsman is, and certainly he was never involved with James in any discussion about the nature of his thought or the efficacy of his writing. That would have meant straying into the field of words and language. It cannot be stressed too much that Sargent's mind was instinctive, and not given to wordy examination of those things which he knew by craftsman's instinct. He might agree to a proposition that was placed before him, but was not himself of a nature to formulate nor to seek vocal arbitration of the slight variances he might have felt with any systematic exposition of thought. And still the fundamentals of pragmatic philosophy, when they were set forth, must have seemed self-evident to him, and hardly new.

The great originality of Sargent's work had always lain in the fact that he was willing to follow to a conclusion the pragmatic solution. He was willing to experiment, and by testing the idea prove it or discard it. The portrait of Mme. Gautreau is naturally the earliest and most obvious example, but other instances of this process are scattered throughout his work, and one of the more outstanding is the large group he did in 1899, *The Wyndham Sisters*. When he tackled this huge work he discovered that the tremendous extension of the value scale he encompassed robbed the separate heads of much of their brilliance. While working on the head of Lady Elcho, on the left, he found that no highlight he could place on it showed well, because of the nearness of such huge masses of sparkling white, and no shadow gave sufficient play to the lights, because the value of shadows was dissipated against the large mass of dark in the background. He went on to sketch the head of the second sister, Mrs. Adeane, on the upper right, and there, where the head stands completely dissociated from the masses of white, he noticed that the first broad sketching, without any of the smaller forms being indicated, seemed to hold its place better than the more finished work on Lady Elcho. The single mass of this head, in so large a composition, was itself a highlight. No other lights were needed on it, and this large, broadly plotted head of Mrs. Adeane did not have the disturbing smallness, the piddling quality, that he saw in his initial attempt at Lady Elcho's portrait. At that point he determined to go back, simplifying what he had done of Lady Elcho until it had the same sparseness as the initial sketch of her sister. With a broad brush he flattened down the modeling he had painfully built up. Then he went further. He began to think of this huge canvas almost as a mural, of the three figures as a single mass of light, without further imposed highlights, eliminating all but the most necessary halftones. Shadows he tried to banish completely from this lower section of the canvas and he succeeded except for the head of Lady Elcho, which was posed and planned before this larger idea had presented itself. But that was all right. It saved the innovation from becoming too obvious, and introduced that touch of naturalism which saved his composition from artificiality. When the third sister, Mrs. Tennant, was finally sketched in, his concept had so altered that he was immediately able to paint her with the broad masses he had evolved. Now so firmly established, he never fully dissociated the hairline from the forehead, giving flesh, halftone, and hair color, in one smooth passage of tone representing them all, leaving her dark eyes as the only accenting tone in the entire head. To some extent, each portrait he did had this same variation of approach, this use of empiric processes to distinguish it from its predecessors. The portrait of Mrs. Widener, done in 1903, is another example of his technical processes being wholly altered to suit a particular need, the resultant product answering with remarkable verve and beauty.

Perhaps the remarkable variety of treatment he employed, due largely to his feeling that in each undertaking the means should be suited to the particular qualities of the sitter, is itself one of the outstanding qualities of his work. Probably no other painter altered his vision so violently and so often to suit the needs of his work, nor produced pictures so varied in their nature. For eventually he evolved a technique whereby he was able to build up powerful masses of pigment that defined the weight and solidity of flesh with wonderful accuracy. When it was needed he could call forth huge strength, producing a shining bald head with all the solidity of its bony structure beneath, as in his portrait of P. A. B. Widener, and he could equally well portray the solid, but soft, jowly flesh of Henry James. The definition of mass and weight came to mean more in his portraits than ever before, but only when these qualities were part of the legitimate need of the picture. For with equal frequency he went to the other end of the scale, flattening out forms to shape them into decorative masses, as in the portrait of Mrs. Huth Jackson, the Wyndhams, Miss Betty Wertheimer, and Lady Eden.

No one since the primitives and Velásquez had made such important use of the silhouette as an artistic element. Its use had been in virtual abeyance through the eighteenth and early nineteenth centuries, finding employment once again, only with the portrait of Mme. Gautreau. In subtler form it appeared that same year in his portrait of Mrs. Henry White, where the outline of the figure was carefully studied, and brought forth praise from R. A. M. Stevenson, writing for a London journal: "The wavering silhouette of the figure, now firmly detached from and now sliding off into its surroundings, may be followed with pleasure even if held upside down. It falls into a perfect scheme of decorative effect, and yet it relieves from its environment with all the consistency and variety of truth." Burnt by the reception of the *Mme. Gautreau* at the Salon, Sargent made no further use of silhouette for several years. When his courage returned he used it again, and employed it not only for decorative effect, but in the postures of Lord Ribblesdale and Theodore Roosevelt he transforms it into an emotional element. In the one it draws attention to the extraordinary elongation of the man, and his exaggerated stylishness, and how subtly he traces the lines that form his censure, and how beautifully! The silhouette employed to fix the characteristics of Roosevelt has an entirely different function, for it is part of the revelation of the man's intensity. The outlining of his posture, the attention given his gesture, all contribute to the immediacy of his tremendous will power, his dynamic energy. Not since Velásquez had silhouette been used with such attention, and such remarkable results.

For all this, technically there was little to differentiate the portrait of Mme. Gautreau from the products of Carolus-Duran. The way the paint was applied to the canvas was virtually the same. The way the picture was laid in was certainly the same. The sense of value and the use of color was exactly in the manner of Carolus. For all his artistic achievement throughout this decade of the eighties, there is never any actual break with the methods of Carolus-Duran. As late as 1890 such portraits as *Mrs. Derby*, painted in New York, bear close relationship to Carolus, and perhaps except for a certain delicacy, the added refinements of his personal revelations of his sitter, they are precisely like Carolus' work. Indeed, periodically some of Sargent's most felicitous works were echoes of similar compositions by Carolus. The little *Robert de Civrieux*, painted in 1879, is a perfect reflection, in composition and technique, even in the selection of stuffs, of a portrait Carolus had done of his daughter five years before. More subtly, too, he frequently made use of Carolus' ideas, as when he took the device of sharply cutting a figure with a cloak, found in Carolus' *Comtesse de Vedal*, and used it when painting *Mrs. Playfair*. Even the later richer manner that he employed appears to have been partially drawn from sketches such as Carolus' *M. Haro*, though Duran himself never evolved this looser manner into a formal technique.

Objectively, the means Sargent employed, until he reached his prime, were essentially those taught him by Carolus-Duran. By shortly after 1890, however, it becomes obvious that he had tremendously expanded those means and added to their plasticity. The very fluency of his work had never been achieved by Carolus, and he built upon that fluency a beauty of paint, of tactile attraction, that Carolus never achieved. The richness of technical resource that he employed to define qualities of weight, depth, and solidity, was entirely new. The extraordinary plasticity of his work done in America in 1890, the head of little Homer St.-Gaudens, the arms of Ellen Loring, were beyond the scope of Carolus' art. Further, he now began to hit a mark in every one of his pictures that Carolus never aspired to nor hoped to achieve.

His figures were detached from their backgrounds more completely than Carolus' ever had been, yet they remained behind their frames and in spatial relationship with the other objects of the composition. His profound knowledge of form and a technical achievement of astonishing range combined to produce amazing results, and his impressionistic eye made everything he painted more real than portraiture had ever been. The combined scope of his accomplishments, when they suddenly matured after that summer of 1890 in New York, made the power and the intensity of his portraits unsurpassed, and the remarkable growth of his reputation and the strength of his influence irresistible. He was a dynamic new force. He simply had to sweep everything out of his path.

The impressionists themselves had not been especially good portraitists. Monet early showed skill in this department, and with an eye on the full-length portraitlike figures that he sent to the Salon it appears that he flirted with the idea of doing them. But Monet was far more interested in landscape work. If perhaps some fine portraits were lost because of this, which appears to be the case, so many fine landscapes were gained that the loss need not be mourned too deeply. Among the impressionists it was Renoir who showed the greatest interest in portraiture, and some of his works in that vein are fine indeed. Especially in the seventies, Renoir exhibited a remarkable inventiveness with the setting of single figures, though his were not the true gifts of the portraitist. He had not the command of draftsmanship that is essential to every fine portraitist. Frequently we see him so taken up with the difficulties of drawing an eye or a mouth that he is unable to individualize the final product. In total, his portraits, purely because of his poor command of the rudiments, lack the incisiveness a portrait must possess, and the personalities of his sitters rarely emerge from a certain decorative blandness. There was another factor that limited the impressionists' success in this field. As the discoverers of a new technical process, they unfortunately were liable to let its exercise run away with them. It was good that they were able to see faces all broken into mottled masses of green, purple, and blue, and no one in this day will deny that a face of those colors can be as true, or more true, than one of the conventional flesh tones. Still, the over-all truth does not lie that way, for these colors are not the dominant gamma. They are the unusual effects that most painters may find more interesting to paint, but which balanced judgment tells us cannot always be painted. Visual truth simply does not lie that way. And so long as the impressionists were to be so wholly taken up with the recording of these unusual moments they limited their effectiveness as portraitists.

Sargent's original training taught him to paint what he saw truthfully and in value. When, after he had already mastered the rudiments of this then-revolutionary but actually, in the larger sense, traditional equipment, he became interested in impressionism. As we have seen, he experimented with it, partially and in pure form, and it was Sargent who finally abstracted all that was of value to portraiture from impressionism and brought it back to the main stream of art. It was Sargent who first posed a model in the conventional north light of his studio, and seeing the penumbra that ringed the head, had the impressionist equipment with which to paint it. It was Sargent who first saw the red edges that floated over blues, the green edges on white, and it was Sargent who realized that gray hair may in all truth be green. He never exaggerated these effects, nor made them dominate the whole, nor gave them greater prominence than they had in nature. Equipped with a knowledge of impressionism, he was able to judge the quality of his highlights more closely than had ever been done before, grasping whether the little touch of white that lit up an eye had the very smallest tinge of blue, or green, or pink, or yellow, and the ochers from which a head projected might perceptibly have an overtone of green. He looked at nature with more and better equipment than any artist had previously brought to bear, and it is no wonder that the speaking quality of his work fascinates and we see a throb of life.

Out of doors he was able to give even wider play to the sharp accuracy of his eye, catching the minutiae of the play of light as it bounced and played upon the surfaces, filling trees with the sparkle of light and casting varied shadows of thin transparency and superb strength. He was able to gauge the opacity of tones with remarkable skill, possessing above all the sound technical equipment with which to translate all that he saw into a work of art. For his was the temperament, the love of nature and art, from which great works flow. And they did flow, for he had the sureness of a sound and perfected craftsmanship to smooth the path. Given such a temperament, plus the outright love of doing complicated pictures, in which a multitude of objects throw off myriad tones and reflections, it is no wonder he was able to produce landscapes and figures that capture all the brilliance of the outdoors. The hackneyed phrases about capturing sunlight were never better suited than to Sargent's paintings, and coming on them in a room one senses the intensity of light and the glare of the sun. They make their fellows look dull by their side. None of the impressionists themselves had painted such full-toned shadow, with the intensity of nature, for fear of losing the brightness of touch they sought. Only Sargent, with the profound wisdom of his eye, saw that in the brilliance of sunlight shadows, too, were intense.

Even in these works there is in Sargent's perception a power that Monet lacks, for as the years progressed the forms passed out of Monet's work. More and more he was producing a vision of the vault of air that intervened between himself and objects. The solidity of the things he painted was totally lost, the substance itself was not felt, but rather glimpsed through the aerial vault of his vision. By contrast, Sargent never gave up the early more solid phase of impressionism, when it was an art that sought to push back the limits of realism and before it became caught up in its own web of technical paraphernalia and so badly entrapped that it allowed realism, which it originally sought, to escape its grasp forever. Sargent's visual perception was remarkably vigorous, and there are times when before an overwhelming subject the vitality of his paint becomes staggering. The underlying structure of his work becomes overwhelmed by impressionist impulses. He builds a thick wiggly surface cut by accenting strokes and modeled by the palette knife until it grows with a life all its own, a mottled vitreous mass, bursting with life and imprisoned energy. The abstracted tactile quality of the surface has all the vitality of his powerful hands as he worked with silent intensity to put his sensations before nature on canvas. Pitted and kneaded, troweled and smudged, the paint applied with knife, brush, and fingers, then mercilessly scraped off and reapplied until he was satisfied — these works have all the brute energy of nature itself.

This same restless vitality became a new quality in formal portraiture. For as he applied his own intense vitality, rivaling that of Rubens, to the field of portraiture, there, too, it became a distinctive feature of his work, too dangerous for anyone else to attempt. The vast majority of his portraits show sitters either in movement or in casual attitudes that imply dynamic intention. They twist and swirl, and the dynamism is as much in the way they are painted, in the force and impetus of the hand applying the paint, plotting the lights and shadows, as in the sitter. This inherent dynamic quality, appearing in everything from his hand, combined with the powerful sense of mass he developed, and his use of pigment, created a portraiture such as had never before been seen. By the time he decided to call a halt he had created a new concept of the portrait and an entirely new standard for following generations to imitate.

By the very nature of his innovations, he was not a revolutionary. He believed emphatically in the past, in the validity of the great masters, in the value of craftsmanship, in academies, and in teaching. He believed in tradition when it was vital, and did not believe in it when it was not. He was never antagonistic to the established order simply because it was the established order. He set about to change the Royal Academy from within, to improve, not to destroy it. His ideas were essentially constructive; not entirely conservative, but certainly not revolutionary, in the sense of destroying institutions because they were institutions.

Sargent's contributions to art were essentially refinements. He expanded the sound technique of Carolus-Duran until it became a first-rate instrument capable of expressing anything from the subtlest to the most powerful. He combined factors others thought antagonistic: strong modeling with silhouette, impressionism with formal portraiture, fine draftsmanship with vigorous painting, decorative backgrounds with intensely living figures. The effects he produced were amazing, their richness, plasticity, life, and vitality remade the portraitist's art until it was totally unlike the placid face-making it had been since the seventeenth century. He made it once more a living tradition, proved it still capable of new treatment. In essence, then, Sargent's genius was the ability to form new correlations, bringing together factors previously existing as wholly separate phenomena. Everything that came within his grasp was revivified by the lifegiving factor of his own tremendous vitality. It was the same skill that Raphael and Tintoretto had in such great measure. Combining the styles of their great predecessors and contemporaries, the qualities of many schools, they, too, formed a newer, more nearly perfect art, fusing this correlated eclectic mass by the sheer force of genius into greatness.

"No More Paughtraits"

BBEY commented in 1898 that Sargent was still "the same
generous, simple-minded fellow, with all his magnificent
position," and through the next decade there was change
neither in him nor in that position. He was the foremost portraitist
of the kingdom, as King Edward himself acknowledged, and as
artists who were competing with him knew in their hearts only too
well. He went on from one fine work to another, striking deeper
tones with the passing time, always progressing, his work constantly varying, showing new and unsuspected qualities. His influence dominated the Royal Academy in a way that made many
an eminent mediocrity despise the sight of his works, yet there
were none who did not admit that his primacy was absolute. The
King again took notice when on January 19, 1907, he wrote to his
prime minister, Sir Henry Campbell-Bannerman:

I strongly recommend the following R.A.'s for Knighthood:

E. A. Abbey (who painted coronation picture)
H. von Herkomer (who instituted a school for artists)
W. Q. Orchardson (who painted *Queen Victoria and Four Genera-
tions*)
J. S. Sargent (the most distinguished portrait painter in England)

Should four be considered too many, two might be made on the
29th June, and two more on 9th November.

The Prime Minister duly informed Sargent, who replied:

> Dear Sir Henry
>
> I deeply appreciate your willingness to propose my name for the high honor to which you refer, but I hold it is one to which I have no right to aspire as I am not one of His Majesty's Subjects but an American Citizen.
>
> > Believe me,
> > With very great respect,
> > John S. Sargent

He was at the very top of the portrait painters' hierarchy and he gave that art a vast supremacy over all others in the public mind. When the Academy doors opened at the beginning of May each year, the first idea in every head was to see what Sargent was showing; at the private view, when his patrons themselves were present, all of London crowded around him. He was the center of attention, his paintings received the most admiration and occasionally were given the spice of derision that was itself an evidence of eminence. His position was unchallenged. When fine portraits were wanted, it was understood that Sargent was the only man, and his refusal, which became more and more common as the decade progressed, doomed people forever to remain without a passport into that special sphere that the possession of his works alone ensured.

He was the mainstay of the Royal Academy as well, for his prestige had reinvigorated that ancient and, during the Victorian era, somewhat ingrown institution. That he used his position inside that body to advocate reforms made the others uneasy, as when on his first tour of the schools during the nineties he returned a report critical of the entire system, claiming that the pupils spent an excess of time assembling a set of drawings for the prizes, while failing to concentrate on the actual work of learning to draw. He disturbed many of the older members and, striving against their opposition, described himself as a "frequent and ineffectual advocate for changes, and a noncomformist to that kind of loyalty that consists in maintaining that everything is perfect." He was also responsible for importing into the Academy members of the revolutionary New English Art Club, which, despite Bernard Shaw's prophecy, had perversely managed to flourish. That, too, infused a new strength, the Academy seeming stronger during this decade than it had been since the end of its prime, which end came with the death of Lawrence.

Most important was the fact that, unlike many another public favorite, he refused to bask in the light of his own glory, but was embarrassed by the constant attention he received. He would not make speeches, he would not be photographed, he would not give interviews. He only allowed his tremendous precedence in the art world to be mobilized in behalf of the Academy itself, in which he believed and which his vitality had saved from its own lethargy. In response to repeated telephone calls from the Prime Minister he agreed to become a member of the newly constituted Board of Trustees for the Tate Gallery, but he soon withdrew, after having discussed the matter with Lamb, the secretary of the Royal Academy. He explained his actions to D. S. MacColl in this way: "I quit as soon as I realized I was the only painter. To elect one painter to a board of that sort looks to me like throwing a possible sop to the body of artists — and his position would be that of the small appendix, or some such survival, in an organism. The fact of my being an Academician also complicates matters more than I can foresee or measure. You, and others on the Board, undoubtedly represent a systematic opposition to the Academy, with influential backing and I don't know what fell purposes with which a member of the Academy cannot sympathize or be associated. . . . So that if I had known the composition when I answered the Prime Minister's laconic calls I would have declined."

In sum, Sargent was the commanding figure of the time.

All the same, there was still an opposition which liked to accuse him of brutality, or horrible literalness, or of being wanting in a sense of beauty. The old line of the Academy was not comfortable under its new master, many of the eminent older members disliking the very presence of his pictures. To them, accustomed as they were to carefully polished surfaces, his new form of realism was brutal in a very true sense and his telling accentuation of his sitter amounted to caricature. They were none of them able to deny that he stood head and shoulders above the rest, but they harped on the idea that this was due to *cleverness*, insisting that he had no suavity of manner, did not seek out idealization, which "it is the duty of every self-respecting painter to discover." That he was no respecter of persons either, and appallingly uncomplimentary, was hailed by the majority, but condemned by this critical opposition.

After the turn of the century there was a new club with which to beat him: increasingly there were portraits by Sargent that were not the vigorous achievements of former days. He was aware of it himself. He had begun to have a strange feeling before the succession of ladies and noble gentlemen who crowded his studio. They did not interest him. Collectively they had not the intellectual energy to motivate a fly. When he took brush in hand it did not move with all the old vigor. He could not account for it himself, and with renewed efforts he insisted that everything leaving the studio must come up to the mark or be scraped out and started afresh. He had begun to spot the sort of people who would bore him, and refused to paint them. He had never done really large numbers of portraits, except on his trips to America. A dozen a year, generally less, were all he thought he could accommodate against the demands of the murals and the London weather. As time passed, the personal trial of each picture became more acute. Now he was refusing oftener, painting fewer and fewer portraits. He would not work on them at all during the long periods that he devoted to the murals. When Mrs. Endicott, for whom he had already done several family portraits, wrote that she was sending her son to be painted, he replied:

> March 13th [1907]
> 31, Tite Street,
> Chelsea, S.W.

Dear Mrs Endicott

I will do my best about your son but there will be so many other portraits on hand at that moment I hope he is not going to make a very brief stay in London, for I would not be able to give anybody more than about 2 sittings a week and have been working at my Boston Library all winter and refused all portraits for a year past, but there are arrears to accomplish and they will come with a will this spring. I must tell you that I am on the

Academy Exhibition Committee this year, and will not be able
to have any sittings before the opening day which is May 6th.

. . .

Yours truly
John S. Sargent

P.S. I have put down Mr. Endicott for May 7th, 9th and 11th at
eleven o'clock unless I hear to the contrary.

He was frankly beginning to experience a growing distaste for
portraiture. What he had once desired with all his heart had been
granted him in such profusion that he was sated. He was too
sensitive an artist to be able to hide the fact that he was bored,
and one is forced to admit that a number of the portraits done at
this time had not the interest of his great works. Each person
mounting the platform was a new face, but more than that, a new
vanity, susceptible to wounds. That had not troubled him when
he was working in Paris, with a single exception, for he had not
the equipment then that he now probed with. His acute eye had
developed with the years, his sense of personality becoming increasingly sensitive. Gentle handling was necessary. He complained that even when women did not ask him to make them
beautiful, he could *feel* them wanting him to do so. The days when
he made friends of new sitters was long gone too, and now he knew
that every portrait he painted made an enemy. Portraiture had
plainly become a trial to his patience, and the routine of it, the
exacting demands, wearied him after so many years of ceaseless
activity. He could no longer completely satisfy himself unless he
became interested in an even deeper probing. One could not do
that with the upper classes, and there was no patronage from below.
He insisted that portraiture was not a game of hide and seek, but
an art, and he was finding that the art of it was increasingly
offensive to his sitters, who took the position that it was his duty
to forge a pleasant mask behind which they might hide.

Whether or not his revelations of his sitters were consciously
conceived is open to question, for he himself tended to deny such
intention. He had to do so, for no one knocked at his door to have

his sins aired. Yet it is certain that he, more probingly than his predecessors, did consciously note the mannerisms of each sitter, that he did study facial expression and the expressive quality of posture. His own claim was that he *chronicled*, he did not *judge*, and we can believe him. For Goya judged, and his standard was such that he gave a pack of fools to the world. Sargent set up no standard. He let the testimony speak for itself, and the record he gave posterity is more complex perhaps than that left by any other portraitist.

For a decade he tried to strike the delicate balance that would please himself and the sitter. The picture had to be good technically, as a composition and as a portrait. To accomplish all that, and still not offend the sitter, was a trial of wills. Furthermore, as his skill continued to develop, he really no longer desired to reach such a balance. Nonetheless, the demands of the sitter, who paid the piper and demanded the right to call the tune, were ever present. There were arguments, caustic remarks, demands for changes, and the advance of each work toward completion was accompanied by a steadily mounting tension. More and more his pleasure lay elsewhere, and his mind preferred to dwell on the murals and on landscape work.

Sargent had always been unwilling to paint royalty, for his was not the swift and fluent art that could catch them in a few short sittings. Nor was his the temperament to make stately personages out of his models without respect to individuality. His absolute refusal in this regard left a clean sweep of royal portraiture to the glib brush of de Laszlo, and Sargent let him have it with good riddance. The Hungarian painter became the special pet of royalty on both sides of the Channel. The slight similarity that his work bore to Sargent's (he, too, had a bold sweep, but his sitters were generally not sufficiently adept to see that the fine sense of mass and weight and the structure of Sargent's work were lacking) made his efforts acceptable with little reservation. Royalty in fact seems to have made little impression on Sargent, and while he was painting Dr. J. William White he refused an invitation to dine with the King and Queen at the American Embassy. "I'd certainly go if I were asked," White commented afterward. "He is more indifferent to such things. They bore him."

By 1906 Sargent was already talking, in an idle way, of giving up portraiture. It would be the means to "regain my manhood," he announced. The portent is obvious. He felt that his work was no longer up to his greatest capacities, that he was becoming entangled in the demands of his sitters. To his friend Lady Lewis he wrote: "I have now a bombproof shelter into which I retire when I sniff the coming portrait or its trajectory."

In 1907 he amused Dr. White by walking through numerous drawing rooms dallying with the "fond illusion" that he was about to give up portraiture and answering all remonstrances with the rather heated statement, "I HATE DOING PAUGHTRAITS," a pronunciation and spelling he now adopted, in derisive reference to the affectations of the London ladies. His refusals could be equally strong and couched in the most positive language, as when he replied to a request from one aristocratic lady: "Ask me to paint your gates, your fences, your barns, which I should gladly do, but NOT THE HUMAN FACE." He would paint only those who interested him now and, oddly, for a few years he seemed to hit a new stride. Lady Sassoon, and A. Augustus Healy, president of the Brooklyn Museum, sent over by McKim, made particularly fine portraits in 1907. Early in that year there was a letter from his cousin Ralph Curtis, with a request that he paint his friend Mrs. Lowther. The reply is a frank revelation of his feelings at the time:

> March 27 — [1907]
> 31, Tite Street,
> Chelsea, S.W.

My dear Ralph

It does not bore me to write that I can't paint a pawtreet, on the contrary it is the greatest joy in life — but I prefer writing it to you than the lady, if you will be good enough to tell her that I have retired from business. Tell her that I now only paint landscapes and religious decorations, that I am a waltzer to delerium tremens or whatever you think may make her congratulate herself on her refusal. I really am shutting up shop in the portrait line. One last Parthian shot tempts me. I did in Rome a study of a magnificent carved staircase and balustrade leading to a grand façade that would reduce a millionaire to a worm — it would be delightful to paint a rather anxious overdressed middleaged lady there, with all her pearls and her bat look, and of course never be chosen to do portraits any more —

. . .

I have just had a musical party and am slowly recovering and getting my place into disorder again.

Obsequies to the Dogaressa. Will you be here this Spring from Saturday to Monday?

Yours
J.S.S.

Apparently the lady he so clearly had in mind for this portrait did not appear. But in June, of all people, President Eliot of Harvard arrived and became the subject of this long-planned insult. The painting, Sargent claimed later, in talking with Endicott, had the only background possible.

He also played with the idea of raising his prices. Perhaps he could make it worth his while to continue doing a few portraits, a very few. With this in mind he approached Sir Edgar Speyer, the banker, who had previously asked if he would do Lady Speyer, and said he was now able to begin the portrait. Sir Edgar was pleased. The details were arranged amicably between them. Though all London knew that Sargent received a thousand guineas for a portrait, Sir Edgar in his gentle way asked Sargent what would be his fee. He explained his price for a portrait was now two thousand guineas, quickly adding that, as Sir Edgar had originally asked him to do it the previous year when his price was only a thousand, he would do it for that. He had chosen his man well, and Sir Edgar responded as expected. "No, no," he said. "That's my loss and your gain." He would pay the two thousand guineas. They talked it over some more, eventually agreeing on fifteen hundred guineas — the highest price he had got to date for a single portrait.

To that extent at least he was successful. But when the opportunity came to annex Germany to his sphere, he would have no part of it. Ethel Smyth had spent the winter of 1902 in Berlin, where her opera was being rehearsed by the Royal State Opera. She met the Kaiser, who was strangely pleased by her outspoken ways. He mentioned Sargent to her, with whom he knew she was acquainted, and though he told her outright he did not like contemporary painting, he did say he liked one by Sargent that he had seen. There is no way of knowing which one it was, though future events seem to imply that it was the *Mme. Gautreau*. Three years later, after ruminating, the Kaiser began unofficial overtures to Sargent, inviting an exhibition of his works in Berlin. It was rather unfortunate that he chose as his envoy none other than Mme. Pierre Gautreau herself, who in 1905 wrote to the artist. Though we can assume that his reply was couched in the usual French courtesies, there apparently was no mistaking the tenor of it. Undaunted, she tried another approach, contacting one of the Roller brothers, who sent word on to Sargent in Venice.

> Palazzo Barbaro
> Venice
> Oct. 3rd, 1906

My dear Roller

I think I know what Mme. Gautreau wants to see me about. She wrote me last year of a matter of vital importance — it was that the Kaiser who was such a dear, thought her portrait the most fascinating woman's likeness that he has ever seen, and that he wishes me to have an exhibition in Berlin of my things. I wrote that I was abroad and couldn't manage it. But to tell the truth, I don't want to do it. It is a tremendous trouble for me to induce a lot of unwilling people to lend me their "pautrets" and Berlin does not attract me at all. So if you are taken into Mme. Gautreau's confidence, and I wish you would tear your shirt for it, please discourage her from giving me the K.K. command.

> Yrs sincerely
> John S. Sargent

The Kaiser never got his wish.

When Sargent returned from that last turn through America in 1903, he resumed work on the remaining portions of his Boston murals. There were lunettes still to be done, and he began to think about the ceilings and ornamentations of the hall, his ideas expanding all the time. There were already enough paintings inserted into the walls. The ceiling itself would more logically be the place for relief work, further extending the symbolism of his religious concepts, as shown in the paintings. He launched into a study of decorative borders, filling sketchbooks with carefully drawn geometric designs, mixing leaf patterns with decorative swirls, and Middle Eastern tile designs from the Alhambra. Turning the pages of these notebooks, he judged them, marking one *TOO BROAD*, finding another too delicate. By 1905 he had decided it would be best to make another trip to the East. Finding no one who could go with him, he went off to the Holy Land alone. He settled into a hotel in Tiberias, surrounded by burning deserts and dark-shrouded Arabs but was generally disappointed, as by much on this trip. There was nothing new, no discoveries he could make in the way of ancient decorative arts, or little. Even the Jews here disappointed him. In London he had found that they were far better sitters than the aristocratic types who normally came his way. Their faces had character rather than a bland ennui, and they were more intense people, with a lively intelligence. He enjoyed the portraits he did for them, and they appreciated his work, too, making him grateful to Mr. Asher Wertheimer, who sent so many of them. He even urged Will Rothenstein to paint Jews, recommending them at once as the most interesting models and the most reliable patrons. But here in the Middle East they impressed him unfavorably, which made him decide he had come upon a decadent generation.

With such a small catch of decorative material, he decided to go out into the desert, where he came on a nomadic band of sheepherders. Joining company with them, he began painting their daily life, from the early morning meal over an open fire to the mothers nursing their babes as the lowering sun cast its last orange beams, setting the desert into fiery opposition of orange dunes and inky troughs. Both water colors and oil had been brought out, and more oils were roughed on canvas than he ever completed. A series of watercolors were done, in every light, while perky goats poked their slim muzzles at him and threatened to eat his paints. And he turned his attention to the desert itself, finding the Dead Sea a brilliant blue in the glowing sands, while the Hills of Galilee, broken, rocky, and unable to support life, looked heat seared and scarred. Fields laid out for cultivation in the sands formed patterns trailing off into vastness. The sky had to be painted too, the sea of the air and the sea of the sand flowing together in liquid washes and opaque touches. The ancient city of Jerusalem offered slender columns, marks of Roman and Greek art, draped figures hurrying past. The heat, the intensity of the sky burning down as he worked, the burning on the back of his neck, and the perspiration dripping through his beard — his pictures give it all.

This was not what he came out for, as he wrote back to London: "Some new material I have secured but it is different from what I had in view and not abundant — no miraculous draught. But I still fish here a while and try to bring back some weightier stuff than lots of impossible sketches and perhaps useless studies." He continued to work, to search, paint, and sketch. In January there was a telegram for him. His mother had died in London.

He replied, begging that the funeral be delayed until he could reach England. It had been an unfortunate trip, and this crowned it. Something of his feelings at that moment went into a letter to Mrs. Hunter, the only one to whom he could write in this way:

> Jan 24th
> Jerusalem
>
> Of course you know that suddenly my mother died three days ago — and that I am still out here — the telegram was brought to me, far in the interior, the very day that a boat left Jaffa — and there is about a week to wait for another boat — next Saturday — today is Wednesday —
>
> With the telegram came a charming letter from my mother, and this was the first I knew of that dreadful burning, which was, I suppose, the thing that proved too much for her strength. And I shall get other letters from her, affectionate and cheerful and telling me that she is getting better and driving out, and that her friends are delightful to know, you among others — Meanwhile . . . what may Emily and Violet be bearing and doing. It is dreadful to be away — I regret deeply not having returned long ago. . . .
>
> Yours J.S.S.

When he reached London he wrote her again:

> Saturday
>
> I have got back . . . I must spend the next evenings with my sisters — but won't you look in here this afternoon after 3, or any time tomorrow . . .

The ceremonial service will be at St. James's Westminster . . .
Monday at 3 — she will be buried at the same hour at Bournemouth — nobody will be there but Emily, Violet and I —

Since writing you from Jerusalem I got your letters saying
you also have had a great grief — I am sorry . . . strange how the
full sense of things seems to come and go by fits and starts. Just
now I seem to feel nothing at all, but I have had bad spells and
will have.

Yours
J.S.S.

One of the things uppermost in his mind was Emily's future.
She had been occupying an apartment in Carlyle Mansions across
the hall from her mother's. In so many ways these two apartments
had been his real home. He had dined there often and spent the
evenings playing chess and frequently inviting Steer, Tonks,
Rothenstein, Harrison, and the others to come along. Perhaps
there had been a certain lack of intimacy with his mother, he
seemed to be as distant with her as he was with other people.
Affectionate they had been, and more than one friend remarked
on the quiet way in which Mrs. Sargent watched over him when
he was in her house. Now Emily was alone, and this presented a
problem. His solution was an offer to set up housekeeping with
her in Tite Street, but fearing that he asked her out of pity, she
refused. His carefully ordered life had so long been spent alone
that she thought another presence would be an inconvenience, and
so she elected to remain where she was.

Mrs. Sargent's estate was small, only thirty thousand dollars, on
the income from which both she and Emily had been living in
London. It was divided equally between John and his two sisters.
But the obvious intention of his mother had been to care for Emily,
her will touchingly stating that her son "through his great talent"
was able to provide for himself and Violet's husband could look
after her, while Emily would have nothing but this inheritance.
She had already given Emily her personal possessions for that
reason and there were really adequate means for Emily to live on,
almost indefinitely, at her modest rate.

It must at this time have occurred to him, suddenly, how great his own earnings were. Compared with his parents, he was fabulously rich. He still lived as simply as ever, collecting pictures, and frames, and furniture, it is true, and lavishing care on his studios and his friends, but he was not the sort to spend extravagantly or unwisely simply because the money was there. Whether he even realized the extent of his income is open to question, for though he was almost avaricious in acquiring it, the money went off to his bankers as soon as it came in. Probably he had no idea at all what was in the bank in his name. Financial statements were dull reading, with no illustrations, and such matter quickly found its way into the wastebasket or was sent off to some solicitor. His affairs were in good hands. All he actually knew was that his income was substantial. The nature of the securities his money was in, their chances of gain or loss, did not trouble him; he did not know a debenture from a debutante.

Earning was a habit nonetheless. Work had to be got out of the house just for fear of the tremendous storage problem consequent on retaining it. There would never be room enough for all he did. The subsequent history of one of the watercolors done in the Holy Land is amusingly suggested in a letter he penned to Mrs. Gardner, who visited London for the last time that summer.

> Tuesday
> 31, Tite Street,
> Chelsea, S.W.

Dear Mrs Gardner

In answer to the mysterious note, do you care enough for the horses to give forty pounds for them? If so they are yours — don't hesitate to say no if you don't want them. Let me know if you do for I shall have to get consular papers and tomorrow morning is my only chance.

Would you like the water colour with its glass and frame packed in a thin box? or should I just take the water colour out so that you can put it in your trunk between cardboards? or roll it up around a cardboard cylinder? This way you could smuggle it easily and there would not be need of consular papers. Also I would sign it. If you want it frame, glass and all, it seems hardly worth while to demolish the framing in order to sign it, but I will if you say so.

Let me know these particulars by tonight or tomorrow first post, in case I must go to the consulate in the city.

> Yours sincerely
> John S. Sargent

The picture, now in the Gardner Museum, Boston, is signed, which suggests that Mrs. Gardner chose the easier, more adventuresome alternative and did not force him to go into the city for consular papers. When he received the check for it, he wrote again:

> Jan 7th 1907
> 31, Tite Street,
> Chelsea, S.W.

Dear Mrs Gardner

Your kind letter and the checque for £40 from Kidder & Peabody arrived the other day.

It is very kind of you to have written me of the comfortableness of the horses in their new abode. I feel that to be worthy of this promotion they ought to have had blue ribands plaited into their tails and manes, like Herod's horses in Flaubert's beautiful Herodiade. You know your sketch was done in Jerusalem but the stalls were not Herod's, but Thomas Cook's who has succeeded him in Palestine.

I hope you will come over every year again, as you used to.

> Yours sincerely
> John S. Sargent

He talked more and more often of giving up portraits. At first it was thought a whimsy of his, and accepted as a new joke. Then, as the idea took root, growing on him, and he experienced more and more the pangs of working on portraits, he said it in earnest. Now he was adopting a new stratagem. After Lady Speyer's portrait was completed and installed in the paneling of her music room in Grosvenor Square, she asked if he would paint Sir Edgar. The prospect did not please him somehow. Speyer was a quiet, thoughtful man, tasteful, and filled with all the Germanic virtues of loving home and family. He seemed really quite dull from Sargent's point of view, with none of Lady Speyer's buoyant temperament. He suggested that he make a charcoal drawing instead of a portrait, as he was then doing with a few others. As he would not do the portrait, the offer of the charcoal was accepted, and both Sir Edgar and Lady Speyer were drawn. This became a common device. Through 1908 and 1909 he did more charcoals than oils, and when he finally decided to give up painting portraits, every inquiry met a counteroffer — a charcoal or nothing. After completing Lady Sassoon and Lady Speyer in 1907 he accepted few portraits. In 1908 there were only seven; in 1909, three. The very last was the aged Earl of Wemyss, father of his friend Evan Charteris and the head of a family that had provided him with many sitters. When at last it was completed he breathed a sigh of relief. It was all over.

The year 1909 was one of changes, great and small. Two events that had a definite bearing on his resolve, now already in force, to be done with portraiture were the sale of a large group of water-colors to the Brooklyn Museum and the death of Charles Follen McKim. McKim's death and Sargent's retirement brought a clean break with all the strategies that had brought Americans to Tite Street. At the end, McKim had been a Trustee of the Metropolitan Museum, and he had left Sargent two friends there, the new acting director, Edward Robinson, who had been at the Boston Museum of Fine Arts, and Frank Millet, who as an associate with McKim in many projects had also become a Trustee. Sargent's life was being swept clear of one career, and readied for another.

The first success of the new life came quickly. It was the sale to the Brooklyn Museum, and arranged through Knoedler's that April, of a group of eighty-three watercolors. Sargent selected the group himself, including in it every type of work he had done in that medium, representing his earliest efforts as well as the most mature. It was the most complete illustration of his abilities with water color that could be got together, and when they were shown at the Knoedler Galleries in New York, A. Augustus Healy, whose portrait had been done two years earlier, came over from Brooklyn to see them. Soon after Healy met with the Trustees of the Brooklyn institution, who raised a special subscription of twenty thousand dollars for the purchase. It was consummated, April 14, 1909, and within a month Sargent had returned to the attack. He was obviously not devoid of interest in his earnings, even though he had completely given up portraiture. His artistic conscience was involved. He did not care to go on with them because they could no longer represent his best work. Yet he was willing to take part in deals that could net him only small profits, or nothing, as it sometimes turned out. Paul Helleu, in Paris, needed help in unloading a picture that he was speculating on. When he sat down to write to prospects, Sargent realized that Helleu and Mrs. Gardner were acquainted. If she knew Helleu was the owner of the picture in question, the two might conclude the matter between themselves. Apparently that would not do.

May 12th [1909]

Dear Mrs Gardner

Whenever I hear of a good picture for sale I think of you, in spite of the rumor that you do not often add to your collection nowadays.

The picture about which I have been asked to inform a few people and Museums is Boldini's portrait of Whistler which belongs to a French artist who wishes to sell it for 25,000 fr.

I suppose you know it. It is first rate Boldini and a wonderful picture of Whistler. If it should tempt you let me know.

I hope you are well, and wish you came over here oftener!

Yours sincerely
John S. Sargent

He put his pen down and looked the letter over. It would do. Mrs. Gardner would never guess that it was Helleu who owned the picture, and it ran smoothly enough so that she would not be attracted to the fact that the name was carefully omitted. In fact, it was pretty good. So he wrote another like it to A. Augustus Healy of the Brooklyn Museum, and then some more. Curiously enough, he was successful, for his word carried extraordinary weight. It was Healy who bought the picture, after bargaining Helleu down to twenty thousand francs. Whether the extra five thousand would have been Sargent's commission or he was doing this merely as a service to Helleu cannot be proved. But the letter to Mrs. Gardner, with its careful elimination of Helleu's name, is suggestive. There were further facts, too. When Healy, who made the purchase personally, turned this Boldini over to the

Museum as a gift he explained that Sargent's opinion had been the decisive factor in the purchase and also that Sargent would prefer that his name not be mentioned in any statement about the acquisition.

And still, he would not paint portraits. Of course, he had good reason not to do anything he found personally bothersome. The income from his capital certainly made it unnecessary to trouble over whether a "mouth had something a little wrong about it." The bother of pleasing people, of being polite when he felt otherwise, of satisfying others at the expense of his principles, all seemed unnecessary. Why allow himself to be kept in London during the heat of the summer months? Why have to attend dinner after dinner? Why have to speak to people he did not know, or like, or care to know, or expect to like, or wish to meet? Why, indeed? And yet he could sell a picture for Helleu, on which he could realize no more than five thousand francs for himself at best. Stories that he had refused a hundred and fifty commissions spread through London quickly and traveled to America, where amazement was great. The idea of Sargent's giving up portraiture seemed incredible. In Philadelphia, friends of Dr. J. William White, who for years had been eager to present a painting of him to the University of Pennsylvania Medical School, suddenly got up a subscription and asked his consent for their project. White in turn penned a letter to Sargent, putting his demands in blunt terms. Would he paint the picture? Would he paint it in June? Would he object too keenly to the scarlet Aberdeen gown?

Well accustomed to White's jokes, when the letter arrived Sargent replied in kind. It took a second letter to convince him that the request was in earnest, and then, like a loyal friend, he bowed his head to the yoke. Just this one more! He wrote to White that his image, clad in dazzling tints, haunted his sleepless nights, "invoking with savage grin the name of friendship to hurl me back to the damned abyss of portraiture, out of which it has taken me two years to scramble." Pitifully, he hoped the friends did not want a three-quarter length. "That would take much longer, and looking at a large surface of scarlet affects me as they say it does army tailors, who have to retire to the vomitorium every three quarters of an hour. You are sure to know all about the close connection between the optic nerve, the colour scarlet, and the epigastrium." Later when the question of the length remained unanswered, he cabled: "Prefer death to three-quarter length."

White sailed for London. Six days before he was expected to land, Sargent wrote a first warmup for the jokes they would be lashing each other with. "By this time I suppose you are on the bridge, practicing a becoming expression. I am also in training for you by a course of drawing from the antique. If you get here on Sunday, the 20th, I shall await you on Monday, at eleven o'clock. Bring your war-paint in the way of gowns, etc." The sittings began on the twenty-first, while Sargent swore vigorously that this would be his last, his *very* last, portrait. Coming over on the ship White had been sunburned until he was a rich, dark red, considerably stronger in tone than the "dazzling" gown he wore. His fiery complexion tones and the equally fiery colors of his portrait, when it was completed, startled Henry James, who came around to see the result. Indignantly White insisted he often was redder, while for his part Sargent expressed the hope that the picture would protect him from further portrait applications. "It will suit my purpose better to let people think that this is my present style than to make a plea for extenuating circumstances," but he also decided, whimsically, that he had made his friend look like a "South African Macaw," which was a pretty good description.

Scarcely a year later, on May 6, 1910, the Edwardian era — the brilliant period of which Sargent stands as chief artistic recorder — came to an end. The King passed away, and lay in state at Windsor, from where royal messengers were dispatched to Tite Street, asking if he would come to do for the dead King what he would not do in life, draw him. He could not refuse, making the trip to sit at the side of the deceased monarch, who had shared many of his feelings toward life, and to draw him. Edward in death was hardly more than his mother's long nose and some whiskers, not much to draw, though he did his best and then was silently ushered out.

It seemed strangely fitting that the death of the King should coincide so well with the end of Sargent's career as a portraitist, for it meant that the Edwardian era and the Sargent era had come to a close together. There is a certain historical neatness about this, as though destiny played a hand in the strange juxtaposition of events. The period ended, and its chief recorder, the man who stood to it as Van Dyck had stood to the cavalier era of Charles I and Holbein to the reign of Henry VIII, brought his work to a close at the same time. A page in history turned.

From the late nineties it had been Sargent's rule to spend the months immediately after his yearly bout with the London ladies recuperating in some Continental hideaway, where he could paint everyone's neck green if he felt that way and the foliage did not care about its expression. Venice had been his first thought when he went on these yearly junkets, these tours back to health and good humor, and almost yearly invitations were extended to him by the Curtises at the Barbaro. Either from there or from some nearby hotel he daily sallied forth, Nicola burdened with a load of papers and paint and canvas and folding easels, to be poled off to some good spot where he could settle down to the water-colors and oils he delighted in. Nothing pleased him better than the multicolored architecture of Venice, its frills and straight walls, its balconies with thousands of penetrations defining the design, and the water everywhere, reflecting and coloring forms, itself picking up the gleam of sky and buildings and posts and carrying it through the depths. The filth of centuries lay on the buildings, looking in the brilliance of the sun like the dabblings of a master decorator, coloring the stone gray, purple, and green where a drain was missing, orange where rust had washed down a wall for centuries, white where pigeons had stood — everything carrying as well the mottled patina contributed by ages of weather. How much of the gentle color transition between water and wall was moss and how much the scattered remnant of human waste in a city that had no adequate sewerage was less important than the color this mysterious substance threw forth, color playing a more important role than people, who were only incidental dots and dashes decorating the fronts of churches and passing along the walks. The dark, mysterious side of the city had to be explored too — long passages shrouded in ancient secrets, steps leading up from the waters to dark alleys, doorways that held their secrets.

Everything appealed to his impressionistic eye, color was everywhere, the task of defining the content of each iridescent gleam becoming his challenge. Each year he felt anew the fascination of architecture, columns and statuary, decorative patterns incised and extruded, capitola and scotias, flutings, filigree and fillisters all fimbriated by the artisans of past centuries, set out to be colored by the seasons and the suns. The patterns of the shadow, the fringed wonders of their falling, lay everywhere, and the gleam of light rising off shining metal and stone was its exact antidote. As his compositions grew more and more compact, his field of vision contracted. He less and less cared to do a scene, concentrating instead on one building, then on part of one building: a façade, the shadows of side entrances, blank walls, a corner of a ledge. More and more his concentration became riveted to the exact quantity of impressionistic light reflected back at his retina by some minor detail in the vast maze of Venice. His sense of architecture, correct in even the earliest works, grew until he was setting down the weight and solidity of walls with deadly sureness, and though done with apparent ease and speed, the volumes are remarkably exacting. Shipping had to be painted in the bay too, and there were barges carrying wares in the side canals. The city had a thousand aspects under morning, afternoon, and evening's failing light. He painted them all, in water colors and, when a subject seemed interesting, again in oil. Venice became his hobby, his mistress, his ladylove, and he paid court to her with no cool analytic devotion but full passion. If only the London ladies had a little of this filth on them, what portraits they would have had!

When the Venetian sun died, late in November, often he went farther south, to Florence or Rome, to find it again where it shone on other monuments and slightly different scenes. As the first decade of the new century passed, he found Venice more and more filled up with "larky Londoners," whose antics he was willing to find amusing but whose interference with his concentrated working habits was an annoyance. Soon he remembered that there were other places in Italy where he could work.

After 1909, with the mantle of the portraitist once and forever discarded, he could go for more extended jaunts. The gypsy streak that had always been in him, deeply a part of the nature he inherited from his mother, and had matured through a childhood spent in railway cars and rented quarters, now asserted itself more strongly, though he had always been a remarkably keen traveler. There was an almost exaggerated junketing, the full extent of which is hard to believe. He went all over the Continent, willing to be absent from London six months of the year, summering in the Simplon, visiting the Curtises in Venice, then off for a final flurry of painting through Italy or Spain or Corfu, lasting almost until Christmas. Only then did he dutifully make his way back to the three empty studios awaiting him in Chelsea. During this travel he produced an enormous amount of landscape work, in both water color and oil, for he was never willing to waste a moment. Landscapes interested him more than portraits had in recent years and, sensitive artist that he was, his feelings toward all things showed in his work. His pleasure, his love of the subjects, and the warm light in which he worked are evident in the finished pictures, which frequently have a lyric quality. They become silent hymns to nature, painted with all the fervor of a heart that had no other voice. Certainly he was happier now than he had been during the last years when the mounting flood of portraits threatened to submerge him, and he battled against the desires of every lady in London to be beautiful. Whether or not he gave any thought to selling these landscapes — and it is altogether possible that he did not, for now he was a wealthy man with a secure income — there was the satisfaction of knowing that among the mass of work there would be, just by averages, a proportion the public might consider attractive. That it was a small proportion did not disturb him. He had no qualms about allowing the mass of his watercolors to be put away in drawers and portfolios when he returned to Tite Street and left there without ever again meeting human eyes. The pleasure had been entirely in the painting, and that was enough. The public was no longer his concern.

Curiously, his very indifference served to raise the prices offered for his things. When he refused portraits, people began to offer him larger sums to change his mind, and the fact that he would not change it did not lessen their persistence. They went gaily on, the prices now mentioned in connection with his pictures seeming fantastic. The landscapes were rising in value too, and there again his complete indifference to whether any of them were sold was playing its part. Few of his oil landscapes saw the light, for they were put away to molder on their stretchers in Tite Street. Some few were periodically selected to be exhibited, and these were fitted into some of the frames he had collected in a small room in number 31. They were quickly sold, but those he selected for this distinction rather force the belief that he did not think too highly of the state of taste about him. The rough, vigorous works that best expressed his vision, and his love of paint, were never among them. Now and again one of these might be given to a friend, but more likely it was the tamer studies that sallied forth. Still, his prices were rising to fantastic heights, culminating years later in the sale at Christies' following his death, when duchesses came to hold hands with duchesses and the auction room took on the aspect of the royal enclosure at Ascot. Canvases and watercolors that had never been seen were brought forth on that occasion, and the opportunity to see so many of his pictures together and for sale, not only on exhibition but actually obtainable, drove a fierce enthusiasm through the crowd. The watercolors came under the hammer first. Starting off at £110 for the first to be knocked down, they soon reached £1,000. The crowd that watched itself in the sale room was pleased, and looking around saw King Manuel of Portugal, the Duchess of Sutherland, Admiral Beatty, and Sir Joseph Duveen, the great art dealer. It was a four-hour session of intensely crowded mania. The large bids were greeted with loud applause, as the watercolors soon reached £1,400, jumping still higher until the *Side Canal at Venice* brought £4,830. Then came the oils! Altogether 237 lots brought a total of £170,000.

Sargent himself never gave any thought to the worth of these pictures that he turned out standing before the manifold splendors of nature. It was a happy life for him, to get off somewhere to paint, to know that he was doing his best work, and the most enjoyable.

One day late in 1910, a letter had come to Sargent from the critic Roger Fry, who was inclined to snipe at him in his reviews of the Academy and the New English Art Club. However, this was rather hat in hand. Fry was requesting that Sargent allow his name to appear on the list of sponsors for an exhibition he was then getting together for the Grafton Galleries. There was nothing unusual about the request except, perhaps, the source, and because he always tried to support a worthy artistic enterprise, it would not have been unusual for him to have joined the Committee of Sponsors. Still, the fact that it was Fry who sent the request made him hesitate, and reading through what Fry had to say of the exhibition he saw a list of names that were quite strange to him. Manet of course he knew, and Cézanne, who had been a friend of Monet's, possibly he had met. At least he had seen Cézanne's works in Paris during the late seventies, and remembered the heavily troweled paint applied with a knife. Cézanne, as he recalled, was very brutal. But what of these others — Matisse, Picasso, Derain, Friesz? He had never heard of them. Others, like Gauguin, Van Gogh, Signac, were familar, but not clear in his mind. Altogether he did not feel inclined to put his name in the hands of a man of such uncertain principles as Fry, and as he had no idea what the exhibition would be like, it seemed downright careless to do so. Therefore, that morning, as he sat down to his correspondence, he included a brief note to Fry, stating that, as he was not familiar with the work of the painters who would be represented, he did not feel he could appear on the list of sponsors. That, so far as he was concerned, was an end to the matter.

When the exhibition opened in November it proved to be an occasion for considerable merriment. The polite ladies and gentlemen who visited the gallery positively demanded a guest book in which they could give forceful expression to their disapproval, and the exhibition generally degenerated into a display of upper-class boorishness. Many of Sargent's friends attended, and though he was not in London at the time, he doubtless heard distant rumblings of the affair, which, when he returned, sent him to see for himself.

The exhibition was truly amazing. Sargent was interested to see that Cézanne had changed his manner, and true to his extreme tendencies, had turned to thin turpentine washes that hardly covered the canvas. Gauguin obviously had some very beautiful color, though why he never bothered to learn how to draw was more than he could understand, nor why the others were willing to sacrifice all the beauties of form and drawing for the limited advantage of overloud color. This was where Monet had led them when he allowed the forms to disappear from his work. Monet was artist enough to make even such canvases beautiful; but much of this looked like plain rubbish to Sargent, though he was pleased to see that, owing to the exhibition, Manet was receiving attention in England. He went the rounds of the walls, stopping at every-thing, examining and carefully searching for things he might con-sider admirable. The amount of admiration called forth was very limited, however, and as he progressed this became evident on his face, which flushed, exaggerating the steely glint of his eyes. Through the tail of one of those eyes he must have seen the critic C. Lewis Hind, an altogether charming and inoffensive little man, who had been pleasant company now and again. But he would have been obliged to speak of this exhibition to Hind, which he did not want to do, moving on as though he had not noticed. For his part Hind, noticing the irritated flush, thought it better not to speak. So he followed around, eager to note reactions, until at length Sargent stalked out without a word to anyone.

He kept his opinions to himself. It seems likely that, if the *Post-Impressionist Exhibition,* as Fry styled it, had not been forced on him, he would never have taken any position on the matter. For it was contrary to his principles to condemn if he could avoid doing so, and when unable to extend the helping hand of praise, he customarily lapsed into silence. Roger Fry, however, found that he was in a dangerous position with this fiasco. Having been induced personally to select and hang this show for the Grafton Galleries, as the first of a series that were to present the work of younger men, both French and English, he found the public had been unable to take the thing seriously. He approached Steer and Tonks to see if they would go along with his plan, explaining that he would use these annual exhibitions, "for a general secession exhibition of all non-academic art of any im-portance including members of the NEAC." They were unwilling to be associated with it. Will Rothenstein's reply was the same, and Fry was desperate. He thereupon wrote a brave article for the *Nation,* which appeared on December 24, and in it listed the champions of post-impressionism, placing Sargent's name in their ranks.

Sargent had never before met anyone who would brazenly

appropriate his name in this way, and such a discreditable action puzzled him. Such culpable dishonesty had to be quashed, or Fry, fond as he was of sniping attacks on his paintings at the Academy, would think he could carry his ears about publicly. Yet, he did not want to act hastily. For two weeks he waited. Then, certain of what had to be done, on January 7 he wrote to the editor of the *Nation.*

Sir,

My attention has been called to an article by Mr. Roger Fry, called "A Postscript on Post-Impressionism" in your issue of December 24th in which he mentions me as among the champions of the group of painters now being shown at the Grafton Gallery. I should be obliged if you would allow me space in your columns for these few words of rectification.

Mr. Fry has been entirely misinformed, and if I had been inclined to join in the controversy, he would have known that my sympathies were in exactly the opposite direction as far as the novelties are concerned, that have been most discussed and that this show has been my first opportunity of seeing. I had declined Mr. Fry's request to place my name on the initial list of promoters of the Exhibition on the ground of not knowing the painters to whom the name of Post-Impressionists can be applied; it certainly does not apply to Manet or Cézanne. Mr. Fry may have been told — and have believed — that the sight of these paintings made me convert to his faith in them.

The fact is I am entirely skeptical as to their having any claim whatever to being works of art, with the exception of some pictures by Gauguin that strike me as admirable in color, and in color only.

But one wonders what will Mr. Fry not believe, and one is tempted to say what will he not print?

Yours,
John S. Sargent

His opinions of the paintings Fry selected had undoubtedly not been flattering. He tended to believe that Fry was actually the instrument of French picture dealers, rather than wholly responsible himself for the selection he had brought over. The whole "movement" seemed to be the invention of sharp French picture dealers, who reveled at the opportunity to buy cheaply and sell dear. Dealers had never been his particular delight, their practices, when they were so outrageous, he was willing to condemn. Roger Fry had rather overstepped the limits of his forbearance by appropriating his name, making him one of the sponsors of this venture, without thought concerning the sanctity of another's name or reputation.

Will Rothenstein had been the first to notice Fry. They were in the Academy Julien together before the turn of the century, and Rothenstein immediately put him down as possessing a very meager proficiency as a figure draftsman. His attempts to make his way as an artist were foredoomed, and his rejection by successive juries at the New English Art Club, and the New Gallery, came each time as proof to him of the failure of those societies. He turned to criticism, leveling his omniscient critical lash on the juries that had rejected him as a painter. He went on to decry the Royal Academy, though as Abbey had observed, "I often think how much better employed some of these chaps would be if they were to try to overcome some of their own shortcomings instead of pointing out the shortcomings of others . . . The poor old R.A. is a very easy mark . . . but it would be well to have a better thing to put in its place before they knock it all to pieces." With the help of a naturally vituperative temperament, Fry went on to lash everything in sight. He was further spurred in his excesses by a succession of futile efforts: to obtain a Slade professorship, to become director of the National Gallery, to sell his soul to J. P. Morgan in return for a curatorship at the Metropolitan Museum, from which appointment he was released after one dismal year. Even his personal life seemed to follow this lamentable path, and the only happiness he had known, that of his marriage, was snuffed out by his wife's insanity.

To be caught making use of another man's name was too much for Fry at this stage. That he did it was certain but, like the boy stealing apples, he was sorry to be caught. He would teach Sargent to treat him in that fashion; and for the rest of his life, in one discreditable, blatantly untrue attack after another, he leveled every weapon at his command at Sargent. Perhaps there was a certain method in this madness too, for if his aim was to demolish the

Royal Academy, in that way to induce the anarchy in the arts he wrote about, Sargent was the logical place to start. He represented the mainstay of the Academy, the great man of huge achievement who gives life and meaning to such an institution. He represented in his own person the new cleansed tradition of the Academy, Victorian bugaboo thrown out, virile forceful methods in its place. To discredit Sargent, the goal that occupied Fry the rest of his life, would mean the complete enfeeblement of the Academy. It was the strategy that one reads in adventure stories: Pick out the biggest and beat him, the others will run away. And so, with an ever-increasing fury, through the years after 1911, Roger Fry called for Sargent's blood. His personal hatred was twisted into attacks on artistry and integrity, and in one way nature allowed him to know a success. For Fry had the good fortune to outlive his prey, giving him the opportunity he had seemed to relish most — to perform a war dance over the recently interred remains.

Sargent's position on the post-impressionists was essentially a reiteration of the stand he had taken with Vernon Lee as far back as 1881. He had no interest in theory, no patience with long dissertations that complacently explained away the shortcomings the eye immediately detected. He was unwilling to confuse incompetence with eccentricity. Slipshod methods met his instant disapproval and aroused his suspicions. When his friend, the critic D. S. MacColl, wrote an article containing a critical estimate of Cézanne in which he pointed out a certain dichotomy between his impressionistic *sketcher's* technical equipment, which was evolved for snatching at effects that would not wait, and the claim that he was seeking eternal verities, Sargent wrote him his agreement: "I have enjoyed reading your article on Post-Impressionism very much — I think it should bring a good many people to their senses." He went on to expose what was in his own mind: "I admire the certainty with which you have refrained from hinting at bad faith on the part of people like Matisse," which showed more understanding than many had at that early date, "or at the theory I am inclined to believe: that the sharp picture dealers invented and boomed this new article of commerce." This last was never far from his mind.

The War Years

NEITHER the assassination of an Austrian prince nor the growing international crisis that filled the chatter of the polite world in 1914 made any impression on Sargent. All he knew was that wars had come and gone in his lifetime, and that they were dull stuff in so far as painting was concerned. As the momentum leading to strife increased, he was busily engaged in packing for his summer's vacation in the Tyrol, where the Adrian Stokes had already reached Seisser Alm, the high grassy plain in the midst of the Dolomites, where Sargent was eager to join them. The very name Seisser Alm brought back memories of childhood days spent in those parts, and in that sentimental mood it seemed a propitious place for outdoor work. The lofty plateau, lying low between jagged, towering peaks, was a likely place to develop compositions with the broad flat plane across the bottom that so nicely drew together the verticals he frequently employed: the verticals would be mountains, the plateau itself supplying the necessary horizontal plane lying perpendicular to them. Voilà! Seisser Alm!

Many of his intimates might have warned him against such a venture at that moment, but he was not seeking advice. Once he arrived, however, the compositions never came off, though he refused to be idle. He managed to keep busy, searching for any little thing that was worth sketching. Silver palings growing in a rather graceful pattern were the material for a watercolor, cattle deep in the gloom of a dim cowshed made another. It was work of a sort, though not what he had envisioned.

And then the thing he had been shrugging off descended on them all. The impossible nonsense became a reality. On July 28, Austria declared war on Serbia, and the following day began bombarding Belgrade. Russian mobilization was speeded, and on August 1, Germany declared war against her, occupying Luxembourg August 2, and declaring war on France the day after.

Immediately the Austrian frontiers were closed, guests at the hotel vanished. Sargent's party, proceeding down to Campitello, found themselves projected into the center of panic. The stations were impossible to get into for the people camped in them, trains were crowded to suffocation, and frequently sidetracked while military specials went through. Worst of all, none of their party had passports nor more money than was required for an ordinary holiday. The little group of six (besides Sargent, the Adrian Stokes and Major Armstrong, there were Nicola and Mrs. Stokes' maid) managed to make the long drive to Colfuschg, where they persuaded the landlord of the inn to take them in. It was a lovely spot, high in the Dolomites, and Sargent for his part was content to settle down and paint.

Then England entered the war and Major Armstrong, a retired army doctor, left for home. Sargent continued work undisturbed. But eventually the struggle engulfing the whole of Europe must be borne in on even this forgotten band. In October came word that Major Armstrong was being held prisoner of war at nearby Trieuil and an appeal was made to Sargent to help. He descended from his mountain fastness and succeeded — perhaps because he was Sargent, whom the Kaiser had honored — in procuring Armstrong's release on parole. Then came word that Robert André Michel, husband of his niece Rose Marie, had died in battle. So this was real. It meant death.

The Tyrol was no place to be. Awaiting the passport he had applied for, he wrote to Mrs. Hunter:

Nov. 9th
St. Lorenzen, Pusterthal
Tirol

I was glad to get your letter, which must have crossed mine I think. . . .

I am only waiting now for arriving Official Passports and permission to travel, and will be off as soon as they arrive — I know from Latimer that boats still run from Trieste to Venice, & that [Thomas] Cook still exists in Venice. So I shall probably go that way, as I can get my pictures and things as far as Venice at any rate, and there hand them over to Cook if I return by land, or arriving there I will see if I find a steamer for England. I know your house has been a haven of refuge for many people. (it always is), the Orosdi, Rodins, etc. I hope you will see Armstrong, & he will tell you all about our summer & his experiences, & his getting loose —

I am aiming at being back by the 20th at latest for my R.A. School —

I hope you are well & not worried —

Yours ever
John S. Sargent

An emergency passport was issued him by the American Embassy in Vienna on November 19, the day before he was to have been in London. Eight days later, by what route is unknown, he turned up at Le Havre, France, where he was forced to apply once more for a permanent passport. A day or two later he was in England.

London was in off season when he returned to resume work on the Boston Library murals. The war was having its effects on the life of the capital. Britain was amazed at the fury of the German advance, at the magnitude of the artillery preparation that leveled everything before the swarming armies of the Hun. The rape of Belgium was an established fact, and "Paris by Christmas" was a hope on the far side of the Rhine and a fear on the near. Perhaps the numbers of uniforms was the first notable feature of this wartime London, and the number of friends who were off with the army in France and Egypt. Lady Speyer had given some of her outbuildings at Overstrand for the care of evacuated French troops and Mrs. Hunter opened a hospital on the grounds of her Essex estate. Tonks went there from Dorchester Heights to put his medical knowledge at their service, and found that everyone was flocking to her house to meet the people returning home on some interesting errand or going to a new appointment at the front. Old Mrs. Curtis came from Venice to stay, and Rodin and Mme. Rodin were permanent guests. The aged sculptor, now on the verge of senility, proved anything but interesting, and all that everyone ever heard him say was "Lord, but the trees are beautiful." The Rodins were given one large bedroom in the house, with a great bed, and were seldom seen except at meals, or sometimes walking together out of doors. The sculptor seemed to break through his haze only when strangers arrived for dinner and the party engaged in worldly talk. Tonks soon had the medical situation in order and then turned the responsibilities of Mrs. Hunter's hospital over to a surgeon from Epping. After he had done pastels of the Rodins and old Mrs. Curtis he joined a Red Cross hospital in Arc-en-Barrois, Haute-Marne, from where he wrote that Sargent had been very generous and he had a good sum in hand for medical expenses.

In this same way everyone seemed to pick out some task for himself, though it must be admitted, as in the case of Mrs. Hunter, it frequently was work that was not too onerous, and left leisure for the normal round of social interests. But there were those who took it more seriously. The Duchess of Marlborough was in Red Cross uniform, Sir Philip Sassoon was off in France, and all the Charteris clan, Lord Elcho and his brothers, had gone. Soon the younger, dreaming members of the nobility, those who wrote poetry and professed socialism at Oxford, were arriving at Tite Street in their uniforms for drawings, and many of them would not be seen or drawn by anyone again.

Henry James was particularly agitated, reading newspaper accounts of German brutality with a shaking fury and organizing an expedition to bring out the raped nuns of Belgium. The war became the cause of his own personal tantrum, and all the energy left in his 72-year-old frame, so long supine, was concentrated in one endless diatribe against Germany and all things German. With Sargent he called on one influential lady who through the years had entertained them both and had charmed Sargent through many long sittings for a portrait nearly ten years before. It was thought that she and her husband had pacifist leanings, and despite her charm and tact, James launched into his own anti-German up-braiding, until the two left with ill feelings. Sargent saw less reason for all this, and James became impatient with him as well. The "inseparables," as they were known in the drawing rooms of London, proved temporarily incompatible, a certain coolness growing out of James's aversion to Sargent's lack of enthusiasm.

Fund raising was in full swing. The British Red Cross Society applied to the leading portraitists to contribute empty frames to an auction held at Christies', the high bidders to sit for their portraits. The device was attractive, for it meant aiding the Red Cross while also receiving good value for the donation, only the painter actually contributing anything. Still, it was impossible to refuse the Red Cross in wartime; every painter who could afford to go along with this humane enterprise agreed to participate. Sargent, however, would not allow himself to be put back into the harness of portraiture, but eventually agreed to a charcoal instead, and then raised the number to two. The sale was held April 16, the result indexing, in the most obvious way, the comparative popularity of the painters who had participated. Of course, as he was not willing to do an oil, Sargent should not be considered in the same scale with the others, and yet the fact remains that his two charcoals were second only to de Laszlo in the bidding, all the other painters having agreed to do oils. The figures were:

de Laszlo	750 G.
Sargent (charcoal)	650 G.
Sargent (charcoal)	500 G.
Orpen	400 G.
Lavery	400 G.
John	210 G.

The auction was such a success that there were hopes of a repetition, with the addition of a Sargent portrait in oil. The artist was not agreeable to that suggestion, but when it was proposed to the Red Cross that a donation of £10,000 would be made outright for a Sargent portrait, he was no longer able to refuse. The offer was then repented of, but Sir Hugh Lane picked it up and Sargent agreed to go along. Henry James, somewhat in want of the proper details, wrote to Dr. White in Philadelphia: "You will no doubt have seen how, at a great auction-sale of artistic treasures sent by the benevolent for conversion into Red Cross money, Sir Hugh Lane bid ten thousand pounds for an empty canvas of John's, to be covered by the latter with the portrait of a person chosen by Lane. What a luxury to be able to resolve one's genius into so splendid a donation! It isn't known yet who is to be the paintee, but that's a comparably insignificant detail."

Hugh Lane appeared to have no definite idea as to whose portrait it was to be, and he took ship to America. He was given a box on the front page of the *New York Times*, offering his rights to a Sargent portrait to anyone who would raise his bid of $50,000. There was speculation about why this was done and who had backed the original bid, the Wideners figuring widely in the talk. Whatever the case, no one came forward to increase the price, and early in May 1915 Lane took passage on the *Lusitania* to return to England.

The sinking of the *Lusitania* on May 7 opened a new phase of the war, for it mobilized popular opinion in Britain as well as America to new heights of anti-German feeling. It was thought at first that the loss of so many American lives on the *Lusitania* would bring America into the war at once. That opinion was whispered about London by many who were believed to have, and themselves did believe that they had, reason to know. But they were not counting on the strange self-mortifying attitude of President Wilson, who suddenly found himself too preposterously proud to fight. The full blast of propaganda and British control of the Atlantic cable were employed to win the American people to Britain's side and bring the New World to the aid of the Old. Anti-German feeling became so extreme in London that Sir George Henschel, knighted and filled with honors since he had sat for his portrait so long before, found himself publishing sonnets to England in the newspapers, to keep the evil eye, and the evil tongue, from his door. Sir Edgar Speyer and Sir Ernest Cassell were "excused" from attendance at the Privy Council: the Speyer family found its home stoned and its four daughters threatened, in the face of which it was forced to go to America. Henry James, by now completely out of sympathy with American policy, impatiently waited for United States entry into the European blood bath before each nightfall. Eventually he, too, yielded to other pressures and saw his solicitors about seeking naturalization, which he intended as one more protest against Wilson. Once he had adopted British citizenship, he tried to explain to Sargent, who foresaw that many Americans would not approve his step:

21, Carlyle Mansions
Cheyne Walk, S.W.
July 30th, 1915

My dear John,
. . .
　Yes, I daresay many Americans *will* be shocked at my "step"; so many of them appear in these days to be shocked at everything that is not reiterated blandishment and slobberation of Germany, with recalls of ancient "amity" and that sort of thing, by our Government. I waited long months, watch in hand, for the latter to show some sign of intermitting those amiabilities to such an enemy — the very smallest would have sufficed for me to throw myself back upon it. But it seemed never to come, and the misrepresentation of *my* attitude becoming at last to me a thing no longer to be borne, I took action myself. It would really have been *so* easy for the U.S. to have "kept" (if they had cared to!) yours all faithfully,

Henry James

　The seriousness of the pressures brought to bear can be gauged by the fact that even Sargent, upon whom much of the situation itself was lost, felt obliged to attempt returning his German honors. He spoke to the American ambassador in London, who communicated with the Secretary of State in Washington:

June 22, 1915

John S. Sargent, the distinguished American artist resident in London, has a decoration conferred several years ago by the German Emperor, which he now wishes to return. He has handed me a note addressed to the proper Court authority in Berlin respectfully returning the decoration, and he asks me if he may return it to you under cover of a letter, requesting you to ask Gerard to deliver it in Berlin or if I under your instructions may send it to Gerard direct. The return of such honors has become quite common between Englishmen and Germans.

He asks me also if he may transmit through Gerard his resignation from two notable art societies in Berlin and Munich.

Sargent makes no criticism of the German Government or German societies in his letters but merely resigns because he is no longer in sympathy with German aims. I await instructions.

American Ambassador
London

The answer was swift, betraying the sensitiveness of Mr. Wilson's government on the subject of German relations.

Washington, June 23, 1915
Not matters with which the Department or its officers abroad can have any connection.

Sargent should reimburse Embassy for your telegram and pay this reply, five dollars.

Lansing

Immediately on his return from the Tyrol in November, Nicola had been put to work photographing the summer's work, and after Sargent had been back a month, and world conditions had not yet sunk in on him, he wrote to Edward Robinson of the Metropolitan Museum, enclosing one of the photographs:

31, Tite Street,
Chelsea, S.W.
Dec. 24, [1914]

My dear Ned
I have been back a few weeks from Tyrol where I was caught by the war and from which it was not very easy to get away. I am gradually getting through the correspondence that has accumulated here since July, and I find your letter of Aug. 31. I am sorry my watercolors have got all jumbled up since my departure. But all the best ones were at the White City.

The two that were here now look to me too rough for a Museum, and I don't think much of the one with shipping that you seem to have liked. I have not done many watercolors this summer, but there are two that are up to the mark. I don't remember you stating any definite number, But I think you said 8 or 10. If the Museum wants 10 it may have these at £50 apiece including the Fountain at that price — never mind my having said 75 before.

I enclose a photo of the best oil picture I did in Tirol last summer. I think it has some good colours, and I feel more justified this time in acting on your repeated suggestion that I should report something that strikes me as worthy of the Museum. I have kept this one back and will not sell it until I hear from you whether the Museum would like to have it. . . .

By January 19, Robinson cabled "Museum takes Tyrolese picture, wants ten watercolours." And in March, with an eye on the war, Sargent wrote:

I ought to have written to you long ago to express the pleasure I feel at the idea that the Museum will buy my Tyrolese interior as well as the ten water colours. I delayed in order to announce to you the departure of the latter. But for the last few weeks the newspapers have been so full of the dangers to shipping that I thought it safer to wait a little while till a few more mines have burst and few more submarines been caught. Things seem to be calming down a little, and I shall soon have the water colours packed by Chenue and sent.

It seems to have been fear of this same shipping situation that induced him, a year later, on January 8, 1916, to write to Robinson that he would be willing to sell the portrait of Mme. Gautreau, which had already crossed the ocean for the Panama-Pacific International Exposition in San Francisco. "Now that it is in America," he wrote, "I feel rather inclined to let it stay there if a Museum should want it. I suppose it is the best thing I have done." Robinson was frankly amazed to hear this from Sargent, for as he explained in his letter to the Trustees on January 24, he had tried to get this picture from him for many years, first for the Boston Museum and later for the Metropolitan, "and this change of decision therefore comes as a complete surprise." Within four days Robinson was able to cable back the unanimous decision to purchase, and three days later Sargent wrote: "By the way, I should prefer, on account of the row I had with the lady years ago, that the picture should not be called by her name, at any rate for the present, and that her name should not be communicated to the newspapers."

It was discovered after the sinking of the *Lusitania* that Hugh Lane had left only a scribbled will, made shortly before he went on board the ship, which did not take into account his bid to the Red Cross nor his apparent possession of an unpainted Sargent portrait. Henry James's *insignificant detail,* "who is to be the paintee," was now an inherent part of Lane's estate, which he left in entirety to the National Gallery of Ireland. It fell to the courts to prove the will, which was tied up more than a year in litigation, and the result produced distant and undreamed-of labors for the artist.

In the meantime a letter came to Tite Street from the American artist Abbott Thayer, who had ideas concerning camouflage that he wanted to bring to the attention of the British Army. Out of the blue, and because he had been one of those watching the painting of Mrs. Fiske Warren in 1903, he selected Sargent as the man to handle this matter for him. On receipt of the letter Sargent seemed to think he might have a try at it. From Boston he was shipped costumes and photographs and armed with these, plus manuscript material prepared by Thayer, and a letter he expected would explain the paraphernalia, he made an appointment to see the quartermaster general, Sir John Cowan. The meeting came off fairly well, and he passed all the materials, including the letters, into the hands of the general's professional advisers. For an hour he stayed on at the War Office, talking about the advantages, as he understood them, of parti-colored versus monochrome. Seizing sheets of papers from a desk, he demonstrated by holding them at different angles to one another that white was not always, nor necessarily, white. He came away with a promise that Thayer's schemes would be examined thoroughly and considered and that he would be notified.

In America, Thayer chafed at the delay, writing for an introduction to Carolus-Duran, who he thought might be influential in official quarters in France. Thus, on the morning of November 12, Sargent sat down to his usual correspondence, in addition penning a note to Léon Bonnat, which he enclosed with the following to Thayer:

I have got your letter this morning saying that you are going to Paris. I enclose a letter to Bonnat whom I know only very slightly but who is certainly the most influential artist in Paris and probably in touch with many generals, etc. Carolus-Duran hates me and would at any rate not be as useful. Besnard is probably in Rome at the Villa Medici. All my other friends are dead. . . .

Unknown to him, Thayer had sailed without waiting for a reply, and appeared in London, demanding an introduction to H. G. Wells, which was given him. Sargent urgently applied at the War Office for a demonstration of Thayer's ideas while he was present, Thayer in the meantime flitting about England so that mail sent to any of the multiple addresses he supplied was returned. The War Office questioned Sargent, who was as much in the dark as they. Then one day, returning to Tite Street, he found that Thayer had come and left a trunk and a note, the latter saying he was going back to America. With the originator of this fuss vanished, the War Office took interest, asking Sargent to send over the trunk, which he had not opened, and come himself to explain. It meant breaking away from the mural work he was doing at Fulham Road in preparation for a new installation in the Boston Library, but off he went to Whitehall. There was a round of handshakes when he met the generals, followed by the business of opening the trunk. Inside were some drawings and an old spotted brown leather jacket with rags pinned to it. The ordeal proved too much for the generals, and the flustered Sargent, who had not known what to expect, could not explain it away. "I am going to Boston," he wrote in a last letter to Thayer, "and shall be anxious to learn what made you vamoose."

Mugs and Murals

W HEN THE *Nieuw Amsterdam* docked at New York, Carroll Beckwith awaited Sargent at the pier, just as he had done thirteen years before. They were both noticeably older now, time having bestowed on each in separate measure the fruits of the years. Sargent arrived visibly fatigued by the voyage, walking with a cane, and favoring a foot that he had injured in his last-minute packing. He would give no interview at the pier, nor after reporters trailed him to Beckwith's apartment at the Hotel Schuyler, on West Forty-fifth Street. Beckwith told them at the door that his guest expected to stay with him for two days, and then go on to Boston. He also had hopes of making a trip out west to paint American landscapes. At the Boston railway station he was met by an architect named Welles Bosworth, sent by John D. Rockefeller to talk about a portrait. While Nicola shouldered huge bundles of materials through the station, they started off to the Hotel Vendome, where Bosworth had helped him get a suite with two windows on the Dartmouth Street side. After the cold outside the steam-heated rooms seemed oppressive, and still favoring his injured foot in its cast and soft slipper, he made his way to the windows, throwing them open in turn and taking deep breaths of the frigid air that wafted in. Bosworth seemed amused, commenting that in Boston there was no trouble about cooling rooms off, only keeping them warm, which set the artist to thinking about the terrible experience he and Abbey

had in the summer of 1895. It would be useful to talk about
vacations at that point anyhow, to put off discussion of portraits,
and he began asking about summer locations, even though in his
own mind he had already decided he would try going to the
Canadian Rockies, which he had heard bore some resemblance to
the Alps. Eventually though, after making objections to Bar
Harbor, because there would be people there, and to some other
famous resorts in Maine, for similar reasons, he permitted the
conversation to turn to portraiture. Bosworth explained, with a
simple, flattering candor, that he had a duty to paint Rockefeller.
He had painted all the great and famous men of the time and it
would be a wrong committed before history were a man of Rockefeller's stature not included in that company. It was an argument
particularly well adapted to Sargent's mental processes, and he felt
it necessary to state that he thought he had *earned* the right to
refuse doing any more portraits. Bosworth switched to telling him
what splendid arrangements Rockefeller would make were he to
come as his guest while the work was being done, how well he
would be treated, and with what consideration. No doubt these
particularly well-chosen arguments took their toll of the painter's
resistance, though he continued to grumble, and object, complaining that people were forever bringing portraits back to him with
requests for changes to an eye or a nose, or the mouth, without
realizing that this necessitated the repainting of almost the entire
head. If only they would accept his portrait as his personal statement of the thing and leave it at that! Here was the sort of opening
Bosworth had hoped to find. Immediately he jumped into the
breach, promising that, if Sargent would consent to paint Rockefeller, the work would be accepted precisely as he left it, without
any requests for changes. He was conscious now of an awakened
interest and tried to press for agreement, but the best he could get
was that the artist would have to think about it.

To Sargent the problem was personal as well as artistic. There
was his conscience to consider, and his vow. Only afterward, when
he became aware of the huge drive for funds still going on for the
British Red Cross, did he find the sort of excuse he needed. He
would give the money to the British Red Cross Society. It would
almost be as though he wasn't painting a portrait at all, and if he

really had any duty to history, well, he would be acquitted of that too. In time he communicated with the Rockefellers, telling them he would do the picture, but not at present, for his injured foot would hamper him in walking back and forth before the easel. He would paint it after some of the present load was eased.

The first threat to be faced was an attempt by the Trustees of the Boston Library to have him give an interview to the press. He was set against it, but finally consented lest his refusal have an adverse effect on the reception given his new and final batch of murals. Thus, one afternoon, he faced a battery of reporters from a chair in the Trustees' room, up a few steps and off the middle of his Hall. He was first asked some innocent questions that went off well enough, then was interrogated about the effects war was having on the arts in England. Well, he did not know. All the artists were off in France anyhow. Were they *all*, Mr. Sargent? Well, some of them were! Orpen, John, and Rothenstein were the ones he knew. Having contradicted himself or run the risk of doing so, he was angry to have the slip picked up by the reporters. He shut his mouth firmly, and sat and glared, poking his foot with the cane. To avoid disaster the officials quickly distributed a prepared statement and ended the conference.

It was widely known that he had come to complete the work on his Hall in the Boston Public Library, though it was not known how much of the work he intended to carry out on the spot. Every part of the room had come under his scrutiny. Every foot of it had been taken into account in his decorative scheme. The vaultings and skylights were all to be fitted with reliefs. Every architrave and archivolt was specially designed after painstaking study. Now he set to work. "I am terribly busy here," he wrote, "with the carrying out of the plaster work of my ceiling — it is progressing well but it will be a long job, and I have to work like a nigger modelling things that the workmen wait to carry off and cast. I doubt if all this is accomplished so that I can put up my paintings before the midsummer heat sets in — when that comes in July or August I shall be off to the Rockies for mountain air and sketching and return to this work in September." Bosworth one day found him cutting stencils rather laboriously in heavy paper. He asked why this sort of mechanical work could not be delegated.

"I have to do it myself, because I cannot find anybody else to do it well enough" was the reply.

Sargent followed his time schedule through the early weeks of July, when he completed all the things he believed had to be done with his own hands, and only then leaving for sketching in the Rockies. Dr. Denman Ross, artist and Trustee of the Boston Museum of Fine Arts, told him of various spectacular waterfalls, which he set out to find. With Nicola and a guide, outfitted with tents and camping equipment, he plunged into the wilderness. Nothing can surpass his own description, written to Mrs. Richard Hale:

August 30ᵗʰ [1916]

Dear Cousin Mary

At the risk of importuning you with this persistent letter writing, here I go again. As I told you in my first or my last it was raining and snowing, my tent flooded, mushrooms sprouting in my boots, porcupines taking shelter in my clothes, canned food always fried in a black frying pan getting in my nerves, and a fine waterfall which was the attraction of the place pounding and thundering all night. I stood it three weeks and yesterday came away with a repulsive picture. Now the weather has changed for the better and I am off again to try the simple life (ach pfui)) in tents at the top of another valley, this time with a gridiron instead of a frying pan and a perforated India rubber mat to stand on. It takes time to learn how to be really happy.

Life was different in the Montana National Park, with the pleasant company of the Livermores. There we toured about over new trails every day. Mrs. Livermore is perfectly delightful *and plays chess*. Alas she went back east, and struck Chicago in a heat wave. The refrigerated dining room at the Blackstone Hotel saved her life, as it did all ours two weeks before. It is worth while flying there from any part of America during a heat wave. You sit in a perfect temperature over an excellent dinner and watch the crowd dying like flies outside the window. Nero or Caligula could not have improved on it.

Please take your courage in both hands and write me a line to this hotel. I will pounce upon it when I get back from my next plunge into canned food — thirty miles away.

Yours ever

John S. Sargent

Despite his amused exceptions to the rigors of camp life, he was obviously enjoying himself, and seems to have prospered. The landscapes he did there have a new flavor unlike his Alpine works. He was able to put onto his canvases something of the feeling of the distinctly American scenes surrounding him. Peculiarly, all the while he was working in the wilderness he seems to have been taken up with attempts to obtain a series of Spanish recordings for Mrs. Gardner, each of his attempts meeting some separate form of disruption. A short note explains:

> Mount Stephan House
> Field, B.C.
> Aug. 31st 1916

Dear Mrs. Gardner

I have just got your letter and am making a last attempt to remove the hoodoo by writing to Charles Deering at Sitges. If he is still there he will be sure to get them, or if his agent reads his letters and can read *mine*, he may have the sense to get them himself.

I have done a picture of a fantastic waterfall, somewhat the sort of night mare as Mrs. Sears' picture, and I am off to another place near here where I expect to find other awful sights. Whether to your liking or not you shall decide.

> Yours sincerely
> John S. Sargent

When he returned to Boston there awaited the task of finally putting in place the lunettes brought from London. He hoped the scaffolding could come down soon to reveal the full nature of what he had done, which he had never yet seen unobstructed from the floor. As he wrote, "Whether or not it is another of the palpable signs that I am getting old, I am rather revelling in the appearance this white elephant of mine is taking on of amounting to something, after all these years." His expectation was that it would be finished before the year was out, allowing him to return to England, where he had been approached to take on another £10,000 portrait for the Red Cross, and perhaps go on to France to do a war picture for the British government.

In the meantime he took a studio in Boston to do various charcoal heads. The murals were progressing with speed and stirring interest throughout Boston, where expectations ran high. In November, the Museum of Fine Arts, which was again adding to its buildings, asked Sargent to undertake a new set of murals for the rotunda dome. He was delighted to have this commission just as his first murals were seeing completion. He began a series of talks with the architects, for he felt that the caissoned ceiling of the dome was not suitable and that no arrangement of panels could properly go with such uninteresting surface treatment. The whole surface of the dome, and to some extent of the supporting dispositions, was therefore modified in accordance with his ideas of how the decorations should be carried out. He had it intersected with plain archivolts on the axes of the dome and pendentives, the skylight at the top surrounded with a perfectly bare ring, and flat ribs projected to spring from the cornice to meet it. Thus the previous area was now divided into eight separate compartments, with interesting penetrations at the base, where shallow arches were cut from the four largest segments of the dome as it was now divided. When it was completed he could place his decorations, which he believed ought to be largely sculptural, into an organic system of design, once again taking into account the architectural needs of the structure.

To begin his studies, he had a model of the dome constructed, which stood six feet tall in his studio and into which he placed studies to see their effect architecturally. The studio he had used during the fall did not seem adequate for these large needs, and he looked for another, finally settling on a loft in the top floor of the Pope Building, 221 Columbus Avenue. There he set to work.

Busy as he was by day, the long habit of social evenings was not forgotten. He found special pleasure with relatives, particularly Mrs. Hale, and Professor Charles Sprague Sargent, the botanist, whose homes he often visited. The professor would send his huge brass-trimmed car to bring him out to Holm Lea, the estate in Brookline, and allowed him the use of it at other times as well. Mrs. Hale's cook, Bridget, always prepared a special fish dish when she knew he was coming, for he had once commented on it. There was no real proof that he enjoyed this more than other dishes, for he seemed to eat anything set before him with a fine disregard of what it was; nonetheless, though it took a day's preparation, combining halibut and whitefish with others, all well seasoned and boiled and baked, she would set about it. The family were all a little shy of his sartorial splendor. His English homespun trousers, which he liked to wear for informal occasions by day, blazed a trail of elegance through their weekends. None of them had ever seen homespun so large, so loud, or so much of it on one man, for not only did it generously cover his large person but there was excess to slop over unconcernedly onto his shoes. His jackets had an equally generous look, for when they hung open the large parts intended to reach around his stomach looked too big for any one man, and flapped like sails in the wind as he reached so constantly into his breast pocket for one of the fifty or more loose cigarettes it was his habit to carry there. His appointment books were crowded with daily luncheon appointments, dinners almost nightly, and evenings spent at the theater or the movies, which he was discovering and from which he derived particular pleasure. Mrs. Gardner became his companion at Charlie Chaplin films. Hers was a long-standing claim on his time, and despite advancing age, she was still a gay hostess, preferring small parties of friends, the sort at which he was comfortable. He gave Mrs. Gardner the Speyers' address on Bay State Road, then met these London friends again at intimate gatherings at Fenway Court. Lady Speyer asked if he was doing any portraits, at which he made a wry face. "No. I'm only painting mountains and niggers." There, too, he first heard Heifetz play and made a little sketch of the youthful performer on a scrap of paper as he fiddled. George Arliss, another from among Mrs. Gardner's society, Sargent did not care for. The shy young Nijinsky, stranded in America after Lady Ripon managed to get him out of Austria, he liked better, and the dancer was likely to turn up at Columbus Avenue at any time, to stand in silence and watch the work as it progressed, dreaming of stage designs and watching the glistening of Negro models beneath the skylight.

The pictures he had sent to the Panama-Pacific Exposition were still an embarrassment, for he did not want to trust them to the ocean just yet. The problem was solved by C. Powell Minnigerode, director of the Corcoran Gallery, who asked if they could be shown in Washington. They were sent, accompanied by a letter that explained in the plainest terms that they were not for sale. Even so, scarcely a month later, Minnigerode wrote that people wanted to buy the pictures and begged him to allow them to go into homes, where they "would always be treated with the most profound respect." The answer was still "No."

By the spring of 1917 the portrait of Rockefeller had been in abeyance more than a year, and Sargent now took up the aged financier's invitation to come to Florida and commence work. He wrote the news to Beckwith, on a portrait expedition to California, who noted in his diary: ". . . A nice letter from Sargent who is going south to paint Mr. Rockefeller. And he hates to paint portraits. I wonder how he was corralled, was it the money?"

The semitropical lands were new and attractive when he arrived at Ormond Beach to do his "Rockefellering," and Rockefeller himself proved a fine model. For the first time in years Sargent began to enjoy a portrait. When his work on Rockefeller was completed he moved over to stay with Charles Deering, painting at the still-unfinished estate being constructed by his brother James. There was sea bathing in breaking surf, and palms grew down to the water's edge. The estate in progress amounted to an amphibious Fenway Court, on a larger scale, with courts, columns, Venetian piers, billowing draperies, and terraces lined by statues reflecting the sun. "It is very hard to leave this place," he wrote back to Boston. "There is so much to paint, not here, but at my host's brother's villa. It combines Venice and Frascati and Aranjuez, and all that one is likely never to see again. Hence this linger-longering."

America had entered the war now, and he was conscious of the rushing events, whether or not he fully digested their import. There was news too that Charlie Hunter was ill, and undergoing surgery, and at the beginning of May, Sargent wrote from the Deering estate at Brickell Point: "With all this noise of great happenings in one's ears it is difficult to write of one's own small affairs — especially if one is out of all that matters. I am fiddling and doing watercolors while Rome is burning and easing my conscience by doing a portrait of Rockefeller for the Red Cross. I should have been back in London by this time, but that my sister was to have come over here for a visit and now the submarines keep us both apart. I am upset from what you say about Charlie Hunter, & from other letters that his end must have come by this time — Poor Mrs Hunter must have had a dreadful ordeal." Yet withal, the work he did was completely dissociated, as it always was, from worldly influences.

He had never before painted palm trees, and found their many colors, variegated by the sun and growth patterns, quite different from the uniform green that Winslow Homer had seen them. Dead fronds lay moldering, swelling with new colors, near the shore, the complexities of their intertwined forms, the colors that crossed, twisted, and fanned before him, all going into watercolors that mounted in number. He found a Negro model and posed him naked in the sun on the ocean beach, his coloring fierce against the jeweled brilliance of the sea. He hated to leave, but eventually the magnetic attraction of Boston grew stronger in the diminishing field of the South.

Sargent was in Boston only ten days when he took a train down to New York, arriving at Beckwith's for Sunday breakfast. The portrait of Rockefeller had been shipped from Florida to Beckwith's studio in the meantime, to be put on new stretchers and varnished before going to the Rockefeller house at Tarrytown. Beckwith was all admiration when he saw it, that same sincere, marveling admiration he had always shown before his friend's work. Sargent remained in and around New York for two days, part of the time looking over the Rockefeller estate, Pocantico Hills, where he had agreed to do a second portrait of the old man. Meanwhile his first effort remained in Beckwith's studio, where it attracted a host of admirers. J. Alden Weir, president of the National Academy, came by. "Weir is a great toady to popularity," Beckwith noted, with the qualification, "but of course John's success fascinates us all." Tuesday the picture was put on its new stretcher, and Rockefeller's son came to see it. There were more visitors — Chase, Orr, Sartain, and Dewing. Then on Thursday in strode Sargent himself. He had come to ask Beckwith to do "some replicas" of Rockefeller portrait, then was off again to Boston.

The next morning he wrote Mrs. Hale:

June 1st

My dear Mary

I got back last night from New York and found your nice letters. I am sorry to say that I cannot go to Bar Harbor just now. In two or three days I've got to go to Pocantico to do my second paughtrait of Rockefeller. I have just come from a tour of inspection there and they are going to be moving somewhere else in three weeks time, so I have got Beckwith the order to copy the other. I expect to go there next Tuesday or Wednesday. Address J. D. Rockefeller Esq., Pocantico Hills. . . .

Rockefeller must have been very impatient, and Sargent seems to have left Boston immediately, for by June 3 he was established at Pocantico. He had Mr. Rockefeller's agreement to a price of fifteen hundred dollars for Beckwith's "replica" of the first portrait, and telephoned Beckwith in New York to say that Rockefeller agreed and that the portrait, which had been shipped out of the studio, would be returned in two weeks' time so that he could copy it.

The visit to the modest Rockefeller house at Pocantico lasted three weeks, during which he stayed in one of the family bedrooms on the second floor. At lunch one day he met a Mr. Inglis, who was engaged by Rockefeller to begin research for his biography, and especially to trace his family in upper New York State, where they had lived before moving farther west. Inglis asked to see the little black-covered account book Rockefeller had kept as a boy when he earned six or eight dollars a week in Ohio. Sargent was interested to note that in the neat little hand there was a record of methodical donations to charities, generally connected with church. On one page he noted fifteen cents "to missionary cause," a dollar for pew rent, twelve cents to "Five points missions," six cents to "missionary cause." What impressed him most was the closeness of the dates, and the systematic way this young man had denied himself to make donations, and it left a much-strengthened belief in his own impressions of Rockefeller. "People think that Mr. Rockefeller gives generously to atone for ruthless business methods," he later told a sitter in Boston. "But I found that giving had been his life habit . . . He is not so bad, I am inclined to think, as people make out."

This second portrait, done in the garage at Pocantico, began to show a somewhat different aspect of Rockefeller — almost unworldly, taking on something of the look of a medieval saint. There is a distinctly religious atmosphere, as though the painter began to sort out some of the characteristics noted in the first portrait but obscured by generalization. It is clear that the character of the man was more opened to him by prolonged observation. To a member of the family he commented, "I have never felt so much as though I were painting St. Francis." Whatever the other people of the world might have thought, whatever the stories he might have heard, he saw Rockefeller in his own way, and it was in this way that he would paint him! He did not allow any outside influence to alter his own perception. His personal reaction could not be compromised. Living with the greatest industrialist and financier of his day, possibly of all time, he saw him as a time-worn man, filled with intellectual vigor despite his years, with his heart at peace and his attitude one of unworldliness. He painted him this way, for he had the honesty to call things as he saw them, and this second portrait of Rockefeller is among his greatest achievements.

Now that he had introduced Beckwith to the bounty of Rockefeller's patronage, he also thought of the young sculptor Paul Manship, whom he had met the year before through Mrs. Sears. Casually he mentioned to the old man one day that he had a fine head for sculpture. When Rockefeller seemed receptive, he went on to say that he knew a good young sculptor. "Why don't you have him do you?" The result was the first of many portraits by Manship, and commissions began coming in increasing numbers from among Sargent's friends.

With his second portrait completed, on the morning of June 24, Sargent and the younger Mr. Rockefeller went to Beckwith's studio to see the copy Beckwith had done. Rockefeller readily approved, but Sargent was able to see what Beckwith had already noted in his diary: "got rattled doing Rockefeller's head — one of John's most subtle bits of painting." He suggested to Beckwith that, as he had some work to do around New York, he would borrow the studio for a few days, and while there perhaps touch over the copy a trifle. He would "oil out" the copy and handle the details of delivering it. That, it seemed, was a part of the price of friendship — redoing what one had hoped a friend could do.

While using Beckwith's studio he did some charcoals, one of young Kermit Roosevelt, who came by in uniform and seemed a likable young man, quite unlike his father. It was the last favor he was to have of Beckwith, though not yet the last he would do for the shy lad who had shown him into Carolus-Duran's atelier. Carroll had not been well of late, his depression growing on him until he had not wanted to accept the order to copy the Rockefeller portrait when it was offered him. It seemed lackey's work to copy a portrait done by the young fellow who had come to Duran's after Beckwith was already a favorite of the master. Only need forced him to accept it.

Toward evening one day late in the year he went out for a stroll. Half an hour later a taxi brought him back. Bertha made the last entry in the diary he had kept since the Rue Notre-Dame-des-Champs days; that touching, sad little life was spent.

It was Beckwith's misfortune in life to stand in the shadow of greatness and, though he had some pleasure and advantage from being so close, there was no doubt he himself was completely engulfed by it. Perhaps, had there been no Sargent, his own frail talents might have seemed more and his training under Carolus-Duran loomed larger in America. He had from the beginning been the most popular teacher, with the largest classes, in the Art Students' League, but it was his misfortune that alongside his friend he looked like nothing, and the further misfortune to be intimate with the source of all his troubles, to feel Sargent's charm and find pleasure in his warm friendship. One last gesture remained. When Bertha organized an auction sale of the pictures left in her husband's studio, Sargent came to New York and retouched those that needed work.

Tremendously enthusiastic about his new murals, Sargent stayed on in Boston through all the heat of the summer of 1917. When friends remonstrated, he explained that summer was the best time to work because everyone was away, and consequently there were no interruptions.

He found that the sketch he had made of Vinton fourteen years earlier was now rather badly cracked and took it to a restorer named Daniel Nolan. Nolan's work on the picture was excellent, for rather than fill in the cracks, he seems to have given the whole canvas an oil bath that made the paint fill out to its former size, closing the cracks. Sargent expressed complete approval, then found Nolan unwilling to take payment, claiming, with his Irish grin, "It's a tribute from one great artist to another!" The vein of this remark rather pleased the painter, and at dinner a few nights later he told about the incident, and the audacity of Nolan, remarking that he must think of something to do in thanks. The natural suggestion was a portrait, for those who knew better than Sargent the conceit of this Irishman thought it a proper gesture indeed, and one that Nolan would appreciate. So he offered to make a charcoal drawing of Nolan, to which Dan, still with impious grin, had the hardihood to offer an amendment, hinting rather broadly that he would prefer a sketch in oils. "Don't you like my drawings?" Sargent threw at him, trying to back him into a corner from which he could not extricate himself. But Nolan was quite equal to the situation. "You know I love them, Mr. Sargent," he began, "but I am thinking of my descendants!"

"What! *Whut?* What's this?" stumbled the artist.

"You see, my wife and I are both Irish, and in our household we sometimes have family discussions. Now, if she should throw her shoe at me, and it happened to go through your charcoal drawing, it would be spoiled forever. But if it just dented an oil painting, I could always fix it up as well as I did the Vinton."

Thus did blarney win another day. The sketch was done in oil, for the descendants of course, and it is one of Sargent's finest, most living achievements.

Ever since Hugh Lane was lost in the *Lusitania* sinking, the National Gallery of Ireland had been involved in complicated legal procedures to establish its right to decide who should sit for the portrait belonging to the Lane estate. Early in June of 1916 the Chancery Division had upheld the will as drawn, and a plebiscite was begun in Ireland to select the sitter. The Trustees of the Gallery now informed Sargent that the selection had been made and, now that the United States was in the war, it would be President Woodrow Wilson. Here was a nasty rap! There was no way out. He was unalterably committed, the right to select the subject had been given the National Gallery by the courts, and they had duly selected the President. Somewhere in the middle of these maneuvers he was caught.

Dutifully, then, if without any enthusiasm, he sat down to write to President Wilson, and the answer came back:

July 18, 1917

Dear Mr. Sargent,

. . . Apparently it is in vain to hope for sittings while Congress is in session and, unfortunately, with the extraordinary dilatory practices possible in the Senate no man would be rash enough to predict how long the present session will last. I do not see how it can very well continue beyond the first of September, and I had in a general way formed the expectation that I might during that month have a chance to give myself the pleasure of seeing you. I should consider it a privilege to do so. . . .

This was all very interesting, whatever it meant. "Extraordinary dilatory practices," indeed! Congress could stay in session as long as it pleased, but not long enough to suit him. In time the summons came:

Dear Mr. Sargent,

Congress has adjourned and my mind turns to the suggestion I made that probably after the adjournment it would be possible for me to sit for the portrait which the Governors of the National Gallery of Ireland so generously desire.

I would be glad to know your own engagements and whether it would be convenient for you to come down next week or the week after.

I would also like to know, if it is possible for you to answer such a question, how much time it would probably be necessary for me to set aside for the purpose.

With the pleasantest anticipations of knowing you,

Cordially and sincerely yours,
Woodrow Wilson

And so now it was back to the White House. The place did not hold happy memories. Sargent had promised himself never to be trapped there again. But what could a man do? Duty was duty.

He arrived in Washington with Nicola, settling into the New Willard Hotel. That first evening there was dinner at Cabot Lodge's, where the wind blew political on every occasion. Lodge announced that he was just delighted about the portrait of the Democratic President: *it was a great opportunity for the artist to serve his party*. Remembering the portrait of Speaker Reed, done nearly thirty years before, Lodge said he was certain there must be some sinister, beastly trait lying hidden in Wilson, and Sargent's job was to ferret that out and reveal it to the world! He would be doing one of his finest, most psychological portraits, while also serving his country. Here certainly was an unhappy thought to lay before the painter. Aside from the laughable idea that he *had* a party, or cared for any party, it dropped him into a realm far removed from his own world of art. All the circumstances surrounding the commission to paint Wilson had been unfortunate. He had never dreamed that his gesture for the British Red Cross would come to this. He had thought it would be one more of the London ladies, another awful *mug* to put on canvas, but certainly nothing of special importance. The selection of Wilson had put that simple gesture, made only with a wish to be helpful in a struggle he hardly understood, into the realm of world events. The light shining on President Wilson, because of his unique international position, was more intense than that on any figure of the time. Now, after his few years of retirement, Sargent found himself once more thrust into the thick of things as a portraitist, with an expectant world hanging on his brush. Until Lodge spoke, however, it had never occurred to him the contending politicians of America would be ready to exploit any flaw in his work, any indication in it of Wilson's character, as an advantage in the political rough-and-tumble. This burden, added to the others, increased his dislike of the portraitist's trade, made it unbearable. If he could have fled Washington he would have done so gladly.

The next day, October 16, Mrs. Wilson received him in the White House, which still looked much the same, except for the changes in the furniture and a different group of portraits that lined the walls. They took a turn around the Rose Room, selected for the north light that streamed through two large windows. He tried to explain what he needed. The housekeeper came to drape

the huge four-poster with dark curtains to form a proper backdrop
to the portrait. He wanted a platform for Mr. Wilson to sit on,
finding it necessary to explain all the uses of a platform and why
the sitter had to be raised to the artist's eye level. Then he needed
a chair that would "paint well." With Mrs. Wilson he toured
the house without luck, for there was nothing proper for a formal
male portrait. Eventually he settled on a rather poor leather affair
that stood in a corner of the upstairs hall. They brought it down,
and with the arrangements apparently completed, stood to chat a
few minutes for the sake of civility. Mrs. Wilson expressed the
hope that all this bother would be made worth while by the production of a fine portrait, a remark that hit him peculiarly.

He was slow to reply. "You know, Mrs. Wilson, I have never
been so nervous over a portrait in my life."

She looked at him in astonishment, and he averted his eyes, putting his hands on the back of the chair and slowly leaning his
weight on them. Cabot Lodge was in his mind, but there was nothing he could say.

It was an awkward moment. Mrs. Wilson seemed eager to
bridge it into more pleasant conversation. "This is a surprise from
the great Sargent," she said, her tone half sarcastic, half coaxing
him into humorous rejoinder. But he had no humor, and there
was a peculiar expression of suppressed pain as he slowly turned his
face up to say, "Well, I only hope I can do it."

The next afternoon at two-thirty the President received him
and gave him a sitting of an hour and a half. This first meeting
with Wilson was a relief in many ways, for he was an interesting
man, with the stamp of intellect on his face, though rather unpre-
possessing otherwise. He was pleasant enough to be with and tried
to make conversation in his urbane way, apparently feeling it his
burden to entertain the silent painter. In comparison with Roosevelt, the "very suave and reposeful" figure of Wilson seemed
strange. "The White House is empty, the habitation of the linx
and the bittern. How different from the days of Roosevelt who
posed or rather didn't pose, in a crowd. . . . " Wilson allowed no
interruptions, and even Mrs. Wilson, though often present, with-
held all opinion. Still, the entire affair lacked interest. Wilson was
dull. Sargent fell into silence, with no string of tales, no mimicries,

no accounts of his former sitters. The following day, Thursday, Wilson sat again at two-thirty and arranged for the next session to be on Saturday. On Monday, Sargent was asked to come to lunch before the sitting, where he impressed Mrs. Wilson as extremely courteous and well bred but, as he had nothing to say, he was also thought uninteresting. There were three more sittings ranged over that week, and on Sunday evening he posted a letter to Mrs. Gardner, telling her that he probably could not leave Washington for another week. "It takes a man a long time to look like his portrait, as Whistler used to say — but he is doing his best, and has been very obliging . . . I have met a good many old friends — Harry White, Mrs George Vanderbilt, the Spring-Rices and others, so I have done less cursing of God and man than I might otherwise have."

The truth of it was that this portrait of Wilson was boring him. As he worked his mind was playing the tricks of a purely technical sort that it did when the subject itself had little to contribute. The head had dry, rather "hard planes," something "like a head hewed out of wood." He noted the dark eyelashes and lighter eyes, and without caricaturing tried to get "the look of those warriors in a Japanese print." His "principal preoccupation was to construct the head on flat planes with very slight modelling" diminishing the halftones to produce the effect he wanted; and even so the square jut-jawed head of the President became no more interesting. "He has not a very paintable brow," he wrote, "& I expect people who expected a political cartoon will be disappointed — He has a very set expression of face and his thoughts are entirely behind the scene, and masked by great suavity of manner. He seems quite serene and not oppressed by his tremendous responsibilities. Very agreeable withal." As sittings progressed, Wilson left his coat behind after each sitting, and Nicola slipped into it, so that the work on the drapery might be continued. On Tuesday the President could spare only an hour at noon, but on Wednesday he gave an hour and a half, and they talked about camouflage. Mr. Wilson was planning to drive out to inspect the American University Camouflage Camp set up outside Washington, and Sargent's experiences with Thayer suddenly made humorous telling. Relieved with the change, after the sitting Wilson suggested that Sargent come along on the drive, as it was to be only a family party. They were six in the open touring car, with chauffeur, that made its way through Washington and out to the camp that afternoon. Officers were waiting, specially assigned to show them around, and were delighted at the unfeigned response of the visitors when a stone moved aside and a soldier emerged. The commandant mentioned that they had been less successful in disguising shell holes in the open country, where they thought it might prove necessary to place men as lookouts. This drew quick response from Sargent. "Line them with black velvet. It absorbs light and reflects nothing." A fine suggestion! Unfortunately, the army engineers were not up to the idea of carting bales of black velvet about the battle front, doubtless from lack of imagination on their part.

After a final sitting on Saturday, November 3, he packed immediately for Boston, leaving the picture, and the controversy that immediately raged over it, for the more pleasant duties of his Hall. In three weeks' time the scaffolding would be coming down.

During the sittings, Wilson had made mention of a statue of Lincoln, to be set up in London as a token of Anglo-American friendship. It had been commissioned of the very talented George Grey Barnard, who turned out a massive work, so trenchantly presenting the Civil War President's physical characteristics as to approach caricature. It was, in truth, an unnaturally elongated figure, with horny face, topped by a shock of unruly hair. Nonetheless, it was a particularly moving, impressive work. Of course it was less a physical copy of Lincoln than an interpretation of him, and his son, Robert Todd Lincoln, sent his objections straight to the White House. He did not like any such presentation of his father, and he would not permit it to be placed in London. When shown photographs of the statue Sargent tended to agree with the objections. The artistic merit of the thing was obvious, but how tasteful a gift it might be to a foreign nation also had to be taken into consideration. He suggested to Wilson that he might look at the statue on his way through New York and report back what he found, so that the President need not be drawn into a controversy that was growing heated. When he did see the statue itself he was "much more favorably impressed with it" than he had been with the photograph. He talked with the sculptor about changes in the posture that might make it less objectionable, then wrote his findings to Wilson, who replied in part:

> Thank you for your kindness in writing us about Mr. Barnard's statue of Lincoln, now that you have seen it. I am very much interested in what you say of it and delighted that the artist is inclined to take your very interesting suggestions about modifying the posture of it. I am reassured, also that you should think that with the suggested changes made the statue will probably be worthy of the very unusual distinction which is to be conferred upon it.

But, for all his efforts, eventually an older statue by St.-Gaudens was copied to be erected in London and the Barnard statue relegated to Manchester. While in Barnard's workshop, he also noticed a *Birth of Eve* that he liked. He mentioned this to Bosworth, who had it purchased and placed in Rockefeller's garden at Pocantico, together with Thorwaldsen's *Cupid and Psyche* which he also suggested. "I am so old fashioned that I like sculpture that has been studied with a view to making it decorative," he explained.

Back at Boston, he had the satisfaction of seeing the ceiling of his Hall in the Public Library unveiled, then picked up his study of the Museum dome, his progress interrupted only by incessant requests for charcoal portraits. Originally he began them to soften his refusal to do oils, but now the charcoals were themselves in demand, and it annoyed him that, in the midst of wrestling with this huge undertaking, two or three mornings of each week would have to be given over to the drawing of "mugs." They fatigued him more and more. In the past two years all the finer qualities that had distinguished them disappeared. The burst of black line they had once had, the compact modeling, the fine placement, the tonal beauty — little remained of any of these. Now they were rather gray sketches, sometimes scratchy, and habitually done in vignette style. Close valued, thin, hazy studies in gray, they were drained of everything that once had made them so fine. And still, regardless even of quality, they were fully digested by the insatiable appetite of his public. He did not like it. He had evolved a quick and easy manner for doing them. It was a simple operation.

But the loss of his time and the break into his thoughts of the dome were bothersome.

The routine was generally the same. He breakfasted at his hotel, put two extra slices of bread into his pocket, then walked out to the street to take one of the waiting cabs to the Pope Building. It was only a short ride. He marched into the tiny lobby of the building, waited for the single elevator and then stood in the open-grilled car as it slowly made its way to the top floor. A step down the skylight-lit hallway and he was in his studio, facing Columbus Avenue. Once inside, he discussed the work with Tom Fox, the architect who had constructed the model and was continuing to aid in the architectural relations of the murals. Ten-thirty was the time set for the *mug* to arrive, and in it walked, to be greeted, in shirt sleeves, with a broad smile and a handshake. Fox would explain that he was going to remain to work on the model, and the sitter's eye generally wandered until it was attracted to the only spot of color in the room, a seascape on the wall, with three dolphins spilling over a very blue wave.

"It's one of Woodbury's," Sargent would explain. "Corking painter of the old ocean, he." The easel stood in the middle of the room, to one side of the two skylights that had been let into the ceiling to accommodate his wish for a top light. On the easel was the paper from which the mug would emerge, and beside it a "curate's assistant," or lectern, with bits of charcoal, and the two slices of bread that served as erasers. After some little conversation, he directed the sitter to a high stool with blue cushion, looking him over, first from one side and then from the other, though likely his ideas had been formed during the previous conversation. Then, throwing his chest forward and with his arm out, he gave his head a gentle turn, and they were off.

Soon he felt a desire to smoke, and offered a cigarette to the sitter, working away amidst the intermittent talk and blowing of smoke. He spoke sometimes of the Japanese fad, and a sitter once made reference to Asher Wertheimer, whom he in turn described as a "good sort." Somewhere along the line he measured the head with a stick. "When you are tired, don't hit me," he would interrupt. "Get down and walk about, but don't look at your picture yet." This invitation few refused, and they took interest in what Tom Fox was doing, working furiously in his corner.

When Charles K. Bolton, librarian of the Boston Athenaeum, sat, Sargent explained that Fox was preparing a roughening for the inner surface of the dome, because gold became light brown unless it overlaid a surface that was broken to catch the light. They went on easily to talk about Rockefeller, and the two portraits that had been done of him; "the latter not flattery," he added, with reference to the reservations of certain critics. He observed that he found men easier to paint than women, adding, "But I lost my nerve for portraits long ago when harassed by mothers, critical wives and sisters."

"Tom," he called. "Come and make your criticism. I say Mr. Bolton looks worried." Fox came over to look at the head on the easel. "Well, worried in the upper half, cheerful in the lower half."

"The lower half is due to your conversation. I don't want to take out those wrinkles in the forehead, even to please Mr. Bolton, for it would make him appear too young. And the eyes are bully." A glance at his watch told him it was 12:45, and he gave the drawing another touch or two.

"I think it's tip-top," volunteered the pleased sitter, pleased not only with the drawing but that he had got Sargent to do it.

"You are very humane," came the reply. Then he helped Mr. Bolton on with his coat, shook hands, and escorted him out to the lift.

When the picture had not been arranged for previously, and Sargent had himself suggested, in that pained way of his, that the mug come along at ten-thirty, there still remained one final difficulty. Generally the mug became restive toward the end and uneasily made some remark concerning payment.

"Oh, anything you like," was the casual reply. "Send me a check for five hundred dollars, if that is satisfactory."

At the Front

CROSSING the ocean by troopship in convoy in April of 1918 he returned to London, to carry out work for the Museum at Fulham Road, and execute a portrait of Mrs. Percival Duxbury and her daughter, for which the Red Cross had once again been given £10,000. To his English friends he looked fatter than ever. "Carved out of beef," remarked one, when with Tonks he went to see the exhibition of Eric Kennington's work at the Leicester Gallery.

The return trip had been marred by the disappearance of Nicola, who had been gone before, only to turn up a few days later somewhat the worse for a losing bout with alcohol but still serviceable. This time he had been away longer, at a time when there were bags to pack and a ship to be caught at New York. His master set about packing them himself, finding it a difficult task costing much energy, and when he was ready to leave and Nicola still had not shown up, there was nothing for him to do but go. Instructions were left with his Boston attorney that, if Nicola eventually did appear, he was to be paid, and discharged; however, Nicola's name was never removed from his will. Thus did Nicola D'Inverno, prophet, pugilist, photographer, and hand servant of the Muses, pass from sight.

In London, Sargent was distinctly lonely for Boston. The one portrait, and the charcoals, were certainly not sufficient to absorb his energies, nor did they give him pleasure. The Zeppelin attacks were an added disturbance. He felt particularly badly when, during his visit with Mrs. Hunter in Essex at Whitsuntide, there was a raid on London in which both his sisters were caught. He found little consolation in the fact that the Germans were over Essex as well with their bombs.

At Tite Street too he was rather at loose ends because of a lack of work to stimulate his mind. Two or three hours a day of a dull portrait were a sad comedown from the routine he had maintained at the Pope Building, where he pondered the throwing of vast panels across architectural expanses. The prospect of an early return to Boston, taking along his two sisters to that safer side of the ocean, vanished too, for Violet would not leave and Emily did not want to go without her. Violet's daughter, Rose Marie, widowed at the very outset of the war, had been attending a Good Friday service in the Church of St.-Gervais in Paris when the Germans unleashed their Big Bertha. The priest had just begun to intone the words "My father, I give my spirit into your hands," when a shell ripped the structure. Seventy worshipers were killed, Rose Marie among them. Her death deeply shocked the family, and her uncle, to whom she had many times posed in landscapes, was particularly affected by it. In that introspective mood he wrote to Mrs. Gardner, "I wish we were dining tonight at the Copley-Plaza and going to see Charlie Chaplin. What night are you free?"

Before leaving Boston he had received a letter from Mr. Yockney, secretary of the War Artists Memorial Committee, of the British Ministry of Information, outlining a plan under which he and other artists were being invited to go to France to paint commemorative pictures of the war. The offer included his expenses, materials, and the sum of £300, for which he would be asked to do the centerpiece of the pictures commissioned. There was a certain flattery in the way Yockney had said, "it is thought very strongly that you should be among the first painters to undertake a composition," and the fact that his canvas was to be larger than the others, and might have different proportions if he chose, also seemed deferential. Painting wars was not his art, however, and his reply had been vague. On his return to London the process of bringing pressure began. He had been back only a month when the big gun was unlimbered, and he received a letter from the Prime Minister:

10, Downing Street
Whitehall, S.W.1
16th May, 1918

Dear Mr. Sargent,

You have heard through Mr. Muirhead Bone and Professor Tonks that it is proposed to commemorate the War with a number of great paintings. These pictures will be preserved in a Memorial Gallery in London, and it is hoped that they will be handed down to posterity as a series of immortal works.

I write to support the suggestion made by the British War Memorials Committee that you should execute one of these large paintings, the subject being, I understand, one in which British and American troops are engaged in unison. If you will undertake this task you will be doing a work of great and lasting service to the nation.

Yours sincerely
D. Lloyd George

John S. Sargent, Esq., R.A.

On June 17, Sargent wrote to Mrs. Hale: "The British Government is sending a lot of painters to the front, myself among their number. I expect to go in about two weeks — it will be interesting whether I am a success as a military painter or not." To Mrs. Gardner he observed, "I hope to have a chance of being well scared," and to Evan Charteris he had already said, "But would I have the nerve to look, not to speak of painting? I have never seen anything in the least horrible — outside of my studio."

Warfare would be a new experience, and at sixty-two he did not know how he would adjust to its new conditions. His talents did not seem particularly suitable to the work asked of him, and he himself wondered how the adjustment would be made, how a portraitist-impressionist turned muralist, and now growing old, would do as a military painter. The question of his outfit for this expedition was considered seriously, and Tite Street, which had seen so many anomalies, was now littered with boots, belts, and a general array of khaki. There was a succession of tryings on, endless packing and unpacking. Buckles suddenly came to play a part in things, and the sheer cussedness of inanimate objects had to be overcome by curses, incantations, trickery, and witchcraft.

On July 2, he departed with Mr. Yockney and Tonks, who had a similar commission to do a medical subject. Little as he resembled an artist, even less could he have been classified with any recognizable military unit. At the station he expressed amusement to Yockney that he, who as an artist might be considered the most peaceful of men, should be thus disguised in uniform, and his strange appearance was set down by one fellow passenger as "a sailor gone wrong." Arriving the next day at Boulogne, he was immediately conducted to the headquarters of Field Marshal Haig, and the scene soon deteriorated into drawing-room comedy. The men were probably the two arch examples of nervous speakers in England, each immediately finding his own mannerisms exaggerated by contact with the other. Sargent, who was shy about beginning his sentences, made his voice just audible in the middle, having employed a wave of the hand to mark the start. Haig was of the contrary school, for he could not finish, and so concluded with extensive handwork instead of words. Altogether the two days they spent in contact were like a tribal powwow — an endless series of pantomimes, which Sargent's friend, Sir Philip Sassoon, on hand as Haig's private secretary, vastly enjoyed.

As the most eminent of the artists coming to France, Sargent received a warm welcome at headquarters, and Sassoon began to initiate him into the mysteries of military life. At least a diligent attempt was made, for at the outset Sargent was discovered to be proof against all distinctions in rank, even the most elementary, and failing the first lesson, all the rest was mostly useless. He stayed the night at headquarters, and the following day, the Fourth of July, was considered appropriate for him to have a look at the fireworks out beyond. Sassoon and he motored to Bavincourt, the headquarters of the Guards Division, some twenty-five miles south of Arras. General Fielding assigned him quarters in a steel tube sunk in the ground to escape enemy detection and to afford protection in the continued bombardments. Sir Philip next thought he might be interested in tanks, then the latest British addition to military science, and had Major Uzzielli take them for a ride inside one of the rolling infernos. It was interesting perhaps, but exquisitely uncomfortable, as the primitive monster went climbing down slopes, running over trenches, jolting up the far side, "looping the loop generally," as Sargent expressed it. Inside they bounced around as though they were the vehicle's enemies, and it had been designed as a torture chamber rather than a means of punishing an enemy presumably on the outside. Later, seeing a row of these vehicles grown obsolescent near Bermicourt, oddly enough, for all the modernity of the contraptions, they reminded him of the ships drawn up before Troy.

On July 13 he accompanied the division up to the line. When, three days later, Tonks joined him, the two worked together. They ate in an officers' mess of about fourteen; breakfast and lunch were impromptu affairs, as each man's duty allowed, but dinner they all tried to have together. Sargent found the officers delightful company and took a huge interest in every going on, understanding nothing, of course, but expressing concern over every trifle brought to his attention and mulling over details of tactics with all the learning amassed from reading Napoleon's campaigns. Nearby he found his old acquaintance Winston Churchill, who had just resigned a cabinet position, complaining that there was not enough work to keep a man occupied, and now in France was busy winning the war singlehanded. His particular hobby seemed to be crawling up to the German lines at night, and he called Sargent's attention to the good luck piece carried on these nocturnal prowlings — a little Greek head dating from 600 B.C. His other habit, firing artillery off into the night until he got response and then telephoning for divisional support, pleased no one.

Sargent accepted his surroundings completely, and went about his work as though quite accustomed to military life. Tonks made further desperate efforts to get him to grasp something about rank, but eventually gave up. One Sunday, while the military band was playing near headquarters, he observed to General Fielding, "I suppose there is no fighting on Sunday." It seemed a natural enough assumption, and he was dismayed by the reception given an innocent remark. Tonks, in fact, came to wonder if Sargent had any idea how dangerous an exploding shell might be, for he never showed the least sign of fear, merely exhibiting annoyance when shells began bursting near enough to shake him. Wheeling his barrow of canvases and sketches about behind the lines, he seemed completely unconcerned. With Tonks he went on to the ruined city of Arras, where the town commandant found them quarters in one of the few undamaged houses in the place. They walked through the rubble-strewn streets, with their high fretwork of lonely chimneys and pathetically silent walls, and for two or three weeks worked systematically recording these modern ruins as they gleamed beneath a brilliant August sun. The ruined cathedral particularly attracted Sargent's attention. Only the few columns that had once supported its main vault were left standing, the huge cavity was filled with rubble, and the entirety was aglow with flooded sunshine. It was a wonderful study, with the same beauty of open porticoes that he had painted in Florence. Here was an expression of tragedy, the falling symbol of man's faith, put up and then pulled down by the powers of his mind and his invention. Sargent did not play upon the dramatic qualities, but painted the ruin as it stood: bleached white columns towering out of the rubble that lay over their bases, while over the top a single thin arch, all that was left of the once-splendid achievement, delicately bridged the chasm.

Everywhere he went he covered the pages of his notebooks with studies of the men in uniform: men in kilts, men with spades in their packs, three pages of men in rain capes, a page of men resting, a sheet of men standing in firing positions in the trenches, troops crowded into an open railway car, and sitting behind trucks. One day he found a group of Tommies bathing in a small creek, their naked bodies brilliant pinks and oranges with blue and purple reflections in the sun. He painted them in the water and again when they climbed out to dry on the grass. He went on to paint gun carriages set in fortifications, underground emplacements, and the mule teams used to haul ammunition. His watercolor sketches had that remarkable combination of free flow and precision that only he was capable of, and while perhaps recording more exactly than he might have done for himself alone, he worked with what Tonks called "surprising skill." Much of what he did is of remarkable beauty, a beauty entirely unrelated to the ugliness of the subject matter, and the more remarkable considering that subject matter. Though he saw with a certain matter-of-factness, never altering the slightest detail nor seeking to find anything but the common denominator of conditions at the war front, he managed nonetheless to confer his own innate beauty of vision upon a ghastly spectacle. All this is very curious, for there is a complete detachment to the pictures he was doing. It was almost as though he was looking down from a safe berth on the moon. All the while painting convulsion and death, bombs and shells exploding about him, his attention was attracted almost entirely by the effects of sunlight on the implements of death and destruction. So long as the sun was shining, the world lit, the tarpaulins showing orange and variegated purples, and the blue of the heavens reflected in the shadows, nothing else really interested him. The very mud lying outside some newly dug trench on a God-forsaken Flanders battlefield became a substance of remarkable, even surprising, beauty.

Late in the afternoon of August 21, he and Tonks heard that a group of men who had been gassed earlier that day were being taken to a casualty clearing station on the Arras-Doullens road. The sun was sinking as the two men motored down in the car assigned Sargent. As they approached the station they came on "a harrowing sight, a field full of gassed and blindfolded men." Submerging all feelings, trying hard to look on it all with detachment, he sat down to draw in his sketchbook. Working first in pencil, then shifting to charcoal pencil to facilitate the movement of his hand, he caught the men as they were being led to a duckboarding by officers and medical orderlies. He noted how the blindfolded soldiers lifted their legs high when told they were coming to a step, and he saw the silent pain of those who lay everywhere in the late evening sun, mutely hoping their turn would come soon. Off to one side were a French boy and girl of about eight, who watched the procession for an hour or so. Tonks thought he worked hard to make notes on the scene, and later, when Sargent asked if he could make this essentially medical subject his own, Tonks consented.

Nine days later word came that the enemy was retiring from the Lys salient, and British patrols pushed out as far as Bailleul, which Sargent soon reached to sketch. The Americans were now going into the line, the 27th Division fighting with British forces in the vicinity of Vierstraat Ridge, and as Sargent had been sent to paint some scene of co-operation between British and American forces, this seemed the best chance to gather material. Accordingly, the headquarters of the British XIX Corps sent along word that he would join the American command. The Americans were operating under somewhat adverse conditions: when they were brought to the front, and the construction of what was called the East Poperinghe line was begun, they had orders from higher British authorities to interfere as little as possible with the unharvested wheat crop. The war itself seemed to be regarded by these Flemish people as an unauthorized interference with their farming activities. It was common to see their old men, women, and even boys and girls hoeing almost on the edge of heavily shelled areas where it seemed impossible that anything could grow. Some attempt was made at camouflaging these fields, and he sketched the huge blinds that were hung in front of the stands of uncut wheat.

The weather began to break now, during which the headquarters of the division was pushed almost into the front lines themselves, for a mire of mud was slowly working to tangle movement behind the front. With difficulty the division commander, General O'Ryan, dissuaded Sargent from going forward during the first few days of his visit, but that was not to his liking and he soon persuaded one of the staff to take him into the trenches. It was a poorly chosen moment, for once back in the pits he was caught in a bombardment of gas shells and, when ordered out, came under bombardment in the ruined city of Ypres.

At headquarters his equipment was still set up outside the steel Nissen hut, his huge white umbrella, with its green lining, looking strange and provocative midst the military surroundings. Everything else was warlike, camouflaged, and serious; only the umbrella was a light touch, which was corrected when an order was issued that it, too, must be camouflaged. Near it a sentry passed up and down the duckboard walk that kept him out of the mud. Sargent came across the rectangle of green before the general's hut and past the orderly who stood outside. Ducking his head at the entrance, he descended the four steps and asked if he might make a sketch of the general. It would take but a short time and would not distract the general from his work of poring over maps. While shells passed over with staccato shriek, whistle, and roar, he sat before the general and continued to draw.

The nights were as ghastly as the days. Troops, trucks, and cars moved along the roads, and when he rode on them at all, he was likely to be shunted to one side as ration parties passed or, if he chose to walk, pushed off the corduroy surface into ankle-deep mud so that a convoy might go past. A thousand indistinguishable sounds filled the darkness, hidden periodically by the explosion of artillery shells. Odors of stray patches of poison gas might be chanced on, lights sparkling in the sky to tell of the return of friendly planes from visits over the enemy. Sudden beads of light that climbed through the heavens were signals sent back by infantrymen to their artillery, and smaller flashes up higher showed that somewhere antiaircraft gunners were at work. Soon swaying columns of light would linger about the sky, crossing and recrossing to form a Jacob's ladder. Spasmodically, too, there was the roar and red flash of the ever-present big guns.

The idea of catching British and American troops acting in some sort of unison was still in his mind, and on September 11, after the 27th Division had been withdrawn from the line and he was once again with the British, he wrote: "The weather is breaking and rain and mud have set in for good I fear, and I hate to consider my campaign over before my harvest of sketches has grown to something more presentable in quality and quantity. The program of 'British and American troops working together,' has sat heavily upon me, for though historically and sentimentally the thing happens, the naked eye cannot catch it in the act, nor have I, so far, forged the Vulcan's net in which the act can be imprisoned and gaily looked upon. How can there be anything flagrant enough for a picture when Mars and Venus are miles apart whether in camps or in the front trenches. And the further forward one goes the more scattered and meager everything is. The nearer to danger the fewer and more hidden the men — the more dramatic the situation the more it becomes an empty landscape. The Ministry of Information expects an epic — and how can one do an epic without masses of men?"

The rain continued, at first with a few days of clear weather between and then more steadily. Late in the month Sargent was struck down with flu, and taken to the forty-first casualty clearing station, near Roisel, where he was a week in bed, "in a hospital tent," as he wrote, "with the accompaniment of groans of wounded and the chokings and coughing of gassed men, which was a nightmare. It always seemed strange on opening one's eyes to see the level cots and the dimly lit long tent looking so calm, when one was dozing in pandemonium." He was placed in the officers' ward, which was warmed by an oil stove, though the tent was muddy and wet inside. There the aftermath of the battlefield constantly passed before him as he read the books provided by the hospital and, bored with that, made a watercolor of the interior of the tent. When able to join the doctors' mess he was an admirable social asset, for everyone liked him and his illness had not stifled his joking propensities, though Orpen, who came upon him at this time and found him much whitened and looking strangely puffy, sent rather cruel caricatures to mutual friends in England. Despite his good humor, he was feeling strange inside, the illness did not seem to leave him, and he wanted to get back to Tite Street, where he would be more comfortable. Three months at the front were enough for a man his age, though at that point the Committee, who sat in London, sent out the suggestion that he ought to take a studio near General Headquarters at Montreuil, France. Muirhead Bone was all set to send out materials to him. At the end of October, when he was still ill, but felt able to travel again, he made his way back to England, the gnawing symptoms of his illness working inside.

Though still not well when he returned to London, Sargent immediately set about the large picture for the Ministry of Information. And again he was being interrupted for charcoal drawings, and there was the bad English light to worry over, but he worked on with his usual persistence. In time his ideas were in order, and a giant frieze of blinded troops was projected on a canvas tacked to the wall in Fulham Road. Ill as he felt, nothing could quell his gusto, as indicated by a letter he wrote to Mrs. Hale: "Having allowed you to get in a word edgewise (I don't know how you managed to do it) I now resume the concentrated drumfire of my correspondence. I have been back a few weeks from my great offensive, which ended in a camp hospital with flu, which I have hardly yet shaken off . . . I have got to do a picture for the British Government, 20 feet long — and must do the work while my memory is fresh — so I can't get back to Boston for several months."

The first applicants for charcoals soon became a stream, and he found himself with an enormous number of drawings to do, his list of sitters becoming a virtual *Debrett's* combined with *Who's Who*. Distinguished personages from every walk of life beat a path to his door, there to meet him, dour and forbidding but willing if necessary to give the one sitting that a charcoal required. He had as many sittings now, for these charcoal portraits, as he would have had were he tied down to more complicated oils; certainly he had as many as when he was in full career as a portraitist. This fiction that he was no longer doing portraits appealed to him, however, and he was so numbed to the brief operation that it went off almost painlessly at times. The charcoal drawings were not demanding, and had he cared enough to total up the money they brought in he would have seen an astonishing figure. For many years now he had been working in charcoal, first employing it in that unhappy Florentine Academy, where he was forced to use stumps, and rub until the paper threatened to crumble. Since that early time he had always employed it in his sketches, and the capacities of the medium had expanded considerably since he began to do his murals. Now, faced with a sequence of heads to do, he further refined it, softening the original bold bursts of line into a thin film that lay imperceptibly upon the paper, only from a distance breaking into gentle distinction of cheeks and smiling lips. What he was able to do with these queer pieces of burnt wood was fantastic, and should one perhaps mourn the loss of the early magnificent improvisations that had been his charcoal portraits, he himself had the answer to that. A cousin wrote that she wanted such a drawing. He lost the letter, and then replied: "I don't know exactly what it is you wanted me to do in the way of a drawing — beyond my getting the impression that it was one of those miraculously successful impromptus, that leave no trace of a hundred preliminary failures, one of those spontaneous brilliant trifles that leave a waste paper basket bulging with discarded experiments. In other words the sort of thing that terrifies me more than making an after dinner speech or than decorating a dome. If I am wrong please tell me, and I shall pull myself together." Improvisation had never been the mainspring of his art, for the improviser is a man who is tied down to his first idea, unable to develop compositions with mature judgment or meditate over the treatment and handling of the parts. He had always been in another category, from the beginning controlling his medium so that if necessary he could mull over the work and the execution at the end would still be fresh. He never relied on spontaneity alone, and the beauty of his work is entirely unlike the surface glitter of those who did, and whose drawing falls apart on inspection and whose color grows muddy with retouching.

But all this was a distraction from the chief work in hand, the war picture, and even that, of course, was a minor distraction from the Museum decorations that still awaited him in Boston. His plan for the war picture had evolved from that day when he came on the "harrowing sight [of] a field full of gassed and blindfolded men." Of all he had seen in France, that made the strongest impression on him, for it most nearly approached the epic proportions of the work expected of him. The drawings made on the spot were unpacked, and from them he developed his frieze of bandaged men as they were led forward onto a duckboarding outside that field station on the Arras-Doullens road. Though he was turning it into a classic frieze, the classicism was all in his viewpoint, for, as Tonks said after seeing the completed picture, "It is a good representation of what we saw." That purpose was uppermost in his mind. No melodrama is attempted. The eye that records is obviously cool. Even the title he finally chose — *Gassed* — was selected, as he explained, with a hope that it would be "very prosaic and matter of fact." Nonetheless, in its quiet statement he has much of the horror of war, as he saw it and knew it to be.

Before he got ready to leave England in 1919, the government had thought of new things for him to do. In those later years England became for him a land of many pressures, as officialdom looked to him for many things that were not within his province. There was forever some new request, some new form of demand. The first scheme was a large group portrait of the generals of the British and Empire forces who had taken notable part in the war. There were to be three such pictures, which Sir Abe Bailey, the

South African, offered to donate to the National Portrait Gallery. They were to represent the political, naval, and military figures of the war, and each painter would receive five thousand pounds for his undertaking. The idea did not appeal to Sargent and at first he refused. However, with his numerous friendships in the official world it was simple for pressure to be brought, and in the end, due to the hammering of those who wanted the work done and perhaps from some sense of duty, he consented. But he made it clear that the work would have to wait until he returned from Boston.

An even more painful surprise awaited him the day he called on Lamb, secretary of the Royal Academy, for an explanation of the new "seventy-five year rule" that was being considered. In his quiet way Lamb explained its purpose: to force the resignation of doddering old Sir Edward Poynter, then over eighty and obviously not sound enough to preside. As that seemed for the general good of the Academy, Sargent tended to agree with its desirability, until he asked who was likely to be elected the new president. Lamb proceeded to explain that Sir Aston Webb, acting president during Poynter's illness, as well as Cope and the other influential members of the Academy, had pretty much decided to elect *him* the new president. His color deepened violently, as it always did when he became agitated, and he strode about the room making wild gestures and protesting his absolute inability to cope with the position, its required speechmaking in and out of the Academy itself, and the necessity of presiding over the discussions of fellow Academicians with whom he was artistically at loggerheads. He knew that many of the older Academicians, those who had viewed his original election with great alarm, still thought him revolutionary and would never willingly permit him to preside over them. He protested also that his powers of persuasion, especially before a crowd, were not equal to the task. He ranted on, explaining that while in a personal sense the older members had always acted in charming fashion toward him, he did not feel in enough sympathy with them to handle their debates. Lamb, in his gentle way, tried to offer reassurance, suggesting that he himself would help with the speeches and mentioning casually that the new rule would eliminate from the Council meetings many of the members referred to. It was not a complete answer though, for Sargent replied — "At the last Assembly that I attended, my dear Lamb, I assure you their eloquence was unimpaired!" — with outflung arms and a look of naïve envy in his eyes.

The kingmakers at the Academy held a private meeting that December, at which they decided on a determined effort to persuade Sargent to accept the position. When, at the conclusion of the meeting, they telephoned Tite Street and asked if he could receive them on a matter of importance, he replied that he would be delighted, then qualified it by adding that, if they intended to make any mention of the presidency, he regretted but he would not be at home. Much as he felt inclined to help the Academy in every way possible, he simply had no intention of being its president. Besides the objections of a purely personal nature upon which he insisted, the demands on his time would make it impossible, as would the yearly banquet at which he would be obliged to address a gallery filled with distinguished people. Further, he was not impressed with the honor, he did not want the knighthood the president traditionally received, nor was he intrigued with the tradition of the president's painting a portrait of the King. He was adamant in his refusal and had spoken so plainly to the group that intended to call on him that they found it advisable to make individual visits on varying pretexts. Again and again he was forced to say a polite "No," to explain his position, qualify his ideas, and hold his temper. When spoken to by Sir Arthur Cope, whom he had recommended together with Sir James Guthrie to paint the other groups for the National Portrait Gallery, he made his final reply: "I would do *anything* for the Royal Academy but that, and if you press me any more I shall flee the country."

The Muralist

THE completeness of Sargent's change into a muralist was astounding. Filled with his new interest in the well-knit composition, he tended to forget that there were other standards in art as well, and with an enthusiasm of condemnation he hurled thunderbolts at his previous works. Sitting with a young artist in the dining room of the Copley-Plaza Hotel in Boston, the very mention of portraits made him hunch his shoulders and clench his fists, with a comical distortion of the face: "I *hate* to paint portraits! I hope never to paint another portrait in my life. Landscape I like, but most of all decoration, where the really aesthetic side of art counts for so much. Portraiture may be all right for a man in his youth, but after forty I believe that manual dexterity deserts one, and, besides, the color sense is less acute. Youth can better stand the exactions of a personal kind that are inseparable from portraiture. *I have had enough of it.* I want now to experiment in more imaginary fields."

His proscriptions upon his early masterpieces were savage and he seemed to bear not even a sentimental attachment to them, forgetting entirely the former enthusiasms, the equally correct, though different, application of his imagination that had given them birth. The *Boit Children*, with its wonderful spatial balance, where each part holds its place not only on the flat surface of the canvas but in the depth of the square picture-box behind the frame, he labeled, "Utterly childish! There is no real composition at all, merely an amateurish sort of arrangement that could find its rebuke in any good Japanese print." He knew well enough that the simile he chose, a Japanese print, was not applicable to his three-dimensional balance, but it made a good illustration for his attempted discrediting of a youthful work. Mention of a self-portrait brought immediate retort: "Do you mean that awful thing in the Uffizi?" No, the reference was to one in the National Academy in New York. At first he could not recall it, then burst out: "Oh, yes, I remember. Terrible!"

The *El Jaleo* fared no better. "I hope to find time to paint an additional figure into it that will help the composition. As it stands the composition is not good, and that is so important." He had definite ideas about that Salon piece, and they were expressed also to Mrs. Gardner, who had finally purchased it and had it hanging in a specially constructed Spanish setting in her palace. "I cannot help thinking," he wrote her, "that if you had seen the Spanish dancers in New York, and the brilliancy of their clothes, and the quality of their performance, you would have great doubts about allowing my gloomy old picture to show its nose. It might be like the mummy at the feast unless I give her 'a new gauze gown all spangles' and pull the sword out of her heart. In other words something tells me that there would not seem, or might not seem, to be the remotest air de famille between the picture and the reality, and that you might be disappointed if the result was a family feud between the old and the new generation."

But the old and the new generation were in reality the alteration in him, brought on by an ever-active mentality, an artistic mind that stopped nowhere, constantly pressing on in its studies. How could he ever be satisfied with one work when, after the passage of time, he, Sargent, was essentially a different organism, with new ideas, new standards, and new enthusiasms? The last time he saw his portrait of Henry G. Marquand his strictures were equally severe. "Chicken, chicken!" he burst out, pointing to the pink skin drawn ever so beautifully over the skull of the aged financier. "I can never think of anything else, when I look at this portrait, but plucked fowl in the markets!"

When in 1924 a huge retrospective exhibit was hung to open the newly organized Grand Central Art Galleries in New York City,

he had little interest in his former products. He would take almost
no part in the organization of the exhibition, aside from allowing
the use of his name and correcting the titles on a sheet sent to him.
He rather disliked the idea of being exposed to his portraits again
in such numbers and refused to attend the exhibition. "If you
should stop a day in New York, you must see a show of my old
paughtraits in the attic of the Grand Central Station," was all he
ever said about it. It had been the same a year earlier when there
was an exhibition in Paris of his watercolors, together with a group
by Winslow Homer and the sculpture of Paul Manship. "I was
almost inveigled into going over . . . for a day or two," he explained,
"by people who said that I ought to go over on account of this show.
But this is the only thing that has stopped [me] . . . from going.
Here nobody knows about it and all is well." Of course, this was
partly the desire not to be caught in an adoring crowd, the fear he had
always shown of becoming a matinee idol, but it was more a fear
of seeing his old works. Any artist who has progressed can understand this, the aching fear that what he had once done and thought
well of, might look downright bad from the new perspective.
Better to retain the old rosy illusions and not become subject to
new impressions. Let the past take care of itself.

But the passage of time leaves marks in a physical sense, and
Sargent was not one to heed warnings. The fact that he did not
shake off the flu so quickly, continuing to feel ill so long after he
had returned from the battlefront, was a hint that he would be wise
to consider time more carefully, taking it more into account.
Otherwise he remained in fine fettle, his spirits, as always, were
high, and perhaps this, too, was a deception, for someone with less
exuberance might have realized that it was time to see a doctor.
Not Sargent. To some extent he did have a notion that he was
slowing down. Some of his remarks about an artist's losing his
manual dexterity, as well as later talk about not being in his best
stride, were taken as marks of his amazing modesty but were probably honest reflections of his thought. Naturally enough, a man of
sixty-three who has always enjoyed good health and who goes
about his work, and the art of living, with all the pleasure he has
ever known, does not feel any awful presence of death. It would
be foolish of him to do so. True, time was passing, but he still

worked with extraordinary energy, and the results still proved that
he had not stopped advancing. A man capable of learning, hoping
one day to master his art in the sincere way that he did, has few
fears about age, for he is always youthful. Perhaps the fact that
he was becoming increasingly subject to colds, that every exposure
brought a continuous cough, then sniffles for weeks afterward,
should have meant something. But he did not want to see doctors.
He only consented to remain in his room, when he did consent,
because of Emily's fears. "He pretends he is staying in bed," she
wrote, "and it is almost the case, for he is lying on a sofa . . . I
hope he will let me send for the doctor." But he rarely did. There
were periods when sniffles sapped his energy and he could say,
"I am feeling quite addled with my cold and have come home to
curl up like a marmot." Yet eventually he managed to snap back,
and then he was able to carry on with all the fire he had shown in
his youth. His dynamic energy, his quick step, were marveled at
by all who knew him. He seemed indestructible. The strength of
his physique was taken for granted by everyone, including himself.
There was good reason for it. He felt well, he still enjoyed his
food, and if he was older than he once had been it seemed to affect
nothing.

Signs of age had crept into his appearance, though. The bald
spot on the back of his head had been there for years, but as few
people were ever able to see the top of his head, the full, rather
bushy, tuft that grew in front belied its existence. His face was
redder than ever, the skin tending to appear puffy, covered by a
network of wrinkles, and there were pouches under his eyes. Up
close, his gray hair and beard made him look rather grizzled, though
from the distance all one saw was the brightness of his large eyes,
which shone with youthful luster. If he chanced to catch sight of
himself in a mirror, one hand would furtively whisk over his bristly
little beard and he had the amusing habit of sitting down stiffly,
with his back very straight, in an obvious attempt to minimize the
remarkable protrusion of his vest.

The Museum murals had been attacked differently than the
Library set. There Sargent had thought about each end of the hall
separately, plotting the Hebraic end first, while for thirteen years

the other stood bare. That he went about it that way no doubt had a salutary effect on the project. For with the demands on his time during those busy years, had he attempted anything like a uniform undertaking he would certainly have lost interest in what had been conceived years before. It was advantageous that he had the added impetus of a fresh conception when he attacked each panel. Not so with the Museum murals, which were conceived as a unit, to be developed and executed in one fell swoop and without distractions. Thrusting his head through the columns of the six-foot model of the dome installed in his Boston studio, he could turn upward to see the effect of each decorative member, calculating how well it was likely to tell. When he made his first studies of the structure in 1917, it seemed that, because the light came from above, at a shallow angle to the decorations, paintings would be less favored than low-relief sculptures. The angle of the light, and the soft shadows, might show such work to perfection, while producing glare on a painted surface. Accordingly, after the primary divisions of the surface were carried out on the model, he arranged the areas to receive a series of relief sculptures, using clay sketches to block out the groupings and study the penetrations. There were no studies for these on paper, each piece, as he completed it, was placed in the model dome, where he noted its individual effectiveness and how it fitted the decoration as a whole. After a year he had the entire decorative plan sketched in this way. To a visitor calling before the summer of 1917 he explained his difficulties.

"Have you ever done any modeling?" he asked. "It's so difficult. I work and work, and somehow it never seems to be any nearer to completion. I find it amazingly interesting though." As always, he asked opinions of his guest that were an embarrassment to give. "Tell me, how does the composition of the group strike you? And for the purposes of wall decoration, do you think a very low relief best, or do you favor a bit fuller approach to the round?"

When the entire system had been sketched in relief, with the exception of small circular panels representing Astronomy, Music, Ganymede, and Prometheus, intended from the beginning to be painted, he decided that the addition of so much sculpture made the dome too heavy. The sense of weight hanging from above was too much intensified, and he found not enough light reaching into all parts of the dome cavity to justify an all-over use of relief. At that point he shifted the large central panels, already sketched in relief, back to painting. This was his final decision, creating a happy balance between the two media and allowing the architectural structure proper treatment with regard to its lighting, while also taking into account its physical limitations. His experimentation had established that painting was the proper medium for those particular spaces, for its modeling was produced by variations in color value independent of the amounts of light received. The other surfaces, set more happily in relation to the light, had proved themselves appropriate for relief work, and there he would work in sculpture.

As the planning of the dome progressed, he went through an army of models, trying to find one that answered his need of a slim, muscular figure. Those sent to him were often older men, long accustomed to posing but no longer possessing classic proportions. He drew each one that applied, whether balding or beer-bellied, noting name and address at the bottom of the sheet, so that each went away with at least one day's wages. Finally, coming down in the elevator at the Copley-Plaza one morning, he noticed that the Negro operator had the desired physique, and this man became his Apollo, Ciron, and Atlas, in fact, serving for most of the figures in the Museum decorations.

Sargent remained in Boston through all the heat of the summer of 1917 to bring the work forward. The only interruptions he allowed during the entire year were the Rockefeller and Wilson portraits. By the time he returned to London in May of 1918 the general scheme for the dome had been established and most of the small-scale models were complete. When he came back a year later, the alterations to the Museum dome had been completed according to his instructions and the surfaces were ready for the moldings, enrichments, bas-reliefs, and painted decorations that he planned. Thus, during this second burst of activity at the Pope Building in 1919, all the bas-reliefs were modeled in full size from the small sketches. Then came the work of casting them, having them put in place at the Museum, making the framework to surround the actual decorative members of his design, getting the moldings manufactured after his drawings, and all the decorative detailing done. In his soiled working clothes, with a cigarette jutting from under his mustache, he seemed to greet visitors to his studio with a reproachful glance. One felt it necessary to apologize when calling, though soon his love of sympathetic company took over and the welcome he extended was very real and warm. If he looked bored it was because he knew he would have to talk about himself, which topic he skirted very nicely by plunging into discussion of the decorations. It took a superior strategist to steer conversation back to John S. Sargent.

Boston, which had been the real center of his activities from 1916, was increasingly becoming his home. He accommodated himself to it well, even though there was a smaller, more limited circle than he was accustomed to in the larger world of London. In many respects the people were like himself, though they lacked his European orientation. In the true sense a *home* was as impossible to him as it had always been. Nonetheless, Boston did become his home to a greater extent than he had ever expected it could, as more and more he fell in with its habits.

With Emily, and his niece Reine, who had come on this trip, he was installed in the Copley-Plaza Hotel, in two bedrooms and a sitting room for Emily and Reine, and a bedroom for himself. He had a table reserved for luncheon and dinner on the terrace of the oval room, where the staff soon became aware of the large quantities of food he was prepared to consume, and he was likely to glance at the plate of anyone eating with him and remark with deep vocal stress that gave obvious reproof, "You eat like a bird."

He was amused to watch the activities of his niece, "mysterious individual," as he labeled her, and there was a new factor in the friendship that sprang up between Emily and Mrs. Gardner. This felicitous warmth between sister and aged patroness brought him into closer contact with Mrs. Gardner than ever before. Together the three attended lectures, which Emily thought "instructive" and Mrs. Gardner regularly enjoyed. They went to the symphony concerts on Mrs. Gardner's tickets, and when unable to go herself, due to the frequent illnesses to which she was now subject, Mrs. Gardner sent her tickets along to the Copley-Plaza in hopes they would go without her. Loeffler was another member of this circle, joining them to eat risotto at the Lombardi Inn. They all planned to see a performance of *Pelléas et Mélisande*, which Sargent never liked though he was willing to hear Mary Garden. After the various illnesses struck, only he and Emily were left to attend, and his conviction was strengthened that the "anemic" tonality of the music was simply not enough to compensate for an "idiotic" play. As the evening progressed, his boredom grew so acute that they left. When later Mrs. Gardner could not attend Ravel's *L'Heure Espagnole*, he posted her on it: ". . . perfectly charming, both musically and as a play. The plot is that of a very broad farce, but treated with infinite grace and finesse. I meant to have sent you the book of the words, but lost it in the scrimmage of getting home in that blizzard!" She sent him tickets to hear Alfred Cortot: ". . . Cortot is so good . . . he drags the piano back among the other instruments so that it does not sound like a separate hail storm on a tin roof but like part of the ensemble." Of Arthur Rubinstein, heard in private recital, he reported: "He shook us like rats, but I think most of us liked the punishment." Telling criticisms, and his remarkably apt comment on Cortot's playing shows the sensitivity of his ear.

He had brought two panels from London to install in the Library, on the wall over the stairway, which until then had remained empty. They represented the two institutions associated with Hebraic and Christian theology, the Synagogue and the Church. His interpretation was according to traditional ideas: the one abased, the other triumphant. This was no idea of his own; it was taken from representations found in the old cathedral at Rheims, and at Strasbourg and Paris, though the question remains whether it was diplomatic, or proper, for him to take these older, clearly bigoted interpretations for use in modern times and circumstances. As soon as the panels had been installed there was objection from the Jewish leaders of Boston, who were offended by the slur on the vitality of their faith. They were not interested in the fact that Christian edifices had employed similar ideas during the Gothic era. They were interested in the present, and in present slurs, which they did not care to see decorating Boston's public library. From Sargent's point of view, he had told a continuous narrative, carrying the development of religious thought through numerous phases of which this was the only possible climax. For the Church, indeed, had emerged triumphant, the faith in Christ was certainly dominant within the Western tradition, while the Synagogue, once the leader, was long toppled.

During this time of dissension, while he was being bullied and threatened and ink was splashed on the offending panel, a note arrived at the Copley-Plaza from C. Lewis Hind, who was in Boston. His wife had a portrait of an Englishwoman, done as a gift many years before, which had recently been sold for taxes. When Sargent had invited them to his room, Mrs. Hind said she hoped he would not mind that the gift picture had been sold. "Not at all. I'm glad she had it to sell," he answered, and then entered into discussion of his Synagogue panel with Hind, who became conscious of Sargent's sensitiveness to criticism. Books were brought out to prove his point, to show that his view was tenable. And later he wrote back to England: "I am in hot water here with the Jews, who resent my 'Synagogue' and want to have it removed — and tomorrow a prominent member of the Jewish colony is coming to bully me about it and ask me to explain myself. I can only refer him to Rheims, Notre Dame, Strasbourg, and other Cathedrals, and dwell at length on the good old times. Fortunately the Library Trustees do not object, and propose to allow this painful work to stay."

As Hind's visit demonstrated, the burden of wartime taxation was beginning to tell on English collectors, and many of Sargent's works were once again being put on the market, as well as some of the collections he had helped to form. When two of his watercolors, once presented to Mrs. Wertheimer, surreptitiously appeared in New York, Mrs. Gardner wired to purchase them at a fancy figure. She drew this response, which also betrays awareness of the sort of criticism Roger Fry and his cohorts were leveling at him:

> The Copley-Plaza
> Boston
> Sunday Feb. 8th 1920

Dear Mrs Gardner

I am shocked at your extravagance. Think of the hundreds of poor childless girls who could have been fed and clothed on the sums you lavish on watercolors that have "no moral lesson in the chiaroscuro." To what excess will a morbid craving not lead a convalescent? How did you elude the vigilance of your nurses? and what will happen if you are disappointed when the things arrive?

I shall be full of anxiety for a week.

> Yours ever
> John S. Sargent

Mrs. Hunter also was feeling an increasing financial strain, struggling to keep Hill Hall, and he seems to have thought it his responsibility to pass on what he could from the collection with which he had burdened her. She first told him that she was willing to part with her caricatures by Max Beerbohm. He let Mrs. Gardner have a series of photographs, with the comment that Mrs. Hunter did not seem to be parting with her Brabazons, which he apparently considered the gems. A month later it was photographs of her drawings by Augustus John that he sent Mrs. Gardner. When she expressed interest, he got the prices by cable.

> The Copley-Plaza
> Boston
> Tuesday 25th [May 1920]

Dear Mrs Gardner

A cable from Mrs Hunter says "Seventy five pounds for the best August John drawings and fifty for the less good." It is a pity it is not the other way around, for there is no doubt about which you prefer!

In haste.

> Yours sincerely
> John S. Sargent

Mrs. Gardner was particularly attracted by a drawing of a woman's head with wild-looking eyes, and she questioned whether it would be considered one of the best or among the less good. He advised her that it was certainly among the best. A full-length drawing of a woman was somewhat slighter, but, as it attracted her, he suggested she might assume doubt about that one and offer fifty pounds. She was uncertain how to word the cable, as the photograph had neither title nor number. Therefore the following Friday he sat down to compose a message: "May I have for fifty pounds the John drawing of a full length girl with hat." He still pressed on her the drawing with the crazy eyes, apparently wanting Mary Hunter to receive the seventy-five pounds. "It is like an old master in its delicacy and finish," he urged her, and this time she agreed. So the next day he sat down once more to compose a new cable: "May I have for seventy five pounds the John drawing of woman's head full face with crazy eyes." At the other end, Mrs. Hunter immediately agreed. Soon he was asking her if he might offer Mrs. Gardner the Brabazon watercolors, waiting impatiently for the prices and photographs to be sent out by mail.

A month earlier he had done a charcoal of the historian James Ford Rhodes, with whom, during the sitting, he had some conversation concerning Theodore Roosevelt. His ideas of Roosevelt had never altered since their sittings in the White House, and he told Rhodes in his own way what he had felt on that occasion. *The Letters of Henry James* had just come out, edited by one of Mrs. Hunter's literary friends, Percy Lubbock. In spare moments Sargent was reading the letters, finding great pleasure in wading through those flourishes about events he remembered, written to people he knew. But he was particularly delighted to come on one written to Dr. White: a diatribe of almost a full page length — against Theodore Roosevelt! He was so pleased to find it, and it so well covered his own feelings, as he had tried to convey them to Rhodes, that instantly he sat down to copy out the entire passage, painfully laboring to make his words legible, and sent it off to Rhodes: "This diatribe is such a splendid amplification of my own frivolous remarks of the other day that when I came cross it I took comfort in knowing that I was not the only one who had felt like a rabbit in the presence of a boa constrictor."

On the other side of the ocean the generals still waited, and eventually their call became too strong to resist. Delayed by work he did not wish to leave unfinished, Sargent's sister and niece sailed for England in May, while he worked on until July. The thought of leaving the murals made him unhappy. Early in May he had written: "I am beginning to see my way clear to getting back to England . . . The Generals loom before me like a nightmare. I curse God and man for having weakly said I would do them, for

I have no ideas about it and foresee a horrible failure." By the
second week in July he was in London, suffering because of the
separation from his murals and the Pope Building. "Here I am in a
London of Bank Holidays and emptiness and boredom — not a
general to put salt on the tail of so far — " His old friend Shakespeare, the singer, called on him as he was about to leave for an
extended tour in unknown parts and apparently in need of money.
The obvious answer seemed to be his Brabazon watercolors, which
were brought to the downstairs studio at number 33, while Sargent
sent off notes to MacColl, Mrs. Gardner in Boston, and others. To
his disappointment Mrs. Gardner wanted only one, though by the
early part of September, when MacColl decided to come look at
them in company with Sir Robert Witt, only a few were left.
Meantime, with the aid of the director of the National Portrait
Gallery, the generals were beginning to arrive at Fulham Road.
There seemed to be a great variety of types among them, and
Sargent hoped to produce something of interest. His sister Emily
noted that he "quite enjoyed" his work on the sketches, and he
confirmed this. "My generals are beginning to congregate, and I
am making sketches and studies of them separately. Each is interesting in himself," though he knew what the trouble was from
the beginning and added, "but united we will fall." "Putting them
all on one canvas is what hangs like a weight on his mind," wrote
Emily. It was true. There was no one background, no place, where
this group of distinguished generals had ever congregated or could
ever congregate. "I am handicapped by the idea that they never
could have been altogether in any particular place — so feel de-
barred from any sort of interesting background and reduced to
painting them all standing up in vacuum." Another objection,
frequently expressed, was "How am I going to paint twenty-two
pairs of boots?"

With a start made on the generals, he was anxious to return to
Boston, finding now that Emily, who had so thoroughly enjoyed
being there, thought Violet had more need of her and elected to
remain in London. Torn between the two, as she so frequently
was, she wished they would stay together in one place. He bought
her a little Pekinese dog to ease her loneliness during his absence
and then, while he began thinking of ships and tickets, a spell of

rainy weather put him to bed again with flu. For ten days he remained there, feverish and coughing, only to find when able to get up that the weather had turned colder; there was snow on the ground and no sign of a thaw, so his cold hung on.

After the turn of the year he wrote to his cousin Ralph Curtis:

31, Tite Street,
Chelsea, S.W.

My dear Ralph

Lo! I am writing you and wishing you a Happy New Year, as you did me while it was yet time — and very nice of you too —

I am off to Boston sailing next week on the 19th for N.Y. where I shall spend a day or two with Helleu — He is there and in the Seventh Heaven of Success — which is amusing as for the last several years he has been beating his breast and giving it up for fear of not having "des commandes" over there — He is over-whelmed with them and says he now has seen so many beautiful and very young girls, and been so much admired by the extremely young. So all is well —

I shall soon see Mrs. Gardner and give her affectionate messages from you. They say she is gaining strength . . .

Yrs ever
John S. Sargent

He sailed for New York on the *Cedric* and arrived on January 30, 1921, looking with jaundiced eye at the press and refusing any statement. He registered at the Ritz-Carlton Hotel, where Helleu was installed, and then, as it was early on a Sunday morning, he took a cab down to 42 Washington Mews, just off the Square, where Manship lived. For an hour or more they talked in the studio, and out of whim he decided to make a sketch of the sculptor. Manship whipped out a sheet of paper without letting the minute pass, and Sargent began to scribble in a figure as the sculptor smoked, straddling his chair. The hand moved rapidly over the paper, watched closely by little Pauline Manship, who ran off to tell her mother, "Mama, Mr. Sargent is drawing Papa just like writing!" In a few minutes he was displeased with what he had done and with a "no good" threw it down. Manship thought otherwise, and asked him to sign it.

Sargent took Helleu out to the Brooklyn Museum to see an exhibition of the last word in French painting. Never bashful, Helleu informed the director that he ought not to hang these things, for he was corrupting taste. Sargent's views naturally were rather broader. Though he could see little merit, he felt that a man like Picasso had a right to experiment if he was so inclined, though he summed up rather caustically: "If the tortured moderns are genuine artists, their execution falls far short of their pretentious titles and conceptions." Their slipshod solution of problems aroused his suspicions, and the complacency exhibited by their defenders irritated him. Still, he kept his criticisms more those of a gentle, much experienced teacher who would have enjoyed seeing improvement and more substantial works produced to support such a heavy weight of theoretical assumption.

In Boston the four large elliptical panels, designed for the central positions of the decorations, still had to be put on canvas and painted, and there were the four smaller ovals to be done as well. They were large projects. After their completion the work of painting and gilding the structural portions of the dome itself remained. He had been in Boston only two weeks when he was again struck down, "succumbed to what seems to be a prevailing epidemic — out-of-kilterness-of ones insides, and I am told I must stay at home. I have been housed ever since Thursday — so it seems rather long, and worthy of more serious illness." Once up, however, he was able to work through the winter. In June he made an excursion "to Montreal to attack one of my generals," and in July he consented to notice the heat. He fled to Schooner Head, where his cousin Mary Hale had a boat and "it is cool most of the time. I had even congratulated myself on feeling cold. No such luck in Boston, I dare say." He had other stops to make, for he was a popular guest. Then he went "on to New York to meet my caravan of sisters," who had sailed from England. In August he determined, by means known only to him, that Boston was again cool enough for human habitation, and again attacked the large panels in the Pope Building. By early October he had finished and, to avoid the unveiling ceremony, immediately took ship back to England. His excuse was the urgency of completing the generals.

When the press was given a look at the dome, the reporters from the newspapers being joined by a "gentleman" from the *Transcript*, the assistant director of the Museum, who arranged the viewing, handed out a succinct mimeographed sheet describing the panels, with a partial explanation of the classic symbolism. Soon attention was drawn to a low relief on which three slim female figures moved in dance postures, entwined by a single long scarf, and it was noticed that there was no title for this on the mimeographed sheet. The three balancing reliefs were *The Three Graces, Aphrodite and Eros,* and *Eros and Psyche.* When the reporter turned to the bemused official, he explained that he had himself asked Mr. Sargent about that before he left and his answer had been "Oh, they're three blokes dancing!" The dome was judged a success, and over in London he was greatly elated by the reports reaching him:

31, Tite Street,
Chelsea, S.W.
Mon. 28ᵗʰ [1921]

Dear Mrs Gardner

It was a great pleasure to get your letter and to know that you had been to the Museum and that the thing as a whole made a good impression on you.

I had that satisfaction myself (further concealment is useless) for they lifted the curtain the day before I left, for a few minutes — and I was relieved to see that the bas-reliefs told quite as much as I wanted them to, and that my empty spaces were not too big, and that the whole thing was better than any separate parts. So my spirits rose and I was ready to meet the accusation of being frivolous, platitudinous, and academic.

And behold! the Museum wants more — they want me to decorate the staircase — and I am most willing, but I think that will be even more of a problem, with less likehood of being able to make architectural changes in case these tempt me.

We are having daily and dense fogs and I am painting my generals in the dark — with the hope of getting back to Boston. I hope you are flourishing.

Yours sincerely
John S. Sargent

If Boston had taken greater hold on him, so his life in England, having gone through a series of changes, now emerged in a rather different pattern from what it had been during the Edwardian, and even the prewar, years. Through the years of absence, and isolation, and through a desire to limit the social demands made on him, perhaps through some final admission that he was not really adapted to the life of a drawing-room favorite, he had withdrawn from that world, from the society through which he and Henry James, "the inseparables," had plodded together. No longer did he go everywhere, and from a personality that one might meet at every important house he had changed more and more to a hermit behind his green door in Tite Street.

Not only Sargent had changed, but the brilliance of prewar society itself had altered, until it practically vanished in an era of higher income taxes, stronger labor unions, fewer servants, and smaller houses. The facilities once brought into play to entertain the scores of people who nightly congregated in the drawing rooms of Grosvenor Square and Park Lane were no longer available. The cost of everything had risen at the same time that the ability to acquire began to shrink. The vast landed estates of England no longer made any substantial contribution toward the maintenance of a great house in London, though the rents themselves had not changed. The banks no longer controlled the exchange of the world, nor did they float the bonds of the New World in the Old. The decline in foreign trade and the curtailed factory production became aggravating factors in a general decline. The coffers of the Empire were nearly empty after four years of unparalleled blood-letting and the treasure of the Empire had been shot off in steel that whistled over no man's land in France. The coal lands on which Mrs. Hunter's fortune rested were less productive in the postwar years. As other forms of fuel began to replace coal, its export was cut in half due to German reparations, and the workers more and more refused to return to the pits generation after generation, the great light that had glowed in Essex dimmed. Now it was a mere ember of its former brilliance with no more than a dozen guests in residence, and those only the old regulars. Sargent still went there, for his friendship with Mary Hunter seemed unaffected

by the fluctuations of the times and was entirely apart from the patroness relationship she once had. Tonks went too, and George
Moore, and Steer. Mrs. Hunter's literary friends were never aware
of a solicitor who somewhere tried hopelessly to total her finances.
Sargent knew. How could he fail to appreciate the circumstances
that brought her to sell such little things as watercolors, bringing
no more than seventy-five pounds? But he seemed to be among the
very few who did, and when it became apparent that her fortune
was fast disappearing, the story went about that Mary Hunter was
being reduced to opulence. Perhaps there was some essence of fact
hidden in the cruelty of that jest, for her stately mansion still stood,
and for one who wandered among the treasures with which it was
filled — the Sargent portraits, the Rodin bust, the Mancinis, the
full Italian room, the Jacobin, Adam and Sheraton pieces, even the
library of three thousand picked volumes — it was difficult to think
that all this stood upon constricted means.

Mrs. Hunter herself had not changed. Her warm personality
still shone through the years, her complete isolation from the value
of money granting her a graciousness of outlook that allowed her
to remain untroubled. She did not become embittered, nor did she
turn her back on anyone, as George Moore later did to her, but
carried on much in her old way, as close to Sargent as she ever had
been when she sent three daughters at a time to be painted in Tite
Street. Charlie Hunter had died during the war. Probably it was
nothing more than her obvious availability that now once more
attracted attention to Mary Hunter's friendship with Sargent.
Perhaps it was the way she more than ever seemed to rely on him,
cultivating his interest. Perhaps it was his consistent efforts to aid
her when he could that made people once again think about them.
Many thought she had definitely made up her mind now to marry
him. It was bruited about until everyone in London suspected he
had seen it first, the situation giving rise to a certain obvious humor.
Little Will Rothenstein was put up to carrying the tale that Steer,
that other stolid bachelor, was about to marry, and he never forgot
the flustered, overboiled look Sargent took on when he realized his
leg was being pulled. The comedy was fully enjoyed, though in
his family there was certainly no thought that he would ever marry
Mary Hunter, or anyone else. The very absurdity of the notion,

as well as the extent of the humor it gave rise to, seems to have caused a rift between the normally good-natured Emily and Mrs. Hunter. Emily refused her invitation to the opera, excusing herself as being too tired and too busy and then rather discouraged another suggestion that they make it tea instead. Violet, for her part, announced that Mrs. Hunter appeared much aged.

With all this swirling about his head, the principal protagonist completely disdained notice. His relations with Mary Hunter remained as they had always been, and he continued to aid her fortunes whenever the possibility presented itself. The idea of taking a wife at his age seemed quite ridiculous to him, and whether Mary Hunter wanted to catch him is itself open to speculation. When mention of their presumed nuptials got into the American press, they took steps together to disclaim the notion:

> Wednesday
> 31, Tite Street,
> Chelsea, S.W.
>
> I couldn't go to the telephone this morning, because I was in the thick of a sitting . . .
> I have sent on your manifesto to Richard Hale in Boston, & told him to have it put into at least one newspaper there and in New York and Washington. I should think that would clear the air of slippers and rice and orange blossoms.
>
> Yrs ever
> J. S. S.

Some few bright spots were still left in a London that now settled into fog more grimly than before. One was the Park Lane mansion of Sir Philip Sassoon, whom the war had not affected nor the times changed. Still a young man, Sir Philip had taste and the ability to live according to his own tenets and was among the few important patrons of the arts in postwar England. He was a frequent caller at Tite Street, where he built up a collection of paintings and was a warm personal friend for whom the rule of "no portraits" was broken. He and his extraordinary sister, Sybil, were special friends of Sargent's, the gulf of thirty years separating them from the artist being a matter of no importance. In the years after the war, Sybil had begun to occupy that special, rather idealistic place where so many others had been, as her image began to blend with the one he carried within himself. Having broken his retirement to paint her in 1913, doing the picture as his wedding present, Sargent agreed to another in 1922. But now, to his horror, he discovered that she was so tanned as to distort the image, and though she assured him she would be quite white by November when sittings were to begin, he nonetheless had Worth design a fanciful gown, the obvious purpose of which was to cover as much of her as possible. It cost him two hundred pounds, and Lady Cholmondeley, as Sybil now was, complained that it only required a mask over the face to be complete. They had "a month of sittings in the fog," during which she spent almost the entire day at the studio with him and was amused to note that his idea of lunch for two was two whole ducks. He carved them with ceremonious vigor, back stiff and elbows wide, and even though she ate little, there was never a bite left over. He was very talkative, his thoughts ranging over a thousand topics, but he had trouble finding words and periodically blew up his red face beneath its beard when one escaped him, then becoming ill-tempered if suggestions were offered. After these sittings he announced, "Sybil is *lovely*. Some days she is positively *green*," which, strange as it may seem, bore all the marks of being intended as a compliment. A little later he undertook the portrait of Sir Philip, catching him with the touch of aristocratic insolence that sometimes stole across his features.

Paul Manship was now installed in Tite Street, and when in time Sargent began urging her to have a bust made, Sybil Cholmondeley was conscious that grist was needed for the mill. Never an admirer of Manship's polished portraits, she had no intention of being sacrificial lamb on this occasion, but her resolve was broken down by persistent bullying. So she shifted to the downstairs studio where her boredom was intense as she had a sculptured portrait done, and Sargent, as impressario of the occasion, frequently came down to interrupt, pointing out the features he claimed the sculptor had missed: one eye was higher than the other, the mouth was crooked, the nose twisted — all of which humorously couched hints Manship studiously avoided in his highly polished, generalized bust.

The four were lunching together now, though we have no count on the number of ducks. Manship and Lady Cholmondeley would file through the passage cut from the downstairs studio to the dining room in number 31, while Sir Philip and Sargent came downstairs from painting in the big studio above. Artur Rubinstein sometimes dropped in to play piano duets with Sargent — *kattermen,* as the artist loved to call them (quatre mains). Margot Asquith, who sometimes made her appearance about this time, let fly with her biting wit, and at every intrusion Sargent pretended indignation, qualifying his pleasure with the knowledge that he ought really to be at work. But he enjoyed these intrusions almost to the same extent that he pretended to dislike them and would certainly have been disappointed had he been left to work all day without them.

Between the gala times he had with Mary Hunter and Sir Philip Sassoon, most of his evenings were still spent in the company of a small group of old friends, the nucleus of which had grown up around him in the New English Art Club of the eighties and nineties. These were the men and women with whom he shared ideals, and who had early clustered about him in Tite Street. With the addition of his and Tonks's solicitor, Nelson Ward, and the critic and former director of the Wallace Collection, D. S. MacColl, they formed a happy group. Frequently they dined together at Emily's flat in Carlyle Mansions, overlooking the spindly little Albert Bridge across the river, or at L. A. Harrison's, where, with the addition of George Moore, they formed a regular company. There were many minor disagreements within this circle; how could it be otherwise with George Moore, all puffed out with his Irish conceit, and MacColl, whose critical attitude toward everything raised Tonks to fits of fury. Evan Charteris was another, sharing with Tonks a devotion to claret that was the disgust of Moore, whose coarse palate cared not at all for talk of wines. Filled and satisfied, he sulked in a corner, while Steer dozed in his chair and the bright light of conversation spread cheer among them with discussion of the classics ("Nellie" Ward and Tonks) and talk of wine (Tonks and Charteris).

Sargent's correspondence was still heavy. He seemed more than ever to enjoy seating himself every morning at the roll-top desk in the dining room to pour out some rather comical expressions on the four sides of his printed letter sheets. He had once told Dr.

White that leaving correspondence unanswered saved half a man's life, and leaving it unread saved the other half, but obviously paid no attention to this himself. That his handwriting was so bad that scarcely half of what he wanted to convey was legible did not in the least disturb him, though he had been told frequently enough. A cousin in Boston sent him stationery with the heading:

J. S. S.
SO HARD IT SEEMS THAT ONE MUST READ
BECAUSE ANOTHER NEEDS WILL WRITE

Delighted, he used it until the supply was exhausted, not however without some allusions to it in letters to Mrs. Hunter, in which he instructed her to ignore it as an old joke that backfired. Every invitation had to be answered in longhand, and it was almost a sacred duty for him to fill the four surfaces with impressionistic crow tracks, but never take another sheet.

When Sir Philip Sassoon planned an entertainment for the opening of his new ballroom at 25 Park Lane, Sargent asked his cousin Mary Potter, about to pass through London, to come along, explaining that it "will probably be the best fuss I can offer you." He laid many plans, and Manship, who was still working in the studio, was a part of them all. They would meet the cousin, have her to lunch, then conduct her through Sir Herbert Cook's collection. When she was unable to arrive in time, he changed plans and notified her that he would be calling on her at whatever hotel she stopped, Manship in tow. Each change in schedule brought new plans. In the meantime he wrote that there was "an international conference of Bostonians here, that knowing your heretical feelings, I dare say say you will not be sorry to miss . . . I am having a purported luncheon party . . ."

Among the guests at Sassoon's, when finally they did get there, was the Prince of Wales, a rather pretty young man, of whom he had once had the misfortune to make one of his charcoals. The Prince had not been impressive in the studio in Tite Street, where the distinguished figures of two generations had come in review. Royalty never interested Sargent much anyhow, and now, with the wine flowing at Sassoon's, there was sudden talk of Manship's doing a bust of the Prince. To Sargent it did not sound like a happy idea, and he leaned over the sculptor to say in low tones, "Don't you do it."

"Why not?"

"He won't sit for you." Then, with ponderous emphasis, "And besides, *he's a very dull young man!*"

The success of the Museum dome was followed by the order for a second group of decorations above the stairs. There was also inquiry from the Trustees of the Widener Library at Harvard about his doing two panels as a War Memorial, to be placed at the head of the stairway. After all the years of quiet plodding effort that had gone into his original Boston Public Library decorations, he was suddenly bursting forth as a full-fledged, one hundred per cent professional muralist. He was very pleased, for it was work that allowed him the utmost freedom and the widest scope for his inventive powers. He delighted in it, and tried to insulate himself further from the insatiable demand for charcoal portraits that ate into his time. One means of choking off requests was to raise his price. In the beginning he had written to Lady Lewis, "I never know what to ask for a mere snapshot, especially if it does not happen to be a miraculously lucky one," and in those days of indecision he accepted as little as twenty-one guineas. By 1916, in Boston, he was getting three hundred dollars, which the Hales thought too little, and at their insistence he asked four hundred, which remained the price until after 1920. The increase of the price had done nothing to decrease the demand, which in fact seemed constantly to grow larger. At the insistence of Professor Charles Sprague Sargent the artist then raised his price to five hundred dollars, and a hundred guineas in England.

To get behind that polished and massive door at 31 Tite Street was now more difficult than ever, whether he was at home or not. And to Londoners the question of whether or not he was inside became a matter for concern, for he had the habit of whisking off to America for a year at a time, just as he had formerly gone to the Continent. There was never any use trying to make an appointment with him, even if the letter was registered, for the postal consignments were huge and frequently remained in bundles until one of his maids looked through for familiar handwritings. The one hope was to take a chance and call, again and again, until perhaps one morning there might be the opportunity to gain five minutes of his time, on the brink of his exodus to Fulham Road, Hill Hall, or America. Likely as not, unless it was his solicitor, Nelson Ward, who approved the application and gave directions how to penetrate the fastness at number 31, all the trouble might be in vain. Even those who succeeded once might find themselves barred forever afterward. Sargent began one letter to Mrs. Hale in Boston, "You are indeed a friend to have staved off a paughtrait," and he meant it as no other painter could, for staving off "paughtraits" had become his great sport, the constant preoccupation of his free hours.

Of course, the twenty-two pairs of boots, replete with khaki and heads too, were still to be finished at Fulham Road. "John has begun work on his generals, but I am sure these dark days, of which there are many, must hamper him a great deal. It is bitterly cold now." So wrote the ever-faithful Emily after his return to London in 1921. However, they were eventually finished, and with Emily he was off again for the studio in the Pope Building.

When I Like

AT THE Boston Museum, Sargent once more found it essential to have architectural changes made to accommodate his new decorations above the stairs. The area of the skylight had to be diminished and the coffers below removed to provide space for his reliefs. For more light, now that the area of the skylight had been critically reduced, the openings into the two courts on either side were made larger and the six columns that stood beside the staircase were regrouped to stand in pairs, an effect reminiscent of the Genoese palaces he had sketched years before. A new model now stood in the Pope Building, and the artist began his studies for the compositions, placing pieces and changing them with great frequency until he arrived at a pleasing balance. This staircase was the least appropriate place he had been called on to decorate, the ceiling over the corridor beside it hanging entirely too low, and from the start he must have been aware that he would be less successful here than he had been with the dome. But that did not change the fact that this was the work he most enjoyed. The confidence of the Trustees in placing this scheme in his hands was much appreciated, and he would do his best!

Passing back and forth before those large windows seven floors above Columbus Avenue, he must often have stopped in moments of perplexity to look out over the rooftops of Boston. There the city lay, spread before him, ugly and colorless, without visible shape or pattern, appearing from this vantage point like a jumble of eroded boulders on a mountaintop. From across the street the rumble of trains passing through the New Haven Railroad cut greeted his ears, and he could see its ugly gash down below behind a row of flat buildings. One wonders if in these odd moments his mind ever strayed to thoughts of the strange career that had carried him up from Italy, out from Paris, flying from London, to this?

Probably not.

More and more, as his life advanced, he ceased to have any sense of retrospect or of future. More and more his mind preferred to dwell in the present, the very moment, and he threw himself into his work with increased absorption to block out the futility that marked his personal existence. There was an underlying bitterness that he, who was such an emotional being, had never managed to find expression for his feelings nor found anyone to return them completely in the way he had dreamed of so long ago. He had, at times, adored certain women, momentarily finding in them a reflected image of what he sought, and this explains much of the attention he was giving to his cousin Mary Potter and to Sybil Cholmondeley. But now that he was a gruff man past sixty-five, the futility of it all hurt even more, and he seemed to have retreated entirely into his work, his whole world becoming centered in a strange, over-accented way on the one picture presently occupying his easel. He lived in his work, he did not care to think of anything very far removed from it, his life and it merging imperceptibly. In that sphere at least, his doubts of himself disappeared and he found honest satisfaction. Why had he not married Mrs. Hunter? Probably because he did not trust his own judgment. Past sixty at the time, he was sensitive to appearances. No doubt she could have made him happy, and with someone's care there is no question but that his life would have continued longer than it did. The last little tragedy of his existence lies in the fact that he never knew, even in his last years, the happiness he so much deserved. Instead, he grew more embittered, more unsure and withdrawn, more heavily reliant upon his work as a form of anesthesia. He was constantly seeking new outlets for his talents, new things to design, and lately was thinking he would like to try his hand at buttons, textiles, and perhaps even furniture — there was no end to what he wanted to do or the things in which he interested himself. It eased his mind, and while absorbed by these distractions he escaped more troublesome thoughts.

There can be no doubt but that he himself realized that his decorations had given him opportunities for greater fulfillment of his gifts than ever existed while he painted the London ladies. He was developing an increasing boldness of line and ever greater sense of dynamic power, and one might believe that in the preparatory drawings made for these later murals, the thousands of figure studies carelessly stacked about in portfolios, he reached his ultimate development as an artist. Never before had he displayed drawing of such strength, with such intimate knowledge of values, such a pure, overwhelming physical vigor. Leaving aside the absolute authority of the handling, the remarkable freedom with which he was able to put down the body lines in thick accents, without need for preparatory development, their brute energy is an intensification of the vitality that always had been the keynote of his art. Here was strength in its purest form, in drawings that were done with no loss of refinement, no concessions to crudity.

It was not long, however, before he was hit by another of his colds, and again shut up in his hotel room, where his sister Emily insisted on calling a doctor, who brought a specialist to relieve some of the pain in his ears. He slept a good deal, "which shows he feels wretchedly," she thought. Impatiently, however, he was up again, and once more returned to the routine of the decorations with breaks for "mugs." Service at the Pope Building closed down on Sundays, when he had to rout out the janitor to take him up in the elevator. One such morning, on the way up, he was asked, "Mr. Sargent, don't you ever take a holiday?" He smiled indulgently. "What would I do for recreation?"

Even at this late date he still, when able, made introductions for Paul Helleu. Sometimes, of course, he thought it wise to add a note of caution: "I have told him that he must show you his beautiful bibelots when you let him know you are back in Paris. I must warn you that he is considered extremely enterprising and makes a jump on any woman who comes within arms length. But he is very nice all the same."

So frequently was he the champion of younger artists, giving them such immense doses of praise that it was often undeserved, that one almost doubts the efficacy of his critical sense. It was acute but he preferred to hide it. It cannot seriously be thought that he lacked the sense, for an artist's progress is made mainly by self-criticism. It is perhaps true that Sargent did not apply the same strict standard to the works of youthful practitioners that he did to himself. But if it were suggested that he abdicated as a critic altogether, the trenchant quality of the remarks he sometimes felt called on to make should lay that idea to rest. "I don't think much of that drawing," he wrote in 1922. "She scribbles very daintily when a correct line would be the thing to try for, and her values are all wrong. I can't understand her making your hair so dark. One of your chief beauties is the originality of a young face with gray hair, and she seems to have missed that entirely. Perhaps she is under the delusion that she is flattering you!" Nor did he think well of the stratagems employed even by his pets to advance their careers. When, after he had been instrumental in interesting two ladies in a sculptor's work, they were invited to have portrait busts made without a definite understanding about price and purchase, he took a dim view. "I expect as how . . . [he] ought to be delerious to you both, in the hope of two splendid paughtraits for his next trip to New York. When you both do sit to him, I warn you that he will be very surprised if you do not buy the paughtraits. This is a tiresome habit of which I have tried to correct him. Otherwise he is not a bad fellow."

He continued to enjoy the theater. Seeing John Barrymore's *Hamlet* in Boston, he was pleased by the opportunity to meet the actor back stage. He showed considerable interest watching him apply make-up, complimenting him on the deft manner he accentuated the frown lines and the highlights of the cheekbones. Sargent had drawn his sister Ethel in 1903, and John rather hoped he could get Sargent to do even more for him, perhaps even paint his portrait. He knew better than to make any outright suggestion, which would certainly have ended the conversation on the spot. But his thought was not hidden, and eventually when Sargent volunteered, "If I were now in oils, I might venture to suggest that you sit for me," Barrymore leaped at this display of telepathy. "It would be the greatest moment of my life," he exclaimed, "just to watch you at work." But Sargent's mind had been made up years before. No, he would not undertake an oil. He had a dread of them. "Besides," he added, as though to soften the disappointment, "you would be a difficult subject for an artist not in his best stride.

Your features are too regular. There is, you know, a bit of caricature in every good portrait."

The discussion was not dropped, and Michael Strange, Barrymore's wife, when she heard what had transpired, was insistent. Once again they discussed the matter, and now Sargent was in a different mood. If Barrymore wanted a charcoal drawing, very well. His price was a thousand dollars, to which the actor agreed. So Barrymore arrived one morning at the grilled lift in the tiny lobby of the Pope Building, and was duly hoisted to the seventh floor, front, where he entered the world of muralizing and "mugging." With the actor once more before him, the artist returned to his original feelings, and set to work. When finished, he wrote across the bottom, "To my friend John Barrymore," as he did with pictures that were gifts, and refused to take any money. "It's a Christmas present for you," he said.

Mrs. Gardner was now in her eighty-third year, and the taunting temptress of the previous century was reduced to a small, thin, much-lined woman, whose face, with its network of wrinkles, reminded Paul Manship of a monkey's in the zoo. She eventually purchased Manship's *Victory*, which Sargent, assuming the role of disinterested onlooker, commented he liked: "all but the egg-shape it is." There was a suggestion that new memorials ought to be made to her now that she had reached advanced age, a statue by Manship perhaps. Neither the sculptor, who was horrified at the idea of tracing out the myriad wrinkles, nor the lady, whose vanity could not have been served in such fashion, was much in favor of this. Still, the idea of a new portrait persisted, and it therefore devolved on Sargent, who thought the most obliging medium, considering her physical condition, would be watercolor. He wrote a little note asking her to appoint a day, and when it was decided, came over to Fenway Court with his equipment and made a small portrait with very indistinct face, the body swathed like an Egyptian mummy. Theirs was a long friendship, but had never been very close except in the way people who are frequently thrown together by chance come to know each other. It was only in the last years of her life, when Emily Sargent came to Boston and became sympathetically attached to this kindly, generous lady, that Sargent and Mrs. Gardner became really close.

Even then their intimacy was limited to concerts, and to little visits by her bedside when he would describe to her what he was doing with the murals. The news of her death in 1924, at the age of eighty-four, was cabled to him in London by Mrs. Monks, her relative and housekeeper in the last years. His comments on receiving the news tell all there is to know: "I had a cable from Mrs. Monks to say that Mrs. Gardner had died peacefully on the 17th. I felt that when I said goodbye to her that it was for good — Before long I suppose we will know what is to happen to her collection." In her will she named him as one of her pallbearers, but he was in London at the time and could not perform this duty.

And still people came for charcoals. He was having sittings on Sundays now to keep his weekdays a little freer. Even his new price, a thousand dollars, did not stop them. They took whatever he did, without regard to quality, it seemed, just to have him draw their mugs. "If only they would let me draw some other part of their bodies!" he burst out to one sitter. They were interested only in how well they looked in their *Sargent*, amusingly borne out by his experience with Dr. Harvey Cushing, the noted brain surgeon. Cushing belonged to the Saturday Club, most of whose members had at one time or another already been "mugged"; among them Major Higginson, Cousin Charles Sprague Sargent, and James Ford Rhodes. It was difficult to refuse another member of the club, and he arranged to do the sketch in his hotel room at the Copley-Plaza. Cushing was afraid he would not prove a good sitter, asking permission to bring along his little daughter Barbara. The reply ran: "You take it like a man, for whom operations have no terror. Any morning at 10 o'clock next week — room 601 Copley Plaza, will suit with a day or two's notice. So take your choice — and bring your anesthetist." When the picture was finished, however, Cushing was not entirely pleased and said, greatly to the artist's exasperation, that he looked as though he had been weaned on a pickle. The drawing, which had been sent off to be photographed and framed at the Copley Gallery, was returned to him, and after he saw it again he wrote: "I confess I did not see the slightest scornfulness to the expression of anything to change in the face. I did lighten a dark under the nose a trifle, but without cosmetics, and I shortened and thickened the neck a little.

I am returning the drawing . . . and I hope you will be satisfied. If you are not, I assume that I am not the right man to do you, and I had rather return the charge and keep the drawing myself. I don't often have such a good head to draw." Which by its firmness did the trick, for it was a *Sargent* that Cushing wanted, however weaned. In afteryears the Cushing family thought the drawing a bargain, considering how frequently the doctor was then able to tell the story.

There were frequent invitations from Mary Potter to come to Holm Lea, where the company appears to have been to his liking and where he could sit on the porch in the evenings, with his feet on the rail, and look out at the sea. Professor Sargent during the early twenties was hard at work on his massive genealogy of the descendants of Epes Sargent of Gloucester, and perhaps hoped his cousin could shed light on his branch of the family, but of this John had a profound ignorance. His further disinterest in family ties, and family pride, was demonstrated late in 1923 when he was amused to receive a letter from a New York art dealer, offering for sale a portrait by Sully which he believed to be of Sargent's grandmother, Mary Newbold. It was rather a nice Sully, of a round-faced girl, about eight, with well-defined, if lumpy, features and dressed in an Empire frock, holding before her, at arm's length, a tousled lap dog. It was known in the family that there had been a Sully portrait of Mary Newbold, but whether or not this was the same picture must be proved. And proved it was, both by the discovery of markings on the back of the canvas, beneath the lining, and by reference to Sully's own notebook, in which the sitters were listed. Even this conclusive identification of the child failed to arouse any spark of enthusiasm. "This amorphous girl, tossing the incestuous product of the rabbit and the carp, is welcome to be my grandmother, but she leaves me cold," was what he wrote to Mrs. Hale, who eventually purchased the portrait.

All the same, his family was his softest spot. He did for them many of the things he would not do for others, and many people applied to his relatives in the hope their influence might get him to do portraits. That was beyond even their capacities, though frequently they did prevail on him to the extent of some charcoal that he might not otherwise have been amenable to. As it happened,

President Calvin Coolidge, locked away inside his secret soul, had a secret and rather surprising ambition to be painted by Sargent, as two of his predecessors had been. A friend suggested that the family might possibly manage this, or at least that they would stand a better chance of approaching the artist than anyone else. So the matter was placed in the hands of Mary Potter, who determined to go about it with all the delicacy at her command. She had previously been successful in getting him to draw several women, and even the American ambassador to France — "your pet Ambassador," as Sargent tagged him — just as Mary Hale had been intermediary with similar requests. Now she arranged to make mention at one of his frequent dinners at Holm Lea. She selected her moment to best advantage, and with knowledge of the habits of her victim she waited until he had finished a good dinner and lit his cigar. He was in a genial mood now, expanding humorously, as he always did, and into this ready situation she dropped gentle mention that President Coolidge would like to have his portrait painted.

Sargent sat back in his chair as though hit by a rifle bullet. His expression changed into the well-known purple apoplectic look and he bellowed, *"You've ruined my whole dinner!"* A note written shortly after completes the story:

> The Copley-Plaza
> Boston
> Thursday [Jan. 3, 1924]

My dear Mary

I hope you have quickly recovered from your motor accident and that you will bring Mrs Zanetti at 10.30. I have had a correspondence with Mrs Zanetti on the earliness of the hour — but it takes two hours and a half to do a drawing and in this season there are no afternoons . . .

You will be pleased to know that I have regretfully declined to paint Mr. Coolidge — I was pale, but firm —

Hoping to see you tomorrow

> Yrs ever
> John S. Sargent

The Queen of Romania received the same treatment, as shown by a letter written that October to Henry H. Pierce:

I am sorry to have to adhere to my telegraphic message, and to repeat that I have entirely given up portrait painting, and have devoted myself entirely to another line of work for the last ten or twelve years. I hope it will be understood that my retirement from portrait painting is a thing of many years standing. I feel greatly honored to have been thought of by Her Majesty the Queen of Romania, and regret very deeply no longer being able to do justice to her commands.

The retrospective exhibition being held in New York at this time was responsible for many of the new requests Sargent was receiving. The Fifth Avenue buses were all decked out with bold-lettered posters proclaiming his name up and down the street. So many brilliant portraits seen together naturally caused inquiries to rear their ugly heads, and he wrote to Walter L. Clark, president of the Gallery, "please choke off any further applications for oil portraits, and say that I am a physical wreck and unable to answer letters." He was further distressed to have a gentleman named Macbeth, who headed a gallery of the same name in New York and had been in contact with him at various times in the past, ask to see him one day at the Copley-Plaza. It seemed uncivil not to receive the man after he had come from New York, and with foreboding he consented to a meeting in his room. Macbeth stated that he was authorized to offer up to twenty-five thousand dollars for a portrait of his client. Sargent made no direct answer, but reaching to the table before him, offered the man a cigarette and then, lighting it for him, explained they were a special brand sent to him. They were very mild. How did he like them? And so the interview went, with never another word about the portrait. At length, when the subject of mild cigarettes had been exhausted, he thanked Mr. Macbeth for coming to see him, rose, shook his hand, and showed him out.

Nor was this the only form of embarrassment his life now contained. For two decades his mere existence as a painter had shown a nasty tendency to slop over from the art columns of the newspapers onto the front pages. It was never anything he himself was responsible for, or could control, any more than he was responsible for the disposition of Sir Hugh Lane's property or the other things that made headlines. Now, nine of the Wertheimer portraits, painted two decades earlier, were being installed in the National Gallery in Trafalgar Square, as a gift to the nation under the generous terms of Wertheimer's will. A certain thrill of horror ran through London that these pictures, so incisively portraying a Jewish art dealer and his numerous family, whose very name was still popularly mouthed with an added Germanic twist, should thus be enshrined in the most important gallery in the Empire. Many respectable people clutched at their pearl-bedecked throats to find old Asher's crafty look and many children so honored. Sargent's name was hurled into the midst of national strike, and socialism, to be the subject of debate in the House of Commons, where Sir J. Butcher, the member for York, rose to ask the Chancellor of the Exchequer on what conditions the Trustees of the National Gallery had accepted this singular bequest — "whether the Trustees had undertaken to keep all these . . . portraits permanently on exhibition in the National Gallery; and what precedent existed for exhibiting the works of a living artist in the National Gallery."

Mr. Stanley Baldwin, the Chancellor, answered that he was "informed that the bequest was not subject to any formal conditions, but that the testator expressed the wish that it might be found possible to exhibit the pictures at the National Gallery." He added that "the Trustees highly appreciated the generosity of the gift," a statement which brought forth cheers from the House, "and in all the circumstances, considered this course more appropriate than the exhibition of the pictures at the Tate Gallery. While the usual practice is against exhibiting work by living artists, no rule exists which debars the Trustees from this course. Indeed they have done so from time to time for the last sixty years. Recent instances are Harpignies, Matthew Maris, and Fantin-Latour among foreign artists, and Watts and Sargent among British artists." But the attack was pressed, Sir. J. Butcher asking whether there was one gallery in which nine full-sized pictures of one family by one artist had been accepted. He was interrupted by a mock request from a fellow member as to whether the Chancellor could arrange for the display of Butcher's own portrait at the National Gallery, which filled the air with ribaldry. Next, Sir C. Oman, the member for Oxford, arose to ask whether the Chancellor could arrange "that these clever, but extremely repulsive pictures, should be placed in a special . . . "

The end of his sentence was lost in laughter and cheers and the demonstration that followed his particular choice of words left little doubt as to what was taken exception to: less the honor done to Sargent, who for reasons politic had been forced to bear the burden of the argument, than the apotheosis accorded a crafty Jewish dealer. It was the kind and generous Wertheimer who was being found "repulsive" and his generosity that had laid him open to such words. Soon after this, Sir Joseph Duveen announced, amid new headlines, that he would offer to the nation as a gift a special new wing at the Tate Gallery in which there would be one room for the exclusive exhibition of the Sargent paintings in public possession. His obvious purpose was to give the Wertheimer portraits a home.

To all this the artist himself was an embarrassed spectator.

The panels that Sargent projected for the Museum were too large to be painted in Columbus Avenue, where the fourteen-foot ceiling would not accommodate them, and so he returned to London, to work in Fulham Road. With him went all the preparatory studies, drawings, and clay sketches for the reliefs, which also would be finished in London that winter. The structural alterations to the Museum staircase were not yet complete, and he had time to get everything ready.

He carried on his normal routine, just as he had in Boston, going each day to Fulham Road and returning to Tite Street or to his sister's for his luncheon engagements, the same groups of people making it a habit to drop in when they knew he was in town. A dealer in Madrid informed him he had a "portrait of a man" by El Greco, and Sargent passed the word on to Edward Robinson of the Metropolitan Museum, which quickly gobbled it up. Emily was ill during the summer, and Dr. Harvey Cushing wrote from Oxford to ask how she was getting on. Sargent mentioned his worries about her. In reply Cushing wrote that he was leaving Oxford on August 9 to catch an eleven-thirty train at Euston Station for Liverpool, and his steamer, and he would manage to look in at Carlyle Mansions at ten-thirty. He did, at the risk of missing both train and ship, to assure the family that all was going well. When winter came on, Violet had pneumonia, and again Sargent was troubled and anxious. But the worst was over by January, and his spirits were back at their normal pitch, as a letter to his wandering cousin Mary Potter amply demonstrates:

> Jan. 23rd 1925
> 31, Tite Street
> Chelsea, S.W.
>
> My dear Mary
>
> It was a pleasure to get your letter of New Year's day and to know that you are safe in civilized countries, for the moment at least. But you can never stay out for long and then you are off again in search of headhunters and cannibals and yellow perils! I am writing a private note to the Captain of the Franconia to say that you must never be allowed on shore without an armed escort — I hope this will put a curb on your spirit of adventure and assure a safe return to everyone's relatives.
>
> . . .
>
> Violet is slowly regaining her strength after her terrible siege of pneumonia — for several days the doctors thought she could not recover.
>
> March seems to be the time when the Museum will be ready for my things, so Emily and I will be leaving for Boston long before you get back there. It will be a treat to see you.
>
> > Bon voyage
> > Yrs ever
> > John S. Sargent

When the decorations were completed, he set to work writing out explicit instructions for those who would install them. Once they were boxed, and ready to ship, he got a reservation for himself and Emily on the *Baltic*, for April 18. Now he noticed a certain finality about having completed all the works for which he had orders and commented to Stokes with a smile, "Now the American things are done; and so, I suppose, I may die when I like."

During the week before his departure he spent several days packing. He was accustomed now to doing this himself and exercised great care doing and undoing, dreading and hating it but gaining satisfaction from each minor victory over his refractory suitcases. Mrs. Hunter questioned the wisdom of these exertions and thought all the lifting of cases bad for a man of sixty-nine, but he disregarded her protests with apparent good nature, and rather high spirits. Lady Cholmondeley called, asking if he might do a drawing of her daughter the next day. It was always a treat when the sparkling Sybil came by and, though he had a sitting scheduled with Princess Mary, he said it was all right, he would put his sitter off for another day. It was cool in his studio that April day, and the child came dressed in a sweater, which refused to stay properly closed about her shoulders. Her mother twisted one of her hair-pins through the wool, holding it together, and he drew it into the little portrait, with a remark about this showing his affection for them both. On the fourteenth, then, he gave the postponed sitting to the Princess, who came to the studio accompanied by her husband, Viscount Lascelles. That evening Emily arranged a little gathering of friends around dinner in her flat: Wilson Steer, Tonks, the Barnard Girls, who had posed for *Carnation Lily, Lily Rose* so long before, L. A. Harrison, Violet, Lady Prothero, and Nelson Ward were the few guests. He was in a humorous mood throughout the evening, acting as host with a good-natured charm. As was the custom in his busy workaday life, the party broke up at ten-thirty. He waved good night and walked away from Emily's down the Chelsea Embankment in the direction of Tite Street. One of the guests lingered long enough to say to Emily, with a laugh, "Do you know, I am still a little terrified of your brother. This is not a case of perfect love casting out fear."

A slight shower came on as he walked, and when a taxi came past he saw Nelson Ward inside. Urged to ride the rest of the way, he at first protested but finally got in and rode the short distance to Tite Street. "Au revoir; in six months," he called back from his door. Inside, he recalled that he had neglected to write an impor-tant note and, rather than wait for morning as was his usual custom, sat down in the dining room:

31, Tite Street,
Chelsea, S.W.

Walter L. Clark
President Grand Central Art Galleries
New York, N.Y.

Dear Mr. Clark

I am afraid I have delayed to inform you that my third contribution was shipped to your galleries on April 2nd by Messrs James Dooley & Co., of 95 Leaderhill Street, consigned to Keer Maurer Co., N.Y. by S.S. Mississippi.

It may reach you before this. I attended to Consular Certificate and paid James Dooley the charges.

The title is "Shoeing Cavalry Horses at the Front." It was done in France in 1918.

I am sailing for Boston (Hotel Copley-Plaza) on the 18th per S.S. Baltic.

Yours truly
John S. Sargent

He closed the envelope, licked the flap, put a stamp on it, and went out to post it. In a few minutes he was back inside, and the maids heard him moving about as he went into the library to find a book, picking a volume of Voltaire's *Dictionnaire Philosophique* out of the complete 1784 edition, which he took along into his bedroom. With his glasses on, he read awhile and then, feeling slightly ill, pushed them up onto his forehead before turning on his left side and going off to sleep.

Notes

CHAPTER ONE

THE ARTIST Winslow Wilson, one of the "few silent students," described the scene in a letter dated August 11, 1954. See also the obituary notice, *Boston Transcript*, April 15, 1925.

E. V. Lucas recalled Sargent's imitation at the home of Adrian Stokes in 1923; *Ladies' Home Journal*, December 1925.

The description of Dr. Sargent is from Vernon Lee, *J. S. Sargent, In Memoriam*, published with Charteris' biography *John Sargent*, The Hon. Evan Charteris, New York, 1927. A photograph of Dr. Sargent can be found in *Epes Sargent of Gloucester and His Descendants*, by Charles Sprague Sargent and Emma Worcester Sargent, Boston, 1923. Dr. Sargent is referred to by his title throughout in conformity with current usage, though in Europe he was always known as Mr. Sargent.

The "porphyry" is mentioned by Mary Newbold Patterson Hale, the Mrs. Richard W. Hale of this book, in "The Sargent I Knew," *World Today*, London, 1927; it was also mentioned by Miss Sally Fairchild in an interview, June 8, 1954.

The work on letters to Philadelphia is mentioned in Dr. Sargent's letters, along with much invaluable information that is not specifically cited. A collection of more than one hundred of these letters was made by Winthrop Sargent as a part of his genealogical study of his family. They are now in the possession of his son, Winthrop Sargent, Jr., of Haverford, Pa.

The extent of Mrs. Sargent's influence within her family is easily seen in these letters as well. That her son John was aware of it is shown by the quotation from the family genealogy, which he doubtless supplied. Winthrop Sargent, Jr., assured me categorically that nothing was inserted into that book without the approval of the interested member of the family.

The sister was Emily Sargent Pleasants, of whom he did an immature portrait reproduced in Charteris. It was assumed in the family that this picture was executed during the American trip of 1876, but technically it is markedly inferior to the works of that year. That her husband visited the Sargents in Brittany during 1875 is established by Dr. Sargent's letters; doubtless she was painted in Paris at that time, a date coinciding better with the floundering style of the portrait.

The derivation of Henry James's *The Pupil* cannot be proved, though the circumstances of the family parallel remarkably those of the Sargents, with the added fact that the characters in the story appear about Europe with dates and places corresponding to the Sargents' appearances. James's original notes for this story seem to have been destroyed in his later life, for they are not included in the published *Notebooks of Henry James*, Matthieson and Murdock, 1947. Mr. Kenneth B. Murdock assured me that this volume contained "the complete text of all the notebooks of Henry James which we knew to exist at the time we published the book. So far as I know no other notebooks have been discovered since." Letter of Aug. 11, 1953. It was my wife, Barbara, who first noticed the singular resemblance between this story and the Sargent family.

The number of Copley portraits is estimated by Winthrop Sargent, Jr., as fourteen.

There was also a previous relationship with the Winthrop family which is rather complicated.

Ship measurements from *The Maritime History of Massachusetts*, Samuel Eliot Morison, Boston, 1921. Details of the voyage of the *General Stark* are from a summary of the ship's log, prepared by Samuel Worcester, in possession of Winthrop Sargent, Jr.

Tonnage of the *Winthrop and Mary* from *Gloucester Ship Reports, 1789–1875*, published by the Essex Institute. The number of vessels was provided by Winthrop Sargent, Jr., and borne out by *Gloucester Ship Reports*, which naturally did not show up ships registered at Boston. "Family tradition has it that Captain Pearce, associated with Daniel Sargent, handled the sandalwood concession from King Kamehameha I." Letter from Winthrop Sargent, Jr., Dec. 28, 1954. Actually there may have been as many as four pyramidings on some voyages; first in the northwest, then at Hawaii, again at Canton, and finally at London. "The English market was best for tea." Letter from Winthrop Sargent, Jr., Dec. 27, 1954.

Brigs *Juliana* and *Mary* from *Shipping and Commercial List, and New York Price Current*, Sept. 3, 1828, and Jan. 21, 1829. The gale in issue of Nov. 7, 1829. The anxiety for the indigo cargo was remembered in after years by Mary Sargent (1806–1898) and told to Winthrop Sargent, Jr. His letter, June 16, 1954.

"The result was bankruptcy." *Epes Sargent of Gloucester* . . . It should be added that "five generations of Yankee enterprise came to an end" only in this particular branch of the family. There are still such enterprises as the Patterson Sargent Paint Company; the Sargent Steel Company became the American Brake Shoe Company and the American Foundries. On the Daniel Sargent line, Charles Sprague Sargent was president of the Boston and Albany Railroad before leasing it to the New York Central, and his family is still interested in banking and brokerage.

Mary Singer "painted in watercolor." One of her notebooks was presented to the Metropolitan Museum by her daughter Violet, Mrs. Ormond.

The amount of Mrs. Sargent's income can be established from the will of her father, John Singer, on file in Philadelphia. "I give and bequeath unto my beloved daughter Mary the sum of 10,000 dollars, to be held in trust for her sole use and benefit." Everything else was left to his wife at her discretion; the total value of the estate, filed Jan. 28, 1851, was $77,019.61. Thus her income would compare favorably with that of her husband, as it can be established from his letter to his younger brother Gorham, dated Nice, Feb. 5, 1869: "I think that $700. a year so early in your career is very encouraging. I never made as much, to the best of my recollection, in any one year, from practice alone." The other income to which he alludes would be from his book, and very small.

"his muscles and bones." Letter quoted in Charteris, *op. cit.*

Nice, the Maison Virello. Paraphrased from Vernon Lee, *op. cit.*, and Dr. Sargent's letters, which show that Vernon Lee, working in after years and from memory, was frequently mistaken in place names.

Emily's "strange disease." Details from Dr. Sargent's letters. The disease itself was probably a spinal tuberculosis.

"Poor little Minnie." Letter quoted in Charteris, *op. cit.*

"a squadron of the United States Navy." From an interview with Admiral Goodrich's daughter, Mrs. C. T. Davis. Vernon Lee, *op. cit.*, also provides much material on the attitude of Dr. Sargent, and his wife's ambitions for her son.

"to help his stricken country." Dr. Sargent presented a copy of this book to John Bigelow, U.S. consul at Paris. The copy in the New York Public Library bears such an inscription in his hand, "with the author's compliments," and there is a letter inserted as a fly leaf dated Paris, Oct. 10, 1863, explaining that certain imperfections in the arrangement of the text were occasioned by "the fact that it was printed in London while I was in Switzerland."

The fleas are mentioned by Mrs. Winthrop Chanler in *Roman Spring*, Boston, 1934.

Descriptions of Rome from Dr. Sargent's letters and Vernon Lee. The actual sketches made in the Vatican are now at the Fogg Museum, Cambridge.

"the particular gallery." " . . . this is, if I remember rightly in the third large Italian room, on the left and perhaps opposite the Correggios." Letter in Charteris.

This Tyrol notebook is now in the Metropolitan Museum, part of a large gift from Mrs. Ormond.

Illnesses and servant problem from Dr. Sargent's letters.

CHAPTER TWO

"awkward and gangling." This early awkwardness is best seen in a sketch of him made by Carroll Beckwith, and published in the *Century Magazine*, June 1896, page 171. Also mentioned by Vernon Lee, *op. cit.*

The descriptions of the studio are from Will Low, *A Chronicle of Friendship*, New York, 1908. There are further descriptions in an unpublished attempt at an autobiography begun by Carroll Beckwith shortly before his death in 1917, and now, together with his diaries, in the possession of the National Academy of Design, in New York. Both are remarkably vivid, and with their aid I was able to find the site in September 1954, only to discover that the buildings themselves had been torn down. The alley and surrounding buildings are precisely as they were, however, and examination of the adjoining walls gave a good indication of the proportions of the place as it was. There are numerous contemporary descriptions of Carolus-Duran, especially by Will Low, *op. cit.*, and Beckwith, *op. cit.* Details of the first interview with Carolus-Duran were written by Beckwith for the *Century Magazine*, June 1896. Carolus' verdict is from W. H. Downes, *John S. Sargent, His Life and Work*, Boston, 1925. The initiation of a new student from Will Low, *op. cit.*

Rue Abbatucci. The address from Dr. Sargent's letters; it was incorrectly given as "Rue Abbatrice" by Charteris.

Beckwith recorded the cost of many of his daily items in a small notebook that he purchased in 1877 to use as a diary for his walking trip through Switzerland. Thus we know that on this trip the notebook itself cost 20 centimes, breakfast 1½ francs, beer 60 centimes, cigarettes 55 centimes, dinner 2 francs 5 centimes, and a barber 60 centimes. The 5-franc cost of a model is recorded at this later date, but could not have differed appreciably three years before. In my possession.

"the most advanced studio in Paris." Accounts of Duran's sessions of instruction are in Beckwith, Low, Charteris, and other works. Will Low is especially helpful, as he states very well the advanced category of Carolus' instruction and gives instances of the disapproval of more academic masters at the Ecole des Beaux-Arts. He also mentions the ban on English and Carolus' particular attentions to his students. Accounts of Carolus' early career appear in all these three sources, and also in *M. Carolus Duran*, Ch. M. Widor, Paris, 1918.

"first in the studio." Obituary notice in the *Boston Transcript*.

"Considering that he had made no use of oil." In later years Sargent was himself uncertain when he had done his earliest studies, and dated one sketch, in the possession of the Marchioness of Cholmondeley, both 1873 and 1874. With this exception I can find no indication that he ever handled oils before he began at Carolus' studio in the spring of 1874. Since he brought no oils to show Carolus, only drawings and watercolors, and since none exist which can be dated by subject matter or anything intrinsic earlier than his debut at Carolus', I do not believe he made any previous use of the medium.

Paul Helleu. When preparing his biography, Charteris interviewed Helleu. Attempting to explore further the relationship between Helleu and Sargent during these years, I interviewed the French artist's son, M. Jean Helleu, in Paris, Sept. 20, 1954. As they were young men together and Helleu was always given to adventures, it seemed the Helleu family might know something of Sargent's life. However, the answer was virtually the same as with all of Sargent's friends through his life: "My father told me, 'Of Sargent I know nothing. He is a puritan. . . .'"

Hôtel des Etats-Unis. Hamilton Mechlin, "Early Recollections of Sargent," *Contemporary Revue*, June 1925.

A letter of Monet's, recounting his first meeting with Sargent, is in Charteris.

Description of living in Paris is paraphrased from a letter of Stanford White's, quoted in *Stanford White*, C. C. Baldwin, New York, 1931.

Gustav Natorp is given in Charteris as "Natop." *Royal Academy*, Graves, London, 1905.

The foundation of the Society of American Artists is recounted in *Reminiscences*, St.-Gaudens, New York, 1913. Two copies of the plaque of Frank Millet are owned by his son, Dr. John Alfred Parsons Millet, who supplied information about his father. The watercolor Sargent traded St.-Gaudens for the plaque of Bastien-Lepage was destroyed in a fire in St.-Gaudens' studio.

Naples and Capri. Sargent's letter to Ben del Castillo recounting this episode is in Charteris. The painting *Rosita, Capri* probably represents this same rooftop.

CHAPTER THREE

Sargent's appearances from Hamilton Mechlin, *op. cit.*, who also states that he commented to Sargent on a picture of Carolus', and Sargent responded that he was flattered because he had done the study in question. It bore Carolus' signature, which had been placed on it, according to this explanation, as a compliment by the master. Similar tales are told of old masters, and in this instance the tale does not seem characteristic of either Sargent or Carolus. This judgment was seconded by Mme. Bagues, Carolus' granddaughter, who never heard of him doing such a thing, though he had many pupils and a few special favorites over the years.

The "splendor" in which they lived cannot be better illustrated than by reference to the classic palaces erected in London by Leighton and Tadema. Beckwith, when he first visited Carolus' home, was tremendously impressed and recorded his astonishment in his diary.

Reynolds and Rubens. It has frequently been stated that Sargent was the greatest financial success of all artists, which is far from the fact. Reynolds's estate was estimated in excess of £100,000, or four times that of Sargent, even without computing the change of values. Details of Rubens's practice can be found in *Sir Peter Paul Rubens, as an Artist and a Diplomatist,* W. Noël Sainsbury, London, 1859; Rubens's confession on page 216, in a letter to Sir Balthazar Gerbier.

The best statement of the significance of the Salon is found in *The History of the Impressionists,* John Rewald, New York, 1946.

M. Haro's portrait is presently in storage in the basement of the Petit-Palais, Paris. Carolus' social flair is recorded in *My Diary,* Wilfrid Scawen Blunt, New York, 1921.

M. Jean Louis Vaudoyer, the distinguished critic and author, kindly told me about Roger-Jourdain and his wife. Interview, Oct. 6, 1954.

M. Robert Bourget Pailleron expressed the belief that his grandfather was impressed by reports of Sargent's fame and picked him up because he believed him certain to be a leader of the new generation. Interview, Paris, Oct. 6, 1954.

"two little children's portraits." Details of the contact with Louis Le Camus, and the subsequent painting of these portraits for the Kieffer family, supplied by Mlle. de Valcourt, granddaughter of one of the children painted and daughter of the present owner of the picture.

"when his parents came to Paris that June." "We feel bound to pay John a visit every Spring to see how he is getting on. And on this occasion we were very much gratified with the progress he had evidently made during the year. He sent to the Salon a portrait of his teacher Carolus-Duran, which was considered not only by his artist and other friends, but also by the Paris critics and the public, to be one of the best portraits exposed at this Spring's exhibition. There was always a little crowd around it, and one heard constantly remarks in favor of its excellence. But as the proof of the pudding is in the eating, so the best, or one of the best evidences of a portrait's success is the receiving by the artist of commissions to execute others. And John received six such evidences from French people. He was very busy during the two months we were in Paris." Dr. Sargent's letter to his brother Thomas, dated St.-Gervais, Savoy, Aug. 15, 1879.

"a full-length portrait." Dr. Sargent speaks of this expedition to the family home of the Paillerons' in-laws, the Buloz; and further accounts were written by Marie Louise Pailleron in her book, *Le Paradis Perdu,* Paris, 1947, in which she also speaks of her later sittings in the Paris studio. Sargent's actual host on this occasion was Mme. Pailleron's mother, Mme. Buloz, whom he presented with a bust-length portrait which she thought very unflattering.

I am much indebted to the distinguished psychiatrist, Dr. John Alfred Parsons Millet, for the aid he gave me in unraveling the inner workings of Sargent's mind during this and later periods. Mrs. Francis Behn Riggs told me of the family tradition that Sargent had loved first one then the other sister.

Velásquez at Madrid. Sargent owned a picture by Ch. Daux, *A Study at Ravello,* which appears in the inventory of his estate. He was also at Seville during that winter, where he first met Henry Adams and his wife. *Letters of Mrs. Henry Adams,* Boston, 1936. A series of the wooden panels painted on this trip when presented to the Metropolitan Museum by Mrs. Ormond still had no varnish.

"traveling for each sitting." That this picture was painted at the sitter's home is shown in a letter to Ben del Castillo, given in Charteris. The subsequent trip to Venice with the Subercaseaux family is recounted in *Memorias de Ochenta Anos,* Ramón Subercaseaux, Santiago, Chile, 1936, Vol. I.

"a knocking at the door." M. Robert Bourget Pailleron told me of this incident in his mother's sittings, which is not mentioned in her published memoir. The excerpts from the diary of Henry St. John Smith were supplied by his daughter, Mrs. Henry G. Beyer.

In an interview with Dr. Pozzi's daughter-in-law, Mme. Pozzi, she thought the portrait might have been done because the doctor had treated Sargent professionally. A subsequent letter from her husband, dated Dec. 1, 1954, made no mention of this.

"In honor of my reconciliation." M. Robert Bourget Pailleron has another drawing by Sargent, of two young ladies lying in a haystack, with this same inscription. This second drawing is also humorously marked with labels; thus the scribbles of hay has "foin" written across it in six places, and the parasol is identified in the same way.

"Doubtless he was hasty." When his father arrived in Paris to see the Salon this picture had already been sold. "The picture was imported by Messrs. Schaus & Co., and sold to Mr. Coolidge of Boston." *Art Journal,* New York, 1882, p. 350.

Palazzo Barbaro. Mr. Ralph Curtis, the present owner of the Barbaro, supplied details of his family's connection with it. During the time of Sargent's stay in Venice four of his artist friends were busily engaged on pictures of Robert Browning. The fact that not only Julian Story, Harper Pennington, and Charles Forbes took part in this, but also Ralph Curtis, shows with what seriousness Sargent at this time took his professional standing, refusing to do the uncommissioned work the others obviously felt might be advantageous to them. Nine years later he tried to do Browning on a commissioned basis. *Robert Browning's Portraits, Photographs and Other Likenesses and Their Makers,* Grace Elizabeth Wilson, Baylor University, 1943; which also supplies additional information on Gustav Natorp.

CHAPTER FOUR

Mme. Gautreau is still remembered by Parisian gossip. Some tales of her can be found in an article "The Tragedy of a Queen of Beauty," by Grace Elison, where a photo of her is reproduced; given me as a clipping by Alfred Yockney. Reference to her American birth appears in Seebold's *Old Louisiana Plantation Homes and Family Trees,* Vol. 2, p. 36. Sargent's letters about her to Castillo and Vernon Lee are from Charteris. The portrait was to have been begun in Paris, as is shown in Sargent's letter of Feb. 10, 1883, from Nice: "In a few days I shall be back in Paris, tackling my other 'envoi', the Portrait of a Great Beauty. Do you object to people who are 'fardées' to the extent of being a uniform lavender or blotting paper color all over?" (Charteris) That serious work on the portrait did not begin until the summer is established by a letter of Dr. Sargent's, written at Nice, Nov. 16, 1883. "John is just now in, or near, Florence whither he betook himself a month ago (his native city, you know!) after having passed most of the summer in Brittany at the Château of a Frenchman whose wife's portrait he was painting."

Mrs. Henry White's choice from *Henry White*, Allan Nevins, 1930.

Marie Louise Pailleron wrote of the history of the butterflies, and the case containing them appears in the inventory of Sargent's estate. Henry James's article is preserved in *Picture and Text*, Henry James, London. The letter about Sargent from *The Letters of Henry James*, Percy Lubbock, London, 1920.

That he was "perplexed by difficulties" is still apparent in the portrait. On examination it shows many alterations which form the basis of the analysis of his work on it as given here.

Judith Gautier. The details of her life and descriptions of her Brittany home from *Judith Gautier, sa vie et son œuvre*, Dita Camacho, Paris, 1939. The house was razed by the Germans during their occupation. Judith Gautier herself wrote an account of her first acquaintance with Wagner in *Wagner at Home*, London, 1910. Some of Sargent's later observations concerning Franz Liszt confirm the notion that he heard much about Wagner and his circle from Judith Gautier, who told her friend Mme. Suzanne Meyer-Zundal that it was because he was painting a portrait nearby that Sargent frequently visited her in the summer of 1883; interview with Mme. Meyer-Zundal, Paris, Oct. 5, 1954. Further accounts of this romance in my article "John S. Sargent and Judith Gautier," *Art Quarterly*, Summer 1955, which reproduces the pictures.

"returned to Paris." Albert de Belleroche, *Print Collector's Quarterly*, 13 (1926), gives his recollections of this and later periods as well as reproducing his own sketch of Sargent asleep in his berth on the train during this junket.

Vernon Lee establishes that he continued to work on it in his Paris studio, as does his own letter to Castillo, which gives Carolus' verdict.

The Boulevard Berthier studio had previously been occupied by Maurice Poirson, with whom it seems likely Sargent was acquainted. He rented it from Poirson's brother, to whom it was left after the artist's death, Oct. 15, 1882. The present occupant of the house, M. Malkovsky, kindly showed me through the interior. The sum of three thousand francs is mentioned from memory by Paul Poirson, Sargent's landlord, in a memorandum prepared for the use of his family. Letter from Mlle. Christiane Poirson, Dec. 3, 1954. Mlle. Poirson had previously taken me to the notary who handled the property, a search of whose archives did not shed any light on Sargent's tenancy, though a series of later leases with Boldini, one in particular from 1921, show his rental was twelve thousand francs. Mlle. Poirson thought that considering changes in the value of the franc this supported the figure given her by her father.

This letter to Miss Popert was purchased by Winthrop Sargent in Rome from an autograph dealer, together with the photo of the sketch. The second letter is in the library of the Metropolitan Museum of Art, New York.

The Salon opening is described in a letter of Ralph Curtis's, in Charteris, which also recounts the later events of the day in which Curtis figured. The attendance figures from *L'Artiste*.

I am indebted to M. D. H. Norton for the translation of the verses from their original French:

> O mon cher peintre, je vous jure
> Que je vous aime de tout cœur,
> Mais quelle drôle de figure!
> Mais quelle drôle de couleur!

En vérité, je suis honteuse
De voir, chaque jour, au Salon,
Mes amis, la mine piteuse,
Me détailer de large en long.

"Est-ce bien elle? — Non — Que sais-je?
— C'est elle, voyez le livret!
— Mais alors, c'est un sacrilège!
— Allons! C'est bien elle! Il paraît!"

Il n'y paraît pas, au contraire,
Et j'avais, j'en jure les cieux,
Quand chez vous je me fis portraire,
Rêvé quelque chose de mieux.

Ce fut un grand tort que j'expie;
Mais, tant pis! Chaque jour j'irai
Me placer près de ma copie . . .
Et le mal sera réparé.

The letter to the editor of *Gaulois* in possession of Adeline Roberts, New York.

Mlle. Beatrice Poirson, present owner of the house on the Boulevard Berthier, told me of the circumstances surrounding the painting of her grandmother's picture. An excerpt from a letter of hers, saying substantially the same thing, appeared in the catalogue of the exhibition of *Sargent, Whistler, and Mary Cassatt*, published by the Art Institute of Chicago, 1954. As he had spent a profitable summer in England, and there should have been money available, it would appear he already had been obliged to pay off arrears. Interview, Paris, Oct. 4, 1954.

Unfortunately I was not able to check Vernon Lee's assertion that he posed for Besnard. A little later he painted a picture of the Besnard family around the birthday cake of their son, the circumstances surrounding which are explained in a letter of Besnard's in *L'Art and L'Artiste*, May 1928. The four drawings for which Besnard says this group was traded appear in the inventory of Sargent's estate, and are dated 1886.

"a double portrait." This picture appears to have been designed almost as a study in composition, and in particular as a reflection of the devices employed in Velásquez's *Prince Felipe Prospero*.

One of the two pictures for which the piano was traded was subsequently purchased by the Worcester Art Museum from the dealer W. Macbeth, of New York. Mr. Macbeth, in his own letter to the Museum of March 2, 1912, quotes a letter he received from Sargent dated Feb. 28, 1896: "The pictures you refer to were both painted in Venice some fifteen years ago. I gave them to their late owner in exchange for a piano of his make." The piano is the same which subsequently figured in Tite Street. It appears in his estate inventory as "an upright pianoforte in ebonized case by C. Bechstein."

CHAPTER FIVE

Besnard's experience in England is in *Albert Besnard*, Roger Marx, Paris, 1893.

"brought forth praise." *Gazette des Beaux-Arts*, Vol. 31, June 1885.

Information concerning the Playfairs from *Memoirs and Correspondence of Lyon Playfair, Lord Playfair of St. Andrews, G.C.B.*, Wemyss Reid, London, Paris, New York, and Melbourne, 1899. It is interesting to note that most of the people Sargent knew at this time in England had American connections.

The conditions of the commission to paint Stevenson were told me by Miss Sally Fairchild, Charles Fairchild's daughter. *The Stevensons*, by Laura L. Hinckley, New York, 1950, supplies an account of Louis's romance where it is left off by Will Low. The "charming, simple . . . " from *The Strange Case of Robert Louis Stevenson*, Malcolm Elwin, London, 1950. An edited text of Stevenson's second letter on Sargent also appears there. The original form, as used here, was kindly supplied me by Bradford A. Booth, who is preparing a collection of Stevenson's letters. The relations with Henry James from *Henry James and R.L.S.*, J. A. Smith, London, 1948, and from *The Letters of Henry James*.

Mrs. J. Comyns Carr, in her *Reminiscences*, speaks of this first meeting with Sargent (London, undated). Accounts of her home from *With Brush and Pencil*, G. P. Jacomb-Hood, London (undated), and mentioned to me by the poet Leonora Speyer, who as a young violinist stayed there.

"abuse" from the *Art Journal*, New York, 1884.

Though it is the recollection of his friends that he lived at the Arts Club, it seems likely that the Club was only his headquarters, and that he lived in various locations about London before taking the larger studio in Tite Street. Bailey's Hotel, Gloster Road, and 17B Elson Road, South Kensington, are addresses which appear on his letters.

Broadway. Much information concerning Broadway is contained in *Edwin Austin Abbey, R.A.* by E. V. Lucas, London and New York, 1921, and *Life and Letters of Sir Edmund Gosse*, by the Hon. Evan Charteris, London. The original large proportion of the garden picture was sketched by Sargent in a letter to his sister (Charteris) and is mentioned in a letter of Abbey's (Lucas). Quotation from Dr. Millet, whose sister Kate has never forgotten the tragedy of her replacement in the picture. That the lilies were painted from a few potted plants is shown by a study in the possession of Dr. Millet, and the photo of Sargent at work which is reproduced, in which they are raised onto a chair.

The letter to Edward Russell in the possession of the Tate Gallery.

"go into business." Winthrop Sargent, Jr., assured me that there were various business opportunities which might have been opened to him in Philadelphia at that time had his father requested that his uncle find a place for him. Most likely was a connection with the Pennsylvania Railroad, in the management of which members of the family long figured.

"willful destruction of his work." By working over the same canvas day after day he was also practicing a form of economy. His care in the use of canvas is notable at this time, especially when he tried to do a portrait of Mrs. Barnard over a piece cut from the garden picture. The catalogue shows how few of his student efforts remain, implying that in his Paris years, and perhaps later, he re-used these unsatisfactory canvases as well, which is corroborated by the number of pictures from this period which appear to have other studies beneath their present surface.

"a second trip to Bournemouth." Two unfixed charcoal sketches for this second portrait are in a sketchbook at the Fogg Museum.

"a thorn in his side." Charteris states that his move to London in 1885 ended his association with Paris, but Dr. Sargent's letter of May 13, 1886, from 4

Rue Longchamp, Nice, states: "John has just left us after a visit of a couple of weeks: he is very well. He spent last winter in London, and is about moving his traps from Paris to London, where he expects to reside instead of Paris, and where he thinks he will find more work to do than in the latter place. He seems to have a good many friends in London, and appears to be very favorably known there. London is a world in itself, with its 4½ millions of people."

Jacomb-Hood, *op. cit.*, mentions the studio upstairs in 33 Tite Street, as well as the initial reaction to him on the street.

Edwin H. Blashfield's account of work on the garden picture from *Commemorative Tribute to Sargent*, New York, 1926.

"the novelist's fussy ways." One imitation of Henry James is recalled by John Bailey, *Letters and Diaries*, London, 1935. He met Sargent at the Athenaeum Club, Feb. 13, 1923, and Sargent spoke "with considerable effect."

Mrs. Gardner was brought to Sargent's attention by both James and Ralph Curtis, and in his first letter to her states they had both "authorized me to call on you."

Jacomb-Hood's recollection of his London work on *Carnation Lily, Lily Rose* in *Cornhill Magazine*, September 1925. In the photo reproduced of Sargent at work on the picture at Broadway there is a larger section of lilies at top than now remains.

Lily Millet's birthday party recounted in Mrs. Carr's *Reminiscences*. Dr. Millet filled in many details for me; the placecards are now in his possession.

George Henschel's recollections of his first meeting with Sargent, and the work done on the river that summer, in his *Musings and Memories of a Musician*, London, 1918. Sargent's own letter to Monet in Charteris.

Development of the New English Art Club from *Life, Work and Setting of Philip Wilson Steer*, D. S. MacColl, London, 1946. In 1888, Sargent and Clausen tied at 44 votes for the Committee of the Club, and were far and away the most popular members inside the Club.

The price of £700 given for *Carnation Lily, Lily Rose* from an unidentified clipping, Journalism Library, Columbia University.

"it was hailed" in the *Art Journal*, New York, 1862, p. 350.

Marquand's invitation and Sargent's mild subterfuge are mentioned by Charteris, and unfortunately I was unable to locate any actual correspondence. The mass of Marquand papers were given the Library of Princeton University, where Mr. Alexander P. Clark, Curator of Manuscripts, informed me that little was known of their contents. At his suggestion I contacted Mrs. Douglas Delanoy, Marquand's granddaughter, who in her letter of Aug. 16, 1954, mentioned that her grandfather was acquainted with Tadema and Leighton, but could throw no further light on the matter.

"three thousand dollars" was the price he received during his first two expeditions to the United States, and probably on the third as well, as it was the price quoted Vanderbilt in 1896 for painting Marquand; Archives, Metropolitan Mueseum.

CHAPTER SIX

The stay at the Torpedo Station was recounted to me by Mrs. Goodrich's daughter, Mrs. C. T. Davis. Descriptions of Newport are paraphrased from *Backward Glance*, Edith Wharton, New York, 1934.

The note was to Mrs. Gardner, the second of 196 he was to write her during his lifetime and which are preserved at Fenway Court in Boston.

"a tour of studios." Beckwith's diary, which frequently accounts for Sargent's whereabouts in day-to-day fashion.

The letter from Frank Millet is in C. C. Baldwin's *Stanford White*, which gives many of the earlier details of White's life.

Mrs. Gardner's difficult posing habits from *Isabella Stewart Gardner and Fenway Court*, Morris Carter, Boston and New York, 1925. Her relations with Dennis Miller Bunker are mentioned in *Dennis Miller Bunker*, R. H. Ives Gammell, New York, 1953, and are also reflected in his letters to her, preserved at Fenway Court. Her affair with Crawford from *Proper Bostonians*, Cleveland Amory, New York, 1947.

The meeting with Loeffler from Charteris, with further information got from Loeffler's letters to Mrs. Gardner, also preserved at Fenway Court.

The opening of the St. Botolph exhibition is described in *Sarah Orne Jewett*, by F. O. Matthieson (undated). That it took place Jan. 30 rather than the previous December was discovered by Channing C. Simmons, Secretary of the Club, who searched the records at my request in March 1952.

The dinners given by Stanford White for Sargent are mentioned in Beckwith's diary, so that we know only of those he attended. Mr. Dave Hennen Morris confirmed the closeness between White and Colonel Shepard at this time, while White was building Scarborough for him, and also recounted the origin of his mother's portrait during the difficulties encountered with his grandmother's. Telephone, July 7, 1954.

Mrs. Gardner's dealings with Ralph Curtis from *Isabella Stewart Gardner and Fenway Court*. That Curtis found them profitable was confirmed by his son, Ralph Curtis, during an interview in Paris, Sept. 29, 1954.

The New York newspapers reported of *Mme. Gautreau* that it showed Sargent "unduly influenced by the prevailing French artistic fashion of painting mere realism to the exclusion of all else." *Art Journal*.

McKim's relations with the great number of artists and sculptors for whom he played King Midas are not treated in the only biography of him, *The Life and Times of Charles Follen McKim*, Charles Moore, Boston and New York, 1929, undertaken by Moore under subsidy from McKim's daughter, who supplied the materials with which he worked. These were later deposited in the New York Public Library. However, in the back it lists the firm's jobs for which McKim was personally responsible, a remarkably high percentage of which can be attached to a Sargent portrait.

CHAPTER SEVEN

The luncheon with the Henschels is described in *When Soft Voices Die*, Helen Henschel, London, 1944.

Macbeth's reception is set forth at length in *Sir Henry Irving*, Lawrence Irving, London, 1951; Sargent's capricious acceptance was remembered by Mrs. Carr, *op. cit.*, while Ellen Terry's sittings are recounted in *The Story of My Life*, Ellen Terry, New York, 1908, and *The Diary of Ellen Terry*, New York, 1933, from which Sargent's attempts to get Irving to pose also are drawn.

Accounts of the Chelsea Arts Club are from Jacomb-Hood's *With Brush and Pencil*, and the memories of Mr. Dean Cornwell, N.A., who, though a member at a later date, heard much of Sargent's attendance in previous times.

Browning's relations with Natorp can be found in *The New Letters of Robert Browning*, DeVane and Knickerbocker, 1950, where he also recounts his meeting with Sargent and their conversation. The incident wherein Pen Browning preserved Sargent's "autograph and scratch of a drawing" on the wall of the Rezzonico is presumably the origin of the similar incident George Du Maurier employed a few years later in his novel *Trilby*.

"they scintillate with sunlight" was the opinion of the *Magazine of Art*, May 1889.

That very few people gave him "credit for insides" was mentioned by Sargent in a letter to Mrs. Van Rensselaer, in Charteris. Though in the context he was referring specifically to critical writings about his paintings, the letter seems to carry further overtones.

Descriptions of the International Exhibition paraphrased from "Carmencita and Her Painters," Lida Rose McCabe, *New York Times Book Review and Magazine*, July 8, 1923. Sargent confirmed to her that he had first seen Carmencita in Paris in a letter dated Jan. 24, 1917, in which he also says, "I think I must have painted her before Chase, because I only learned from your letter that Chase did paint her"(!). The notebook in which he attempted to sketch the Javanese dancers is in the Metropolitan Museum.

Gabriel Fauré's son, M. Philippe Fauré-Frémiet was unable to throw any light on when his father and Sargent first met. Interview, Paris, Sept. 21, 1954.

The fund raising for the purchase of the *Olympia* is covered at length in *Claude Monet, sa vie, son temps, son œuvre*, Gustave Geffroy, Paris, 1922, in which the lists of contributors and Mme. Manet's letter are given. A further letter of Sargent's telling Monet whom he has approached and the amounts they promised is in Charteris. Sargent owned a watercolor of Iris which was given him by Manet, with whom he appears to have been friendly, and also a study for the *Balcony*, which possibly was given him by Mme. Manet at this time.

The Fladbury Rectory was very accurately mirrored by Abbey in a letter written while he stayed there (Lucas). Further memories of it were given me by Miss Sally Fairchild. When I visited it in September 1954 I was surprised at the accuracy of what Abbey had written. An account of her stay there with Kit Anstruther-Thomson was written by Vernon Lee in *Art and Man*, London, 1924. That she was "all bones and art" was the happy expression of Sir Gerald Kelly.

Helleu's pastel study of his wife, reflecting a simultaneous composition of Sargent's, is owned by his son, M. Jean Helleu, Paris.

The Mote House period from Mrs. Carr's *Reminiscences*.

CHAPTER EIGHT

That Sargent arrived in December rather than January is shown by the Beckwith diaries. The studio he took belonged to Mrs. Candace Wheeler; *Carmencita and Her Painters*. His call on Booth was written of by Booth to his daughter; *Edwin Booth*, Edwina Booth Grossman, New York, 1894. The advice of T. B. Aldrich from his wife's *Crowding Memories*, Boston and New York, 1920. I have never succeeded in understanding how Sargent managed to paint in The Players' fireplace; the room itself is too dark for him to have worked in, and it would have required transporting a very large unfinished canvas down from 23rd Street, then back again, where it was first viewed by the Committee.

Still, it appears to have been painted "from life," and I know of no sketch from which it might have been done.

Carmencita's dance and conversation from clippings in the Music and Theatre Collections of the New York Public Library; the jewelry she was acquiring was worn when she was photographed by Sarony. Sargent's admission of the costliness from Charteris, his change of address shows in the letters to Chase. Beckwith records that it was a stiffish party, of which further descriptions were supplied Charteris by Mrs. de Glehn, who was present. Sargent's second party is mentioned by Mrs. Daniel Chester French in *Memories of a Sculptor's Wife*, New York, 1928, and is not to be confused with the descriptions of Beckwith's initial party written by J. J. Chapman in *J. J. Chapman and His Letters*, M. A. De Wolfe Howe, Boston, 1937. Chase's portrait of Carmencita is in the Metropolitan Museum, the head and the indistinct drawing of the hands reflecting the imperfections of Sarony's photographs.

CHAPTER NINE

The difficulties of obtaining funds for the Boston Public Library murals is touched on in *The Life and Times of Charles Follen McKim* and *Stanford White*. Many of McKim's letters to his associates are in the New York Historical Society, some of which show that he was carrying the project for short periods on his own slim savings rather than suspend work. McKim's letter to the Trustees is in Charteris and Abbey's letter is in Lucas.

The computations from dollars to pounds to francs was described by Sargent to Miss Sally Fairchild, who told me of them. Miss Fairchild also provided information concerning the stay at Nahant, and photos of Sargent lying in the grass before the house with her younger brother Gordon are in a scrapbook owned by Mrs. Richard W. Hale.

CHAPTER TEN

The mummies were mentioned by Miss Sally Fairchild; other geographic references from Charteris. Most of his sketches from this trip now in the Fogg Museum.

That Reed's portrait was painted in his studio is mentioned by Belleroche, *op. cit.* The letter showing Charles Fairchild's part from *Thomas B. Reed, Parliamentarian*, William A. Robinson, New York, 1930. I was unable to define Lodge's role because his papers, in the Massachusetts Historical Society, have been closed. Reed's own letter from *Memoirs of an Editor*, Edward P. Mitchell, New York, 1924.

Whistler's entrances into Tite Street are given in an article by Sargent's valet, Nicola D'Inverno, *Boston Sunday Advertiser*, Feb. 7, 1926. The account of the two dinners at Foyot's from *The Life and Times of Charles Follen McKim*, and corroborated by Mr. Lawrence Grant White, who in a letter dated June 9, 1954, mentioned that McKim had told him the same story.

The episode of the boots recalled by G. P. Jacomb-Hood, *op. cit.* Charteris is authority for the story of the farmer; Henry Adams's letter published in *Henry Adams and His Friends*, Harold Dean Cater, Boston, 1947.

Sargent's letter to McKim from *The Life and Times of Charles Follen McKim*. Preparatory drawings for Beckwith's murals are in the Cooper Union Museum, New York.

The letter to the National Academy of Design in their files.

That *A Street in Venice* was presented to his father by the Misses Chanler was told me by Lawrence Grant White in his letter of Aug. 24, 1953.

W. Graham Robertson's memoirs were published as *Life Was Worth Living*, London, 1939, and also contain the letter from Ada Rehan. Four of Sargent's letters to Mrs. Whitin were published in *Art in America*, July 1941.

The *Carmencita* had been sold to the Luxembourg in November of 1892, after appearing at an exhibition of the Société Nationale des Beaux-Arts. M. Germain Bazin, Curator of Paintings and Drawings, in his letter of Dec. 21, 1954, because of the regulations was unable to tell me the actual price, but the Luxembourg policy of paying little and conferring much honor is well known.

Sir William Rothenstein's *Men and Memories*, New York, 1937, is the source of Sargent's letter to him, as well as much other material invaluable for understanding this period. There are numerous accounts of the failure of *Guy Domville;* I have relied principally on that contained in Robertson's memoirs.

CHAPTER ELEVEN

That Sargent went to the expense of having his murals mounted on a vaulted support for their showing at the Royal Academy is proved by photographs of them taken while they hung in place, which are now in the Frick Art Reference Library. The place in which the photographs were taken was unknown, but comparison of the skylight and background moldings appearing in the pictures prove it is the Royal Academy. Sargent's requests for this special position, that he be allowed to bring an assistant to help assemble the panels, and that he be allowed to photograph them in place, all appear in the Council minutes of the Royal Academy. Doubtless he hoped he might for his pains attract further mural work in England, in which he was disappointed.

The portrait of Patmore is yet another that Sargent undertook because of the prominence of the sitter. He had asked Gosse to see if he could get Patmore to sit; Patmore's reply was in part: "He seems to me to be the greatest, not only of living English portrait painters, but of *all* English portrait painters; and to be thus *invited* to sit to him for my picture is among the most signal honours I have ever received." Letter dated May 9, 1894, in *Memoirs and Correspondence of Coventry Patmore*, Basil Champneys, London, 1900. A further letter of September 7 tells Gosse the picture is finished. His inclusion among the prophets contained in *Life and Times of Coventry Patmore*, Derek Patmore, London, 1949.

An enlightening discussion of the London model hierarchy is given in *Victorian Olympus*, William Gaunt, London and New York. Colarossi modeled also for Frank Millet at Broadway, and photos of him there are in the possession of Dr. Millet. Nicola D'Inverno's arrival was recounted by him in his memoir, *op. cit.* Sargent noted "Nicola D'Inverno, 189 High Holborn, Saturday" inside the cover of his sketchbook; now in the Metropolitan Museum.

The installation of the Boston murals explained in Lucas. The lists of invitations, and replies, for this Boston Social of McKim's now in the New York Public Library. Sargent's encounter with the elderly lady is mentioned by McKim in his letter of Dec. 19, 1896, in *Life and Times of Charles Follen McKim*.

Abbey's letter from Lucas. The talk of a portrait and the incident of touching a wet picture mentioned by Lawrence Grant White in his letter of Aug. 24, 1953.

Henry James's description of Biltmore from *The Letters of Henry James*. I am obligated to Laura Wood Roper, who is writing a biography of Frederick Law Olmsted, for providing the dates of Sargent's stay with Vanderbilt. Her letter, May 18, 1953.

Sargent's passage to Spain was the occasion of his meeting with Dr. J. William White; *J. William White*, Agnes Repplier, New York, 1919.

It is possible that Mrs. Hunter and Sargent actually met in Venice at the Curtis'; this was the recollection of Lady Cholmondeley, who was friendly with them both, though I was unable to confirm it. Much information concerning her can be found in her sister Ethel Smyth's various books of memoirs: *A Three Legged Tour of Greece*, London, 1927; *What Happened Next*, London, New York, Toronto, 1940; *As Time Went On*, London, 1936; *Female Pipings in Eden*, London, 1933; *Impressions That Remained*, London, 1919, and *Streaks of Life*, London, 1921; as well as Edith Wharton's *Backward Glance*. Sargent's direct "You ought to have her paint your children" was told me by the poet Leonora Speyer, who figures in this book as Lady Speyer. That the approach was successful is still proved by the portrait of her three daughters done by Mrs. Swynnerton.

Ethel Smyth's conducting was done at private concerts given in the Speyers' London home.

Mr. Lord kindly gave me his recollections of Sargent when I stopped at his tobacco shop after visiting the Fulham Road studio, Aug. 24, 1954.

His literary tastes are spoken of by Ethel Smyth, *op cit.*, and Eliza Wedgwood, in a memorandum she prepared for the use of Charteris in 1925, a copy of which is now in the Frick Art Reference Library.

Gabriel Fauré's own references to his stays at Tite Street can be found in *Lettres Intimes*, Philippe Fauré-Frémiet, Paris, 1951. In an interview (see p. 414) M. Fauré-Frémiet gave Sargent tremendous credit for his father's early acceptance in London, even believing Sargent had managed to arrange for a recital his father gave at Buckingham Palace.

Percy Grainger's memoir of Sargent is contained in Charteris.

The curious dichotomy of belief about Sargent still persists in London, where many people who remember him hotly maintain one or the other thesis. The letters to Mary Hunter are now in possession of her granddaughter, Miss Elizabeth Williamson.

Emily Sargent was famous within her own circle for her wit, and her brother frequently asked friends, "Have you heard Emily's latest?" Her letters are unlike her talk in that respect, for they are the quiet expressions of a very sympathetic personality. One of her tearful eruptions is recalled by Eliza Wedgwood, *op. cit.* Mrs. Campbell's tease is from *Naphthali*, C. Lewis Hind, London.

Henry Adams's unusual attempt at praise from *Henry Adams and His Friends*.

Emil Fuchs's recollections are published as *With Brush, Pencil and Chisel* (undated). Sargent's invitation to him is in the New York Public Library.

The rumored engagement to Ena Wertheimer was mentioned by her husband, Robert Mathias, Esq. The idea that Sargent was in love with her was persisted in by her sister Betty for many years after. He doubtless was attracted to her, as he was to many women, and wrote her a series of letters now in the possession of her husband. As the principal members of the Wertheimer family have passed on, I was unable to confirm definitely on what basis so many portraits were painted, though when I explained the probability to several of Wertheimer's grandchildren they each mentioned they thought they had heard some such thing.

The letter to Stanford White from *Stanford White*.

The catalogue of the Copley Hall Exhibition is in the New York Public Library. The request of the Philadelphia Museum, and its subsequent exhibition of Wertheimer alone, reported in the *Philadelphia Times*, Aug. 30, 1899.

The reporter's visit to Tite Street, and Sargent's response to his obituaries, given in the *New York Sun*, April 14, 1899.

The third description of Sargent from *My Diary*, Wilfrid Scawen Blunt, which also provides details of the Wyndhams' sittings. Two snapshots of him at "Temple" were shown me by Robert Mathias, Esq.

I do not know for certain when the purchase of number 31 took place, but the earliest change I find on his stationery is in 1901.

Major Higginson's letter to McKim is in the New York Public Library.

Ribblesdale's sittings recounted in *Impressions and Memories*, Lord Ribblesdale, London, 1927. Sargent had actually solicited Ribblesdale to sit when he spoke for the Artists' Benevolent Fund some three or four years prior to the time the picture was undertaken.

The stay at Welbeck from the *Memoirs of the Duke of Portland* (undated).

I was told of the little gathering at the Arts Club in a letter from Sir Sydney Cockerell, dated May 2, 1953.

The Prince of Wales's astonishing question from *J. William White*. This commission to Abbey seems to have bearing on the report of March 13, 1901, that King Edward had commissioned Sargent to do his portrait. (Clipping in Journalism Library, Columbia University.) No such picture was done, and I was assured by Sir Owen Morshead, Librarian of the Royal Archives, that no record of any such commission has survived, "and I think it would have." Sir Owen thought it very unlikely that this first portrait after King Edward's accession, and thus an official state portrait, would have been "passed over the whole body of English painters in favour of an American." Letter, July 7, 1954. Regardless, in the case of Abbey the entire body of English painters were passed over, and King Edward's regard for Sargent is shown in his remarks and his later desire to knight him. It therefore seems likely that at least unofficial overtures were made, the length of Sargent's sittings perhaps proving an impossible condition.

The "four beautiful faces" letter from *Time Remembered*, Frances, Lady Horner, London (undated). Chase's letter from William Merritt Chase, Katherine M. Roof, New York, 1917.

The letter to Alfred Wertheimer appears to have been passed on to his sister Ena, for it is now in the possession of Robert Mathias, Esq., together with Sargent's letters to her and the Rothenstein lithograph inscribed to Alfred.

CHAPTER TWELVE

McKim's exhorting letter from *The Life and Times of Charles Follen McKim*, which also has Mrs. Roosevelt's letter about pictures. Abbey's picture *Fiammetta's Song* did arrive safely, and McKim's client was Henry A. C. Taylor, who then commissioned two companion pictures from Abbey: *A Poet* and *A Measure* (Lucas). In 1905 McKim also equipped him with a Sargent portrait.

Theodore Roosevelt's three letters are in the Theodore Roosevelt Collection, Harvard College Library, which also has his covering letter to Henry White and the dispatch to Kermit.

The announcements of his plans and the *New York Times* editorial in clippings, Journalism Library, Columbia University.

Pierside interview in unidentified clipping, in my possession.

The lunch at Satterlee's from Beckwith's diary.

Mrs. Endicott and Mrs. Warren kindly gave me details of their sittings, June 9, 1954. Sargent had at first refused to take on the portrait of Mrs. Warren until his return to Boston from Washington. Some years ago she mentioned to Dr. Millet that she had deliberately sat next to him at a party at Mrs. Sears' for the purpose of inducing him to begin before he left. Dr. Millet thought Sargent's irresolution on this point, and his ultimate accession to her wishes, was expressive of continued anxieties over how long he might remain fashionable.

Ethel Smyth is authority for all Boston incidents in which she and Mrs. Hunter figure.

The Tintoretto from *Isabella Stewart Gardner and Fenway Court*. I did not find this letter among those preserved at Fenway Court.

The exploration of the White House from *Across the Busy Years*, Nicholas Murray Butler, New York and London, 1940, Vol. II.

The note to John Hay in possession of Mrs. James W. Wadsworth.

Sargent mentioned feeling "like a rabbit" in a letter to James Ford Rhodes, dated April 19 (1920), in the Massachusetts Historical Society, which also has Henry Adams's mention of the snow in a letter of February 22.

Sargent's interview concerning the Roosevelt portrait in the *World*, March 29, 1903.

Information concerning the exercises at the University of Pennsylvania was provided me by Edward F. Lane, Assistant Secretary of the university, in his letter of June 1, 1954. *Leonard Wood, A Biography*, Hermann Hagedorn, New York and London, 1931, is the source for the meeting at Philadelphia and the subsequent painting of the portrait. I have taken the liberty of changing the Sargent quotation on p. 403 of this book from "Do you think he would *let* me paint him?" to "Do you think he would *want* me to paint him?" in the belief that Sargent desired to do a commissioned portrait, which this second wording solicits. The "bananas" supplied by Martin Birnbaum in *John Singer Sargent, A Conversation Piece*, New York, 1941.

Henry Adams's appraisal of Sargent's call from *The Letters of Henry Adams*, Boston, 1930. That Adams habitually received in his library mentioned in John Hay, William Roscoe Thayer, New York, 1916.

The *World* mentions the secrecy surrounding Roosevelt's picture before its public view.

The Redemption criticized in *Boston Daily Advertiser*, March 7, 1903.

The prices sent John Lambert now in the Library, Princeton University.

That McKim arranged Major Higginson's sittings mentioned in *The Life and Times of Charles Follen McKim;* further authority on Higginson is *Henry Lee Higginson,* Bliss Perry, Boston, 1921.

Sargent's request for the obscure Eakins from *Modern American Painting,* Peyton Boswell, Jr., New York, 1940. Dr. White's disinterest in Eakins's portraiture from *Eakins,* Lloyd Goodrich, New York, 1933.

The student with the "intelligent question" was Mr. Joseph Cummings Chase, who told me of the experience.

Sargent mentions the fact that the Wideners were being done at home in one of his letters to Mrs. Gardner.

Riley's sittings from the *Letters of J. W. Riley,* Indianapolis, 1917; description of his voice from a 1909 recording.

Portrait of Mrs. White and accompanying letters from *J. William White.*

Little Kate Haven, now Mrs. William Osborn, remembered that her picture was done in the morning of the day Sargent sailed.

CHAPTER THIRTEEN

The morning ritual at Tite Street from the memoir by Nicola D'Inverno, *op. cit.* The estate inventory specifies where each article of furnishing stood, and further impressions of the house at this period were given me by Leonora Speyer and Lady Gosford. The roll-top desk was shown me by Mrs. Ormond in her sitting room, August 1954. Sir Gerald Kelly, who received frequent summons, recalled Nicola's form of invitation. Interview, Oct. 8, 1954.

The "completely unconscious" Duchess from *King George VI,* Hector Bolitho, Philadelphia and New York, 1938. Jenkinson's sittings from *Francis Jenkinson,* H. F. Stewart, Cambridge, 1926. Pulitzer from a letter to the editor of the *London Sunday Times,* published Feb. 2, 1926.

Leonora Speyer has kindly given me her recollections of Sargent in many conversations. Her ovation at Queen's Hall, which she never mentioned, from *Memoirs,* Henry J. Wood, London, 1938.

Elsie Swinton's sittings from a letter of hers in W. H. Downes, *op. cit.*

Mrs. Ernest Franklin's sittings from Winslow Wilson's letter of Jan. 29, 1955.

The *Four Doctors* from the *Johns Hopkins Alumni Magazine,* Vol. II, November 1913–June 1914; *William Henry Welch,* Simon Flexner and James T. Flexner, New York, 1941; *The Life of Sir William Osler,* Harvey Cushing, New York, 1940.

The letter concerning changes from Charteris. One such gesture with the presentation of a frame is recounted by Sir Osbert Sitwell in *Right Hand, Left Hand,* Boston, 1944, and has been mentioned to me by numerous of his sitters.

According to the estate inventory, one small room of his house contained 126 carved frames he had collected and 21 were in other parts of the house.

Mr. Timothy Cole, N.A., gave me his recollections of this call on Sargent in January 1954.

The use of Marlborough's robes for *A Vele Gonfie* was recounted by Robert Mathias, Esq., who also explained the swordlike object at the lower right of the picture as a broom handle which Mrs. Mathias held under her cloak to simulate the movement Sargent wanted to convey in its folds!

The "boy keeps getting older" from *Ananias or the False Artist,* Walter Pach, New York and London, 1928, which also quotes his refusal to sell. His refusal to part with his works at this time was consistent. In June of 1908 the Carfax Gallery in London held an exhibition of 46 watercolors, of which he would not sell any. The exhibition also included his *Nude Egyptian Girl,* one of the *Javanese Dancers,* and the *Mme. Gautreau;* clipping from *New York Daily Telegram* at Journalism Library, Columbia University, which also has clipping from the *New York Herald* which shows that in 1903 he held his first one-man show in England, this time also refusing to sell any of the works included.

A copy of this letter to Miss Popert was given me by Winthrop Sargent, Jr.

Lady Speyer's hesitation about mentioning her pearls to Sargent told me by her sister, Mrs. Paul Fande. Interview, June 11, 1954.

All the various Endicott letters from Sargent and reporting on the sittings in the Massachusetts Historical Society.

Mrs. Patrick Campbell's second round from *Haply I May Remember,* Lady Cynthia Asquith, London, 1950. Sargent's pronunciation of "dae*mons*" brought to my attention by Miss Elizabeth Williamson, his only intimate to initiate mention of his voice. I had asked numerous people, all of whom agreed it was of a middle register and pleasant tone. She added that it seemed to rise from his chest with a certain richness and was an important part of his personal charm.

The Sitwell affair from *Right Hand, Left Hand.*

This further technical analysis of the portrait of Mme. Gautreau, like that given in Chapter Four, is based upon examination of the many changes which can be seen in the work. The area surrounding her right arm is particularly labored, showing a series of ridges where the edge of the arm was at various times in the course of the work. The change in the position of the table is shown by ridges under the present surface, following the present highlight on the table's edge, indicating where it had formerly been. The surface of the *Wyndham Sisters* likewise tells its own story, with the added help of some preliminary compositional sketches in one of the notebooks now at the Fogg Museum. The order in which the portraits were done is specified in *My Diary,* Wilfrid Scawen Blunt.

R. A. M. Stevenson's mention of Mrs. White from the *Art Journal.* An engraving accompanying this article shows that at the time it was first exhibited the portrait was much different from its present state. The head was then in front face rather than three-quarter view, the fan was held open rather than closed, and the lower parts of the skirt had not yet been covered in halftone. The technique of the present head indicates that the changes must have been made about the time Sargent was first established in England. The original head has begun to come through the background covering it.

CHAPTER FOURTEEN

King Edward's letters from *King Edward VII,* Sir Sidney Lee, New York, 1927, Vol. II; Sargent's reply from Charteris.

The minutes of the Council of the Royal Academy note Sargent's first report on the schools; it was a subject he returned to at later times. The "frequent and ineffectual advocate" letter to MacColl in the possession of René MacColl.

The dichotomy of opinions concerning Sargent is well set forth in "The Art of J. S. Sargent, R.A.," by A. L. Baldry, *Studio,* March 1900.

That he was "too sensitive an artist to be able to hide the fact that he was bored" was the perceptive thought of Sir Gerald Kelly, in his letter of June 29, 1954. The refusal of an Embassy dinner from *J. William White.* The remark about "regain my manhood" was made to Leonora Speyer. The quote to Lady Lewis from Charteris. "NOT THE HUMAN FACE" from *Sargent, Whistler and Mary Cassatt.* "Parthian shot" letter in the possession of Ralph Curtis.

The letter to Roller in Charteris. Sargent did, however, compromise with the Kaiser's wishes by sending eight portraits to the 1907–8 exhibition of the Prussian Academy of Arts, and was appointed a member of the Academy at the close of the exhibition on Jan. 10, 1908. Letter from the office of the Senator for Cultural Affairs of the City of Berlin, dated Nov. 29, 1954. It was the recollection of Robert Mathias, Esq., that one of his pictures had been borrowed for this purpose that began my inquiries.

The "too broad" designs at the Fogg Museum; the "no miraculous draught" letter from Charteris.

His offer to set up with Emily in Tite Street and her fear he acted from pity later told by Emily to Eliza Wedgwood, *op. cit.* The will of Mary Newbold Sargent on file in Philadelphia.

The transaction of the Boldini portrait from the records of the Brooklyn Museum. Healy acquired it Oct. 23, 1909, directly from Helleu, and his letter of transference to the Museum is dated Nov. 12, 1909.

The portrait of Dr. White from *J. William White.*

The Sargent Sale at Christies' is characterized in *A Story of Christies,* Percy Colson, London, 1950. A priced catalogue is in the New York Public Library, and further information was provided by Sir Alec Martin. Interview, Sept. 7, 1954.

Roger Fry's impertinence from the columns of the *Nation,* Jan. 7, 1911. Fry made a lame attempt at explanation, claiming he had in his possession a letter from Sargent expressing admiration of Cézanne, which undoubtedly was nothing more than Sargent's polite refusal to join the sponsoring committee. *Nation,* Jan. 14, 1911. Authority for Fry's life is *Roger Fry,* Virginia Woolf, New York, 1940, and Will Rothenstein, *op. cit.* Sargent's appearance at the exhibition from *Naphthali.* Fry's final war dance in *Transformations,* Roger Fry, London, 1926. "That Sargent was taken for an artist will perhaps seem incredible to the rising generation, but I can testify to the fact. . . ." Sargent's letter to MacColl in possession of René MacColl.

CHAPTER FIFTEEN

Sargent in the Tyrol mostly drawn from an article by Adrian Stokes in the *Old Water Color Society Club Third Annual Volume, 1925–26.* It was verified by Mr. Thad Page, of the National Archives, where the correspondence Sargent had with the American Embassy at Vienna now reposes. Letter of Aug. 16, 1954. Photostats of the applications for passports filled in by Sargent were supplied me by Mrs. R. B. Shipley, Director, Passport Office, Department of State.

England in wartime from *The Life of Henry Tonks,* Joseph Hone, London, 1939. Henry James under siege told me by Leonora Speyer and Mrs. Richard W. Hale.

The second Red Cross Sale from a letter of Sargent's, Dec. 13, 1917, to C. Powell Minnigerode of the Corcoran Gallery, now in their archives.

Notes

Diplomatic correspondence over the German honors from *The Life and Letters of Walter Hines Page*, Burton J. Hendrick, New York, 1925. Sargent did carry out his intention of resigning, though at a later date. A letter has recently been found in the files of the Prussian Academy of Arts in Berlin, dated October 1919, in which he made his resignation. Letter from Senator for Cultural Affairs of Berlin, Nov. 29, 1954.

Correspondence with Metropolitan Museum from their archives.

The Thayer incident from *Abbott H. Thayer*, Nelson C. White, New Haven, 1951. Sargent's belief that Carolus "hates me" is a mystery to both Sargent's sister and Carolus' granddaughter, with whom I tried to check it. It is apparent they had some disagreement prior to the time of the letter to Russell, written in 1885, which seems to have been completely forgotten by the older man, while it magnified with the years in Sargent's mind.

CHAPTER SIXTEEN

Arrival on the *Nieuw Amsterdam* and refusal of interviews from clipping, Journalism Library, Columbia University.

Mr. Welles Bosworth is authority for his own part in the Rockefeller negotiations, and subsequent details of the stay at Pocantico. The interview at Boston also from clipping in Journalism Library, Columbia University. It is Mr. Bosworth's recollection that prior to taking the studio on Columbus Avenue he had some sort of working space in the Hotel Vendome itself.

Developmental sequence of Museum Murals from *Decorations of the Dome of the Rotunda* and *Decorations over the Main Stairway and Library*, both prepared by Thomas A. Fox, who assisted in the actual work, and published by the Museum.

The brass-trimmed car recalled by Edward Rotan Sargent; Mrs. Hale told me of the "favorite" fish dish; Winthrop Sargent, Jr., of the homespun, and Miss Elizabeth Williamson of the appearance of his jackets.

Nijinsky from *Nijinsky*, by Romola Nijinsky (1934), and *Nijinsky*, by Paul Magriel, New York, 1946.

The letter concerning Mrs. Hunter's ordeal written to Lady Cholmondeley, and in her possession.

Letter to Mrs. Hale in her possession.

The man who came to lunch at Rockefeller's from "Sitting to Sargent," by Charles K. Bolton, *Boston Transcript*, April 15, 1925. That it was Inglis is shown by repetition of the incident in *John D. Rockefeller*, Allan Nevins, New York, 1940.

Paul Manship is authority for his manner of coming to Rockefeller's attention. Interview, June 10, 1953.

Blashfield, *op. cit.*, mentions the retouching of Beckwith's works.

Nolan's blarney from Downes, *op. cit.*

Chancery Division's action from *New York Times*, Dec. 24, 1916.

Wilson's letters from *Woodrow Wilson, Life and Letters*, Ray Stannard Baker, New York, 1938. Further accounts of his visits to the White House from *My Memoir*, Edith Bolling Wilson, Indianapolis-New York, 1938, which also recounts the dinner with Cabot Lodge. The technical preoccupations during the painting of Wilson are well expressed in Sargent's own letter to Timothy Cole in *Timothy Cole: Wood Engraver*, by Alphaeus P. Cole and Margaret Ward Cole, New York, 1935. That Wilson had bored him was mentioned outright to his cousin, Mrs. N. B. Potter.

The manner of drawing a charcoal head from *Sitting to Sargent*.

The "satisfactory" price from a clipping, *Boston Transcript*, in my possession.

CHAPTER SEVENTEEN

The crossing in convoy is mentioned in the letters written on board to Mrs. Hale and Mrs. Gardner.

That he was "carved out of beef" was the opinion of Charles Ricketts, R.A., in *Selfportrait*, edited by Cecil Lewis, London, 1939.

Mrs. Hale told me of Nicola's disappearance. His own contradictory account in his memoir of Sargent (*op. cit.*) was probably caused by his desire to find another similar position. If he was given the reference he states Sargent wrote out on Copley-Plaza stationery it was at a later date. According to the Boston Directory he was a *photographer, cleaner,* and then *barber* before he dropped from its record in 1925.

Yockney's letter was dated April 26, 1918; a copy was supplied me by W. P. Mayes, Keeper of the Art Department of the Imperial War Museum, who also supplied the letter from Lloyd George. Alfred Yockney told me of going to the station with Sargent and Tonks. His arrival at headquarters from *Haig*, by Duff Cooper, London, 1936. The pantomimes from *The Sassoon Dynasty*, Cecil Roth, London, 1941.

Life in the trenches from "Sargent's Studio of Shellfire," *New York Times*, March 23, 1919, and *The Story of the Twenty Seventh Division*, Major General John F. O'Ryan, New York, 1921.

The sketches he did are now in the Fogg Museum, the watercolors in the Imperial War Museum, and the residue in the Metropolitan Museum.

His sketching of the blinded troops recounted by Henry Tonks in a letter to Alfred Yockney, dated March 19, 1920, a copy of which was given me by W. P. Mayes.

Orpen's caricatures were sent Lady Cholmondeley, who kindly showed them to me.

Sir Walter Lamb told me of the attempts to make Sargent president of the Academy, supplying both excerpts from his diary, and his memories. Interview, Sept. 5, 1954.

CHAPTER EIGHTEEN

The "young artist" was Walter Tittle, who wrote "My Memories of John Sargent," *Illustrated London News*, April 25, 1925.

Tittle confirmed, in his letter to me of Nov. 29, 1953, that Sargent was perfectly serious about adding a figure to the *El Jaleo*.

The "chicken" remark was made before Mr. Welles Bosworth, who had taken Sargent and his sister to the Museum. He displayed no interest in seeing his own works, for which his sister had particularly come, and Bosworth had been obliged tactfully to haul him back from wandering into other galleries.

The quotations from Emily Sargent are from her letters to Mrs. Gardner, preserved at Fenway Court.

The hand over his beard was recalled by Mr. Antonio de Navarro; D. S. MacColl recalled his sitting posture in *Life, Work and Setting of Philip Wilson Steer.*

The visitor to his studio was Walter Tittle, *op. cit.*

Many of the sheets with models' names and addresses below a sketch now in the Fogg Museum and the Corcoran Gallery. The elevator operator from "As Sargent Goes to Rest," Thomas A. Fox, in the *Boston Transcript,* April 24, 1925.

His rooms at the Copley-Plaza from a letter to Mrs. Hale, asking her to reserve them. The reserved table mentioned by Lloyd Carswell, general manager of the Sheraton-Plaza (as it is now called), who got his information from Spencer Sawyer, the assistant manager in Sargent's time. Letter June 28, 1954.

"You eat like a bird" was said to Martin Birnbaum. Interview, Aug. 2, 1954.

The "Synagogue" controversy from *Art News,* June 10, 1922.

Hind's call from "Sargent," by C. Lewis Hind, in *Outlook,* April 29, 1925. Hind requested that Sargent sign the picture, which he did, going out in a blizzard the following day to get the proper paints.

The letter to Rhodes in the Massachusetts Historical Society.

His arrival and refusal to talk to the press from a clipping, Journalism Library, Columbia University.

Lady Cholmondeley told me of her sittings. Interview, Aug. 30, 1954. Sargent's letters to her in her possession.

The letters to Mary (Mrs. Nathaniel Bowditch) Potter in her possession.

CHAPTER NINETEEN

The talk on the elevator from a letter of Winthrop Sargent to Evan Charteris, dated Dec. 21, 1925, a copy of which was given me by Winthrop Sargent, Jr.

The drawing of Barrymore from *Confessions of an Actor,* John Barrymore, Indianapolis, 1926, and *Good Night, Sweet Prince,* Gene Fowler, New York, 1944.

Dr. Cushing's sittings and the letters from *Harvey Cushing,* John F. Fulton, Springfield, Ill., 1946.

The portrait of Mary Newbold by Sully is reproduced in *International Studio,* August 1925, p. 378.

The story of the Coolidge portrait told me by Mrs. Potter. Interview June 4, 1954.

The letter to Pierce from Downes, *op. cit.*

The letter to Walter L. Clark has been quoted in varying forms.

Robert McIntire of the Macbeth Gallery is authority for the call Mr. Macbeth made on Sargent in Boston.

The debate over the Wertheimer pictures is from a clipping dated March 13, 1923, given me by Alfred Yockney. The operative clause in Asher Wertheimer's will reads as follows: "I give the said portraits to the Trustees of the National Gallery for the benefit of the Nation and I desire but without imposing or intending to impose any binding or legal obligation on them that the said Trustees shall keep the said portraits and to exhibit them together in one room in the National

Gallery." The quote supplied by Mr. John M. Mathias, his letter of Sept. 29, 1954.

The El Greco incident from the files of the Metropolitan Museum.

His last letter from the *New York Times*, April 26, 1925.

The cause of death was established by an autopsy as heart disease, due to fatty degeneration of the cardiac muscles. His heart was twice normal size. An advanced arteriosclerosis also was found, as well as chronic Bright's disease. *New York Post*, April 16, 1925.

The will was proved June 16, 1925, and the gross estate found to be £25,703. The entire estate was left in trust for his two sisters, except for a legacy of £5,000 given Mrs. Barnard. As she predeceased him, the money went to her daughters, the little girls who posed for *Carnation Lily, Lily Rose*. Nicola was left £200, without taxes.

Catalogue
of
Sargent's Works in Oil

EXCEPT for the sale held by Sargent's executors at Christie's in 1925 and the Royal Academy's 1926 memorial exhibition, which are accepted as assurances of a picture's absolute authenticity (though not of correct titles) no work has been admitted to this catalogue by trust or hearsay or merely by report. Nor is an old provenance sufficient recommendation. The artist himself reported to a cousin, December 25, 1922: "You must warn your father that America swarms with forgeries of my things . . ." Several thousand oil paintings attributed to Sargent are here reduced to 1080 authentic pictures known to the author. Each has been thoroughly examined and its inclusion predicated on style, technique, drawing, structure of the facture, brushing, and nature of its materials. Where personal examination has not been possible study has been made through persuasive media such as photographs. The author takes full responsibility for these pictures and also for the elimination from this catalogue of others equally well known.

The first list comprises portraits only. It is right that these should be considered apart from Sargent's other efforts for they represent the bulk of his professional work and are the largest category in his *oeuvre*. It is also of some importance to Sargent's position in the artistic hierarchy that his commissioned portraits rarely if ever were painted with the special pallette reserved for his outdoor work (see

427

Preface to the Third Edition). Portraits therefore were always a phenomenon distinctly apart in his mind, and for the purposes of this list a definition is adhered to pedantically: only those works undertaken to fix the likeness of specific individuals are included. The chronologic order adopted in earlier editions was not helpful in a book of general reference and has been replaced by alphabetic arrangement. For the second list, *works other than portraits,* chronologic order retains its logic and now is augmented by place names showing where Sargent wielded his brush each year.

Before first publication of this catalogue in 1955 lists of their pictures were circulated among members of Sargent's immediate family. This tallying of their private holdings was resumed in 1963 and the lists grew, note also being taken of new dispositions following the death of the artist's second sister, Violet (Mrs. Francis Ormond). To make a permanent record my photographer visited each member of the family to photograph their holdings. Pictures never listed now appeared, and this was no less surprising than the omissions. Quantities of youthful studies and the vast preparations for late murals either have disappeared or are put away so well they are forgot. "I am afraid that I am at a loss to answer even as much as one of your questions" was the reply of Sargent's nephew to proddings over these pictures. Such "lost" works are recorded as the property of their last owner, the artist's sister Miss Emily Sargent, who died in 1935.

A further rationalization of the catalogue has been carried out on the premise that Sargent painted specific places when he visited them. This logic forced the scrapping of many established dates. In some cases the artist's own misdating possibly prevents final solutions. His habit was to add the signature and year not when the picture was completed (the majority of those left at his death were neither signed nor dated), but when it passed out of his studio to an exhibition or into the hands of a purchaser. A writer who approached him in the last year of his life found that "in the matter of dates he was more than uncertain . . .," yet during this time when asked to sign and date the works of his youth he obliged.

The sometimes fanciful names under which Sargent exhibited pictures is epitomized by *Carnation Lily, Lily Rose,* completed in 1886, but the preoccupation in different forms continued throughout his life. *"The Twin Falls,* or *Yoho Falls* sounds better," and "it might be well to call the alligator one *Muddy Alligators* to explain their whiteness," are from letters referring to the fruits of his last landscaping expeditions in America during 1916 and 1917. Later owners frequently developed their own purely descriptive names for pictures on whose titles Sargent had bestowed a certain restrained artistry of his own. For example, they exchanged his evocative *Gethsemane* for *Near the Mount of Olives, Jerusalem.* In this instance, as in many others, both titles crept into published catalogues as though for separate works and numerous duplications were created. It is hoped that all such duplicate titles now have been discovered and are married in a single entry.

More arbitrary alterations also have been made where personal familiarity with the places Sargent painted, particularly in Italy, has enabled wrongly identified sites to be correctly titled. Thus *San Geremia,* a title from the 1914 Royal Academy, has been matched up to its picture, also entitled *The Labbia Palace* at the Royal Academy in 1926 and *Palazzo Labia, Venice* at Birmingham in 1964. Other examples among many are studies of the Venetian Church of San Staë (previously wrongly called *The Gesuiti*) and *A Window in the Vatican* which is transported back to the Villa Papa Giulio where it belongs.

Sizes are indicated in inches and unless otherwise stated all works are painted on canvas. To add identification the name of the last known owner is given, an asterisk (*) denoting pictures untraced since leaving that ownership.

PART ONE

PORTRAITS

A

number
in
previous
editions

ABBOTT, Holker.
1920, Boston; 28 × 22. Signed and dated. Tavern Club, Boston. 201

ACHESON, The Ladies.
1902, London; 106 × 78. Signed and dated. Chatsworth. 0218

ADDICKS, Miss Florence.
1890, Nahant; 30 × 25. Signed and dated. Toledo Museum. 9035

AGNEW, Lady (of Lochnaw)
1893, London; 49½ × 39½. Signed. National Gallery of Scotland. .. 931

AGNEW, Mrs. Philip L.
1902, London; 34½ × 28½. Signed and dated. The Tate Gallery. 0212

ALEXANDER, Mrs. Charles B.
1902, London; 58 × 38. Signed and dated. Mrs. Arnold Whitredge. 0214

ALLEN, Lancelot.
1894, London; 35 × 23. Signed and dated. Miss Rachel Allen.* 941

ALLENBY, Field-Marshall The Viscount.
1922, London; 22 × 16. (Study for group portrait *The Generals*.)
National Gallery of South Africa. 224
1922, London; 22 × 16. (Study actually employed for group portrait
The Generals.) City of Leicester Museum. 223

ALLHUSEN, Mrs. Angus H. E.
1906, London; 59 × 39. Signed. Deering Library, Northwestern University. 0615

ALLOUARD-JOUAN, Mme.
1884, Paris; 29½ × 22. Inscribed: A. Mme. Allouard-Jouan témoignage
d'amitié John S. Sargent. Petit Palais. 841

ALMA-TADEMA, Sir Laurence.
1886, London; @ 30 × 25. 8715

ANDERSON, Mrs. Garrett, M.D.
1900, London; 33 × 26. Signed and dated. Sir Alan Anderson.* 051

ANSTRUTHER-THOMSON, Mrs. Charles F. St.-Clair.
1898, London; 58 × 38. Signed. Baron John Bonde. 9817

ANSTRUTHER-THOMSON, Caroline.
1889, Fladbury; (sketch for full length). Baron John Bonde. 8927
1889, Fladbury; (full length). Lord Kilmany. 8919

ASTOR, Viscountess.
1908, London; 59 × 38. Signed. Viscount Astor* 082

ASTOR, Miss (Mrs. Spender-Clay)
1902, London; 98 × 50. Signed. Lt.-Col. H. H. Spender-Clay. 0227

AUSTIN, Mrs. Isabel Vallé
1882, Paris; (three quarter length). Signed and dated. Mrs. Robert
Brookings.* 826

AUSTIN, Mary T.
1880, Paris. Inscribed: To my friend Mary John S. Sargent.
Williard W. Cummins 8021
1880, Paris; 18 × 15. Inscribed: To my friend Mary John S. Sargent.
Gladys Green 8020

B

BACON, Ruthie Sears.
1887, Boston; 48¾ × 36. Signed and dated. Mrs. Austin Cheney. 876

BACON, Mrs. Edward.
1895, Biltmore; 82 × 36. Signed and dated. Biltmore House. 901

BAKER, The Rev. Dr.
1901, London; 37½ × 27. Signed and dated. The Merchant Taylor's
School, Northwood, Middlesex. 012

BALFOUR, Earl of.
1908, London; 101 × 58. Signed and dated. Carleton Club. 083

BARENTON, Jacques.
1883, Paris; 22½ × 18½. Signed and dated. Edna Levinson Ripin. 833

BARNARD, Dorothy.
1889, Broadway; 27¾ × 15½. Fitzwilliam Museum. 891

BARNARD, Mrs. Frederick.
1885, Broadway; (unfinished) Painted on a strip cut from "Carnation
Lily, Lily Rose." Dr. J. A. P. Millet. 857
1885, Broadway; (second version) 40 × 21½. Inscribed: To Alice Bar-
nard John S. Sargent. (Part of older inscription visible at bottom right).
The Tate Gallery. 856

BARNARD, Polly.
1889, Broadway; 32 × 26 (called *Girl in White Muslin Dress*) Inscribed: To Miss Anstruther-Thomson. Knoedler* 893

BARRETT, Lawrence.
1890, New York; 30 × 25. Signed and dated. The Players, New York. 908

BATTEN, Mrs. George (singing)
1895, London; 34 × 16½. Inscribed: To Mrs. G. Batten John S. Sar-
gent. Glasgow Art Gallery. 954

BAYARD, Thomas Francis.
1897, London; 59 × 41. Inscribed: Offered to Mrs. Bayard John S.
Sargent 1897. Mrs. Thomas F. Bayard. ....

BELLEROCHE, Albert de.
1882, Paris; 27½ × 19½. Inscribed and signed. Colorado Springs Fine
Art Center. 8217
1882, Paris. 24 × 18. Inscribed: To Baby Millbank John S. Sargent.
Count W. de Belleroche (on loan to Travellers' Club, London). K8225
1884, Paris; 25 × 16½. Wildenstein, Scott & Fowle. 845

BELLEROCHE, Mme.
1884, Paris; 75 × 36, (unfinished). Count W. de Belleroche (on loan to
Travellers' Club, London). 8420
1884, Paris; 22½ × 17½. Mr. & Mrs. Philip I. Berman. 8424

BERESFORD, Lady Charles.
@1900, London; 28⅞ × 23⅝. Inscribed: To Lady Charles Beresford
John S. Sargent. Municipal Gallery of Modern Art, Dublin. X1

BIRDWOOD, Sir William, Bart.
1920, London; 16 × 22 (study for portrait group The Generals). Signed
and dated. National Gallery of Australia. 202

BLANCHE, Jacques-Emile.
1891, Paris; 32 × 20. Inscribed: A mon ami Blanche. Musée des Beaux-
Arts, Rouen. X14

BOIT, CHILDREN, (group portrait)
1882, Paris; 87½ × 87½. Signed and dated. Museum of Fine Arts, Bos-
ton. 8211

BOIT, Edward Darley.
1908, London; 35 × 24. Signed and dated. Julian M. Boit. 084

BOIT, Mrs. Edward Darley.
1887, Boston; 59 × 41½. Signed. Museum of Fine Arts, Boston. 878

BOOTH, Edwin.
1890, New York; 87½ × 61¾. Signed. The Players, New York. 907
1890, New York; 24 × 20 (sketch). Signed. Guy Ayrault. 906

BOUGHTON, Miss.
@1886, London. Manuscript letter addressed to Miss Boughton from 13,
Tite Street, asks that "our last sitting" be put off. "This ain't no time to
be painting portraits even in Fiji costume." Not located.

BRABAZON, H. B.
1893, London; 22 × 15½. Signed. Brabazon Museum, Oaklands, Sed-
dlescombe* (Museum now defunct). 937
1893, London; 28 × 16½. Inscribed: To Mr. Brabazon John S. Sargent.
Mrs. R. E. Danielson (in storage at Museum of Fine Arts, Boston). 938

BRANDEGEE, Mrs. Edward D.
1907, London, 60 × 38. Signed. Edward D. Brandegee. 072

BRICE, Senator Calvin S.
1898, London; 58 × 38. Signed and dated (twice). The Allen County,
Ohio, Historical Society. 983

BRICE, Miss Helen.
1907, London, 58 × 34. Signed and dated. Mrs. Brice Allen. 073

BROOKS, Miss Eleanor, (Mrs. R. M. Santonstall)
1890, Boston; 60 × 37. Mrs. George Lewis, Sr. 903
1890, Boston; 20 × 17 (sketch). Signed: J.S.S. Mrs. Leverett Salton-
stall, Jr. 902

BROOKS, Peter Chardon.
1890, Boston; 27 × 24. Signed and dated. Mrs. George Lewis, Sr. 904

BROOKS, Mrs. Peter Chardon.
1890, Boston; 50 × 40. Signed and dated. Peabody Museum, Salem,
Mass. 905

BROWNLEE, William.
1902, London; 60 × 37½. Signed and dated. Dundee Museum. 0213

BULLOCK, Mrs. Alexander H.
1890, Boston; 30 × 25. Signed and dated. Chandler Bullock. 9036

BULOZ, Mme. Francois. (Christine Blaze)
    1879, Savoy; 20½ × 17. Inscribed: A mon ami M. Buloz John S. Sargent Roujoux 1879. Madame Bourget Pailleron. 797
BUNKER, Dennis Miller.
    1887, Boston; 18 × 14. Inscribed: To Bunker with a Merry Xmas John S. Sargent. Tavern Club, Boston. 8712
BURCH, Miss Cara.
    1887, New York; 30 × 25. Signed. New Britain Museum of American Art. 8714
BURCKHARDT, Edward.
    1880, Paris; 22 × 18. Inscribed: To my friend Valerie John S. Sargent June 1880. Mrs. Francis Behn-Riggs. 803
BURCKHARDT, Mrs. Edward, and her daughter Louise.
    1885, Paris. 79¼ × 56¼. Signed and dated. James Graham & Sons. 853
BURCKHARDT, Louise.
    1882, Paris; 84 × 44. Inscribed: To my friend Mrs. Burckhardt John S. Sargent 1882. Metropolitan Museum. 823
BURCKHARDT, Valerie (Mrs. Harold F. Hadden)
    1878, Paris; 36 × 29. Gavin Hadden* 781
    1882, Paris; 24 × 21 (called "Gigio"). Sir William Orpen.* 8010
BUSK, Sir Edward H.
    1923, London; 35½ × 27½. Signed and dated. University of London ... 232
BYNG, General Lord, of Vimy.
    1922, London; 22 × 16 (sketch for group portrait The Generals). Signed. National Gallery of Canada, Ottawa. 224
BYWATER, Professor Ingraham.
    1900, London; 58 × 38. Signed. The Tate Gallery. 0010

C

CAGNIARD, Mlle. Louise.
    1882, Paris; 20 × 16. Signed. Prof. de Gennes. 8215
CARMENCITA
    1890, New York; 90 × 54½. Signed. Museum of Modern Art, Paris. ... 9019
    1890, New York; 28½ × 19½ (sketch in the act of singing). Jean Louis Ormond. 909
CAROLUS-DURAN
    1877, Paris; 46 × 37¾. Inscribed: A mon cher maître M. Carolus-Duran, son élève affectioné John S. Sargent 1877. Sterling & Francine Clark Institute. 771
    1877, Paris; 13½ × 10. (Wood). Christies 1925, No. 210 (Martin)* 772
    1877, Paris; 13½ × 10. (Wood). (seated in an armchair). Christies 1925, No. 211 (Stevens & Brown to Miss Jane Nichols)* 773
CARTER, James C.
    1899, London; 57 × 38. Signed. Harvard Club, New York. 991
CARTER, John Ridgeley.
    1903 (repainted and dated 1908) New York and London; 33½ × 26½. Signed. Mrs. Bernard S. Carter 081

CASSATT, Alexander J.
1903, Philadelphia; 58 × 38. Signed. Pennsylvania Railroad. 033

CASTILLO, Countess Nünez del.
1903, London; 33½ × 27½. Signed. Count Nunez del Castillo. 0312

CAVAN, General the Earl of.
1922, London; 22 × 16 (study for group portrait The Generals). National Portrait Gallery, London. 225

CAZALET, William M.
1902, London; 100 × 65. Signed and dated. Peter Cazalet. 0221

CAZALET, Mrs. William M., and her children.
1900, London; 100 × 65. Signed. Peter Cazalet. 008

CHADWICK, Francis Brooks.
1880, 12⅝ × 9 (wood), Haarlem. Inscribed: To my friend Chadwick John S. Sargent Haarlem. Edmund J. McCormick. 8022

CHAMBERLAIN, Joseph.
1896, London; 63½ × 37. Signed and dated. National Portrait Gallery, London. 963

CHAMBERLAIN, Mrs. Joseph. (Mrs. W. Hartley Carnegie)
1902, London; 45 × 32. Signed and dated. National Gallery, Washington. 0225

CHAPMAN, Beatrix.
1882, Paris. Destroyed by enemy action, London. 8216

CHAPMAN, Eleanor J. (Mrs. Richard Mortimer)
1885, Richard M. & Maxime J. Furlaud. 855

CHAPMAN, Mrs. John J. (Miss Chanler)
1892, London; 40 × 30. Signed and dated. Mrs. Richard Aldrich. 927

CHASE, William Merritt.
1902, London; 62½ × 41⅜. Inscribed: Copyright John S. Sargent 1902. Metropolitan Museum. 0215

CHIERCATI, Countess.
1894, London; 26 × 17¾. Inscribed: To the Countess Chiercati John S. Sargent. Mrs. John E. Greene, Jr. 948

CHOATE, Joseph Hodges.
1899, London; 58 × 38. Signed. Harvard Club, New York. 992

CHOLMONDELEY, Sybil Marchioness of.
1913, London; 34 × 26½. Inscribed: To Sybil from her friend John S. Sargent 1913. Sybil, Marchioness of Cholmondeley. 132
1922, London; 63½ × 35½. Signed and dated. Sybil, Marchioness of Cholmondeley. 221

CLARY, Countess Therese.
1896, London; 90 × 48. Seized by Russian Army 1945. 961

CIVRIEUX, Robert de.
1879, Paris; 33 × 19. Signed and dated. Museum of Fine Arts, Boston. 791

COHEN, Arthur.
1906, London; 29½ × 25. Signed. Miss Cohen* 0614

COHEN, Mrs. Arthur.
1897, London. (Exhibited at New Gallery 1898) 979

COMYNS CARR, Mrs. Alice.
1889, Kent; 25⅜ × 19⅞. Inscribed (twice): To Mrs. Comyns Carr
John S. Sargent. J.B. Speed Museum. 984

CONNAUGHT, Duchess of.
1908, London; 63 × 42½. Signed and dated. Windsor Castle. 087

CONNAUGHT, Duke of.
1908, London; 63 × 42½. Signed and dated. Windsor Castle. 086

COOKE, Mrs. Russell. (Mrs. Ashton Dilke)
1895, London; 35 × 28. Signed. Parke-Bernet, September 25, 1968* 953

COWANS, General Sir J.S.
1922, London; 21 × 17 (sketch for group portrait The Generals).
Viscount Cowdray. 226

COWDRAY, Viscount.
1907, London; 63 × 39. Signed and dated. Viscount Cowdray. 079

COWDRAY, Viscountess.
1906, London; 63 × 39. Signed and dated. Viscount Cowdray. 068

CRAM, Miss Charlotte.
1900, London; 34¾ × 24. Signed and dated. Mrs. Robert L. Fowler. 0011

CRAM, Henry A.
1893, London. Mrs. Robert L. Fowler. 939

CROMBIE, Mrs. J.W.
1898, London; 39 × 29. Signed and dated. Aberdeen Art Gallery. 984

CROMER, The Earl of.
1902, London; 57½ × 38. Signed and dated. National Portrait Gallery,
London. 027

CURRIE, General Sir A.W.
1922, London; 22 × 16 (study for group portrait The Generals). Sir
Arthur Currie.* 2216

CURTIS, Mrs. Charles P.
1903, Boston; 60 × 35. Signed and dated. Mrs. Lewis Iselin, Jr. 031

CURTIS, Ariana W. (Mrs. Daniel Sargent Curtis)
1882, Venice; 28 × 21. Inscribed: Venice 1882 John S. Sargent to his
kind friend Mrs. Curtis. University of Kansas Museum of Art. 822

CURTIS, Ralph (on the sand at Scheveningen)
1880, Scheveningen; 10 × 12. Inscribed: J.S. Sargent Scheveningen
1880. Mrs. Schuyler Owen. 8015

CURTIS, Mrs. Ralph.
1898, London; 90 × 48. Inscribed: To Ralph and Lisa Curtis John S.
Sargent 1898. Ralph W. Curtis. 9816

CURZON, Marquis, of Kedleston.
1914, London; 39½ × 30½. Signed and dated. Royal Geographic Society. 141

CURZON, Marchioness, of Kedleston.
1925, London; 59 × 40. Signed and dated. Currier Gallery of Art, Manchester, New Hampshire. 251

D

D'ABERNON, Viscount.
1906, London; 37 × 27½. Signed and dated. Viscountess D'Abernon.   0611

D'ABERNON, Viscountess.
1904, Venice; 63 × 42. Inscribed: John S. Sargent Venice, 1904. Viscount D'Abernon.   0413

DAINTREY, Arthur.
Date unknown; 22½ × 18. Inscribed: To my friend Daintrey. Julius Weitzner.* X19

DALHOUSIE, The Earl of.
1900, London; 60 × 40. The Earl of Dalhousie.   006

DAVIDSON, Randall, Archbishop of Canterbury.
1910, London; 51¼ × 41½. Signed and dated. Church Commissioners, Lambeth Palace.   101

DAVIS, Mrs. Edward Livingston, and her son.
1890, Worcester; 86¼ × 44¾. Signed. Sold at Parke-Bernet, March 1969.   9024

DEERING, Charles (at Brickell Point)
1917, Miami; 27 × 21. Inscribed: To my friend Charles Deering John S. Sargent Miami 1917. Mrs. R. E. Danielson.   175

DELAFOSSE, Léon.
1894, London; 37 × 22. Inscribed: A. M. Léon Delafosse souvenir amical John S. Sargent.   9412

DEMIDOFF, Princess.
1896, London; 66 × 38. Signed. Toledo Museum.   962

DERBY, Mrs. Richard H.
1889, New York; 77½ × 39½. Signed and dated. Mrs. Robert T. Gannett.   892

DEVITT, Sir Thomas L. Bart.
1904, London; 57 × 37. Signed and dated. Sir Thomas C. Devitt, Bart.   042

DEVONSHIRE, The Duchess of.
1902, London; 57½ × 36. Signed and dated. The Duke of Devonshire.   0217

DEWEY, Mrs. Frances H.
1890, Worcester; 36 × 28. Signed. Mrs. Rockwood Bullock.   9010

DICK, Archibald Douglas.
1886, London; 58 × 38. Signed. Hon. Mrs. Charles Noel.   8613

DICK, Mrs. Douglas.
1886, London; 63 × 36. Signed and dated. Mrs. R. Drummond Wolff*   851

D'INVERNO, Nicola (called *a Gondolier*)
1904, Venice; 27½ × 21½. Ralph W. Curtis.   0714

DOCTORS, The Four (Group portrait of Drs. Kelly, Halsted, Welch, & Osler.)
1905, London; 114 × 84. Signed. Johns Hopkins University.   0512

DOVERDALE, Lord.
1902, London; 36 × 28. Signed. Lord Doverdale.   0220

HAMMOND, Mrs. Gardiner Greene, Jr.
1903, Boston; 35 × 25⅛. Signed and dated. Worcester Museum. 035
HARRISON, Cecil.
1887, London; 70 × 33. Signed. Southampton Public Art Gallery. 8713
HARRISON, Lawrence.
1899, London; 22 × 19. Signed. Michael Harrison. X17
HARRISON, Lawrence A. (Peter)
1902; 30 × 20½. Inscribed: To Peter Harrison John S. Sargent. Michael
Harrison. 0224
HARRISON, Mrs. Lawrence A. (Alma Strettel)
1889, Kent; 26½ × 21½. Inscribed: To my friend Miss Strettel John
S. Sargent. Nicholas Harrison. 895
HARRISON, Mrs. Robert.
1886, London; 62 × 32. Signed and dated. Philippa J.M. Harrison. 865
HARRISON, Sylvia.
1913, London; 58 × 33. Signed. (An Australian Art Gallery?) 133
HAVEN, Kate.
1903, New York; 26 × 20. Inscribed: To my friend Mrs. Haven John
S. Sargent 1903. Mrs. William Osborn. 032
HAY, John.
1903, Washington; 30 × 25. Signed and dated. Clarence L. Hay. 038
HEALY, A. Augustus.
1907, London; 32½ × 28½. Signed and dated. Brooklyn Museum. 076
HELLEU, Paul
1883, Paris; 28½ × 19½. Signed. Ellen Helleu-Orosdi 835
HELLEU, Mme. Paul.
1889, Fladbury; 39⅞ × 31⅞. Signed. Henry D. Irwin. 896
HEMENWAY, Mrs. Augustus.
1890, Boston; 32 × 25. Signed and dated. Mrs. Auguste Richard. 9015
HEMY, Napier C.
1905, London; 26½ × 20. Inscribed: To my friend Napier Hemy John
S. Sargent 1905. Hubert N. Hemy. 054
HENSCHEL, Sir George.
1889, London; 24 × 20. Inscribed: To my friend Henschel. Miss G.
Henschel. 897
HEWER, William F.
1893, London. Inscribed: To Mr. Hewer John S. Sargent. Mrs. W. F.
Hewer. 934
HIGGINSON, Major Henry L.
1903, Boston; 96 × 60. Signed and dated. Harvard University. 036
HILL, Miss Octavia.
1899, London; 39½ × 30½. Signed. National Portrait Gallery, London. 993
HILLS, Mrs. Ernest.
1894, London; 61 × 40. Signed. National Gallery of Scotland. 949
1905, London; 58 × 38. Signed. Bradford City Art Gallery. 9413
HIRSCH, Mrs. Adolph (later Mrs. Cornwallis-West)
1905, London; 48½ × 37 (oval). Signed. Mrs. Richard Pinto. 053

HIRSCH, Mrs. Leopold.
1901, London; 57 × 36½. Signed. Major John H. Hirsch. 019

HORNE, General Lord.
1922, London; 22 × 16 (study for group portrait The Generals). Scottish National Portrait Gallery. 228

HORNER, Cecily (Mrs. George Lambton)
1897, Mells; 24 × 16. Inscribed: To Mrs. Horner Mells '97 John S. Sargent. Charles Bolles Rogers. 976
1897, Mells; 24 × 16. Signed (and incorrectly dated 1910). American private collection. 977

HUNNEWELL, Mrs. Arthur.
1910, London; 35 × 27. Signed and dated. Miss Jane B. Hunnewell. 102

HUNT, Richard Morris.
1895, Biltmore, North Carolina; 100 × 55. Signed and dated. Biltmore House. 955

HUNTER, The Misses.
1902, London; 89½ × 89½. Signed and dated. The Tate Gallery. 0223

HUNTER, Mrs. Charles.
1898, London; 57 × 34½. Signed. The Tate Gallery. 9811

HUNTER, Mrs. Colin.
1896, London; 36 × 24. Inscribed: To my friend Colin Hunter John S. Sargent 1896. Detroit Art Institute. 964

HUNTINGTON, Jane, Lady.
1898, London; 92½ × 50. Signed. Brooklyn Museum. 988

I

INCHES, Mrs. Charles E.
1887, Boston; 34 × 24. Signed and dated. Mrs. Henry Seton. 873

IRVING, Sir Henry.
1889, London. (Destroyed) 8910

ISELIN, Mrs. Adrian.
1888, New York; 60½ × 36½. Signed and dated. National Gallery, Washington. 883

J

JACKSON, Mrs. Huth.
1907, London; 58 × 39. Signed and dated. Hans Christian Sonné. 077

JAMES, Henry.
1913, London; 33½ × 26½. Signed and dated. National Portrait Gallery, London. 131

JAY, Peter Augustus (as a child)
1880, Paris; 18 × 14¾. Signed and dated. Mrs. Peter A. Jay. 816

JEFFERSON, Joseph.
　　1890, New York; 36½ × 28¼ (as *Dr. Pangloss*). Signed. The Players,
　　New York. 9016
　　1890, New York; 19 × 14 (sketch). Signed: J.S.S. Reine Pitman. 9017
　　1890, New York; 20 × 16 (sketch) False signature. Parke-Bernet,
　　1944* 9018

JENKINSON, Francis J. H.
　　1915, London; 35½ × 27½. Signed and dated. University Library,
　　Cambridge. 151

JOACHIM, Dr. Joseph.
　　1904, London; 37½ × 32½. Signed and dated. Art Gallery of Toronto. 046

JOURDAIN, Mlle.
　　1879, Paris; 23⅛ × 17¼. Inscribed: A mon amie Madame Jourdain
　　John S. Sargent (date illegible). Sterling & Francine Clark Institute. 796

JUILLERAT, Eugène.
　　1878, Paris; 16 × 13. Inscribed: A mon ami Juillerat J. S. Sargent. Mrs.
　　Calvin P. Foulke. 782

K

KEITH, Master Skein.
　　1892, London; 30 × 26. Inscribed: To my friend Mrs. Keith John S.
　　Sargent 1892. T. Skene Keith 922

KELLY, Mrs. Edmonde.
　　1889, France; 44 × 32. Signed and dated. Shaun Kelly*. 8923

KIEFFER, Jeanne.
　　1879, Paris; 17 × 14. Signed and dated. Mme. de Valcourt. 792

KIEFFER, René.
　　1879, Paris; 17 × 14. Signed and dated. Mme. Jean Merzeau. 793

KING, Leroy.
　　1888, Newport; 30 × 25. Leroy King. 888

KISSAM, Benjamin.
　　1890, New York; 32 × 26. Signed and dated. Mrs. William Brunet. 9039

KISSAM, Mrs. Benjamin.
　　1888, New York; 60 × 36. Signed and dated. Biltmore. 887

KNOWLES, Mrs. Arthur, and her sons.
　　1902, London; 73 × 60. Signed and dated. Butler Art Institute. 0219

L

LANE, Sir Hugh.
　　1906, London; 29½ × 24½. Signed and dated. Municipal Gallery of
　　Modern Art, Dublin. 065

LANGMAN, Mrs. A. L.
　　1907, London; 59 × 39½. Signed and dated. Lady Langman. 078

LORING, William Caleb.
1903, Boston; 56 × 40. Signed and dated. Supreme Court of Massachusetts. 0310

LOTHROP, Thornton K.
1882-3, Paris; 28 × 21. Signed and dated. Mrs. Edward W. Moore. 8310

LOWELL, A. Lawrence.
1923, Boston; 54⅞ × 38¾. Signed and dated. Harvard University. 233

LUCAS, J. Seymour.
1905, London; 26 × 21. Inscribed: To my friend Seymour Lucas 1905
John S. Sargent. Mrs. Grubbe* 055

LUCY, Sir Henry W.
1904, London; 28½ × 21½. Signed and dated. National Portrait Gallery, London. 044

LUKIN, Major-General Sir Henry T.
1922, London; 22 × 16 (sketch for group portrait The Generals).

M

MACMILLAN, Daniel.
1887, London; 16 × 14. Signed and dated. Rt. Hon. Harold Macmillan. 872

MACMILLAN, George A.
1925, London. Signed. Dilettanti Club, London. 252

MALDONER, Carl.
1914, Austrian Tyrol. 143

MANCINI, Antonio.
1894, London; 26 × 20. Inscribed: Mancini ringrazia devotamente M.
Sargent che e così buono per il pittore cattivo . . . Londra Mai. Museo di
Arte Moderna, Rome. 942

MANSON, Mrs. Thomas Lincoln.
1890, New York; 56 × 44. Signed. Hirschl & Adler. 9033
1890, New York; 17 × 14. High Museum of Art, Atlanta 9044

MARLBOROUGH, The Duke and Duchess, with family.
1905, London. Signed and dated. Blenheim. 056

MARQUAND, Henry G.
1897, London; 51 × 40½. Signed. Metropolitan Museum 971

MARQUAND, Mrs. Henry G.
1887, Newport; 66½ × 42. Signed and dated. Mrs. Douglas Delanoy
(on loan to Marquand Library, Princeton Univ.) 874

MASON, Mrs. Alice.
1885, London; 61 × 41. Signed and dated. John Balfour. 858

MATHIAS, Robert.
1906, London; 39½ × 29½. Signed. David Mathias. 0616

MEAD, Mrs. Frederick.
1893, Fairford; 33¾ × 24. Inscribed: To Mrs. Abbey from her friend
John S. Sargent 1893. Yale University Art Gallery. 935
1893, Fairford; 26 × 20⅜. Yale University Art Gallery 9310

MEYER, Lady, and her children.
1896, London; 79½ × 53½. Signed and dated. Sir Anthony Meyer, Bart. 968

MILLET, Mrs. Frank D.
1886, Broadway; 35½ × 27½. Inscribed: To my friend Mrs. Millet John S. Sargent. Dr. J.A.P. Millet. 867

MILLET, John Alfred Parsons.
1892, England; 35½ × 23½. Inscribed: To my friend Mrs. Millet John S. Sargent 1892. Dr. J.A.P. Millet. 923

MILLET, Kate.
1886, Broadway; 16 × 14. Inscribed: To my friend Lily Millet. Mrs. Lisbeth Bazeley. 8611

MILLET, Lawrence.
1886, Broadway; 18 × 15 (unfinished). Adams Gallery* 8610
1887, Broadway; 29½ × 20. Inscribed: To Mrs. Millet John S. Sargent 1887. Dr. Chester J. Robertson. 868

MILNE, General Sir G. F.
1922, London; 22 × 16. Inscribed: Sir. G. Milne. Scottish National Portrait Gallery. (study for group portrait The Generals) 229

MITCHELL, Dr. Silas Weir.
1903, Philadelphia; 34½ × 23. Signed. Mutual Assurance Co., Philadelphia. 0311

MONET, Claude.
1887, Giverny; 16 × 13. Signed. National Academy of Design, New York. 8921

MOORE, Madame.
1884, Paris; 28 × 20. Signed. Museum of Modern Art. Paris. 843
1884, Paris; 71 × 45½. Signed and dated. Huntington Hartford Museum. 847

MOSENTHAL, Mrs. George.
1906, London; 35½ × 28½. Signed and dated. Mrs. Dorothy Mosenthal. 067

Mc

McCORQUODALE, G. F.
1902, London; 57½ × 37½. Signed and dated. Mrs. J. L. Wood. 022

McCULLOCH, Alec.
1902, Norway; 27 × 22. A. McCulloch* 0229

McCULLOCH, George.
1901, London; 27 × 21½. Exhibited at The Royal Academy 1909 number 247. 0115

McCURDY, Richard A. C.
1890, New York; 50 × 37½ (cut down from full length). Robert Mccurdy Ames. 9038

PRIESTLEY, Miss Flora.
1885, Broadway (?); 25 × 19. Reine Pitman. 8510
1889, Fladbury; 35½ × 24½. Signed. The Tate Gallery. 8913
1889, Fladbury; 18 × 12 (cut down) Singing by lamplight. Inscribed:
To Miss Priestley. Partial signature. Reine Pitman. 8920
1889, Fladbury; 26 × 19. Robert C. Barton. 8914

PROBY, Sir Ballyraine.
1903, Eton; 58 × 38½. Inscribed: John S. Sargent Eton 1903. Mise
Féiht.

PROBY, Hely-Hutchinson.
1906, London; 37½ × 32½. Signed and dated. Sinn Féin Hall, Black
Rock.

PULITZER, Joseph.
1905, London; 38½ × 28. Signed and dated July 1905. 058

PULITZER, Mrs. Joseph.
1905, London; 58½ × 38½. Signed and dated. 0515

PUMPELLY, Mrs. Raphael.
1887, Newport; 30 × 24. Signed. Berkshire Museum. 8716

R

RAMBAUD, Mme. André.
1889, Paris; 82 × 44. Inscribed: Camaret à Mont Thabor souvenir
amical / John S. Sargent 1889. David Stolit.

RAPHAEL, Mrs. E. G.
1905, London; 63 × 44. Signed and dated. Cyril E. Raphael. 059

RAPHAEL, Mrs. Louis E.
1905, London; 57½ × 38. H. E. Raphael. 0518

RAPHAEL, Mrs. William.
1906, London; 56 × 41. Signed and dated. Lady Hothfield. 069

RAWLINSON, General Lord.
1922, London; 22 × 16 (study for portrait group The Generals) National Portrait Gallery, London. 2210

REED, Thomas Brackett.
1891, Paris; 32 × 26 (cut down from full-length). Speaker's Lobby,
Capitol Building, Washington. 911

REHAN, Ada.
1895, London; 93 × 50. Signed. Metropolitan Museum. 951

RIBBLESDALE, Lord.
1902, London; 100 × 55. Signed and dated. The Tate Gallery. 023
1902, London; 33¼ × 24 (preliminary study). Lady Wilson (1927)* K993

RICHARDSON, Henry.
1902, London; 58 × 38. Signed and dated. Laing Art Gallery. 0228

RICHMOND, Sir David.
1900, London; 95½ ×52½. Signed and dated Glasgow Institute of
Arts. 003
1900, London; 58 × 38. Glasgow Institute of Arts. 004

RILEY, James Whitcomb.
  1903, Philadelphia; 36× 29. Signed. John Herron Art Institute. 0315
RIPON, The Marchioness of.
  1914, London; 34 × 26. Mrs. John Edward Tennant. 144
ROBB, Mrs.
  Unfinished portrait referred to in manuscript letter dated November 6,
  [1913]. Not located.
ROBBINS, Royal E.
  1890, Boston; 29¾ × 24⅜. Signed and dated. Weiner's Antique Shop.   877
ROBERTS, Field-Marshal Earl.
  1906, London; 64 × 41. Signed and dated. National Portrait Gallery,
  London. 0610
ROBERTSON, Mrs. Graham Moore.
  1894, London; 63 × 40. Signed. G. F. Watts Art Gallery 947
ROBERTSON, W. Graham.
  1894, London; 89½ × 45. Signed and dated. The Tate Gallery. 946
  1894, London; 36 × 28 (sketch for the full-length). O. A. Harker*
ROBERTSON, Field-Marshal Sir William.
  1922, London; 22 × 16 (study for group portrait The Generals). The
  Clothworkers' Company. 2211
ROBINSON, A. Mary.
  1881, London; Mme. le Docteur Duclaux Appell. 818
ROBINSON, Edward.
  1903, New York; 55 × 36. Signed and dated. Metropolitan Museum. ... 0314
ROCKEFELLER, John D.
  1917, Florida; 58 × 46. Signed and dated. John D. Rockefeller, Jr.*.... 172
  1917, Pocantico; 58× 45. Signed and dated. John D. Rockefeller, Jr.* 173
RODIN, Auguste.
  1884, Paris; 18 × 14. Inscribed: A mon ami Rodin John S. Sargent 1884.
  Musée Rodin, Paris. 8411
ROLLER, Mrs. Frederick.
  1895, London; 88 × 43½. Signed. Knoedler* 952
ROLLER, Madge.
  1902, London; 23½ × 17½. Inscribed: To my friend Nettie John S.
  Sargent. Mrs. Eugene Rolland. 024
ROOSEVELT, Mrs. R. B., Jr.
  1890, New York; 64½ × 37½. Signed and dated. National Gallery,
  Washington. 9020
ROOSEVELT, Theodore.
  1903, The White House; 58 × 40. Signed and dated. The White House. 0321
ROTCH, Mrs. Arthur Lawrence.
  1903, Boston; 55 × 36. Signed. Museum of Fine Arts, Boston. 0316
ROTHERMERE, Viscountess.
  1906, London; 57 × 37. Signed and dated. Viscount Rothermere. 064
RUSSELL, Lady Charles.
  1900, London; 41½ × 29½. Signed and dated. Sir Charles Russell,
  Bart. 005

SEARS, Mrs. Montgomery.
1896, London; 58 × 38. Signed. Benjamin Sonnenberg. 9611

SHAKESPEARE, Mrs.
1894, London; 29 × 24. Inscribed: To my friend Shakespeare John S.
Sargent. Ferargil Gallery* 9411

SHEPARD, Alice V. (Mrs. Dave Hennen Morris as a child)
1888, New York; 22× 20. Signed and dated. Dave Hennen Morris, Jr.   885

SHEPARD, Mrs. Elliott F.
1888, New York; 84 × 48. Signed and dated. Mrs. De Welle Ferguson
Ellsworth. 884

SITWELL, (Family Group; *conversation piece*)
1900, London; 67 × 76. Signed. Sacheverell Sitwell. 007

SMITH, Mrs. Colin Hugh.
1904, London; 42 × 32. Signed and dated. Lady Bicester. 0410

SMITH, Henry St.-John.
1880, Paris; 24 × 19½. Portland Art Museum. 804

SMITH, Mrs. Henry St.-John. (later Mrs. Charles D. Barrows)
1883, Paris; 25 × 20½. Inscribed: John S. Sargent Paris 1883. Portland
Art Museum. 831

SMUTS, General.
1922, London; 31½ × 25½ (sketch for group portrait The Generals).
On the same canvas sketches of the appropriate decorations worn by
French, Allenby, Robertson, Cowan. National Portrait Gallery, Lon-
don. 2212

SORCHAN, Marius.
1884, Paris; Inscribed: To my friend Lachaise John S. Sargent 1884.
Mrs. Horace Binney* 8414

SPEYER, Lady.
1907, London; 58 × 36. Signed and dated. The Royal College of Music.   071

SPICER, Captain John E. P.
1901, London; 62 × 38½. Signed. Captain Frank Spicer. 0112
1901, London; 25 × 17½ (sketch). Christies July 18, 1935, lot 18. 0111

SPICER, Lady Margaret.
1901, London; 105 × 59. Signed. Captain Frank Spicer. 0113

STANLEY, Lady Victoria.
1899, London; 77½ × 41½. Signed and dated. Sir Malcolm Bullock,
Bart. 996

STEVENSON, Robert Louis.
1884, Bournemouth; 20 × 24½. Inscribed: John S. Sargent Bournemouth (and wrongly dated) 1887. Taft Museum. 846
1885, Bournemouth; 20½ × 24½. Inscribed: To R. L. Stevenson from
his friend John S. Sargent 1885. 852

STRAFFORD, Cora, Countess of.
1908, London; 62 × 44½. Signed and dated. Earl of Strafford. 085

SUBERCASEAUX, Ramon.
1880, Paris; wood, 14 × 10½. Inscribed: A Mme. Subercaseaux hom-
mage de John S. Sargent. Dr. Frederick K. Sargent. 801

WERTHEIMER, Asher.
1898, London; 58 × 38. Signed and dated. The Tate Gallery.   981

WERTHEIMER, Mrs. Asher.
1898, London; 62 × 40 (in white). Mrs. Wilson-Young.   982
1904, London; 64 × 42. Signed and dated. The Tate Gallery.   0412

WERTHEIMER, Betty (Mrs. Euston Salaman).
1906, London; 48 × 37. Signed. Smithsonian Institution.   018
1906, London; 21½ × 18 (sketch) Inscribed: To Comyns Carr John
S. Sargent. J. Goldschmidt.

WERTHEIMER, Edward
1902, Paris; 63 × 38½ (unfinished). The Tate Gallery.   025

WERTHEIMER, Ena. (Mrs. Robert Mathias) "A Vele Gonfie."
1905, London; 64 × 42½. Signed. Trustees of the Estate of Robert
Mathias.   057

WERTHEIMER, Conway, Almina, & Hylda.
1902, London; 73½ × 52. Signed and dated. The Tate Gallery.   0211

WERTHEIMER, Ferdinand, Ruby & Essie.
1902, London; 63 × 76. Signed and dated. The Tate Gallery.   0216

WERTHEIMER, Hylda. (Mrs. H. Wilson-Young).
1901, London; 84 × 56. Signed and dated. The Tate Gallery.   013

WERTHEIMER, Betty & Ena.
1901, London; 73 × 51½. Signed and dated. The Tate Gallery.   017

WHITE, Mrs. Charles J.
1883, Nice; wood 14½ × 10½. Mrs. Charles J. White.   8311

WHITE, Mrs. Henry.
1883, Paris; 87 × 55. Signed and dated. Corcoran Gallery   836
1883, Paris; Inscribed: To Mrs. White John S. Sargent. Destroyed in
Silesia World War II.   837

WHITE, Dr. J. William.
1909, London; 36 × 28. Signed. University of Pennsylvania.   093

WHITE, Mrs. J. William.
1903, Philadelphia; 30 × 25. Inscribed: To my friend Mrs. White John
S. Sargent 1903. Philadelphia Museum of Art.   0322

WIDENER, Mrs. Joseph E.
1903, Elkins Park; 60 × 38½. Signed and dated. Mrs. Cortwright
Wetherell.   0317

WIDENER, Peter A. B.
1903, Elkins Park; 58 × 38. Signed. National Gallery, Washington.   0318
1903, Elkins Park; 58 × 38½. Signed. P.A.B. Widener, III.   0324

WILLIAMSON, Dorothy.
1900, London. G. M. Williamson (1901)*   0012

WILLIAMSON, Lady.
1906, London; 58½ × 42½. Signed and dated. On loan to Paisley Art
Galleries.   0619

WILSON, Mrs. Harold C.
1897, London; 59 × 37. Signed. Harold C. Wilson.   975

UNIDENTIFIED PORTRAITS

PART TWO

WORKS OTHER THAN PORTRAITS

number
in
previous
editions

1874 A STAIRCASE, 21½ × 18⅛. Sterling & Francine Clark Institute. K741
HEAD OF A WOMAN, 12¾ × 15¾. Inscribed: J. S. Sargent Paris
Dec. 1874. Knoedler* 741

1875 WINEGLASSES, 18 × 14½. Signed and incorrectly dated 1874.
Sybil, Marchioness of Cholmondeley. K752
RESTING, 8½ × 10½. Signed. Sterling & Francine Clark Institute. K753

1876 STUDY OF A MAN WEARING LAURELS, 17⅜ × 13. Los
Angeles County Museum. 8019
HEAD OF A FEMALE MODEL, 17½ × 14⅜. Inscribed: A Mon
Ami Lacombe. Sterling & Francine Clark Institute. 764

at sea and in America

THE ARTIST'S MOTHER ABOARD SHIP, wood 10¾ × 7½.
Signed: J.S.S. Mrs. H. R. Thurber* K764
THE COOK'S BOY, wood 10¾ × 7½. Inscribed: To my friend
Bacon John S. Sargent. Mrs. H. R. Thurber* K765
THE SAILOR, wood 13¼ × 10¼. Inscribed: To my friend Bacon
John S. Sargent. Mrs. H. R. Thurber* K776
MID-WINTER, MID-OCEAN, 12½ × 16½. Inscribed: To my
friend Henry [Bacon] John S. Sargent 1876. Mrs. H. R. Thurber* K763
THE STEAMSHIP TRACK (AN ATLANTIC STORM), 23⅜ ×
31¾. Drury W. Cooper. K762
AN AMERICAN INDIAN (called "Gitana"), 28 × 24. Signed.
Metropolitan Museum. 761

1877 STUDY FOR CAROLUS-DURAN'S 'TRIUMPH OF MARIE DE
MEDICI', 32 × 25¾. Portland Art Museum.
STUDY FOR CAROLUS-DURAN'S 'TRIUMPH OF MARIE DE
MEDICI', 32 × 25¾. Robert Carlen*
WOMAN WITH BASKET, 10 × 10¾. Inscribed: To my friend
Mrs. Roach. Ralph W. Curtis. K806
TWO OCTOPI, 12¾ × 16. Signed and incorrectly dated 1875.
Nelson C. White. K751
BEACH SCENE (CANCALE), 33½ × 22½. Knoedler* K772
BEACH SCENE (CANCALE), 33¼ × 22½. Knoedler* K773
IDLE SAILS (LOW TIDE, CANCALE HARBOR), 18⅞ × 11.
Signed and dated. Museum of Fine Arts, Boston. K774
STUDY FOR OYSTER GATHERERS, 9¾ × 12½. Inscribed:
To my friend Beckwith John S. Sargent. Mrs. John E. Jenkins. ... K771
STUDY FOR OYSTER GATHERERS, 16¼ × 23¾. Signed. Mu-
seum of Fine Arts, Boston. K775

1878 THE OYSTER GATHERERS OF CANCALE, 31 × 48½. In-
scribed: John S. Sargent Paris 1878. Corcoran Gallery. K783

REHEARSAL OF THE PAS DE LOUP ORCHESTRA AT THE CIRQUE D'HIVER (monochrome), 21¾ × 18¼. Inscribed: Rehearsal at the Cirque d'Hiver John S. Sargent. Museum of Fine Arts, Boston. K784

REHEARSAL OF THE PAS DE LOUP ORCHESTRA AT THE CIRQUE D'HIVER, 39¾ × 36½. Inscribed: to G. Henschel John S. Sargent. Mr. and Mrs. Chauncey McCormick. K785

TWO STUDIES OF A BLUEBIRD, 20 × 15. Metropolitan Museum. K7810

A SUMMER IDYLL, 12¾ × 16. Inscribed: To my friend Walton John S. Sargent. Brooklyn Museum. K789

Naples and Capri

NEAPOLITAN BOY (three-quarter face), 18½ × 13½. Alvin T. Fuller* 785

NEAPOLITAN BOY (profile), 18½ × 14. Signed. Alvin T. Fuller* 784

ITALIAN BOY, 15 × 18. Inscribed: To my cousin Kitty Austin John S. Sargent 1878. Mrs. William Spickers. 786

ITALIAN GIRL, 17½ × 14. False Signature. Art Gallery, Canajoharie, New York. 787

STUDY HEAD FOR THE CAPRI GIRL, 9 × 10. Jean Louis Ormond. 783

THE CAPRI GIRL, 34½ × 25. Inscribed: John S. Sargent Capri 1878. Museum of Fine Arts, Boston. K787

THE CAPRI GIRL, 31 × 25. Inscribed: To my friend Mrs. Sorchan. Mrs. Walter Binger. K786

NUDE GIRL ON THE SANDS, CAPRI, 10 × 13½ wood. Guillaume Ormond. K7811

HEAD OF A CAPRI GIRL (called Sicilian Girl), 17 × 12. Inscribed: To Philip John S. Sargent. Sybil, Marchioness of Cholmondeley. 788

HEAD OF A CAPRI GIRL (called Mlle. L. Cagnard), 18 × 14. Sir Alec Martin. 789

ROSITA, CAPRI, 25¾ × 19¾. Inscribed: John S. Sargent Capri. Knoedler* K781

A STAIRWAY, CAPRI, 32¼ × 18¼. Signed, incorrectly dated 1875. Dr. George Woodward. K782

1879 FEMME AVEC FOURRURES, 10¾ × 8¼. Inscribed: A mon ami H. Vergèses John S. Sargent. Sterling & Francine Clark Institute. K815

RAPHAEL'S WAX HEAD AT LILLE. Richard Ormond. XK16

TWO BOYS MODELLING IN A STUDIO (on reverse) PENETENTIA, wood 18¼ × 11¼. Kennedy Galleries. K7923

JAPANESE BOY AND A BLOSSOMING BOUGH, 36½ × 25¾. Signed. M. R. Schweitzer Gallery.*

LUXEMBOURG GARDENS AT TWILIGHT, 24¾ × 35½. Inscribed: John S. Sargent Paris 1879. Philadelphia Museum. K793

LUXEMBOURG GARDENS AT TWILIGHT, 28½ × 36. Inscribed: To my friend McKim John S. Sargent. Minneapolis Institute of Arts. K792

BOYS ON BEACH, 10⅝ × 16¼. Signed and dated. Sterling and Francine Clark Institute. K7927

INNOCENTS ABROAD (study for Boys on Beach), 10 × 13½. Conrad Ormond. K788

Spain

SORTIE D'EGLISE EN ESPAGNE, 56 × 35. Signed. K7918

COURT OF LIONS, ALHAMBRA, 18¾ × 31½. Wildenstein Scott & Fowles. K795

THE ALHAMBRA, 20½ × 17. Guillaume Ormond. K794

THE LITTLE FRUIT SELLER, 13¾ × 10¾, wood. Inscribed: To my friend Mrs. Contemosi John S. Sargent 1879. Knoedler* K791

A SPANISH CHRIST, WITH ALTAR, 22½ × 15½. Emily Sargent 1935* K7922

A SPANISH MADONNA, wood 6 × 13. Inscribed: To Mrs. Gardner John S. Sargent. Isabella Stewart Gardner Museum.

MONK'S CELL (or The Moor), wood 13 × 11. Conrad Ormond. K8024

Copies made at Madrid

VELASQUEZ: MARTINEZ MONTANES, 24½ × 20. Francis H. Clarke. K7912

LAS MENIAS, 43½ × 38½. Conrad Ormond. K7911

APOLLO FROM 'THE FORGE OF VULCAN', 18 × 10⅝. Sir Alfred Beit. K7915

A DWARF. Conrad Ormond. K7929

THE IDIOT OF CORIA, 42 × 32½. Christies October 27, 1961. K7928

INFANTA MARGARETA, wood 13½ × 9½. Knoedler* K7910

HEAD OF AESOP, 18 × 14½. Agnews* K796

A BUFFOON OF PHILIP IV, 20½ × 16½. Sybil, Marchioness of Cholmondeley. K797

PRINCE BALTHAZAR CARLOS, 17½ × 14. Agnews* K7914

PRINCE BALTHAZAR CARLOS (Head), 21½ × 17¾. Van Der Neut (1925)*. K7913

LAS HILANDERAS, 23 × 28. Sir Alfred Beit. K799

THE DWARF DON ANTONIO EL INGLES, 55½ × 41½. Knoedler* K798

CARDINAL INFANTE DON FERDINAND, 16½ × 11. Ralph W. Curtis. K7926

PHILIP IV, 17 × 11. Ralph W. Curtis. K7925

RUBENS: THREE GRACES, 18 × 12. A. W. Kincade, Sr. K7917

EL GRECO: A PIETA, 31½ × 21. Sybil, Marchioness of Chol-
mondeley. K7916

TITIAN: PHILIP II, 17½ × 10½. Reine Pitman. K7920

GIROLAMO DA TREVISO: ST. GEROME, ST. ROCH, ST. SE-
BASTIAN, 31½ × 31½. Dartmouth College Art Gallery. K7919

GOYA: (from an Archway at San Antonio, Madrid), wood
13½ × 9½. Lady Dorothy Charteris* K7921

THE ENTOMBMENT (A Fresco in a Church in Granada), wood
14½ × 17. Saxe (1925)* K7924

1880
North Africa

BEDOUIN WOMEN, wood 10½ × 13½. Nicholson Gallery* K8025

TUNISIAN STREET SCENE, wood, 10 × 13½. Knoedler* K801

COURTYARD, TETUAN, wood 10⅜ × 13¾. Metropolitan Mu-
seum. K8026

OPEN DOORWAY, wood 13⅞ × 10⅜. Metropolitan Museum. K8027

COURTYARD WITH MOORISH DOOR, wood 10⅜ × 13⅞.
Metropolitan Museum. K8028

MOORISH HOUSE ON CLOUDY DAY, wood 10½ × 13⅞. Metro-
politan Museum. K8029

LANDSCAPE WITH HILLS, wood 10⅜ × 13⅞. Metropolitan Mu-
seum. K8030

MOORISH BUILDING IN SUNSHINE, wood 10⅜ × 13⅞.
Metropolitan Museum. K8031

BALCONY (on reverse) TWO NUDE BATHERS NEAR WHARF,
wood 13⅞ × 10⅝. Metropolitan Museum. K8032

MADONNA IN FESTIVE ROBE, wood 13 × 10¼. Metropolitan
Museum. K8033

THE COAST OF AFRICA (called The Coast of Algiers), wood
10½ × 13½. Leggatt (1925)* K8019

TWO MOORISH FIGURES. Metropolitan Museum. K8018

BOY LYING ON A BEACH, wood 10½ × 13½. Sutro (1925)* K8020

MAN AND A BOY IN A BOAT, wood 13½ × 10¼. Henry Tonks* K8021

THREE DONKEYS IN A DESERT, WITH SQUATTING FIGURE,
wood 10½ × 13. Guillaume Ormond. K8034

SEASCAPE WIH ROCKS, wood 10½ × 13. Guillaume Ormond. ... K8035

INTERIOR WITH STAINED GLASS WINDOW. Conrad Ormond.

INTERIOR WITH MOORISH COLLONADE. Guillaume Ormond.

TUNISIAN GIRL, wood 9¾ × 7½. Signed. K8018

OUTDOOR STUDY (Related to Fumée d'Ambre Gris), wood 10½
× 13½. Emily Sargent (1935)* K8023

Paris

STUDY FOR FUMÉE D'AMBRE GRIS, 31½ × 21. Jean Louis
Ormond. K809

FUMÉE D'AMBRE GRIS, 54 × 35¾. Inscribed: John S. Sargent Tanger. Sterling Francine Clark Institute. K808

STUDY OF A MAN, 25 × 30. Signed and incorrectly dated 1876. Mrs. Dudley Olcott. K802

WOODED LANDSCAPE (incorrectly called Les Chênes), 25⅞ × 21¼. Signed and dated. Knoedler* K805

EVENING SEA WITH ROWBOAT, wood 10½ × 13. Conrad Ormond. PUMPKINS, wood 10½ × 13½. Mrs. Ormond* K8022

AT SEVILLE (also called SPANISH DANCE), 33½ × 35½. Signed. Hispanic Society, New York. K803

STUDY FOR AT SEVILLE, 19 × 28½. Signed. J. W. Middendorf II. K804

STUDY FOR AT SEVILLE, 19 × 13½. Guillaume Ormond. K8226

Holland

COPIES AFTER FRANS HALS:

STANDARD BEARER OF THE ST. JORIS DOELEN, 25 × 23. Alvin T. Fuller*. K8015

TWO HEADS FROM THE ST. JORIS DOELEN GROUP, 22½ × 25. Mr. & Mrs. Robert L. Henderson. K8017

ADMINISTRATORS OF THE OLD MEN'S HOSPITAL AT HAARLEM, 30 × 42. Parke-Bernet, Dec. 14, 1933, No. 32* K8014

TWO FIGURES FROM THE ADMINISTRATORS OF THE OLD WOMAN'S HOSPITAL AT HAARLEM, 50 × 22. Christies, Dec. 1, 1961, No. 40* K8016

SCENE IN HOLLAND, 11 × 15. Mr. & Mrs. Roy Wildsmith.

Paris

CARMELA BERTAGNA, 23½ × 19½. Inscribed: A mon ami Poirson John S. Sargent / Carmela Bertagna/ 16 Rue du Maine. Columbus Gallery of Fine Arts. 8013

BEGGAR GIRL, 25¼ × 17¾. Inscribed: A mon ami Edelfeldt John S. Sargent. Chicago Art Institute. K8010

Venice

ONION GIRL, 33 × 24. Inscribed: A. M. Lemercier souvenir amical John S. Sargent. Sam Baraf. K807

COPY AFTER TINTORETTO'S BIRTH OF HE MILKY WAY. Conrad Ormond.

GONDOLAS, 14¾ × 18¼ wood. Anderson Galleries, May 10-11, 1933*. K8013

RAMON SUBERCASEAUX IN A GONDOLA, 18½ × 25. Luis Subercaseaux. 8017

SCENE ON A SIDE CANAL, VENICE (actually Scala di San Rocca), 16¾ × 13. Knoedler* K8213

GRAND CANAL, 33½ × 23½. Ralph W. Curtis. K8218

A STREET IN VENICE, 18 × 21½. Timothy Ormond. (Sottoportico di Calle Longo)

AN ITALIAN COURTYARD, 18 × 21½. Richard Ormond.

1881

SPANISH GYPSY, 18¼ × 11¼. Signed. Edward K. McCagg. K811

SPANISH GYPSY, 18 × 10¾. Inscribed: John S. Sargent A mon ami Chabrier. Daniel H. Farr Co.* K814

JACOB AND THE ANGEL, 6¾ × 6⅜. Signed. Howard Young Galleries* K812

AT ASSISSI. Emily Sargent (1935)* K813

1882

EL JALEO, 94½ × 137. Signed and dated. Isabella Stewart Gardner Museum K8221

SKETCH FOR EL JALEO. 32 × 25¾. Fogg Museum. K8223

SKETCH FOR EL JALEO, 31 × 23¼. Fogg Museum. K8222

Venice

LADY WITH A FAN, 50 × 100. Signed and dated. The Hon. Laurence Curtis. 8213

A VENETIAN WOMAN (Study for Woman With Fan), wood 16¾ × 12⅝. Joseph V. Reed. K8217

STUDY OF A VENETIAN GIRL, 20½ × 14. Mr. & Mrs. Charles Kohlmeyer, Jr. K8228

STUDY OF A VENETIAN GIRL, 20½ × 14. Ralph W. Curtis. ... K8229

THE VENETIAN GIRL (called Capri Girl), 16½ × 13. Signed and incorrectly dated 1880. Fogg Museum. 805

GONDOLIER (Study of a Man) 17¼ × 22. Signed. Knoedler* 806

THE SULPHUR MATCH, 23 × 16¼. Inscribed: John S. Sargent Venice 1882. Mrs. Louis Curtis. K825

VENETIAN WATER CARRIERS, 25¼ × 27. An inscription, probably to Bechstein, removed. Signed. Worcester Art Museum. K821

VENETIAN BEAD STRINGERS, 22 × 31. Inscribed: To my friend Lawless. National Gallery of Ireland. K8227

VENETIAN BEAD STRINGERS, 26 × 30. Inscribed: To my friend J. C. Beckwith. Albright-Knox Art Gallery. K826

VENETIAN INTERIOR, 18¾ × 25⅝. Inscribed: To my friend Litazia (?) John S. Sargent. Sterling & Francine Clark Institute. K8219

VENETIAN INTERIOR, 26⅜ × 34. Signed. Carnegie Institute. K824

VENETIAN GLASS WORKERS, 22 × 33½. Signed. Chicago Art Institute. K8220

VENETIAN COURTYARD (called Spanish Courtyard) 27½ × 31⅞. Signed. John Hay Whitney. K8212

SIESTA TIME IN THE DOGE'S PALACE, 20 × 30. Mrs. Ogilvie Grant. K8036

THE WINE SHOP (called Street in Venice), 28¾ × 20¾. Inscribed: John S. Sargent Venice. Sterling & Francine Clark Institute. 8211

WOMAN AT A WINDOW, 30 × 19¼. Mr. David Daniels.

STREET IN VENICE, 17½ × 21 wood. Signed. National Gallery, Washington. K822

A STREET IN VENICE, @22 × 31. Exhibited St.-Botolph's Club, Boston, 1887: illustrated in ART AMATEUR, 1888, page 5.

VENICE PAR TEMPS GRIS, 20 × 27½. Inscribed: A mon ami Flameng John S. Sargent. Trent Park, Barnet, Herts. (National Trust). K823

STREET SCENE IN VENICE, 16 × 20. Mrs. Schuyler Owen K8215

THE GUIDECCA, 11½ × 16. Inscribed: J.S. Sargent to R.W.C. Venice 1882. Mrs. Schuyler Owen. K8214

ST. MARK'S VENICE: THE PAVEMENT. 21 × 28½. Signed. Conrad Ormond. K8210

ST. MARK'S, 18× 24. Mrs. Schuyler Owen. K8216

INTERIOR OF ST. MARK'S, 18 × 23¾. Inscribed: A Helleu de John S. Sargent ne pas plier. Gabriel Semence.

RIO DEI MENDICANTI, wood, 14 × 10. (on the reverse a study of an Italian fountain) M. Kennedy & Co.

PRESSING WINE IN A CELLAR. Exhibited at The Fine Art Society, London, 1882.

GENOA HARBOR, wood 10 × 13½. Guillaume Ormond. K8224

1883 *Nice*

FLOWERING BORDER, wood. Victor Spark Gallery.*

ALMOND BLOSSOMS, NICE, 22× 28. Conrad Ormond. K833

ORANGE TREES, 18 × 15. Inscribed: Nice. Reine Pitman. K834

ALMOND BLOSSOMS, NICE (Garden With Hedged Beds in Bloom), 18 × 26. Reine Pitman.

ORCHARD IN BLOOM NEAR NICE, 23⅝ × 29. Mr. & Mrs. Norman I. Schaflen. K831

LANDSCAPE VIEW NEAR NICE, 23½ × 28½. Christies, June 30, 1939, No. 129. .... K832

1884 *England*

A DINNER TABLE AT NIGHT, 20 × 27. Signed. The Hon. David Pleydell-Bouverie. K841

Nice

IN A GARDEN, 24 × 29. Conrad Ormond.

1885 *Nice*

A ROAD IN THE SOUTH, 12¾ × 18. Sterling & Francine Clark Institute. K855

ROSES, 9½ × 21½. Guillaume Ormond.

MEADOW AND STREAM, Board 14⅝ × 24¼. Inscribed: a mon ami . . . (Signature re-enforced). Detroit Institute of Arts.

THE BREAKFAST TABLE, 21¾ × 18¼. Inscribed: A mon ami Besnard John S. Sargent. Fogg Museum. K853

Paris

THE BESNARD FAMILY (The Birthday Party) 24 × 30. Minneapolis Museum. 859

England

WHITBY FISHING BOATS, 19 × 27. Inscribed: To my friend Mrs. Vickers John S. Sargent Whitby. The Hon. David Pleydell-Bouverie. K8511

THE HOME FIELDS, 28½ × 38. Inscribed: To my friend Bramley John S. Sargent. Detroit Institute of Arts. K856

SKETCHES FOR CARNATION LILY, LILY ROSE
  1. 28 × 18. Lily Millet* K851
  2. 28 × 18. Christies, April 18, 1969, No. 149 .... K852
  3. 23½ × 19½. Sotheby's, Nov. 21, 1961, lot 56. .... K8513
  4. 19½ × 15½. Reine Pitman.
  5. 22 × 13½. (Roses on a Trellis) Robert C. Barton.

HOLLYHOCKS, 39¾ × 33. Knoedlers* K854

LADY WITH CANDLEABRA, 20¾ × 26¼. Signed and dated. Mr. & Mrs. Gilbert Schafer. K8516

THE OLD CHAIR, 26½ × 21½. Mrs. J. L. Hughes. K8510

LANDSCAPE WITH ROSE BUSHES, 20½ × 25. Guillaume Ormond. K8514

PICKING ROSES, BROADWAY (Mrs. Millet & Kate), 36 × 24. Mrs. Lisbeth Bazeley. K8517

THE THRESHERS, 28 × 36. Metropolitan Museum. K8512

GARDEN SKETCH. Estate of Dr. Frederick S. Pratt.* K8515

LADY WITH POPPIES. Exhibited at Copley Hall, Boston, 1899, No. 112.

1886   *England*

CARNATION LILY, LILY ROSE, 68½ × 60½. Signed. The Tate Gallery. K864

A GIRL WITH A SICKLE, 23½ × 15½. Inscribed: To Lily Millet from her old friend John S. Sargent. Dr. J.A.P. Millet. K861

THE GARDEN AT BROADWAY, 27, × 35. Dr. J. P. Millet K862

AT BROADWAY, 1886, 17½ × 23½. Mrs. Robert Osborne. K863

1887   *Giverny*

CLAUDE MONET PAINTING, 20½ × 25½. The Tate Gallery. K893

CLAUDE MONET PAINTING IN HIS STUDIO-BOAT. Gene Thaw.

MME. HOSCHEDÉ AND HER SON AT GIVERNY, 25½ × 27¾. Samuel Spector.

England

FIVE MONOCHROME ILLUSTRATIONS FOR SPANISH
AND ITALIAN FOLK SONGS' BY ALMA STRETTELL.
Given in charge of Thomas Fox (1926). Disappeared.
1. FATE. Signed J.S.S. K871
2. GARDEN SKETCH. K872
3. SPANISH DANCER. Signed J.S.S. K873
4. SPANISH CRUCIFIX K875
5. MONOCHROME (Statue of the Virgin) K876
LADY AND A BOY ASLEEP IN A PUNT UNDER A WIL-
LOW. Signed. K877
THE BLUE BOWL, 27½ × 23. Signed J.S.S. Milch Gallery* K878
UNDER THE WILLOWS, 26 × 21. Signed J. C. Shepherd* K879
MY DINING ROOM, 28½ × 23½. Smith College Museum of
Art K8710

1888 *England*

BY THE RIVER, 20 × 27. Signed. (An inscription: *A Otto,*
éxchange amical, has been removed.) Mrs. James D. Cameron
Bradley. K882
DENNIS MILLER BUNKER PAINTING AT CALCOT,
27 × 25. Signed. Mrs. William C. Breed. K886
A BACKWATER AT CALCOT NEAR READING, 25 × 30.
Knoedlers* K883
THE BACKWATER, CALCOT MILL, NEAR READING,
20 × 27. Kennedy Galleries. K884
ST. MARTIN'S SUMMER (called Fladbury Rectory, but actu-
ally painted at Calcot), 36¼ × 28⅛. Signed and dated. Knoed-
lers* K881
WARGRAVE BACKWATER, 30 × 25. Milch Gallery. K887
THE MORNING WALK (Violet Sargent). Jean Louis Ormond. K885

1889 *England*

A BOATING PARTY (called Calcot, but done at Fladbury Rec-
tory), 34⅜ × 36. Rhode Island School of Design. K592
AUTUMN ON THE RIVER, 30 × 19¾. Signed. Estate of
Charles Deering. K891
PAUL HELLEU SKETCHING WITH HIS WIFE. 26 × 32.
Signed. Brooklyn Museum. K8910
RIVER BANK NEAR OXFORD, 16 × 20. Robert C. Barton.
TWO GIRLS IN A PUNT (Violet Sargent & Mme. Helleu),
18 × 14½. Guillaume Ormond. K8918
SKETCH OF TWO GIRLS ON A LAWN, 21⅛ × 15¼. Metro-
politan Museum. K896
TWO GIRLS WITH PARASOLS AT FLADBURY, 29½ × 25.
Metropolitan Museum. K897

FISHING, 28½ × 21. Inscribed: To Reine, John S. Sargent.
Mrs. J. L. Hughes. K898

FISHING, 72 × 38. Tate Gallery. K899

THE LOWEST TERRACE, FLADBURY (Unfinished), 30 ×
24½. Conrad Ormond. K8916

MISS PRIESTLEY AND MME. ORMOND, 22 × 16½. Reine
Pitman. K8917

IGHTHAM MOTE HOUSE, KENT, 56¼ × 90¼. Signed.
Parke-Bernet, May 11, 1966. .... K894

PISTOL IN THE SNOW (Illustration from Shakespeare's Henry
V), 25 × 30. Metropolitan Museum. K895

THE GLASS OF CLARET (BY CANDLELIGHT). Exhibited
Copley Hall, Boston, 1899, No. 78. .... K8915

Paris

JAVANESE DANCER:

1. 68 × 32. George P. Gardner, Jr. K8911
2. 68½ × 31½. Jean Louis Ormond. K8913
3. 68½ × 30. Mrs. J. L. Hughes. K8914
4. (At her Toilet) 25½ × 21. Wildenstein, Scott & Fowles. K8912

1890 *Massachusetts*

TREES AND POND, 25 × 30. Mrs. R. M. Saltonstall. K901

1891 *Egypt*

BEDOUIN ARABS (heads):
1. 25 × 18½. Signed. Sybil, Marchioness of Cholmondeley. 914
2. 27½ × 21½. L. Sutro, Esq. (1925)* 919
3. 28 × 22. Christies 1925, No. 196. 9110
4. 20½ × 16½. Christies 1925, No. 190. 918
5. 31½ × 23¼. Museum of Fine Arts, Boston. 9112

TWO BEDOUINS, 15½ × 28½. D. Croal Thomson (1925)* K9113

BEDOUINS, 10 × 17½. Otto Gutekunst. K9114

EGYPTIAN WOMEN (heads):
1. A FELLAH WOMAN, 25 × 19. Signed. Sybil, Marchioness
of Cholmondeley.
2. GIRL, 25½ × 21. Metropolitan Museum. 916
3. GIRL, 28 × 21¼. Metropolitan Museum. 915

EGYPTIAN GIRL (nude study), 73 × 23. Signed. Mrs. Chauncey McCormick, Mrs. Richard E. Danielson. K911

EGYPTIAN INDIGO DYERS, 25 × 21. Metropolitan Museum. K915

NILE WATER CARRIERS. Guillaume Ormond.

NILE WATER CARRIERS. 21 × 25. Chicago Art Institute. K9110

SUNSET, CAIRO, 24½ × 29. Knoedlers* K918

THE TEMPLE OF DENDERAH, 29 × 24. Sotheby's, Dec. 11,
1957, No. 126. .... K9111

DOOR OF A MOSQUE. Museum of Fine Arts, Boston.

TWO ARCHITECTURAL VIEWS ON ONE CANVAS. Museum of Fine Arts, Boston.

STUDIES OF EGYPTIAN SCULPTURE, 24 × 29. M. R. Schweitzer Gallery. K916

Constantinople

INTERIOR OF SANCTA SOPHIA, 32 × 24½. J.B. Speed Museum. K912

INTERIOR OF SANCTA SOPHIA, 31½ × 24¼. Metropolitan Museum. K914

CEMETERY, CONSTANTINOPLE, 18½ × 23½. Guillaume Ormond. K9116

CEMETERY, CONSTANTINOPLE. Guillaume Ormond.

Greece

THE ERECTHEUM (also called The Beggar), 18½ × 23½. Guillaume Ormond. K919

SKETCH AT CORFU. Exhibited at Copley Hall, 1899, No. 91. K982

Versailles

COUR D'HONNEUR, 19½ × 24. Gabriel Semence.

1892 *England* (Preparations for Boston Library murals.)

MAJOR GEORGE C. ROLLER AS A PROPHET, 26 × 26. Inscribed: To my friend Roller. Mrs. John Mathias. 9212

THE PROPHETS (Two heads of a bearded man), 24 × 36. Harry W. Anderson. K921

MOSES, 31 × 23. The Norton Galleries. K922

HEAD OF A MALE MODEL (HEAVY MUSTACHE), 14½ × 19. Nelson C. White. 9617

STUDY FOR THE PROPHET HOSEA'S DRAPERY, 33 × 23½. Mrs. C. Nichols Greene (1940)* K924

STUDY FOR THE FRIEZE OF PROPHETS, 22 × 28. Museum of Fine Arts, Boston.

STUDY FOR THE FRIEZE OF PROPHETS, 47 × 74. Emily Sargent (1935)* K926

EARLY STUDY FOR HEBRAIC END OF BOSTON PUBLIC LIBRARY, 39 × 44. Emily Sargent (1935)* K925

1893 *England*

COUNTRY ROAD IN WINTER (Probably Fairford), 25 × 29½. Parke-Bernet* K927

A JERSEY CALF, 29 × 25. Inscribed: To Mrs. Mead with a Merry Christmas. Yale University Art Gallery. K931

(Preparations for Boston Library murals)

ASTARTE:
1. Inscribed: To my friend Fred Leighton John S. Sargent.
   Isabella Stewart Gardner Museum. K932
2. 38⅝ × 12. Metropolitan Museum. K933
3. 64 × 22. Emily Sargent (1935)* K937
4. 78½ × 35½. Print Department, Boston Public Library K935

MOLOCH:
1. 57 × 18. Museum of Fine Arts, Boston. K936
2. 78½ × 35½. Print Department, Boston Public Library. K934

1894 *England*

A PERSIAN CARPET, 54 × 40. Christies 1925, No. 179 (Martin) K941

1895 *Spain*

SPANISH COURTYARD, 22 × 28. Estate of Charles Deering. K125

SKETCH OF SPANISH COURTYARD, wood. Jean Louis Ormond.

1896   (Preparations for Boston Library murals)

AN ITALIAN MODEL, 24 × 17⅜. City Museum & Art Gallery, Birmingham. 9616

ITALIAN SAILOR WITH ROPE, 25 × 18. Signed. Wildenstein, Scott & Fowle. 9613

AN ITALIAN MODEL, 24 × 18. Christies, March 23, 1962, No. 194.

A YOUNG ITALIAN(MAN IN BLACK), 23 × 17½. Private Collection, California from Barbizon House (1926). X7

HEAD OF A GONDOLIER, 23½ × 19½. Trent Park, Barnet, Herts. (National Trust) 9614

MONOCHROME BIBLE ILLUSTRATIONS:
1. David in Saul's Camp, 26 × 28. Knoedler* K961
2. David Playing Before Saul, 22½ × 30½. Signed. M. R.
   Schweitzer Gallery* K962
3. DAVID AND JONATHAN SWEAR A COVENANT. Ex.
   hibited at Copley Hall, Boston, 1899, No. 108. .... K963
4. DAVID THE SHEPHERD, 17½ × 24. Christies 1925,
   No. 212 (Smith)* K964

1897 *Sicily*

VIEW IN SICILY, 22 × 27½. Inscribed: John S. Sargent Girgenti. Lady Dorothy Charteris* K971

1898 *Ravenna*

STUDIES FROM THE MOSAIC DECORATIONS INTENDED
AS PREPARATIONS FOR THE BOSTON LIBRARY MURALS
  1. A FLOOR, 17½ × 26. Sybil, Marchioness of Cholmon-
     deley. K917
  2. A FLOOR, 14 × 17½. Guillaume Ormond. K9115
  3. A SAINT HOLDING A BOOK, 26¼ × 18⅛. Knoedler* K989
  4. VIRGIN AND CHILD, 26¼ × 18⅛. Knoedler* K988
  5. VIRGIN AND FIVE FEMALE SAINTS, 26 × 18.
     Knoedler* K983
  6. A CEILING DECORATION, 14½ × 18½. South Afri-
     can National Gallery, Capetown. K981
  7. VIRGIN AND HEAD OF CHRIST, 26 × 17½. Museum
     of Fine Arts, Boston. K984
  8. HEAD OF CHRIST, 26 × 18. Museum of Fine Arts,
     Boston. K987
  9. A MOSAIC, 18½ × 21½. Sybil, Marchioness of Chol-
     mondeley. K985
  10. A MOSAIC, 18 × 13½. Sybil, Marchioness of Cholmon-
     deley. K986

1899 *Venice*

THE ROCCOCCO MIRROR, wood 23 × 18. Jean Louis Ormond.

AN INTERIOR IN VENICE (Palazzo Barbaro), 25½ × 31¾.
Signed and dated 1899. The Royal Academy, London. K991

INTERIOR OF THE DUCAL PALACE, 20 × 27½. Signed.
Earl of Harewood. K042

1902 *Norway*

TORRENT IN NORWAY, 22 × 28. Christies 1925, No. 146
(Martin)* K021

ON HIS HOLIDAYS, 52½ × 96. Signed. Lady Lever Art Gal-
lery. K022

A SALMON. George McCulloch* K023

1903 *Switzerland*

NO NONSENSE (His Studio), 21 × 28. Signed. Museum of Fine
Arts, Boston. K041

PADRE SEBASTIANO, 22½ × 28. Signed. Metropolitan Mu-
seum. K089

1904 *Venice*

A CANAL IN VENICE, 19½ × 14. Inscribed: To my friend Sir
Frank Swettenham. Christies November 22, 1946, No. 17

GONDOLAS AT THE PIAZZETTA, 19¾ × 13¾. Inscribed:
To my friend Sir Frank Swettenham. Sotheby's, Dec. 11, 1957,
No. 125.

THE PIAZZETTA, 13 × 18. Signed. Christies November 13, 1964.

MOSAIC FLOOR (San Marco?) Unfinished. 23½ × 28½. Semence et Fils.

THE FLOOR OF SAN MARCO, 21¼ × 28¾. Signed Wickersham Gallery.

GRAND CANAL, 23½ × 29. Signed. Wickersham Gallery K137

SCENE IN VENICE, REFLECTIONS, 20 × 28½. Signed. Hirschl & Adler. K829

TRATTORIA (called Venetian Wine Shop), 21 × 27½. Signed. Jean Louis Ormond. K047

THE CHURCH OF SAN STAE:
    1. 21½ × 27½. Trent Park, Barnet, Herts. (National Trust) K044
    2. 28 × 22. Signed and dated. C. Ledyard. K045

THE CHURCH OF THE SALUTE:
    1. 12 × 16. Signed. Henry Goldman.
    2. 28½ × 40½. Signed. Johannesburg Art Gallery. K046
    3. 25 × 36. Fitzwilliam Museum. K043
    4. 23½ × 28½. Signed. Meyer P. Potamkin.

BEHIND THE CURTAIN (Marionettes), 28½ × 20. Conrad Ormond. K1011

1905   *England*

THE GREAT HALL AT BLENHEIM, 20½ × 17. Julian George Lousada* K992

The Holy Land

JERUSALEM:
    1. 27½ × 21½. Signed. Emily Sargent (1925)* K0513
    2. 18½ × 23½. Violet Ormond (1925)* K0512
    3. (Pavement) 19 × 23. Violet Ormond (1925)* K0517
    4. 21 × 27½. Richard Ormond. K053

GETHSEMANE, 26 × 38½. Fitzwilliam Museum. K0515

FRANCISCAN MONK IN THE GARDEN OF GETHSEMANE, 27 × 22. Signed. Portland Art Museum. K055

PALESTINE (Bedouin Lying in Foreground), 22 × 28. Knoedler. K0519

THE DEAD SEA, 22 × 28. Christies 1925, No. 125 (Stevens & Brown)* K0518

THE MOUNTAINS OF MOAB, 25 × 43. Signed. The Tate Gallery. K057

PLAINS OF ESRAELON, 27½ × 43. The Tate Gallery. K0511

HOLY LAND MOUNTAINS, 13¾ × 24¾. Metropolitan Museum. K058

VALLEY OF MAR SEBA, 25 × 37½. Edwin T. Kasper K054

ARABS IN CAMP, 21½ × 27½. Signed. Sold privately by Christies, May 18, 1936. .... K052

SYRIAN STABLES, 22 × 28.

SYRIAN GOATS, 22 × 28. Estate of Charles Deering. K056

WOMAN GOATHERD (unfinished), 24½ × 31⅞. Metropolitan Museum. K059

A DONKEY, 20 × 27. Knoedler* XK4

1906 *Rome*

THE VILLA PAPA GIULIO:
1. 21½ × 27¼. Conrad Ormond. K064
2. (The Exterior Portal), 27½ × 22. Jean Louis Ormond.
3. (Study of a Balustrade), 28 × 22. Trent Park, Barnet, Herts. (National Trust). K062
4. (The Garden Terrace: called "Window in the Vatican"), 28 × 21½. Trent Park, Barnet, Herts. (National Trust). K065

STEPS OF S. DOMENICO E SISTO, 21½ × 27½. Ashmolean Museum, Oxford. K063

A TEMPLE IN A GARDEN, 19 × 23. Signed. Christies, June 19, 1964.

A HOTEL ROOM, 24 × 17½. Conrad Ormond. K066

NICOLA READING, 22 × 25. Reading Public Museum & Art Gallery. X8

Siena

OXEN RESTING, 21½ × 27½. Signed. Lady Dorothy Charteris* K074

SHOEING THE OX, 21½ × 27½. Signed. Corporation of Aberdeen. K105

Bologna

THE FOUNTAIN, 20 × 28. Signed. Trent Park, Barnet, Herts. (National Trust). K067

1907 *Florence*

A FLORENTINE FOUNTAIN, 22 × 18½. Signed. Knoedler* K001

THE STATUE OF PERSEUS BY NIGHT, 36 × 50½. Signed. Santa Barbara Museum. K0710

Frascati

GARDENS OF THE VILLA TORLONIA:
1. 27 × 34½. Signed. Jean Louis Ormond. K076
2. 28½ × 22. Signed. Chicago Art Institute. K077
3. 21½ × 27½. Signed. Guillaume Ormond. K073

FALCONIERI GARDENS, 20½ × 28. Signed. Knoedler* K071

STATUE OF VERTUMNUS AT FRASCATI, 29½ × 22. Signed. Municipal Gallery of Modern Art, Dublin. K075

A VILLA, 14¾ × 23½. Goldschmidt.

number
in
previous
editions

1908 *Switzerland*

CASHMERE, 27½ × 42½. Signed. Nicholas Benson. K0812
THE BROOK, 21½ × 17½. Signed. The Tate Gallery. K0816
THE BROOK, 21½ × 27½. Inscribed: To Violet John S. Sargent. Guillaume Ormond. K123
DOLCE FAR NIENTE, 16 × 29. Signed. Brooklyn Museum. ... K088
THE CHESS GAME, 21½ × 27½. Signed. Albert Sneck. K086
GROUP WITH PARASOLS, 21½ × 27½. Inscription undeciphered. Signed. Daniel & Rita Fraad. K0822
THE SKETCHERS, 22 × 28. Mrs. Schermerhorn. K0821
THE HERMIT, 38 × 38. Signed. Metropolitan Museum. K087

Majorca

HORSES:
    1. 21⅞ × 28. Knoedler* K084
    2. 20× 28. Addison Gallery of American Art. K0818
THISTLES:
    1. 22½ × 28. Miss Grace Nichols* XK1
    2. 22 × 28. Christies 1925, No. 198 (D. Croal Thomson)*.... XK3
    3. 22 × 28. Christies 1925, No. 202.
POMEGRANATES:
    1. 22 × 28. Henry Lowey. K081
    2. 27½ × 22. Wildenstein, Scott & Fowle. K082
    3. 36 × 28. Mrs. Thomas Ware. K083
ILEX WOOD, 22 × 28. Knoedler. K0819
ROOTS, VALDEMOSA, 22½ × 28. Knoedler* K085
GIRLS GATHERING BLOSSOMS, VALDEMOSA, 28 × 22. Parke-Bernet, May 15, 1968. ...... K0815
A SIESTA (The Mosquito Net), 22 × 28. The White House, Washington. K0810
MOSQUITO NETS (Miss Wedgewood & Emily Sargent), 22 × 28. Conrad Ormond. K0811
MAJORCAN FISHERMAN, 27½ × 21½. Signed and dated. Viscount Rothermere. K0817

1909 *Switzerland*

RECONNOITERING, 22 × 28. Signed. Pitti Palace, Florence. K114
PRINCESS NOURONIHAR, 22 × 28. Signed. Parke-Bernet* K1013
COMING DOWN FROM MONT BLANC, 36 × 44½. M. R. Schweitzer Gallery. K0813
ALPINE POOL, 30½ × 44. Parke-Bernet* K1012
DRY STREAM BED, 17½ × 18½. J. S. Maas & Co.
SHADED ALPINE POOL, 27½ × 38. Metropolitan Museum. K1017
SIMPLON PASS, 28 × 36½. Signed. Corcoran Gallery. K1010
GLACIER STREAMS, THE SIMPLON, 34⅝ × 44¾. Signed. The Springfield Museum of Fine Arts. K107

STUDY IN THE ALPS, 20 × 28. Signed. Victoria National Gallery, Melbourne. K108

THE MORAINE, 21½ × 27½. Signed. Viscount Rothermere. K149

MONT BLANC, 35½ × 38. Signed. The Tate Gallery. K0814

BRENNER GLACIER, 36½ × 46½. Signed. Municipal Art Gallery, Johannesburg. K091

Corfu

OLIVE GROVES:
1. (Albanian Olive Gatherers), 37 × 44½. Signed. City of Manchester Art Gallery. K0910
2. 20 × 24. Irving W. Rabb. K097
3. 26½ × 36. Breckenridge Long. K098
4. (unfinished) Conrad Ormond. K094
5. 22 × 28. Inscribed: Corfu (incorrectly dated 1912) Fitzwilliam Museum. K0913
6. 22 × 28. Signed. Knoedler* K093

THE WHITE HOUSE, 27 × 21. Sotheby's, Dec. 11. 1957, No. 127. .... K096

GARDEN IN CORFU, 21½ × 27½. Signed. Viscount Rothermere. K0912

LANDSCAPE WITH GOATS, 22 × 28. Signed. Freer Gallery. K0919

CYPRESSES AND PINES, 28 ×36. Signed, R. J. Edwards. K095

TWO GIRLS RECLINING UNDER CYPRESS TREES, 28 × 35½. Barbizon House (1925)* K0911

THREE FIGURE AND PLUMBAGO. Matias Errazuriz. K0925

ORANGES AT CORFU, 21½ × 27½. Signed. Worcester Museum. K099

BOY AND GIRL IN AN ORANGE GROVE, 55 × 22. .... K079

VESPERS. Sir Thomas Brock sale, May 4, 1928. .... K0914

FIG TREE (Foliage Study), 22 × 28. Knoedler* K0916

London (Preparations for Boston Library murals)

THE MESSIANISTIC ERA:
1. 33¼ × 66¼. Smith College Museum. K0917
2. 35 × 68½. The Royal Academy, London. K9020
3. Lewis F. Perry K0923

JUDGMENT:
1. 33¼ × 66¼. Smith College Museum. K0918
2. 69½ × 59. Emily Sargent (1935)* K0922

ISRAEL LEARNING THE LAW, 30 × 58. Mrs. C. Nichols Greene. K0915

MURAL STUDY. Lewis F. Perry K0924

1910 *Switzerland*

ON THE SIMPLON PASS, 27½ × 35½. Signed and incorrectly dated 1912. Lt.-Col. E. A. Armstrong. K1215

THE SIMPLON, CHALETS IN A VALLEY, 28 × 36. Viscount
Rothermere. K1015

A VIEW IN THE SIMPLON VALLEY, 37 × 45. Fogg Museum.   K1014

A WATERFALL, 28 × 44¼. Signed. I.B.M. Collection K106

VAL D'AOSTA:
    1. (Stepping Stones), 22 × 28. Knoedler* K101
    2. (Mountain Stream), 17 × 21. Knoedler* K103
    3. (Man Fishing), 22 × 28. Addison Gallery of American Art.   K109
    4. (A Stream Over Rocks), 22 × 28. Neville Orgel. K104
    5. (Rocks and Torrents), 22 × 28. Knoedler* K0820
    6. (The Cashmere Shawl), 28 × 22. Inscribed: To my friend
       George Roller John S. Sargent. Babcock Gallery. K102
    7. (Two Girls Fishing), 22 × 28. Signed. Cincinnati Museum.   K124

Florence

STUDY OF ARCHITECTURE, FLORENCE, 28 × 36. Tooth
Gallery. K1018

VILLA TORRE GALLI:
    1. Ladies in a Garden, 28 × 36. Diploma Gallery, Royal
       Academy, London. K1016
    2. Breakfast in the Loggia, 20¼ × 28. Signed. Freer Gallery.   K1019
    3. The Loggia, 22 × 28. Signed. Mrs. Charles S. Payson. K1020
    4. In the Garden, 21½ × 27½. Milch Gallery* K1021

London   (Preparations for Boston Library murals)

THE FALL OF GOG AND MAGOG:
    1. 27½ × 54½. Print Department, Boston Public Library. K1025
    2. 33⅛ × 66¾. Fogg Museum.
    3. 35 × 68½. The Royal Academy, London. K1023
    4. 30 × 60. Print Department, Boston Public Library. K1024

1911 *Venice*

THE RIALTO:
    1. 21½ × 26. Jean Louis Ormond. K113
    2. 22 × 36. Philadelphia Museum. K112

NONCHALOIR, 22 × 28. Signed and dated. National Gallery,
Washington. K115

Carrara

MARBLE QUARRY, 28 × 22. Inscribed: John S. Sargent Car-
rara (and misdated) 1913. R. Langston Douglas* K116

MARBLE QUARRIES, 28 × 36. Signed. Metropolitan Museum.   K117

Switzerland

THE BROOK, 21½ × 27½. Timothy Ormond. K118

THE PINK DRESS, 21½ × 26. Guillaume Ormond. K1217

TWO GIRLS IN WHITE DRESSES, 22 × 28. Signed. Trent Park,
Barnet, Herts. (National Trust). K111

1912   *Spain*

SPANISH GYPSIES, 28 × 36. Addison Gallery of American Art. K1213

THE COURTYARD, 22 × 28. Signed. Albany Institute of History and Art. K121

MOORISH COURTYARD, 28 × 36. Signed. (misdated) 1913. James H. Clarke. K126

GRANADA: SUNSPOTS, 27½ × 21½. Richard Ormond. K1210

GARDEN IN GRANADA, 15 × 22. Reine Pitman.

FOUNTAIN AT ARANJUEZ, 22 × 28. Inscribed: John S. Sargent Aranjuez 1912. Asscher & Walker (1925)* K122

HOSPITAL AT GRANADA, 20 × 27½. Signed. Victoria National Gallery, Melbourne. K128

THE WEAVERS, 22 × 28. Signed. Freer Gallery. K127

SPANISH LANDSCAPE, 21½ × 27½. Signed. K1210

THE SIERRA NEVADA, 22 × 25½. Signed. H. W. Henderson (1926)* K1212

1913   *Venice*

SAN GEREMIA (& Palazzo Labbia), 21½ × 27½. Signed and dated. Conrad Ormond. K048

THE PIAZZETTA:
  1. 20 × 24. Mr. & Mrs. Robert Cooper, Jr.
  2. 21½ × 27½. Conrad Ormond. K138

LA SCALA DI SAN ROCCA, originally 25 × 31 cut down by the artist to 25 × 26. Signed. Harry W. Anderson.
  Strip cut away, 6¼ × 24. Russell Cooke (destroyed 1940-45) K829

STUDY FOR FIGURES IN LA SCALA DI SAN ROCCA. Guillaume Ormond.

SAN GIOVANNI EVANGELISTA, 22 × 28. Signed and dated. Fogg Museum. K134

San Vigilio

CYPRESS TREES AT SAN VIGILIO, 28 × 36. Knoedler* K133

CYPRESS TREES AT SAN VIGILIO, 28 × 36. Phillips Andover Academy. K1311

SAN VIGILIO, 25 × 45. Christies 1925, No. 81

LANDSCAPE AT SAN VIGILIO, 36 × 45. Lord Milford. K1312

SAN VIGILIO, 27½ × 71. Signed and dated. Beaverbrook Museum. K1320

A BOAT WITH A GOLDEN SAIL, 22 × 28. Nicholson Gallery. K135

TWO SAILING BARGES IN DOCK AT SAN VIGILIO, 22 × 28. Signed. Knoedler* K132

THREE BOATS IN THE HARBOUR OF SAN VIGILIO, 22 × 28. Signed. Estate of Charles Deering. K136

1917 *America*

INTERIOR OF VISCAYA. Destroyed by fire, 1920.
FOUNTAIN AT POCANTICO HILLS, 28 × 22. Signed. J. D.
Rockefeller, Jr. K174
FULL LENGTH STUDY OF A COLORED MODEL. K171
MALE MODEL:
    1. (Pillow behind his shoulders) 21 × 17. Arthur V. Newton.*   K176
    2. (Resting: *Nicola*), 22 × 28. Mrs. John Gardner Greene. XK14
THE HESPERIDES (mural preparation), 15½ × 35½. Jean
Louis Ormond. K173

1918 *France*

RUINED CATHEDRAL AT ARRAS, 21½ × 27½. Inscribed:
John S. Sargent Arras Aug. 1918. Sybil, Marchioness of Chol-
mondeley. K183
ARRIVAL OF AMERICAN TROOPS AT THE FRONT,
17½ × 28. Knoedler.* K181
AMERICAN TROOPS GOING UP THE LINE, 14½ × 27½.
Sybil, Marchioness of Cholmondeley. K187
THE ROAD, 15 × 26½. Signed and dated. Museum of Fine
Arts, Boston. K185
ARMY CONVOY, 9⅜ × 14⅜. Richard Ormond. K188
SHOEING CAVALRY HORSES AT THE FRONT, 22 × 25.
Signed. Grand Central Art Galleries (1947)* K182

London

GASSED, 90½ × 240. Signed and dated Aug. 1918. Imperial
War Museum. K184
STUDY FOR GASSED, 10 × 27. Inscribed: To Evan Char-
teris John S. Sargent. Lady Dorothy Charteris* K186

1919 *America*

SPHINX AND CHIMAERA (mural study). Jean Louis Ormond.   K191
REVENGE, 28 × 24. Fogg Museum. XK8

1921 *America*

SKETCH OF ONE SIDE WALL OF THE BOSTON PUBLIC
LIBRARY, 22½ × 62. Print Department, Boston Public Library.   XK18

(Preparations for murals in the Museum of Fine Arts, Boston)

ORESTES AND THE FURIES:
    1. 29 × 24¼. Yale University Art Gallery.
    2. 35 × 28. Christies 1925, No. 176 (Mathews)* K212
HERCULES AND THE HYDRA:
    1. 27 × 24½. Christies 1925, No. 175 (Leggatt)* K211
    2. 45 × 33½. Emily Sargent (1935)* K213

DUBLIN, NEW HAMPSHIRE, 24 × 18. Knoedler.

1922 *America*

THE ARTIST SKETCHING, 27¼ × 27¾. Signed and dated.
Mrs. Richard T. Crane. K229

(Preparations for Museum of Fine Arts murals)
UNVEILING OF TRUTH:
1. 25 × 47. Fogg Museum. K224
2. 36 × 47. Christies 1925, No. 167 (Cooling)* K223
3. 38 × 58. Guillaume Ormond. K228
THE WINDS:
1. 24 × 58½. Christies 1925, No. 172 (Van der Neut)* K222
2. 37 × 36½. Emily Sargent (1935)* K226
THE DANAIDES:
1. 32 × 60. Christies 1925, No. 173 (Willard)* K221
2. 44 × 75. Jean Louis Ormond. K225
APOLLO WITH THE HOURS. Emily Sargent (1935)* K227

1923 *America*

(Preparations for Museum of Fine Arts murals)
PHILOSOPHY, 13⅝ × 7¼. Metropolitan Museum. K232
ASTRONOMY, 13⅝ × 7½. Metropolitan Museum. K231

UNDATED

SEACOAST WITH A WRECK, 16¾ × 13¾. Mrs. H. W.
Jefferson. K175
PEASANT BOY, 24 × 18. Christies 1925, No. 138
THE FLIGHT INTO EGYPT, 21½ × 17½. Guillaume Or-
mond. XK10
EXPECTANCY: A YOUNG GIRL, 39½ × 33¼. T. de Mattos.
COMYNS CARR AND MISS HUXLEY IN A BOAT (Sketch
from Memory), 24½ × 29½. Mrs. Huxley Roller* XK2

MALE MODELS:
1. Head of a Young Man, 17½ × 9½. C. J. Conway (1925)*   X4
2. (Reclining on the ground) 16 × 20. Christies 1925, No. 206
(Price)* XK12
3. (With folded arms) 27½ × 13½. Christies 1925, No. 141.
(Greenstreet)* XK15
4. (Lying on the ground) 12 × 18. Christies 1925, No. 189.
(Saxe)* XK13
5. (Standing before a stove) 27½ × 22. Christies 1925, No.
199. (Smith)* XK6

Index

481